WHITE-COLLAR CRIMES

WHITE-COLLAR CRIMES

GIRISH MISHRA

BRAJ KUMAR PANDEY

GYAN

GYAN PUBLISHING HOUSE

NEW DELHI-110002

WHITE-COLLAR CRIMES

(*Current Affairs, Crime, Education, Literature, Media, Politics, Religion, Sociology*)

ISBN: 81-212-0596-4

Published in 1998 in India
by Gyan Publishing House,
5, Ansari Road, Darya Ganj
New Delhi-110002

Laser Typesetting at A.S. Printers, Delhi.

Printed at Mehra Offset Press, Delhi.

Dedicated to
The memory of our dear friend,
Late Mr. R.K. Garg, Senior Advocate,
The Supreme Court of India, who inspired
the idea of this study in no small measure.

Dedicated to

The memory of our dear friend,
Late Mr. R.K. Garg, Senior Advocate,
The Supreme Court of India, who inspired
the idea of this study in no small measure.

Contents

Preface

For quite a few years, there has been an increasing clamour against growing criminalisation of socio-economic life in India. In addition to traditional or petty crimes and street criminals, over the years; new types of crimes and criminals have come to the fore which have assumed menacing proportions as underlined by various scams and media reports. Even the Prime Minister and Parliament both have acknowledged this fact. The rich and influential people are also involved in these crimes. They are unlike the petty criminals with whom we have been familiar for ages.

The new breed includes criminals who are apparently suave, soft-spoken, well-dressed and well-educated in the formal sense and socially respectable, politically influential and economically sound. They have come to the fore and proliferated with the rise of modern industrial capitalism. Their origin can be traced to the mid-eighteenth century in Britain. From the early nineteenth century and onwards they have prospered in other European countries and North America.

While in the West, there have been a number of serious studies on this type of crimes and criminality and novelists like Charles Dickens and Balzac, among others have treated them in their novels at length but in our country there has been a singular indifference. Except media write-ups and government reports, no research work of comprehensive nature has been produced to enlighten on the genesis and growth of this phenomenon. There may be empirical studies which do not take us very far except that they satisfy the funding agencies. Our efforts have been to fill up this gap. If the present study succeeds in throwing light on the large area of darkness that envelops the crimes of the rich and influential, we shall think our efforts are successful. It is our firm belief that without the entirely understanding the phenomenon of clarion calls whether given from the ramparts of the Red Fort or from the Parliament House will succeed.

Our interest in the crimes of the rich and influential in general and the growing nexus among business, bureaucracy, politics and mafia in particular was aroused during the second half of the 1980s, when the late Pandit Kamalapati Tripathi, Mr. Krishna Kant and our dear friend late Mr. R.K. Garg began actively campaigning against them by organising discussions. We then realised that these people, however, well intentioned they were; did not have a proper perspective and they viewed the phenomenon in a narrow context.

We have studied the phenomenon in a wide historical perspective and all its interconnections.

We shall welcome comments, criticisms and suggestions from the readers, which may help us in our future studies.

26 January, 1998

GIRISH MISHRA
BRAJ KUMAR PANDEY

Acknowledgements

We acknowledge our debt of gratitude to all the authors and publishers whose books, journals and newspapers we have relied on for preparing this study. We are also grateful to the Ratan Tata Library of Delhi School of Economics; the Nehru Memorial Museum and Library, Teen Murti House, the American Center Library; the Indian Institute of Public Administration Library and the Kirori Mal College Library for making books and journals available to us.

A number of friends helped us in bringing this work into existence. We are particularly thankful to Mr. Ganesh Shukla, Mr. R. Raina, Mr. Arun Bose, Prof. K.N. Kabra, Dr. Nirmal Kumar, Dr. Anurag Mishra and Mr. V.D. Chopra for their encouragement and academic cooperation. Last but not least we are grateful to the Directors of Gyan Publishing House for bringing-out this study without any delay.

Introduction

Almost a century ago, the Grand Old Man of India, Dadabhai Naoroji was troubled by the question: why was India poor and backward notwithstanding its immense natural and human resources? He was restless till he found ar appropriate answer, after devoting a great deal of his time and energy to look into government publications and archival materials both in India and Britain. The answer he found was that India was poor not because its people were lazy, but owing to the fact that a large part of what they were producing was being drained away by foreign rulers through an intricate mechanism and was, thus, not available either for consumption or capital accumulation in India. Thus, crime of robbery was being regularly committed by foreign rulers against the people of India though this act was in accordance with the existing laws. Hence, the Britishers could be called licensed robbers.

Today we have not only licensed robbers and thieves, but unlicensed ones too. Those who indulge in manipulation of stocks and prices are licensed ones because they act in accordance with the law. But at the same time there are a number of others who contravene the existing laws and procedures to rob the people and the public exchequer. In recent years various scams which have come to the light underline this. One common feature of most of them is that a part (of course substantial) of the loot has been stashed away in foreign banks, whether on-shore or off-shore, or invested in various kinds of illegal activities in both India and abroad. The figures revealed by the media are mind-boggling. A front-page report in *The Times of India* (Delhi ed., 30 January, 1997) states: "An unofficial estimate by the International Monetary Fund (IMF) saying Indians have stashed away at least $100 billion in foreign banks seems to get substantiated by the findings of a research study by three US economists. They have concluded that the capital flight from India to the United States alone in 1994 and 1995 must have ranged from a maximum of $11,300 million to a minimum of $3,875 million." The study authored by Prof. John Zdanowicz, Prof. William W. Welch and Prof. Simon J. Pak of the Florida University originally appeared in *Finance India*.

Not only this, public land, mines, forest resources and moveable assets like cars, refrigerators, air conditioners are being used for private purposes. Licences and permits, funds, grants and subsidies are being fully or partially cornered for personal enrichment. Power and positions both are being used for personal gains. Discretion is used by a number of people in decision-making positions without any objective basis or criterion. If one takes the lists of persons allotted government quarters or petrol pumps or LPG dealerships or the people nominated to legislative councils or the Rajya Sabha on the ground of their possessing special qualifications as laid down in the Constitution, there immediately emerges a prima facie case of quidproquo.

The people involved in the above-mentioned acts have clearly violated the trust reposed in them by the people, the law and the Constitution. If the social institution of trust, which today forms the foundation of our nation is destroyed, then India cannot survive and chaos and anarchy cannot be avoided. In the recent times this foundation has been considerably shaken.

These influential people are not ordinary criminals. They are poles apart from the common street criminals who snatch away bags and gold chains, pilfer shops and godowns, loot trains and houses, commit murders, indulge in burglary, kidnap for ransom and so on. They are suave, soft-spoken, well-dressed, well-educated, possessing university degrees and distinctions and membership of professional and academic bodies in India and abroad, lovers of arts and patrons of literature and culture, belonging to the upper segments of society. They do not frequent roadside eateries and tea stalls-cum-gossip centres. Instead they go to five-star hotels and high class clubs. They smoke expensive cigars or cigarettes and drink foreign-made liquors, not hashish or bidis or country-made or illicit liquors. Their company is sought by the high and mighty. They are interviewed by media on important issues and happenings and their views and opinions make news and are hotly discussed in important fora and influence the decisions-making process at the governmental level. They fly or travel by *Rajdhani* or *Shatabdi Express* trains as their time is extremely precious. The problem of analysing the nature and character of the crimes of such people was taken up first by an American sociologist in the beginning of this century, though perceptible remarks on such crimes are evident in the works of celebrated novelists of the nineteenth century like Honoré de Balzac and Charles Dickens, besides some analysis of such criminal characters.

In John Reed's classic account of the Bolshevik Revolution, *Ten Days that Shook the World* (Penguin, 1966, p. 29), we find the very opening lines talking of an unnamed American scholar: "Towards the end of 1917, an alien professor of sociology visiting Russia came to see me in Petrograd. He had been informed by businessmen and intellectuals that the Revolution was slowing down. The professor wrote an article about it and then travelled around the country, visiting factory towns and peasant communities where, to his astonishment, the Revolution seemed to be speeding up."

This unnamed professor, mentioned by John Reed was Edward Alsworth Ross (1866-1951) whose paper "The Criminaloid", appearing in *The Atlantic Monthly* (no. 99,

January 1907), focused for the first time on this new sort of crime, affecting the American society where Ross had lamented that, while there was nothing to quarrel with society's attitude towards traditional crimes and criminals, the social view of what he called "the quasi-criminal" was not correct. The society regards them as successful people, worthy of emulation. They are felicitated on birthdays and are eulogised. Unlike ordinary criminals, their arrest is lamented and, at times, the news of arrest is suppressed even by media and the government. Yet, in the ultimate analysis, they are worse than ordinary thieves and robbers as they do more damage to society and nation as will be brought more clearly in the course of our discussion. He wrote that, "The shocking leniency of the public in judging conspicuous persons who have thriven by anti-social practices is not due, as many imagine, to sycophancy. Let a prominent man commit some offence in bad odour and the multitude flings its stones with right goodwill. The social lynching of the self-made magnate who put away his faded, toil-worn wife for the sake of a soubrette proves that the props of the old morality have not rotted through. Sex righteousness continues to be thus stiffly upheld simply because man has not invented new ways of wronging woman."

Here in India the Jnanpith and Moorti Devi awards given by Sahu Jains' outfit have become a matter of great prestige and achievement for recipients while the jury consists of top people of the country. Award-giving ceremonies are graced by the high and mighty of this land, who, day in and day out, pontificate on morality, but they seldom look at the background of those who have instituted them.

If one looks carefully, one will find that a Ram Krishna Dalmia or a H.D. Mundhra or a Dharam Teja or a Sahu Shanti Prasad Jain inflicted greater damage on the nation than one N.C. Jain. But on this we shall have more to say later in the course of our discussion.

In recent years we have witnessed that far more social indignation was aroused by the very mention of the name of Sushil Sharma while the cases of various scamsters, who are involved in cases of defrauding the country of billions of rupees and the case of a former Prime Minister charged with a number of crimes, have eclipsed the notice of many.

This is all because the traditional type of morality still has a strong grip over our society. None of our scriptures have dealt with new kinds of criminal activities which have come up in the world ever since the dawn of modern industrial capitalism. Thus, white-collar crime became a phenomenon to be reckoned with only after the Industrial Revolution. In other words, it is only about 200-year old. Modern industrial capitalist economy which came into being was complex in nature as it had a large network of banking and a growing commercial nexus of insurance, stocks, credit, transportation and so on. It gave rise to a complicated legal system and the intricacies of property rights and laws that necessitated the emergence and proliferation of lawyers who aided and abetted white-collar crimes. Looking around, we find a large number of legal consultants whose main job is to advise the rich and influential on how to evade and avoid taxes and launder their black incomes and wealth, file and successfully realise their bogus insurance and other claims. We also find, especially in New Delhi, various kinds of liaison officers acting as power brokers, facilitating the giving and taking of bribe.

In recent times, we have seen how a big hue and cry was raised when a noted eye surgeon of Delhi, N.C. Jain was sent to jail to serve his sentence for his complicity in the murder of his wife, but no such social uneasiness was witnessed when Ram Krishna Dalmia was imprisoned for his business and financial misdeeds and he and his son-in-law Sahu Shanti Prasad Jain were held guilty on various counts by Mr. Justice Vivian Bose. He was reported to have been caught at the Palam Airport (New Delhi) for allegedly attempting to smuggle in a substantial amount of foreign exchange. Lately, in the year 1997, his son Ashok

Jain has been charged by the Enforcement Directorate of the Finance Ministry with the same crime.

Vishnugupta Chanakya surely could not be aware of the phenomenon symbolised by H.D. Mundhara, Harshad Mehta, Haji Mastan, C.R. Bhansali, Dharam Teja, Tulmohan Ram and others. Thus, Ross was fully correct when he asserted: "Overlooked in Bible and prayer book, their obliquities lack the brimstone smell. Surpass as their misdeeds may in meanness and cruelty, there has not yet been time enough to store-up strong emotion about them; and so the sight of them does not let loose the flood of wrath and abhorrence that rushes down upon the long-attained sins."

Ross's criminaloid, a term of Latin-Greek origin just like "asteroid", "crystalloid" and "anthropoid", stands for those who prosper by resorting to underhand and illegal ways and means which either escape the general public scrutiny or the society has not been able to formulate its attitude towards them. Sometimes they may be held guilty by law but not by general public opinion. Consequently, society does not view their activities as criminal. Thus, 'so long as morality stands stock-still in the old tracks, they escape both punishment and ignominy'. The result is that "unlike their lowbrow cousins, they occupy the cabin rather than the steerage of society. Relentless pursuit hems in the criminals, narrows the range of success and denies them influence. The criminaloids, on the other hand, encounter but feeble opposition and since their practices are often more lucrative than the authentic crimes, they distance their more scrupulous rivals in business and politics and reap an uncommon world of prosperity."

Looking around, we find a number of such criminals having signboards of legitimate business and are being protected by their connections with political leaders, bureaucracy and all others who matter. They are hailed as great benefactors of the society and their help and support are solicited for various institutions from charitable to commercial. Quite often a corporate criminaloid is social. He donates lots of money for relief to the people affected by natural calamities. He is religious and builds places of worship and endows them with property and subsidises the publication of low-priced religious books to attract the attention of religious minded people. He is a philanthropist and donates lots of money for the promotion of science, arts, literature and culture. All these expressions of large-heartedness are at the expense of the corporate entities he controls and their shareholders, most of whom have no say in these decisions and the expense of public exchequer in order to refurbish his own image. The same may be said of a political criminaloid. This explains why people of the home town of a criminaloid or of the constituency or clan of a political criminaloid think that a good man is being maligned whenever the long arm of law tries to reach him. They suspect some conspiracy or unholy alliance against their benefactors. When some VVIPs grace some occasion, criminaloids are requested to associate themselves with the reception committees. With their financial resources and influence they enjoy social and political respect and leverage which no common criminal can dream of. Thus, a criminaloid is more dangerous than a common robber or murderer because the latter deprives a person only of his earnings or life but leaves the ideals of the society intact while the former takes away the ideals of the society and corrupts youth by setting-up wrong precepts. Balzac wrote, exposing the dual standard adopted by the society, "a burglar or a chicken-stealer in an inhabited area is sent to the galleys, whereas a man who ruins whole families by fraudulent bankruptcy gets off with a few months' imprisonment at the worst... by sentencing the burglar, the judges are upholding the barriers between rich and poor. If these were overthrown, social order would come to an end. Whereas the bankrupt, the clever rogue who diverts an inheritance, the banker who brings a business to ruin in order to line his pockets, is merely an instrument by which fortunes change hands." And "Present-day society, no longer worships the true God, but the Golden Calf! That is the religion of your Charter, which politically speaking takes no account of anything but property."[1]

There is one more difference between an ordinary criminal and a criminaloid. While the former is prompted by an evil impulse, the latter is morally insensible. A person who sells spurious drugs and adulterated food and drinks, speculates in the stocks of his own company on the basis of inside knowledge and lends his own depositor's money to himself under "diverse corporate aliases" is nothing but morally insensible or devoid of scruples. Similarly, a person occupying a position of power in a political party grants party tickets for fighting election on monetary considerations, ignoring the criteria of merit and eligibility is obviously devoid of all moral sensibility and belongs to the category of criminaloid. Any number of such examples can be furnished to illustrate this, yet, let us refer to a few more common instances.

A labour leader who either instigates or calls off strikes in expectation of pecuniary rewards, a minister or official who grants exemption from entertainment tax to some run-of-the-mill film, a publisher who bribes the authorities in order to get his books prescribed as textbooks in schools, a professor who plagiarises somebody else's book and gets it published under his own name and so on are all from the class of criminaloid.

Look at their faces, they are, as Ross would have found, perfectly normal, "nothing of the wolf or vulture. Nature has not foredoomed them to evil by a double dose of lust, cruelty, malice, greed or jealousy. They are not degenerates, tormented by monstrous cravings. They want nothing more than we all want—money, power, consideration—in a word 'success', but they are in a hurry and they are not particular as to the means."

There is another vital difference between a petty criminal and criminaloid. While the former preys upon a specific or marked victim with whom, in most cases, he comes into contact, the criminaloid does not know for certain who his victims are. In fact, the victims of the criminaloid remain anonymous and there is both a time as well as distance gap that separates him from his victims. In most cases he may not know them at all. This may well be illustrated with a simple example. Take, for instance, the producer of a spurious drug. He does not know who his victims will be. The sufferings of the victims will, in most cases, not be witnessed by him, so there is no question of his sleep being disturbed. Not only this, the likely victims may not have been born in some cases. This is more true when a bridge, being built by some contractor supposed to last for 50 years, but collapsed just after 25 years, when a bus carrying schoolchildren passed over it because of the use of sub-standard materials and inferior craftsmanship. The contractor and the governmental supervisory staff who are involved in this, may not be alive to witness or hear of the tragedy. Maybe their own progeny are among the victims.

In some cases a criminaloid may show apparent moral sensibility but this may be purely for refurbishing his public image which seldom has anything to do with his real image. For example, when his car knocks down a cyclist, he shows great concern for the victim, takes him to a doctor and spends money and bestows every care till he recovers. He may even look after his family till the victim fully recovers and resumes earning his livelihood. More often people at large are deceived in regarding him as a benevolent person.

Generally, a criminaloid works through a network of middlemen. He is all the time conscious of the difference between committing a crime and getting it committed through some others. In our own country we have seen him capturing polling booths, instrumental in calling off labour strikes, smuggling narcotics out and gold and electronic goods in, purchasing legislators, kidnapping executives of business firms and committing a host of other crimes not personally, but through a string of intermediaries. He never dirties his own hands and boots. He is, thus, able to keep his hands neat and boots clean. Thus, in the words of Ross: "he becomes a consumer of custom-made crime, a client of criminals, often a maker of criminals by persuading or requiring his subordinates to break the law. Of course, he must have 'responsible' agents as valves to streamline the flow of guilt from such proceedings. He shows them the goal, provides the money, insists on 'results', but vehemently declines to know the foul method by which alone his followers can get these 'results'. Not to bribe, but to employ and finance the briber; not to lie, but to admit to your editorial columns 'paying matter', not to commit perjury, but to hire men to homestead and make over to you claims they have sworn were entered in good faith and without collusion; not to cheat, but to promise a 'rake-off' to a mysterious go-between in case your just assessment is cut down; not to rob on the highway, but to make the carrier pay you a rebate on your rival's shipments; not to shed innocent blood, but to bribe inspectors to overlook your neglect to instal safety appliances—such are the ways of the criminaloid. He is a buyer rather than a practitioner of sin and his middlemen spare him unpleasant details." Obviously, the criminaloid partakes the characteristics of a mafia don or godfather.

The area or space of operation of the criminaloid is much larger than that of a common criminal. It may be nationwide or even global. The producer of 'duplicate' spare parts of a Maruti car may extend his area of operation to the entire India or even overseas where this car is used. Similarly, a vendor of pseudo-spiritualism may have all sorts of people from all continents of the world as his victims.

Ross was not very clear as to how to fight out the phenomenon of criminaloid. He merely stated: "the criminaloid flourishes until the growth of morality overtakes the growth of opportunities to prey".

The treatment of the crimes of the rich and influential remained for more than three decades where Ross had left it. A major breakthrough could come only in 1939 when the doyen of US sociologists, Edwin H. Sutherland, as president of the American Sociological Society brought in the term "white-collar crime" to encompass criminal activities in corporate, commercial, professional and political spheres within its purview. He defined it as "a new class of crime: the crime with the multi-victims and the uncertain victims".[2]

Even though both sociology and criminology have been the subjects of teaching and research for more than six decades in our country, we do not find any light in this area. There is neither an authentic book nor a series of papers discussing the crimes by the rich and influential in all their aspects. What we have consists mainly of newspaper reports, mixed with quite a lot of sensational stuff to make them saleable.

With the changing socio-economic scenario and growing linkages with the outside world as a result of both revolution in information and communication technology and globalisation of the economy, the crimes by the rich and influential are bound to grow rapidly in the coming months and years. Any worthwhile understanding of this new type of criminality and new breed of criminals requires clarity in approach which, in turn, reaps profits from the works done in the West, especially Britain, France and the USA, because they have already encountered them in their journey on the path of capitalism.

Thus, before embarking on a study of the Indian situation, it will be fruitful if we attempt a brief survey of important theoretical and historical studies of the crimes of the rich and influential. An attempt towards this direction shall be made in the subsequent chapters.

REFERENCES

1. Honoré de Balzac, *Lost Illusions*, Harmondsworth, 1981, p. 647.
2. Gilbert Geis and Robert F. Meir (eds.), *White-Collar Crime: Offences in Business, Politics and the Professions*, New York, 1977, p. 2.

1

The Crimes of the Rich and Influential

White-collar crime has many features which distinguish it from a petty crime. To begin with, it is seldom an object of popular focus and reflected in regularly published crime statistics which generally refer to criminals and their illegal activities, investigated and handled by the police, judiciary and jail authorities, and which most often includes crimes such as murder, assault, burglary, robbery, theft, pick-pocketing, sex offences and so on. Experts make these statistics on the basis of their theorisation and pontification about various facets of criminal behaviour and proffer suggestions for keeping the crime under control. These theorists have found that "since crime is concentrated in the lower class, it is caused by poverty or by personal and social characteristics believed to be statistically associated with poverty, including feeble-mindedness, psychopathic deviations, slum-dwellers and "deteriorated" families."[1]

Crimes of Lower and Higher Classes

Engels regarded criminality among the labouring classes as a primitive form of expression of insurrection and a response to deprivation and oppression, though he at the same time cautioned against idealising it and regarding it as a satisfactory form of politics.[2] Generally, labouring classes resort to crime as a form of insurrection only in the early phase of the development of capitalism and before they themselves become a political force and acquire proletarian consciousness. Thus, it cannot be the beginning of a conscious rebellion against capitalist oppression. It is only a transitional phase.

Looking at the society after the emergence and development of industrial capitalism, focusing attention only on the crimes of lower classes gives an incomplete picture, and is, thus, misleading as it leaves out "vast areas of criminal behaviour of persons not in the lower class.[3] The latter type of criminal behaviour, covering these vast and ever-expanding areas is white-collar criminality,[4] whose sanctums are corporate boardrooms, politicians' parlours and the meeting places like clubs, hotels, restaurants, etc. where bureaucrats, businessmen and politicians enjoy each other's company and factories where spurious drugs and adulterated foods and drinks are produced and "duplicate" goods are turned out, on which no excise duty is paid or which may be completely fake except for the appearance. Thus, "a pattern of crime can be found to exist outside both the focus of popular pre-occupation with crime and the focus of scientific investigation of crime and criminality.[5]" Charles Dickens wrote of the financial institutions of the city of London after the working hours in these words: "the deserted counting-houses, with their secrets of books and papers locked up in chests and safes; the banking-houses, with their secrets of strong rooms and wells, the keys of which were in a very few secret pockets and a veryfew secret breasts; the secrets of all the dispersed grinders in the vast mill, among whom there were doubtless plunderers, forgers and trust-betrayers of many sorts, whom the light of any day that dawned might reveal; he could have fancied that these things, in hiding imparted a heaviness to the air."[6] While laying bare the real character of capitalist financier, Merdle, he said: "He, the uncouth object of such widespread adulation, the sitter at great men's feasts, the roc's egg of great ladies' assemblies, the subduer of exclusiveness, the leveller of pride, the patron of patrons, the bargain-driver with a Minister for Lordships of the

Circumlocution Office, the recipient of more acknowledgement within some ten or fifteen years, at most, than had been bestowed in England upon all peaceful public benefactors and upon all the leaders of all the Arts and Sciences, with all their works to testify for them, during two centuries at least—he, the shining wonder, the new constellation to be followed by the wise-men bringing gifts, until it stopped over certain-carrion at the bottom of a bath and disappeared-was simply the greatest Forger and the greatest Thief that ever cheated the gallows"[7].

Corporate boardrooms and politicians' parlours are seldom under surveillance by Intelligence Bureau (IB), Central Bureau of Investigation (CBI) or Enforcement Directorate (ED). These agencies listen to and monitor telephonic conversations generally of criminals like smugglers and terrorists, but not of a high corporate functionary or a serving Prime Minister who was found merrily watching television and neglecting his duty to protect a disputed structure, thereby pushing the country and its ideals towards a disastrous situation. There is insufficiency of first hand observation about white-collar crimes.

Influence of the White-Collar Criminals

Whatever little we know of white-collar crimes has come from reports of commissions of enquiry and newspapers. They, however, show only a small fragment of the total picture. In fact, the experiences of this country as well as of other countries show that white-collar criminals are so powerful that official investigating and prosecuting agencies are seldom in a position to dig out all the skeletons and present a complete picture in all their complexities before the public. In India, this truth has been underlined times without number. In recent times, a Chief Minister of a very large, but one of the poorest Indian States seems to have presided only over scams and scandals which have drained away its meagre resources and condemned its inhabitants to a position of perpetual backwardness and misery, yet he had been moving scot free with all his civil rights intact and presiding over the destiny of not less than 100 million people: He was neither shadowed nor was his telephone taped. If such a person is scornful of law and legal processes, no one should be surprised.

In many cases, both here and abroad, it has been noticed that white-collar criminals as well as judges and prosecuting officials belong to the same class with similar outlook and attitude and interests if not bound by marriage and other ties. The result is that the latter are seldom very serious about their duty unless there is tremendous public pressure. In the case of evasion of the provisions of land reform laws, this fact has been underlined time and again by experts from India and abroad.

Those who indulge in white-collar crimes are so powerful and influential that the state instead of bringing them to books, toes their line and protect their interests.[8] As early as 1904, Henry D. Lloyd in his book, *Wealth Against Commonwealth*, wrote about the Standard Oil Company that "it has done everything with the Pennsylvania legislature except to refine it.[9]

The American President, Mr. Theodore Roosevelt, during the early years of this century, stated: "Swindling in stocks, corrupting legislatures, making fortunes by the inflation of securities, by wrecking railroads, by destroying competitors by rebates—these forms of wrong doing in the capitalist society are far more infamous than any ordinary form of embezzlement or forgery; yet it is a matter of extreme difficulty to secure punishments of the men most guilty and most responsible for them".[10]

White-collar crime whether in this country or elsewhere, if properly and thoroughly studied, indicate the distribution of power in society. This is obvious after a perusal of legislative enactments and government orders, which shows what crimes are kept out of their purview or sought to be treated leniently. To illustrate this, take the enactments made against black money. From time to time, there have been voluntary disclosure schemes and bearer bonds or gold bond schemes. It has been underlined by one Finance Minister after another that it is the high rate of personal taxation and controls that have led people to hide their incomes and wealth and indulge in the creation of black money. In other words, the primary responsibility is placed on the shoulders of the government and its wrong policies. Since the country is short of investible resources, black moneyholders need to be induced and propitiated to bring their hidden incomes and wealth in the open and put them in legitimate activities where no penalty is levied. The same attitude, however, is not shown or adopted towards common criminals' assets. Those who are found in the possession of stolen or looted cash and assets from banks, other organisations or private individuals are immediately arrested while those amassing black money by indulging in hoarding, profiteering, bribe-taking, smuggling and so on are treated with leniency and tenderness.

Gilbert Geis and Robert F. Meir have rightly said: "White-collar crime provides an indication of the degree of hypocrisy present in a society. Such hypocrisy may be seen as leverage by means of which the society may be forced toward congruence between its verbal commitments and its actual conduct. In regard to white-collar crimes, hypocrisy exists when fraud among the lower classes is viewed with distantee and punished, while upper-class deception is countenanced and defined as nothing more and malevolent than shrewd business practice".[11]

Financial cost of white-collar crime is many times greater than the total sum involved in the activities, traditionally regarded as criminal. Though precise figures are not involved, yet one may hazard a guess that the total amount looted from the public exchequer in Bihar by fodder scamsters is much more than the nominal value of all cash and assets grabbed by traditional robbers and thieves all over the State or take the sum siphoned-off by the CRB Capital Markets and compare it with the total amount lost as a result of traditional crimes in all the metropolitan cities of the country and we are sure, the former will exceed. Taking all the scams, big or small, the sum involved in them will be staggering. The point we are stressing is that white-collar crimes are much more serious as regards loss than traditional ones.

In addition to financial cost, white-collar crimes bring distrust and lead to social demoralisation and disorganisation. Take, for example, CRB Capital Markets episode. It is bound to create-social distrust. For quite some time, people will not entrust their savings to financial companies even though they secure and flaunt certificates of high credit rating. Distrust has been created for not only financial companies and credit rating agencies but also for government's capability of regulating non-banking financial companies. This is bound to result in demoralisation on the part of victims and it will adversely affect the financial sector in general. In recent years, we have quite often found people cynically saying that all are corrupt and an auto-rickshaw driver remarking: "Why do you resent, when I ask for a few rupees more than the actual fare; when Ministers, Chief Ministers and bureaucrats have looted crores and crores and yet, you did not protest? In this connection one is reminded of Sutherland's remark that: "The financial loss from white-collar crimes, great as it is, is less important than the damage to social relations. White-collar crimes violate trust and, therefore, create distrust, which lowers social morale and produces social disorganisation on a large scale. Other crimes have relatively little effect on social institutions or social organisations." Thus, 'white-collar crime is real crime.[12]

The emergence and growth of white-collar crimes indicate changing socio-economic life. We still come across traditional grocers though declining in number in various parts of the country. They weigh their merchandise by hand and, in most cases, deal with their customers on a personal basis. They have a limited scope and inclination to defraud the customers since turnover is limited and they have personal relations with many of the customers. This is not true in the case of large departmental stores or the firms which market packaged merchandise, where each packet is supposed to carry the weight. It has been found that, in several cases, they indulge in short weighing while the propitiated officials of weights and measures department just wink at it. They have no personal contact with customers and are not afraid of social sanctions.

Over the years not only the number of white-collar crimes in India has gone up but their spread and variety have also increased. In daily newspapers, one will find incidents of white-collar crimes occupying quite a substantial amount of space and there is hardly any sphere of life untouched by them. Once when Gulzari Lal Nanda told his Prime Minister that as many as 80 honourable MPs were regularly beholden to a particular business house, it created quite a sensation in the country and a storm in Parliment. But today episodes like Jharkhand Mukti Morcha MPs bribery case or the use of material incentives to win over elected representatives of people do not create any consternation.

Till the beginning of the Second World War, one came into contact in their day-to-day dealings with mostly small traders who personally handled their customers. The scope for defrauding a customer was limited to short-weighing and a few other tricks. They did not have much distance separating them from their customers.

Noble Professions: The Days of Nobility have Gone

Likewise, before 1950, we quite often came across a postal employee or a bankman or a cashier or somebody working at district treasury embezzling money entrusted to his care or a petty official or employee in some government department taking bribes. The incidences of white-collar crimes were limited in its extent. The high-officials in administration accepted only gifts (known in Bihar and U.P. as *dali* or *dal*). In other words, most of the people, committing white-collar crimes were just "grass eaters", unlike today when most of them are "meat eaters". At present white-collar crimes are not only widespread but formalised and systematised. Development of capitalism with a dominant role of the government in it, has contributed to it in a big way. Not even the medical profession has remained untainted. We find illegal vending of alcohol and narcotics being carried out under the alibis provided by doctors. Quite often, country liquor is sold by Ayurvedic stores under fake labels of tonics. Doctors provide bogus certificates of illness to members of the underworld and tender false evidence in cases of contrived accidents, prescribe unnecessary drugs medicines tests and receive cuts and commissions from medical stores and laboratories for helping them fleece the patients. The Judiciary too is not untouched. One finds a former High Court Judge illegally sending out valuable foreign exchange, and a sitting Metropolitan Magistrate being hauled-up for running brothels! It has come to light in the process of investigation into fodder scam in Bihar how chairmen of legislative committees helped and protected the scamsters who looted crores of rupees from the State exchequer. The academic world too is in the grip of white-collar criminals. "Respectable" academicianes are found manipulating results, marksheets and appointments for money. Not many years ago, the computer centre of the University of Delhi was found guilty of manipulating the results of the pre-medical tests.

The Roots of the White-Collar Crimes

Now, let us turn our attention to the roots of white-collar crimes. What motivates people to commit them? As has already been pointed out, those who indulge in such crimes belong neither to deprived strata of the society nor are they uneducated and influenced by the company of undesirable people. They are neither unemployed nor without economic security. They are neither exploited nor oppressed and humiliated to such an extent that they should resort to crimes to attempt destruction of the existing society and socio-economic relations. On the contrary, they are well-off, suave and formally well-educated and they have every reason to refrain from destabilising the existing pattern of society.

Among the earliest explanations for crimes of the rich and influential is the one given by Aristotle: "Men may desire superfluities in order to enjoy pleasure unaccompanied with pain and, therefore, they commit crimes". He was of the view that "the greatest crimes are caused by excess and not by necessity."[13] This, however, needs to be qualified because the mere aspiration for superfluities cannot by itself lead a corporate executive to indulge in embezzlement or evasion of personal income from taxation or some such white-collar crimes. There are other options too before him. He may give up his desire for superfluities or may satisfy them by cutting expenses on other items. Or he may try to increase his income by working on weekends or taking some other assignments. However, it needs to be stressed that this desire for superfluities is only an indispensable condition not the cause for inducing people to commit white-collar crimes. Hence, Aristotle's explanation needs to be qualified and supplemented rather than totally discarded.

R.H. Tawney tries to search the motive for criminality of the rise of industrial capitalism which has given birth to acquisitive society which, in turn, has thrown "an invitation to men to use the powers with which they have been endowed by nature or society, by skill or energy or relentless egotism or mere good fortune, without enquiring whether there is any principle by which their exercise should be limited. It assumes the social organization which determines the opportunities which different classes shall in fact possess and concentrates attention upon the right of those who possess or can acquire power to make the fullest use of it for their own self-advancement. By fixing men's minds, not upon the discharge of social obligations, which restricts their energy, because it defines the goal to which it should be directed; but upon the exercise of the right to pursue their own self-interest, it offers unlimited scope for the acquisition of riches and, therefore; gives free play to one of the most powerful of human instincts."[14] This society does not seem to impose any moral restrictions on acquiring riches as regards the means and methods used. "It assures men that there are no ends other than their ends, no law other than their desires, no limit other than that which they think advisable. Thus, it makes the individual the centre of his own universe and dissolves moral principles into a choice of expediencies."[15]

Consequently, people do not discriminate between different sources of wealth and do not bother whether property has been earned legitimately or not. This is the way most of our rich and influential people have emerged.

The criminality of the rich and influential is witnessed almost everywhere in present day society, be it in business or the professions or politics. It may, however, be added here that white-collar crimes do not include murder, rape, arson and kidnapping for ransom by the rich and influential. Generally, among these crimes; we include acts such as embezzlement, bribe-taking, stock fraud, misleading advertisements in order to dupe the people, falsification of accounts, misrepresentation of asset values, insider trading and so on. "Since modern business and professional relationships are largely based on trust, white-collar crimes can be further defined as breaches of trust within business and professional communities or between those communities and the general public. Trust is that evanescent quality without which the operations of modern business would be impossible. Trust enables people to turn over their hard-earned savings to banks or stockbrokers rather than burying it in basements or stuffing it in mattresses. Trust enables the directors of large corporations to rely on the honesty of their employees rather than tallying every penny themselves. By widening our definition of white-collar crimes to include breach of trust, we, therefore; include behaviours widely held to be unethical and immoral as well as that which violates the letter of the law."[16]

The cases of white-collar crimes mentioned in course of our discussion mostly underline the breach of delegated or implied trust. Many of them involve duplicity. Hence, a person indulging in white-collar crime 'holds two antagonistic positions, one of which is a position of trust that is violated... generally in the interest of the other position.'[17] This may well be illustrated by citing the example of a cricket player who is trusted to play with all his energy and devotion for the victory of his own team, but betrays his team by accepting bribes from the other side and "misses" the chances to make runs or "drops" the catch.

Another important fact to be noted about white-collar crimes is that it is deliberate, pre-planned and, in most cases, organised. The organisation may be formal or informal. For example, there may exist a formal organisation for selling spurious drugs or vending country liquor under the label of some Ayurvedic tonic. Similarly, many registered and formally organised firms operating in business, industry or finance defraud their customers. But the racketeers who corner cinema tickets or railway seat/berth reservations to resell them at a premium may be organised, yet not formally. Similarly, as has been revealed, officials, businessmen and politicians involved in various scams were organised but only informally.

Mafia all over the world is well-organised but without any formal basis. It is neither registered nor does it have a written constitution or set of guidelines. That is why, when a don was asked about his mafia connection, he pretended complete ignorance and, when further pressed, he shot back: "What is mafia? I do not know." A cursory look at the smuggling network shows that it does not have any formal organisation while in actuality it is the opposite.

Industrial Capitalism and Criminality

The rise of industrial capitalism in the eighteenth century opened a new chapter in the history of crimes and criminality. In fact, the very origin of industrial capitalism lay in coercion and robbery. Before we come to it, let us state briefly what we mean by capitalism. In the words of V.I. Lenin: "Capitalism is the name given to that social system under which the land, factories, implements, etc. belong to a small number of landed proprietors and capitalists, while the mass of the people possess no property, or very little property, and are compelled to hire themselves out as workers. The landowners and factory-owners hire workers and make them produce wares of different kind which they sell on the market. The factory-owners, furthermore, pay the workers only such a wage as provides a bare subsistence for them and their families, while everything the worker produces over and above this amount goes into the factory-owner's pocket as his profit."[18]

From this explanation, three conditions seem to be essential for the emergence of capitalism:

(i) The vast majority of the people in the society do not have any means of production of their own;

(2) Being deprived of the means of production and, therefore, of the means of subsistence, these people have no alternative but to sell their labour-power or hire themselves out in order to earn a living. These people have personal freedom in the choice of occupation and the place of work. It means, there is no restriction on their mobility.

(3) The means of production and a large amount of money get concentrated into the hands of a handful of people in the society.

The process of the emergence of these conditions was subsumed by Karl Marx under the term "primitive accumulation", while Adam Smith had called it "previous accumulation".

There is absolutely no factual basis for the assertion that it was thrift and industriousness that made some people capitalists while others remained poor and were obliged to become wage earners. Barring one individual here and there, thrift and industriousness played a very insignificant role in the rise of the capitalist class and capitalism. In fact, the division and polarisation in the society into those who were deprived of the means of production and those in whose hands they came to be concentrated witnessed one of the cruellest and utmost coercion found 'in the annals of mankind "in letters of blood and fire".[19]

Primitive accumulation took away from direct producers such as craftsmen, peasants, village artisans, etc. their tools and other means of production. The urge to earn as much profit as possible led to the routing of English peasants from the land on which they had been settled for generations in order to facilitate sheep farming. This had prompted Sir Thomas More to remark that the sheep were eating men! The uprooted people were forced, irrespective of their age and gender, to work in newly-established factories just for survival. There was no limitation on hours of work. Quite often, working-hours stretched to 16 or more. Even the God-ordained Sunday as holiday was not meant for a worker. It deprived the workers of fresh air, usurped the time needed for growth, development and healthy maintenance of the body. It deprived children of their play time and ruined the family life by driving all—father, mother and children—to work in the factory.

Everybody knows how industrial capitalism of Britain had exploited, looted its colonies and committed acts of barbarism. In view of this, Marx was not wrong when he said: "In actual history it is notorious that conquest, enslavement, robbery, murder, chiefly force, played the great part.... As a matter of fact, the methods of primitive accumulation are nothing but idyllic".[20]

The colonialists, whether Dutch or British, enslaved people and forcibly took them to work on their plantations, be they located in Java, West Indies, Mauritius, Fiji or somewhere else. The system of indentured labour was the result of nothing but deception and symbolised criminality.

According to British parliamentary papers, in just ten years (1757-66) the East India Company and its employees extorted 6 million pound sterling by way of "gifts" from the Indians. Thus, the very structure of industrial capitalism was rooted in crimes and criminality.

Industrial capitalism brought about a sea change in the values and attitudes of people. Its high priest Adam Smith extolled the virtues of self-interest. Now, amassing money became the sole aim of the members of the newly emerged capitalist class because money meant power, prestige and status. There, thus, began a rat race to grab as much money as possible by hook or by crook. This ideal gave to the strong and powerful unfettered freedom to use their skills and position to enrich themselves without bothering about the impact of their actions on the society at large or on their fellow beings. Why should an industrialist care for the impact of effluents being drained into the river, flowing nearby so long as it reduces his costs and increases his profits and why should he bother about morality of his methods and means to achieve his ends? If somebody has some qualms of conscience, there was always church, saints and priests in the West to take care of it. In India, there have always been ways to get rid of one's sins and there have been Chandraswamis, Rajneeshs, Murari Bapus and so on to relieve one of mental problems and provide spiritual peace.

So far as the weaks are concerned, they always nurture the hope that they too may one day be in a position now occupied by the strong and powerful to enrich themselves. It is what is called the "bandwagon effect"—follow the leader. Tawney rightly remarks: "Before the eyes of both it suspends a golden prize, which not all can attain, but for which each may strive, the enchanting vision of infinite expansion. It assures men that there are no ends other than their ends, no law other than their desires, no limit other than that which they think advisable. Thus, it makes the individual the centre of his own universe, and dissolves moral principles into a choice of expediencies. And it immensely simplifies the problems of social life in complex communities. For it relieves them of the necessity of discriminating between different types of economic activity and different sources of wealth, between enterprise and avarice, energy and unscrupulous greed, property which is legitimate and property which is theft, the just enjoyment of the fruits of labour and the idle parasitism of birth or fortune, because it treats all economic activities as standing upon the same level and suggests that excess or defect, waste or superfluity, require no conscious effort of social will to avert them, but are corrected almost automatically by the mechanical play of economic forces."[21]

Modern capitalism not only changed the values, attitudes and outlook, but brought into existence enormous possibilities to realise the goal of acquisitive society. New techniques of production developed, modern factory system came into existence and mass production of goods became the order of the day. Production was not only for local or national market, but to be sold in far-off lands. There came about a revolution in the field of transport and communications which enormously increased the total volume of goods entering world trade. Even perishable commodities could be transported from one continent to the another. Refrigeration facilities kept such goods fresh for weeks and even months. Faster means of transportation eliminated the danger of piracy on high seas. Metalled roads made transportation of goods possible throughout the year irrespective of weather. Railways and airways brought certainty and speed in transportation.

In the political sphere, there were changes establishing law and order in most parts of the world. The forms of business organisation changed and joint-stock firms came to be adopted to overcome the shortage of capital, infinite liability and legally impermanence of existence.

Alongside, the role of finance increased tremendously. Both capital as well as money market developed and banking and insurance became important constituents of these markets. These developments gave rise to professionals like brokers, financiers, bankers, insurance agents, forwarding and clearing agents, chartered accountants and so on.

Lawyers saw their activities expanding to these new areas of business, finance and commerce. The entire gamut of mercantile law came into being. Since the role of the government and its agencies also became increasingly vital in the course of time, liaison people emerged, whose role was to take care of bureaucratic and political hurdles.

With these developments, there opened a great scope for fraud, bungling, swindling, deceit and so on. This scope went on expanding its base and new innovations are witnessed almost everyday to circumvent the new laws and rules. They are not limited to one country but to many countries and in some cases, to the world.

Take, for example, the fodder scam of a backward State like Bihar; its proliferation is limited not only to various parts of the country but to far-off Switzerland, Britain, Ukraine and also to the USA. Similarly, the urea scam is alleged to have the involvement of a company of Turkey and the banks of Switzerland and the USA. Thus, not only the geographical scope has widened but complexity has also deepened. Thus, Mihir Bose and Cathy Gunn are not wrong when they assert that fraud has become the growth industry in the present-day world.[22]

With accelerated changes in technology and growing complications in different spheres of economy, white-collar crimes or what we say the crimes of the rich and influential have too become more subtle, sophisticated and full of complexities and it is not very easy to detect them. With fast changes in information technology, it is beyond the capacity of most of the Third World countries to detect them, not to speak of forewarning.

Among these crimes, those committed in the sphere of the corporate sector account for a fairly large proportion.

REFERENCES

1. Gilbert Geis and Robert F. Meir (eds.), *White-Collar Crime: Offences in Business, Politics and the Professions*, New York, 1977, p. 2.
2. 'The contempt for the existing social order is most conspicuous in its extreme form—that of offences against the law. If the influences demoralizing to the working-man acts more powerfully, with more concentration than usual, he becomes an offender as certainly as water abandons the fluid for the vaporous state 80 degrees, Reaumur. Under the brutal treatment of the bourgeoisie, the working-man becomes precisely as much a thing without volition as water and is subject to the laws of nature with precisely the same necessity: at a certain point all freedom ceases. Hence with the extension of the proletariat, crime has increased in England and has become the most criminal in the world.' Frederick Engels, *The Condition of the Working Class in England*', London, 1984, p. 159 and also pp. 161-62. Commenting on Engels' writings on crime, Steven Marcus writes: "Crime is a primitive form of insurrection, driven by need and deprivations, an incomplete but not altogether mistaken response to a bad situation and coming into active existence only by overcoming the resistance of inherited values and internalized sanctions... Nevertheless, an inescapable part of the meaning of

crime is its essential failure. It is insufficiently rational and excessively, or too purely, symbolic and symptomatic. Most of all, in it the criminal remains socially untransformed: he is still an isolated individual pursuing activities in an underground and alternate market place; if he is successful, he is a small-time entrepreneur; at best, he is the member or leader of a gang. At this, he capable of organizing a movement to withstand the institutional forces that are arrayed against him. He lives in a parallel and parasitic world whose horizon is bounded and obscured by the larger society upon which it depends." Steven Marcus, *Engels, Manchester and the Working Class*, New York, 1974, pp. 223-224.

3. *Ibid.*
4. Albert Morris has called it "upper world crime" in his book *Criminology*, New York, 1935, pp. 152-158.
5. Donald R. Cressey's foreword to Edwin H. Sutherland, *White Collar Crime*, New York, 1961, p. xii, cf. 'The greatest evil is not now done in those sordid "dens of crime" that Dickens loved to paint. It is not done even in concentration camps and labor camps. In those we see its final result. But it is conceived and ordered (moved, seconded, carried and minuted) in clean, carpeted, warmed and well-lighted offices, by quiet men with white collars and cut fingernails and smooth-shaven cheeks, who do not need to raise their voices. Hence, naturally enough, my symbol for Hell is something like... the offices of a thoroughly nasty business concern,' C.S. Lewis, *The Screwtape Letters and Screwtape Purposes*, New York, 1961, p. xxv.
6. Charles Dickens, *Little Dorrit*, London, 1994, p. 542.
7. *Ibid.*, p. 710.
8. Girish Mishra and Braj Kumar Pandey, *Sociology and Economics of Casteism in India*, Delhi, 1996, pp. 265-266.
9. Henry D. Lloyd, *Wealth Against Commonwealth*, New York, 1904, p. 315.
10. Theodore Roosevelt, *The Roosevelt Policy*, New York, 1908, p. 2: 687.
11. 'Introduction' by editors, Gilbert Geis and Robert F. Meir, *White-Collar Crime: Offenses in Business, Politics and the Professions*, New York, 1977, p. 19.
12. Edwin H. Sutherland, *op. cit.*
13. Aristotle, *Politics*, Macmillan, London, Book II, Chapter 7, p. 65.
14. R.H. Tawney, *The Acquisitive Society*, Sussex, 1982, p. 32.
15. *Ibid.*, p. 33.
16. George Robb, *White-Collar Crime in Modern England: Financial fraud and business morality, 1845-1929*, Cambridge, 1992, pp. 4-5.

17. Edwin H. Sutherland, *op. cit.*
18. V.I. Lenin, *Collected Works*, Vol. 4, Moscow, 1964, p. 311.
19. Karl Marx, *Capital*, Vol. I, Moscow, 1977, p. 669.
20. *Ibid.*, p. 668.
21. R.H. Tawney, *op.cit.*, pp. 32-33.
22. Mihir Bose and Cathy Gunn, *Fraud: The Growth Industry of the Eighties*, London, 1989.

2

Corporate Sector Crimes

Though the media quite often talk of crimes in the corporate sector, yet, not only the people at large but even those who claim to be educated and conscious are familiar neither with the extent nor of the damage inflicted by them. Even those who claim to be knowledgeable are not in a position to grasp the intricacies involved in them. Notwithstanding the increase in public awareness in India of such crimes in recent years, especially since 1992; there is still a great deal of ignorance, misinformation and mystification. This is so because a corporate crime is generally invisible as a result of careful and sophisticated planning and meticulous execution along with laxness on the part of supervisory and regulatory authorities in addition to lenient laws which are always full of loopholes to the advantage of its perpetrators. Moreover, the public vigilance and social sanctions against corporate crimes have always been lacking or deficient. Generally, such crimes are underplayed by the media because of the class bias and/or the control exercised over them directly or indirectly. Directly whether in India or abroad, the print media have been largely owned by business houses and indirectly because they have been dependent on the corporate sector formost of their revenues by way of advertisement.

Between 1945 and 1972, the two-volume *Criminology*

Index listed 3,700 books and articles dealing with crimes and criminology, but "there were only ninety-two, or about 2.5 per cent, dealing with white-collar or corporate crime. And if the former is subtracted on the grounds that crimes against corporations are dissimilar to crimes for corporations, then just over 1 per cent of the listed material referred to corporate crime".[1]

Popular television crime serials, films and stories generally concentrate on conventional crimes rather than on the crimes of the corporate sector. Wherever they deal with the crimes of the middle and upper classes, these are conventional crimes like murders resulting from frustration in love, lack of fidelity in marriage or straightaway property disputes. Did not we witness a great deal of noise in connection with the Vidya Jain murder case in which her husband, an eminent eyesurgeon was involved or the murder case in Bihar in which the husband, a senior civil service officer, Nagmani's involvement was alleged? In the past during the British period, there were Bhwal Sanyasi cases and the Pakur Raj murder case and in the post-independence time, there were sensational cases like the Ahuja murder in which a high-ranking naval officer Nanavati was involved and the murder of a doctor in Lucknow by his beloved who thought herself to be betrayed or the Syed Modi murder in which the scion of a Talukedar family was said to be involved.

The credit, to a large extent, goes to Sutherland in focusing public opinion on white-collar crimes in general and corporate sector crimes in particular. It was he who demonstrated that these crimes posed far greater dangers than conventional crimes and they entailed much larger and lasting social costs.

While dealing with the corporate sector crimes, we shall include in our purview only those crimes which are committed for, or on behalf of the corporate sector in order to benefit it along with the crimes committed by people who are privy to its secrets for their own benefit. Among the latter, we certainly include insider trading. We exclude the crimes which are committed against the corporate sector. In other words, we keep aside the acts of vandalism, embezzlement, pilferage, thefts and so on whose purpose is to damage one or more constituents of the corporate sector. For example, if an irate crowd of workers burns a factory or beats it manager on the death of a workman as a result of negligence of safety regulations on the part of mangement, it is not a corporate crime, but the death of the worker is certainly a corporate crime for the simple reason that inadequacy of safety arrangements was meant to save some money for the company concerned.

There is a difference between the crime committed by the irate crowd of workers and the crime involved in the neglect of safety arrangements. Workers demonstrate their disdain not for the humanity at large but only for a particular company and its negligent management while the company shows its disdain not for a particular worker who has accidentally died but for all workers who work or will come to work, that is, its disdain is for humanity in general and acts of omission or negligence should also be included among corporate crimes.[2]

NBFC: Cheating the Gullible Investors

There are corporations or companies, set up with the sole purpose of pursuing criminal activities like smuggling, defrauding and cheating people and government. In India we have seen a number of NBFCs (Non-banking Financial Companies) mushrooming with the deliberate aim of defrauding gullible investors who are lured away by them through attractive gifts and unbelievably higher rates of interest. Before the advent of the SEBI (Securities and Exchange Board of India), companies were floated to gather subscriptions to share capital and then to decamp with the money. One may name any number of such companies which have not even held a single annual general body meeting of shareholders and their whereabouts are unknown. Among them are Sehgal Carbonless Paper (which was launched in the 1970s with great fanfare with advertisements on TV and newspapers), Bagrian Shoes, Gangappa Paper, Wrapaid, Rama Fibres, Mayur Syntex, Sidha Syntex, Padma

Paper, 5S, Multitech International and so on. It is said that in Delhi there have been 400 such companies. It needs to be noted that the society as well as the government gets agitated when the number of pickpockets increases and they freely roam about and carry-on their activities, but no such agitated attitude is witnessed when criminal companies mushroom and loot people's hard-earned money, at times with the connivance of the stock exchange and public sector banks. It took a number of decades for the government to realise and bring in SEBI in order to curb the operation of white-collar pickpockets, but even now these operations are not completely curbed. In the course of our discussion, we shall talk at length on certain criminal corporations.

How the so-called promoters cheat investing public, may be illustrated by referring to a typical example cited in *The Annals*, the journal of the American Academy of Political and Social Science. It can very well be applied to India of post-independence years. It is as follows: 'At the age of 16, Barry Minkow had started a carpet cleaning service in his garage. By the time Minkow was 21, ZZZZ Best Carpet Cleaning had become a public company valued at more than $200 million on Wall Street. One of the hottest stocks, ZZZZ Best sold $15 million in shares in one week.

By 1990, Barry Minkow was financially broke and serving 25 years in prison. "There was only one problem with the company and me," Minkow said from prison, "We were both frauds".

'Minkow's meteoric rise in the business world was aided unwittingly by a so-called Big Six public accounting firm. When Minkow first started doing business, his immaturity and ego conflicted with the daily grind of running a company. When he began to lose money, rather than admit it, he concocted a series of frauds to hide his true financial condition. Minkow borrowed money at banks using false financial statements. When that credit ran out, he turned to loan sharks. And when that credit ran out he owed so much money that the only thing that would save him was a public stock offering.'

'With the aid of several key lieutenants, Minkow bought a defunct Nevada corporation listed at one time on the stock exchange. Thereafter, he contracted with auditors of a public accounting firm to do the necessary, "due diligence" required with a stock offering. By phonying-up key documents, Minkow convinced his auditors that his company had made millions. In reality, it was hopelessly insolvent. But the auditors did not discover Minkow's fraud and gave him the necessary stamp of approval needed to engage in public stock offering.'

'For several months, Minkow's stock climbed steadily. He then brazenly decided to issue more stock. He was within days of raising an additional $ 80 million to buy a competing carpet cleaning service when a housewife complained to the *Los Angeles Times* that Minkow had defrauded her by overcharging her for carpet cleaning services. The reporter conducted an investigation and discovered that Minkow had cheated hundreds of customers in the same way. An expose appeared in the newspaper and the price of Minkow's stock fell through the floor. It was later discovered that more than 80 per cent of the assets Minkow listed on his financial statements did not exist. The assets of his $ 200 million company were eventually sold for less than $ 50,000. In Minkow's view, the auditors were too accepting and too believing in him. "They had no idea I was committing fraud," Minkow said.'

'Is the Minkow case an exception? According to his claim, "... there are a lot of Barry Minkows out there".'[3]

Surely, this claim is not wrong as far as India is concerned. We have not one but many Minkows here, resorting to fraud and falsehood to cheat the unsuspecting public. It is a well-known fact that when a company, listed on a stock exchange, comes out with a right or ordinary issue of its stocks, its promoters generally indulge in manipulation of share prices in such a manner that they start climbing up rapidly, creating an illusion in the minds of prospective buyers and once the issue is over-subscribed and allotment is made, prices fall and promoters corner the shares at much below the par value. In this machination, promoters play the role of proverbial pied-piper and lead the investors to their ruin.

Harshad Mehta: Ruined a Number of Investors

In 1992 Harshad Mehta sent the share prices sky-rocketting luring the gullible investors to buy shares and get rich overnight. In this process, quite a substantial number of them went to their ruin when the bubble burst after fictitious trading rings came to light and the banks found themselves cheated of $ 1.4 billion. In 1995, Pawan Sachdeva, chief of MS Shoes East, a little known company of Delhi spurred more or less a similar crisis with a $ 4.3 million default. With the help of brokers R.S. Jhaveri in Mumbai and Sareen & Co. in New Delhi, he tried to boost the prices of his company's shares. This was done with the aim of raising resources for his hotel and textile projects, to quote *Far Eastern Economic Review* (April 20, 1995), 'through a complicated double-whammy stock issue'. *Result*: The Bombay Stock Exchange was shut down for three days in late March as the MS Shoes issue unravelled, to their consternation.

".... As recent studies show, ramping of share prices before local or Euro-market issues is routine in India for fish much bigger than Sachdeva."

"At issue is the securities board's approval of a gap longer than the stipulated 30-day (maximum) between the two parts of the MS Shoes issue. Sachdeva was attempting to raise 4.28 billion rupees ($ 136 million) through an issue of fully convertible debentures, followed by a rights issue. The board allowed him up to 60 days between the two issues, ostensibly to straddle the late-February/early-March period, when the government's budget tends to cause sharp market fluctuations.

The delay mattered. Investors subscribing to the

debentures were left unaware that the value of MS Shoes shares would fall sharply after the rights issue because of dilution of capital. Their funds would, meanwhile be available to the company before the rights issues closed, allowing Sachdeva to buy his own rights entitlement.

'Moreover, the rights issue could have failed, leaving the double issue less than 90% subscribed and entitling the public to a refund. But by that stage, their cash would have been out of the hands of the issue managers and in the pockets of the company. Indian companies are notoriously slow to make such refunds.'

Sachdeva's misfortune was that, at that time authorities were trying to clean up the bourse and he got exposed in that process. It turned out that he was allegedly helped by two officials of the SEBI, besides two executives of public sector SBI Capital Markets. Thus, there appeared to be a nexus among a tycoon, sharebrokers and the bureaucracy. It is interesting to note that Sachdeva was arrested, hand-cuffed and paraded, but till now no trial has taken place. The softness of the prosecuting agency is quite intriguing.

Accounting and auditing firms and certain government departments help in facilitating the fraudulent activities by simply neglecting their assigned duties or by actively conniving. Whether it is Harshad Mehta's manipulative activities at the Mumbai Stock Exchange in 1992 or C.R. Bhansali's alleged defrauding of depositors in his company, public sector financial institutions and auditing firms have been said to be actively aiding. It is well-known that as late as, 1918, a major function of accountants and auditors was uncovering fraud and manipulative activities. Then gradually they shifted away from this major duty of theirs. In recent times, they seem to be going back to this old function, but not willingly. "Indeed, one of the major reasons auditors and accountants are now concerned about fraud has nothing to do with the huge costs our society pays and they are worried that the lawyers will drive them out of business by alleging they have been negligent in their professional responsibilities."[4]

In 1992, accountants in the USA faced more than 4,000 liability suits, claiming $15 billion in damages while in 1985, such suits were half of this number. Most of the suits were due to the failure to uncover fraud. In India, we do not find even government auditors, not to speak of private ones, very serious and sincere about their job and this is testified by the reports concerning animal husbandry scam in Bihar where for years, even glaring discrepancies and lapses could not be detected. In the 1950s embezzlement of provident funds in the Champaran District Board was uncovered. This embezzlement had been going on for more than two decades but no auditor could point it out though auditing was an annual affair. There was a strong suspicion that auditors were properly tackled!

The earliest example of the Minkow-type defrauding was again committed by John Law. Originally from Scotland, he landed in France in 1716 as a fugitive who was wanted in his native land in connection with a murder. He was an ace gambler and lived on it for some time in Italy. With the help of his contacts in high places in France, he secured permission to establish a bank - Banque Royale, with branches at several places. Later, he formed the Mississipi Company and skilfully manipulated price of its share so that it began skyrocketting. The demand for its shares exceeded the supply manifold and the result was thousands of applicants lining-up day and night outside the offices of the company and within six months, the shares of the company were selling at a premium which was nine times the nominal value. People employed all kinds of ingenuities to enter Law's office to secure some shares. His secretary amassed a big fortune out of bribes from people seeking rapport with Law.

Formally, the promoter was gathering funds for the development of the Louisiana wilderness in America, but, in fact, they were going to pay for the expenses of the government of France. Law was helping his patron, the Regent. Law's operations were a bit complex. Law was regarded as a genius till the crash came. When it came, Law fled the country, leaving the investors high and dry.

It will not be proper to blame corporate crimes which are committed for the organisation by an individual or groups of officers, responsible for decision-making. In fact, these officers or executives work in order to realise the goals set by the organisation itself and they are neither informed by the organisation nor are the manifestation of personal motives of officers concerned. 'Rather, organizational goals are what they are perceived to be by officials who have been socialized into the organizational 'way of life' and who strive in a highly co-ordinate fashion to bring collectively about their realization. Of course, these strivings to realize organizational goals may become crystallized in standard operational procedures. These confront new employees at all bureaucratic levels as 'solid facts' to be learnt and practised rather than queried and altered'.[5]

The victims of corporate crimes may not always be people at large or governments and countries, but other members of the corporate sector too. For example, quite often firms bribe foreign or domestic government officials or go in for dumping, mergers, advertisement war to spread false propaganda against the rivals, dumping, espionage and so on to drive the rivals out of the market or ruin them though in the ultimate analysis, the victims turn out to be human beings who have to suffer as shareholders, employees and wholesale and retail traders of ruined companies. In case, the ruined company belongs to the public sector, taxpayers of the country concerned will have to suffer because they may be asked to make-up for the loss to the government.

Corporate Criminals: Playing with the Lives of Innocent People

Corporate crimes lead to killing, injuring, maiming and robbing. Any number of such instances can be cited to illustrate how corporate crimes result in deaths of workers, customers and the people at large. We can cite the examples such as Dhori and Chasnala coal mine disasters, where negligence of management as regards safety measures led to the deaths of a large number of people. This negligence is generally the outcome of the desire of the company to minimise its costs and increase its profits. Adulterated and substandard products are thrust on customers in order to increase profits but they sometimes lead to deaths. For example, substandard pressure stoves, LPG cooking ovens with defective regulators, substandard electric gadgets, lax quality control as regard automobiles and so on cost many lives. When effluents are drained into rivers from where people draw drinking water, lives of people at large are endangered. Take the case of the gas tragedy in Bhopal owing to negligence on the part of the management of Union Carbide Limited which cost not only thousands of lives but made many people, including the next generation to suffer. These deaths are always avoidable, but they are not avoided intentionally because the corporate sector has scant regard for human beings as compared to the profit deity. In fact, it is worse than killer gangs who kill one another or people who resist their activities.

Spurious drugs and adulterated food items and drinks impair the health of customers. The cases of food poisoning are the outcome of stale meat or fish preparations or unhygienic way of cooking. Accidents in factories due to non-compliance with safety regulations, polluting rivers and atmosphere and so on injure or maim a large number of people every year. Quite often we read about the collapse of bridges, buildings and flyovers because of the use of substandard materials and/or poor workmanship, injuring and killing lots of people. Sometimes a building under construction collapses and injuries and deaths result because construction companies do not take proper precautions. One may recall the disastrous consequence of the use of the untested drug, thalidomide, during the 1970s under medical advice. As many as 8,000 pregnant mothers gave birth to deformed babies in North America, Australia, Brazil, Germany, Britain, Spain, Ireland, Sweden, Italy and Japan. The company which marked the drug was Chemie Grunenthal of Germany. It had deliberately falsified the results of the test and suppressed the truth about its after-effects.

Robbery on the part of the corporate sector takes many forms such as profiteering, marketing substandard goods and services, taking deposits from public and neither paying interest nor repaying the principal, evading taxes and other dues and packaging goods in less quantity than declared on each packet.

Corporate sector crimes, as we have seen, entail physical, economic and social costs. Like conventional crimes, they kill, maim and injure people. They lead to avoidable industrial or occupational diseases and accidents. We do not have reliable statistics for India, but estimates about the USA should rid people of the illusion that conventional crimes are the bigger killer. According to one reliable estimate by Reiman in 1972, the number of deaths resulting from industrial diseases and accidents in the USA was 1,14,000 while only 20,000 deaths occurred owing to being shot, cut, beaten, or poisoned and being termed as a case of homicide. Had there been a time clock for murder, it would show one murder in every twenty-six minutes. A leading criminologist Reiman adds: "If a similar crime clock for industrial deaths was constructed and recalling that this clock ticks only for that half of the population that is in the labour force—this clock would show an industrial death about every four-and-a-half minute! In other words, the time it takes for one murder on the crime clock, six workers have already died "just trying to make a living"![6]

During 1973-79, there were 11,436 deaths from occupational accidents and diseases as against 3,291 homicide deaths. Two things need to be noted in connection with this comparison. First, most of the deaths resulting from industrial accidents and diseases were avoidable. Had the companies concerned adhered to safety regulations besides providing proper rest, periodic medical check-up and adequate treatment, many lives could have been saved. Second, while deaths from homicide relate to the entire population, the deaths from industrial accidents and diseases pertain only to those who are included in working population, employed in the organised sector. Thus, those who could be done to death by corporate murderers constitute less than fifty per cent of the total population! In addition, there are genuine doubts about the number of deaths resulting from industrial accidents and diseases. While homicide deaths are more or less correctly recorded, other type of deaths are not, because of underplaying and some other factors entering to cloud the real cause.[7]

So far as deaths at the hands of common criminals are concerned, they can be avoided, to a large extent, by remaining confined to one's homes and houses, but this safety is not available in the case of corporate sector criminals. Improperly tested or spurious drugs and adulterated food and drinks can kill people even when they are in their own homes which are no longer safe. There may be an accident like the one that happened in the Union Carbide factory at Bhopal, killing or maiming people even though they were sleeping comfortably in their bed. Growing pollution of air and water, caused by factories has been slowly poisoning people to death. Such factories have been correctly termed as "silent killers at work".

Then there are injuries and diseases, caused by corporate sector dealing with activities which do not lead to deaths. If such incidents are added to avoidable deaths resulting from industrial accidents and diseases, we may get an inkling of corporate criminal violence. Comparing it with conventional criminal violence, one finds that the latter pales into insignificance.

Now, let us turn our attention to economic costs, inflicted by corporate sector crimes. Unlike common crimes, corporate sector crimes are generally non-violent in nature. Even a person belonging to religions or sects for which killing even an insect is supposed to be anathema can merrily deprive an old man or a widow with nobody to care about of his or her entire savings and reduce him or her to complete destitution without any qualms of conscience. This kind of robbery is committed not with the help of fire-arms, but with cunningness and deception. Woody Guthrie in "Pretty Boy Floyd" says:

'Now as through this world I ramble.
I see lots of funny men,
Some rob you with a six gun,
And some with a fountain pen.'

Corporate sector criminals rob people in various ways both directly and indirectly. Manipulating prices in such a way as to peg them to a very high level is a common form of robbery. For this, shortages are wilfully created by indulging in hoarding, cutting output, combining with other producers, bribing corrupt officals and ministers in several other ways. Thus, buyers have to pay more than what they would have paid had there been competitive conditions in the market. Walter Lippman, the celebrated American journalist has rightly remarked, "Competition has survived only where men have been unable to abolish it".

Over the years, everywhere in the world, the priority of businessmen in general has changed 'to a considerable extent from efficiency in production to efficiency in manipulation, including manipulation of the government for the attainment of preferential advantages.[8]

Illegal mergers and take-overs, deliberately leading the company into the red and then into bankruptcy, besides other shady deals are resorted to defraud shareholders and creditors. In India banks have been forced to write-off huge amounts as bad or irrecoverable debts because the companies who borrowed them have been rendered sick by their promoters-cum-management. There is seldom any stringent punishment given for this kind of fraud. Rendering a company knowingly or wilfully sick is a very profitable business in this country. It is a convenient device to cheat the investing people and the public exchequer and then the government is approached to put in more money through financial institutions and accord tax concessions and subsidies to nurse it back to health on the pretext of saving jobs of workers. It is strange that there is neither any investigation nor search for the culprits who wilfully reduce the company to the state of sickness.

In India, there is no verification of the credentials and competence of promoters before giving permission to enter primary market to gather subscriptions to equity capital and launch production. In U.P., Bihar and other parts of the country many a sugar factory has been rendered sick because of mismanagement and siphoning off of funds and neglecting maintenance and modernisation work. After a sugar factory becomes sick, its inability to make payments to cane-growers and keep itself running, creates big noise and political pressure is exerted on the government to come to its rescue. The government writes-off or postpones the recovery of cane cess and other dues, pumps in money to keep it going, but seldom are the factory owners hauled up for their neglect, mismanagement and siphoning off of funds. This may be because the powers-that-be are not interested as there is *quid pro quo.* Sugar factory owners provide men and materials to politicians during normal as well as election times. This shows why the politicians keep themselves confined only to verbal attacks on sugar factory-owners. Sugar industry is no exception. One can see same things happening in cotton, jute and a host of other industries.

Cheating is an indispensable means of becoming a successful businessman or industrialist because generous and honest souls make poor businessmen. And this cheating can be even in the name of religion and God. To verify this statement, let us go to any wholesale grain market in north India. We usually find a box in every dealer's shop, marked with the word *dharmartha seva* (for religious purpose) and whenever a deal is struck, some money is deducted from or added to the total amount to be paid and is put in the box. The amount so collected is supposed to be spent for religious purposes. On enquiring, one will find that the religious purposes also include the marriage of daughters and grand-daughters of the grain dealer. Ask him about this and he will tell you that performing the marriage ceremony of a girl is, according to scriptures, a great religious act. He will retort 'Is *Kanyadan* not an act of great religious significance?'

Thus, public money is appropriated for private purposes. Not only this, the *seth* builds temples, dharamshalas, digs wells and makes donations to schools, etc. to perpetuate the memory of his father, mother and other relations. A Lakshminarayan temple built with public money (coming from companies at the expense of shareholders and government) may become a Birla Mandir or JK Mandir and full size statues of the businessman or his father/mother may be installed in front of a temple or dharamshala. If one goes to Rishikesh, one's attention will be immediately attracted by such statues.

There are a number of educational institutions in India, established to perpetuate the names of industrialists like Birlas, Tatas, Singhanias, Modis, Shankarlal and his elder brother Shri Ram (both of whom were knighted by the British for their loyalty) and so on, and then there are various foundations named after them. All of them have been built with the money which should have gone to shareholders as dividends, or to the government as tax. Here arises a pertinent moral question. What right have these people got to use money belonging to others to build institutions and foundations and confer awards in their own names? If they spend out of their own income, there can be no objection. They are in a position to pick the pockets of their shareholders and the government because of the law that one who manipulates to have a majority at the annual general meeting can impose one's will on others. Nobody till now has given a thought to prevention of this kind of cheating and fraud.

We know of one trader who made lots of money by indulging in blackmarketing in grains and other essential items during the Second World War. His activities must have caused a great deal of misery and sufferings to common people. Profiting by such miseries and sufferings, he, later, set up educational institutions to perpetuate his name and put a gloss over his black past. One of them is located in Delhi and every year on Founder's Day, he is eulogised!

Balzac's Experience

It is not only in India but elsewhere too that public misery has come handy to businessmen and industrialists as a source of profit. Let us refer to what the great novelist Balzac says of France of the early years of the nineteenth century: "The foundations of his (Goriot's) fortune were laid in the time of the scarcity (real or artificial), when the price of grain of all kinds rose enormously in Paris. People used to fight for bread at the baker's doors...' It was during this year that Goriot made the money which, at a later time, was to give him all the advantage of the great capitalist over the small buyer."[9]

Balzac adds: "Goriot was an authority second to none on all questions relating to corn, flour and "middlings", and the production, storage and quality of grain. He could estimate the yield of the harvest and foresee market prices. He bought his cereals in Sicily and imported Russian wheat."[10] He indulged in hoarding to create an artificial scarcity where there was none. It reminds one of the role of M/s M.M. Ispahani (later, a big industrial house of Pakistan) and their sub-agents M/s Hanuman Bux Vishavanath in the Bengal famine of 1943. They indulged in hoarding and profiteering while people with insufficient purchasing power were starving and dying in the streets of Calcutta.

This story is repeated time and again when an artificial scarcity is created by businessmen and industrialists by conniving with government agencies. Balzac's Goriot like the Ispahanis, who 'was in the secret of the famous scarcity of grain and laid the foundation of his fortune in those days by selling flour for ten times its cost'[11] appears again and again in our country.

Thus, behind every great business fortune or corporate empire, there is invariably a great deal of cheating, fraud and other criminal activity. If one looks around, it will be seen that a number of smugglers and other underworld operators are emerging as great tycoons. In our metros they have come to acquire real estates and have set up companies to undertake trading, financing, capital market operations, newspaper publishing, air transportation, manufacturing and so on. Some of them have made great strides and their political leverage is also substantial. They have unhindered access to bed chambers and ante-rooms of a number of decision-makers.

At the very outset of this chapter, we stated that we would be discussing two types of crimes, namely, the crimes committed for corporations and those committed by certain individuals who are privy to certain decisions and information directly or indirectly by virtue of their positions in them. Both these crimes are committed against the people at large. The most important among the latter is insider trading.

Generally speaking, working on the basis of inside information to which one has access to has always been regarded as unfair. For example, if a question paper setter reveals fully or partially its nature or direction or a Minister or Civil Servant discloses the operative part of the policy or proposals to his near and dear ones either free or for some consideration, this is regarded not as unethical, but, in most cases, a criminal or corrupt practice. Both the society and the law view it with seriousness.

In the world of business, insider trading has been in existence for quite a few hundred years, though it has been made a criminal activity vis-a-vis the corporate world relatively much recently. It is quite interesting to go a bit in the history of insider trading.

By insider trading we mean trading in stocks on the basis of "materials information" unavailable to other. In other words, basing one's activity on non-public information to which one is directly or indirectly privy by virtue of one's position of trust. Rule 10b-5 of the US Securities and Exchange Commission declares it as an offence "to employ any device, scheme, or artifice to defraud in connection with the purchase or sale of any security." Here what Elizabeth Szockyj says needs to be taken note of. To quote the same: "Corporate officers and major shareholders are restricted as to when and on what grounds, they may trade company stock, but insider trading is not illegal in the United States. On the contrary, allowing officers and directors of corporations to own and to deal in stock in their company is supported in order to reward past performance and to supply an incentive for future profitability. What is illegal is when an insider trades on information that is confidential or not available to the general public, such as advance knowledge regarding a new product or unanticipated profits or losses. Trading on non-public information, or tipping other people who then trade, is said to undermine the fair and honest operation of our securities markets'."[12]

Insider trading in stocks is as old as the modern bourse. The first instance of insider trading which has been studied at length occurred more than two centuries ago on the Wall Street in which an Assistant Secretary of Treasury, William Duer, took advantage of his inside knowledge of governmental decision-making process and passed the information to which he was privy onto private parties with whom he had a secret arrangement for sharing the gains.

With his guidance, speculators purchased and sold public securities at right moments and obtained tremendous amounts of profit. Inside information considerably reduces risks by removing most of the uncertainties about the future. When two Dutch firms and a leading banker joined hands to speculate on the Wall Street and sent their agent Brissot de Warville to America and instructed him that, before clinching a deal, he must 'Study it, and if at first view it looks romantic, find the means of saving it from that objection; converse upon it with intelligent persons; find such as are sufficiently attached to great objects, to be willing to concur in them with zeal, when they are designed for the aid and consolation of humanity'.

On arrival in New York in 1788, Brissot spotted Duer and began cultivating him and, as a result, got valuable inside information as regards the direction of government policies and their likely implications. Brissot's masters, with the help of Duer's inside information, contrived a sustained bull market and there set in a veritable mania which inspired poets to write verses. When the bubble burst in 1792, William Duer landed himself in jail for violating the oath of office and secrecy, where he died in 1799.

The fear expressed by the *New York Daily Gazette* at last came true. It had published a poem in 1791 when James Madison had told Jefferson that 'stock and scrip (are) the sole domestic subjects of conversation.' The last six lines of the poem are sure to remind an Indian reader of the situation prevailed here some years ago when the Big Bull Harshad Mehta was in a commanding position:

'Touched by the wand of speculation,
A frenzy runs through all the nation;
For soon or late, so truth advises,
Things must assume their proper sizes;
And sure as death all mortal trips,
Thousands will rue the name of the SCRIPS.'

There is a widely circulated story that the London branch of the well-known bank of Rothschild made huge gains on the basis of intelligence about Wellington's victory over Napoleon. It came through a carrier pigeon. It is said that the Rothschilds first spread the rumour that the trend of the battle was unfavourable to the British and Napoleon's victory looked like a certainty. To impart credence to it, they began selling their holdings of British government bonds. Others followed suit, but when prices nose-dived, they cornered a huge number of bonds and, after Wellington's victory, made a great fortune.[13]

Kennedy: Made Huge Profit

Joseph Kennedy, the father of John F. Kennedy, profited a great deal on the basis of inside information that the Ford Motor Company was working towards the acquisition of Pond Creek Coal and, within a few months, he was able to gather a profit of $650,000 on an investment of just $24,000.[14]

During those days these deals were, however, not

illegal as there was no law in the statute book banning them. The US Congress woke up to the evil consequences of insider trading only after the abuses started mounting up during the 1920s. It created the Securities and Exchange Commission (SEC) in 1933 and President Franklin Roosevelt appointed Joseph Kennedy as its first head. Kennedy knew all the intricacies and all the players involved in the game. It was just like appointing Jacques Collin alias Vautrin, the underworld don of Balzac's novels incharge of controlling crimes in Paris and he did successfully discharge his commission.[15]

It will not be out of place to mention that Kennedy was also an ace smuggler who had seen to it that the prohibition law was reduced to a joke in practice. He made huge profits out of his smuggling venture. He was later appointed as US Ambassador to Britain.

Roosevelt was anxious to see the SEC restore common investor's confidence in the stock market after the Great Crash of 1929 and create a level playing field for all investors. As ill luck would have it, the Commission could not achieve much, as it was not easy to prove the charge of insider trading convincingly and conclusively in a court of law. In the cases where convictions did take place, punishment was limited only to pecuniary fines. One big drawback in the law was that what constituted insider trading was not unambiguously defined. Some insider traders argued that curbing insider trading would deprive speculation of its charm and they quoted John Maynard Keynes in their support. He had remarked: "The game of professional investment is intolerably boring... to anyone who is entirely exempt from the gambling instinct".[16]

But, here we are not concerned with the proposition whether insider trading is desirable. We only want to state that a number of countries found it as an evil practice and made enactments to curb it by branding it as a criminal activity. Britain took notice of it more than half-a-century after the Americans had put their laws on the statute book. The Financial Services Act, 1986 of Britain provided the legal basis "to regulate the carrying on of investment business," which specifically took note of insider trading.

Britain's amended insider-dealing law terms a person guilty of insider-dealing "if, knowing all the relevant facts, he takes advantage of inside information".[17] The public debate over the law at its enactment stage was not only lively but it had reflected a genuine concern on the part of London on the damage insider-trading had been doing. '*The Economist*' reported: "City-dealers may have depended on inside information for their profits in the past, but most now accept that the practice damages a market's integrity."[18]

It was pointed out that the biggest problem with any such law was how to make its enforcement effective. "Since 1987, when the existing Act came into force, the London Stock Exchange has referred more than 100 cases of suspected insider-dealing to the Department of Trade and Industry. Yet there have been only 27 prosecutions and these have produced just 12 convictions. Given the profits that can be made by judicious insider-dealing, such a record is hardly likely to deter crooks."[19] As against this, there were, on an average, 35 convictions a year in the USA mainly because the law was more stringent and the SEC had greater expertise in catching and hauling the culprits before the court of law.

Ivan Boesky: 'Greed is Good'

The immediate provocation for this British enactment was the Ivan Boesky insider trading scandal in the USA in the early 1980s. His operations had within their purview Britain too. It is not only interesting but instructive too to have a look at this scandalours hero. Boesky, a Jew, was the son of a Russian-born businessman. He was a lawyer by training and had become, within a very short time, nothing less than a legend on the Wall Street just like our Big Bull Harshad Mehta on the Dalal Street a decade later. His motto was "greed is good." He had acquired a personal fortune of around $200 million and was included among the 400 richest Americans, published by Forbes. His Ivan F. Boesky Corporation came to have around

$ 1billion at its disposal for use in arbitrage deals. Through a subsidiary, Seemala Corporation which was named after his wife Seema, he had a seat on the New York Stock Exchange. He had controlling interest in a British investment trust — Cambrian and General Securities PLC. His holdings in this company came to $ 50 million. Along with his wife he owned 53 per cent of the prestigious Beverly Hills Hotel, valued at more than $ 100 million. 'Boesky was so successful that Wall Street flattered him by emulating him. If word leaked out that Boesky had plunged into a stock position, that alone was enough to bring in a horde of copycat investors after him. He could move the market all by himself. His reputation was so secure that an investor who wanted to jump on the Boesky bandwagon and pour money into his arbitrage fund had to agree to give him 40 per cent of all profits, while absorbing 90 per cent of all losses.'[20]

According to one of his accomplices in insider trading, who also had to go to jail: "Over the years he had used some of his fortune, rather overtly...in an attempt to buy respect. After he contributed hundreds of thousands of dollars to Harvard University, he was appointed to an advisory panel at the school, and, thus, qualified for membership at New York's Harvard Club. Donating $2 million to the Jewish Theological Seminary of America, the school named a library for him and his wife. For five years he was reported to have contributed more than $ 100,000 to the campaign coffers of national political candidates; in turn, he was appointed an adviser on Jewish Affairs to the Chairman of the Republican Committee.'[21] Incidentally, another big insider trader of the USA, Michael Milken, was also a generous contributor to public causes and charitable organisations. He too was convicted and sentenced to a jail-term of ten years. This was the longest sentence handed over to an operator on the Wall Street. Earlier, this dubious distinction belonged to Paul Bilzerian, a former Chairman of Singer, who was sent to jail for four years for giving false information to SEC. In 1992, he appeared in Court to testify against Alan Rosenthal, a former colleague at Drexel Burnham Lambert.

When the Ivan Boesky insider trading scandal broke out into the open, the joke which made the rounds was "knowledge is power, inside knowledge is power squared."

It is not only difficult to prove the crime of insider trading, but those indulging in this activity devise novel ways to evade the net. For example, Denis Levine and his friend, Wilkis, decided to profit by insider trading and an agreement was reached among them which had the following terms and conditions:

1. Each of us will only trade on the other's information.

2. We will never share tips with other members of our family or with friends and we will keep our activities secret even from our wives.

3. We will trade stocks only through secret foreign accounts.

4. We will share information only in person and when we speak to each other by phone, we will refer to one another by a code name so that no one will notice our association.

5. We will use common sense.[22]

Alas! even after this kind of agreement to keep their business of insider trading extremely secret and using the Bahamas branch of a Swiss bank as the conduit, Levine was caught. He was accused of using non-public information to trade in securities of not less than 54 companies. Within a few years, Levine had his trading activities spread over to Panama where there were two companies, namely, International Gold Inc. and Diamond Holding S.A., controlled by him. Three things emerge out of what we have said above: (a) insider traders have their activities spread over many countries, (b) their public faces are quite different from their real ones and (c) they are very cunning people who are difficult to catch.

According to Levine, nothing can stop a really determined insider trader. He can pierce the Chinese Wall which consists in preventing one department of the company from having access to the information available to other departments in its entirety. It is more difficult to get the culprit punished. In a typical American company "as many as one hundred people, ranging from corporate executives to secretaries, may be privy to inside knowledge concerning a given deal; the very nature of the work requires that even the most junior people encounter non-public information; how can anyone prove who knew what?"[23]

Even before the Boesky and the Milken scandals, there was the Prudential-Bache scandal which till today remains the costliest financial scam. It began in 1981 and involved Prudential-Bache, a stockbroking firm which fraudulently sold to lakhs of Americans investments worth billions of dollars in its capacity as a subsidiary of Prudential Insurance, one of the oldest firms in the field of life insurance. It itself admitted that it had for years, circulated fraudulent literature to dupe the prospective investors.

Years after the Boesky and the Milken scandals had subsided and the moral indignation over insider trading and junk bonds that had blackened the face of Wall Street had waned, there arose another spate of scandals involving the Salomon Brothers, Merril Lynch, Union Bank of Switzerland, Smith Barney and American Express. The Salomon Brothers admitted in August, 1991 that it had attempted to corner a May Treasuries auction, faking customer orders in that sale and others and all these irregularities were suitably covered up.

Less than a year after this, to be exact, in February 1992, a prolonged trial resulted in a judgement that held four persons operating in the city of London guilty of fraud. One of them had worked for a big stockbroking firm and the three for a subsidiary of National Westminster Bank. The scandal involving these four came to be known as the Blue Arrow affair. The story behind this scandal was as follows: The Blue Arrow, a British employment agency tried to raise $1.4 billion through rights issue. It needed funds to take over an American company, Manpower.

Unfortunately, the issue evoked a discouraging response from the shareholders. Only 38 per cent of the issue was subscribed. In this, the County, British merchant banking organisation also had a big stake. Its success would have boosted up the standing of the County. A scheme to salvage the situation was hatched. The remaining shares were to be sold by placing them with the investing institutions who were to find buyers by spreading the falsehood that the rights issue had been a grand success. After the closure of the rights issue, the County and other conspirators bought the shares to bring the proportion taken-up to 49 per cent. The County, in all, acquired 13.5 per cent of Blue Arrow equity but did not disclose to the authorities who were to be informed of any holding exceeding 5 per cent under the existing company law.

Unfortunately, on October 19, 1987, there was a crash of stock prices and the share price of the Blue Arrow went down by 50 per cent which dashed the hope of the County to enrich itself substantially. The manipulations by the County and others led them into deeper troubles and the culprits were caught.[24]

If this is the situation in the USA, one may imagine how difficult it will be in a country like India to curb this menace. Here, SEBI lacks expertise and infrastructure to enforce ban on insider trading by successfully catching the offenders and bringing them before courts of law. Japan could enforce legal sanctions against insider trading as late as 1989.

In Germany insider trading was not punishable by law till as late as 1991 and it was made an offence as a result of pressures from other European countries. Till then, Germans relied on a voluntary "Code of Good Conduct", drawn in 1970 and subsequently amended to make it more effective. Those who were likely to have an access-to inside information had undertaken to abide by the code. Among them were the bankers, company directors, auditors and so on. Stock exchanges were to probe alleged trading on the basis of inside information which was non-public. Once somebody was caught violating the Code, he was boycotted by his fellow businessmen and this was supposed to act as a big deterrent. But the critics were not convinced of the efficacy of the Code. They asserted that there was widespread bending of the rules, even by those trading on stock exchanges on behalf of banks, the committees of bourses to look into the alleged violation of the Code were not effective and scandals were very quickly and cleverly swept under the carpet. At one point of time some high-ups of the Deutsche Bank were alleged to be aiding inside-traders.

India has begun thinking of tackling it only since the formation of the SEBI in the 1990s. Under the stewardship of G.V. Ramakrishna, the first Chairman of the SEBI, an insider trading code was formulated and three or four cases were investigated, one of which involved the TISCO, but nothing concrete came out.

In India, there is a thread that binds brokers, big investors, directors and executives in the corporate sector, government officials and politicians in power and they help one another to manipulate the market and stock prices.

It is an open secret that when the Congress Working Committee met in the 1940s to consider the Crips Mission proposals in New Delhi, the wherewithal was provided by a leading business house. Its intelligent executives were deputed as Seva Dal volunteers to serve tea, coffee and snacks to participants while the meeting was on and its progress was monitored by a top person from that business house, who reported the trend to high ups in Bombay and Calcutta, who acted accordingly at the bourses and made lakhs of rupees. The point to be stressed is that the relevant information was fraudulently acquired by this business house while it was non-public. Hence, other players in the market were in a disadvantageous position. This practice of securing non-public information material to operation at the bourses continues and one can daily find lots of people who are on the payroll of business houses, hanging around the offices of important political parties, leaders, ministers and top bureaucrats with the sole purpose of gathering helpful intelligence. In this work, editors and correspondents of newspapers, owned by big business are also used. It is not without significance that Indian business houses and multinational companies employ in their service close relations of top bureaucrats and politicians in power and pay them high salaries and perks which their qualifications and capabilities rarely merit. Many a time, top bureaucrats and military officials are employed by them after retirement in order to reward them for their past services and use them to gather intelligence from the offices where they still continue to have influence.

Whenever a company is about to issue bonus or right shares, insiders try to corner as much stock as possible to gather profits after the relevant decision is announced by the Board of Directors. In this operation, some bureaucrats and politicians are also brought in so that they can also make substantial gains. Likewise, if a company is heading towards an imminent disaster, this fact is suppressed as long as possible and prices are pegged and stocks are disposed of. Most of the buying and selling activity is carried on *benami* (in somebody else's name) or in fictitious names so that the real operator is not caught.

Futures Trading: An Old Corporate Sector Crime

There is yet another type of corporate sector crime. It occurs in the sphere of futures trading. Since most people are not aware of what this kind of activity means, it is difficult for them to comprehend the crime relating to it. In simple terms, futures trading pertains to an agreement to buy or sell any particular commodity in a specified quantity at some future date. The agreement sets out in standardised terms (wherever this kind of trading is legal), the quality and quantity of the commodity and the place of delivery. Its history shows that this sort of trading arose in the past mainly in order to reduce wide price fluctuations resulting from shortages and excesses in certain important produces harvested and marketed within short spans of time. The forerunner of futures contracts was forward contracting under which contracts were entered upon, fixing the terms of sale in advance of the date of delivery of the goods. Since uncertainty about weather and/or other unforeseen circumstances could affect the supply and demand of the goods, market prices so established in forward contract agreements could considerably deviate from the actual prices obtaining at the stipulated delivery date. These deviations naturally opened the scope for the entry of speculators who came forward to buy or sell futures contracts in order to make profits. According to Kip Schlegel, 'Such speculation in futures markets is considered beneficial to the market, as it increases the number of buyers and sellers, which increases the likelihood of firm commitments for delivery at set prices, thus, reducing uncertainty for producers and processors.'[25]

Historical records show futures trading having come into existence with the advent of merchant capitalism in the 17th century when the Dojima Rice Market was established in Osaka (Japan) has now become a worldwide phenomenon. It has been going on in the USA since 1848. Even where it is banned, it has been going on merrily.

To understand criminal activities in futures trading, we must have a brief look at how it operates. Basically, it consists of two activities, namely, hedging and speculating. Hedging requires taking a particular position in the futures market that is equal and opposite to a position held in the cash or spot market and it serves to protect against any future adverse price changes. Losses likely to result from decline in price in future are sought to be offset by an opposite and equal gain in the value of futures contract.

Hedging serves as an important protective device for those taking to futures trading. Investment firms take recourse to it to hedge treasury bills and bonds against inflation while MNCs use futures market to protect themselves from fluctuations in international exchange rates. For example, an Indian firm, planning to open an office in London will enter into futures contracts in the pound sterling for its stock of US dollars so that it does not face any difficulty in its initial operations.

While hedgers try to lock in a price for a commodity

or financial instrument for delivery at a specified date, speculators, no matter whether they are individuals or institutions, buy or sell in the expectation of prices going up or down in ensuing days with the aim of making a profit. Quite often speculators base their decisions on sophisticated analysis of market and the factors that affect conditions in it. They employ modern forecasting techniques and gadgets. There are, however, speculators who are sometimes swayed by rumours.

Kip Schlegel has described the formal structure of futures trading 'along a linear path consisting of three central entities: commission houses, exchanges and clearing houses. Orders are placed by customers, who may be individuals or institutions—either hedgers or speculators. Clustering around customers are a range of satellite occupations to assist their entry in the markets—commodity pool operators, commodity trading advisers and introducing brokers. Orders are placed... to commission houses—referred to as futures commission merchants—which serve the gate-keeping role, ensuring that those who wish to trade have sufficient financial backing to secure their end of the contract. Commission houses may serve one or more of the exchanges with their employees acting as sales representatives. Customers deal with the sales agents, who secure a specific cash amount for each contract. This figure constitutes "the margin," collateral signifying an obligation to the terms of the contract. Having secured the necessary margin, the commission houses become legally liable for the contracts traded by them'.

"Once the margin is established, the commission house agent will time-stamp the order and a runner will rush it to a floor trader working in the appropriate pit of the exchange. Generally, there are three types of floor traders. In the first group are brokers employed by trading firms whose sole duty is to fill orders from those firms. The second group of traders, known as locals, trade only for their own accounts. Many locals reap profits by quickly moving in and out of commodities, termed "scalping", taking advantage of small changes in prices rather than assuming major positions. A third group consists of independent brokers who trade on their own accounts but will also execute orders for customers for commissions, usually a couple of dollars per contract. The locals and independents are viewed as vital to the exchanges as they add liquidity to the markets, liquidity meaning the quantity of bids and offers; the narrower the spread between them, the better the price for customers".

'In the pits, via the open-outcry system, brokers and traders shout and gesture prices as they negotiate and compete to determine the going price of a particular commodity. Once the order is filled, the trader will write a ticket recording the price, quantity, time of execution and the identity of the trade counterpart. The broker will report the price to an exchange price reporter, who relays price changes to the central quotation computer. The computer will then transmit the current price to the electronic price-boards facing the trading flour and send it around the world via computerized information systems'.

'The various orders for the day are recorded and settled at a clearing house. Using cards to represent each trader, the representative from the clearing house verifies the sale and purchase of each contract, debits and credits each account and guarantees payment and delivery. In essence, the clearing house ensures market integrity by serving as "buyer to all sellers and seller to all buyers"'.[26]

Criminal acts in the sphere of futures trading relate to, not honouring the commitments as regards the delivery, quality and quantity of the commodity and combining together to manipulate prices. At times, speculators combine to spread rumours about some impending scarcity or abundance of some product or the other in order to create panic in the market.

In recent years, the collapse of the Barings Bank has been the result of the fraudulent acts of its 28-year old operator, Nick Leeson, who is at present serving a long prison sentence in Singapore. Before it came to be taken over and merged with another European bank, depositors and investors of this 233-year-old merchant bank, spent many a sleepless night. In addition, there prevailed an utter confusion in both forward trading business and financial markets all over the world. A reputed financial journal wrote: 'Armed with little more than a computer screen and the Barings name, 28-year-old Nick Leeson, went on a spending spree and racked up losses that until recently would have required the resources of a large Latin American country.' It went on to add that Leeson's trading activities 'apparently have accomplished what centuries of financial panics have failed to do—destroy the House of Barings, a merchant bank that sometimes appeared more powerful than the governments it financed, whose clients include the Queen of England and whose emerging markets financing stretches back more than two centuries.'[27]

The collapse of the bank was the result of Leeson's miscalculations as regards Japanese stock prices. Operating on the Singapore International Monetary Exchange (Simex), and on the Osaka Securities Exchange, he had built up massive positions in futures contracts betting that Japanese stock prices would rise. Over a span of few days, he entered into futures contracts to buy huge amounts of Japanese shares without any formal authorization from his superiors based in London, though it was claimed that he had been informally given a go-ahead signal. If this claim was true, it meant his superiors were also responsible for the disaster brought upon the bank. Had Leeson succeeded, his superiors could also have shared the gains. His failure cost the Barings PLC more than $1 billion and its independent existence. Commenting on this affair, Gary Silverman wrote: "Leeson's speciality was trading futures contracts on Japan's Nikkei Stock Average, instruments sold on the Simex and in Osaka. Traders buy the contract to bet on the direction of the stock benchmark—a financial instrument linked to the value of an underlying security, currency or index".

"Derivatives trading has recently produced a series of spectacular losses—everywhere from China to

California's Orange County—but nearly all those deals involved clients who later claimed they did not understand the derivatives they had bought. Barings is saying something different. It claims it did not really understand one of the derivatives traders it had hired".

'However, Leeson's activity was no secret to the markets. In Osaka, where brokerages' exposure is a matter of record, Barings' outstanding loan positions soared from slightly more than 3,000 in early January to more than 20,000 by mid-February—nearly eight times more than any other player'.[28]

What emerged out of the Baring's episode was the conclusion that Leeson and his superiors who were supposed to keep a watch on his activities and regulate them were guilty of criminal irresponsibility.

REFERENCES

1. Steven Box, *Power, Crime and Mystification*, London, 1983, p. 18. Box refers to Clinard and Yeager who have stated: 'Of 28 social problems textbooks published between 1964 and 1978, a total of only 110 pages discussed the importance of large corporations to society; Of these pages only 11 mentioned corporate crime and all but one of these pages were contained in two textbooks published in 1978. Approximately 96 per cent of all social problems textbooks mentioning, generally briefly, either corporations or corporate crime were published in 1972 or later.' *Ibid.*, p. 19.
2. Cf. 'if a person intends doing *someone* harm, it cannot be assumed that s/he displays a disdain towards humanity, although it is clearly directed towards the particular intended victim. However, if indifference characterizes the attitude, a person has towards the consequences of his/her action, then s/he are indifferent as to who suffers—it could literally be anybody—and this does display disdain for humanity in general. In this sense, the intent to harm someone may be less immoral (or at least no more immoral) than to be indifferent as to whom is harmed. Evil should not be unrecognized merely because it is as banal as indifference; indifference rather than intent may well be the greater cause of avoidable human suffering, particularly in the case of corporate crime...corporate crime should be conceptualized so as to induce acts of *omission* as well as the more obvious acts of *commission*.' *Ibid.*, p. 21.
3. "Accountancy and White-Collar Crime" by Joseph T. Wells in *The*

Annals of the American Academy of Political and Social Science, January 1993, p. 84.

4. *Ibid.*, p. 85.
5. Steven Box, *op. cit.*, p. 21.
6. Quoted in *Ibid.*, p. 26.
7. 'The cause of death is frequently ambiguous and pinning it down to occupational environments, which may have been experienced years or even decades ago, is clearly no easy matter. Furthermore, in the processes of socially constructing the cause(s) of death, there are considerable social forces directed towards minimizing the number of deaths certified as occupationally induced.' *Ibid.*
8. Edwin H. Sutherland's paper "Crime of Corporations" in Gilbert Geis and Robert F. Meir, *op. cit.*, p. 82.
9. Honoré de Balzac, *Pere Goriot*, New York, 1962, p. 87.
10. *Ibid.*
11. *Ibid.*, p. 76.
12. Elizabeth Szockyj's paper "Insider Trading: The SEC Meets Carl Karcher" in *The Annals of The American Academy of Political and Social Science*, Vol. 525, January 1993, p. 47.
13. Denis B. Levine, *Inside Out: An Insider's Account of the Wall Street*, New York, 1991, p. 58.
14. *Ibid.*
15. Honoré de Balzac, *A Harlot High and Low*, London, 1970.
16. Quoted in Denis B. Levine, *op. cit.*, p. 58.
17. *The Economist*, November 7, 1992.
18. *Ibid.*
19. *Ibid.*
20. Denis B. Levine, *op. cit.*, p. 135.
21. *Ibid.*, pp. 135-36.
22. *Ibid.*, p. 73.
23. *Ibid.*, p. 63 Cf. 'Illegal insider trading has been one of the good rackets. The criminal risks little. Detection is unlikely, but if one is caught, punishment for a first-time offender normally is light. The potential rewards, on the other hand, are great'. *The Annals of the American Academy of Political and Social Science*, Vol. 525, January 1993, Preface by special editors of the volume Gilbert Geis and Paul Jesilow, p. 10.
24. For details, see *The Economist*, March 7, 1992.
25. Kip Schlegel's paper "Crime in the Pits: The Regulation of Futures Trading", *Ibid.*, p. 60.
26. *Ibid.*, pp. 61-62.
27. *Far Eastern Economic Review*, March 9, 1995.
28. *Ibid.*

3

BCCI: The Rogue Corporation

Greed and fraud have been at the root of corporate sector crimes ever since the dawn of industrial capitalism and the emergence of joint-stock form of business organisation. How greed and fraud have operated has changed with changing times.

Abedi: An Evil Genius Tycoon

Globalisation and the revolution in information technology have given a free rein to crimes and they now play with very few constraints. This can be very well illustrated by the rise and fall of the BCCI (Bank of Credit and Commerce International). The story of this rogue banking corporation is of special interest to the people of the Indian sub-continent because its founder Agha Hasan Abedi, an evil genius, belonged to it.

Abedi was born in the early 1920s in U.P. but migrated to Pakistan after the partition. There, he came to have a commercial bank of his own—United Bank Ltd. which prospered till 1972 when it was nationalised by Zulfikar Ali Bhutto. But Abedi was not to change his line of business. What he did, was to operate on an international plane rather than within the national boundaries of Pakistan. He realised that offshore banking with no control from any central bank had enormous possibilities and opportunities for a person like him. It was a completely unregulated world of banking whose contours were not even imagined by any earlier authority on modern banking from Walter Bagehot to R.S. Sayers. Nor could Marx and the theorists of imperialism have any inkling of its potential. Off-shore banking offers greater protection and opportunity to all kinds of racketeers than the Swiss banks with all their rules of secrecy. Talking of the BCCI, *The Economist* wrote as follows: "It is starting to read like one of the lesser John Buchan novels, the sort that brought the global conspiracy theory into the pages of English literature. A fiendishly cunning gang of financial crooks, with origins somewhere, east of Cyprus, silently worms its way into the world's money markets and then, by a mixture of favour and terror, gets itself involved with the operations of some of the world's most respectable governments. When the moment is ripe the veil is ripped aside, the wriggling pile of scandals is exposed, honest politicians blench, markets plunge, the end of decent society is nigh".[1]

Abedi arranged for just $2.5 million as seed money from the Bank of America and floated the BCCI whose two main arms were incorporated in Luxembourg and the Cayman Islands though most of its top executives operated from London where its head office was located and the Bank of England could discover this fact after as many as 14 years!

It prospered without any interruption and at a break-speed and within less than two decades it became one of the largest privately-owned financial institutions in the entire world and its assets came to $20 billion with branches in as many as 72 nations. It had a core of 3,000 customers around the globe, most of them were corrupt and crooked but there were a number of careless and innocent people among them too. Villainous drug-traffickers, including one of their kingpins—a former dictator of Panama, terrorists, members of ruling families of the Arab world, intelligence agencies like the CIA and the ISI, the mafia dons and smugglers of different varieties patronised it. The launderers of the dirty money found it specially convenient.

Its customers came to include top businessmen and politicians of the world. Among its customers were Ferdinand and Imelda Marcos of Philippines, Saudi arms dealer, Adnan Khashogi, the Duvalier family of Haiti and a lot of top military brass of Pakistan and Nigeria besides the bigwigs from the Arab world.

Abedi had very close connections with Jimmy Carter of the USA and the German socialist leader, Willy Brandt. Carter was among his friends and defenders. The following report is quite revealing.

'Inside the entrance to the Carter Center and presidential library in Atlanta, opened in 1983, the Pakistani banker's name is carved in stone as one of two chief donors who contributed $575,000. He also served as co-chairman of Carter's Global Inc., a foundation designed to promote Third World agricultural and environmental projects, to which he... donated $9.2 million... His co-chairman, Ryoichi Sasaka, who once called himself 'the world's wealthiest fascist'.'[2]

The other recipients of Abedi's largesse included the 84-year-old Clark Clifford, a former Defence Secretary under Lyndon Johnson and Adviser to every Democratic President from Harry S. Truman onwards and Andrew Young, a former Atlanta mayor and Carter's Ambassador to the UN. Clifford was once described as "one of Washington's most distinguished power brokers." Young admitted of having received $57,500 annual retainer from Abedi for more than 10 years in return for introducing Abedi to prominent players in economy and politics of the Third World.

The former Labour Prime Minister of Britain, James Callaghan, hailed Abedi as a person of "deep moral concern." And the then UN Secretary-General, Javier Perez de Cuellar, had no hesitation in availing himself of helicopter services provided by Abedi on behalf of the BCCI.

Not only this, the BCCI successfully tried to enter the Soviet Union and China. In the latter, it had its offices transacting banking business. It needs to be underlined that the BCCI was the first Western-style bank permitted to function on the Chinese mainland.

This was partly 'because of Abedi's early support of CITIC, the Chinese investment company that is doorway to China's military-industrial complex.'[3] In his efforts to have ties with China, his friendship with the former US President Jimmy Carter, proved very helpful. Carter took Abedi with him to meet the Chinese leaders. Their association was as good as a reference for Mr. Abedi. China lost about $400m as a result of trusting Mr. Abedi and worse, felt that foreigners had made it look foolish.'[4] China's tangible gain was that, with the help and Islamic connections of the BCCI, it could promote the sale of its Silkworm missiles to Iran and the Arab nations.

Greed for large profits from trade with the Soviet bloc prompted Abedi to visit Moscow in 1985. He wanted to promote arms deals with it and persuade the Soviet authorities to permit the BCCI to open its offices in the USSR. As ill luck would have it, Mikhail Gorbachev in the meantime, came to power and with him came '*perestroika*' which upset Abedi's applecart. It is said that Abedi had propitiated and persuaded greedy government officials and managers of enterprises to support him in his endeavour, but the fact of payoffs came to the surface and these people were removed from their positions under the Gorbachev dispensation.

Abedi: A Champion of the Third World

Abedi posed himself as a champion of the Third World in general and of the Islamic countries in particular. He moved around and met the leaders of the Third World, tried to impress upon them the need to support and strengthen the BCCI which, in turn, would help them meeting their needs of both capital and modern technology.

Abedi funded a seemingly radical international journal *South* which received warm welcome from Leftist intellectuals from all over the world, including India. Gauhar Ayub Khan, the present Foreign Minister of Pakistan and a son of one-time military dictator of Pakistan was closely connected with it. It needs to be noted that the only Third World leader who kept Abedi at a safe distance, was Mrs. Indira Gandhi.

One international business associate of Abedi later testified: "In the West, Abedi presented one face, but in the Muslim world, he and his bankers have always promoted themselves as a Third World, Muslim bank that would eventually dominate global finances by using oil dollars and Abedi's network of influence. And he whispered in the ears of the Sheikhs and the Generals that he would bring them the Muslim bomb."[5]

Muslims in England, Pakistan, Bangladesh, India (especially in Mumbai) and elsewhere reposed great confidence in Abedi and the BCCI. They rushed to deposit their lives' entire savings in the bank. 'As many as 1 million or so depositors were Asians who had believed that the bank was a better home for their savings than the banks of 'colonialist' countries. Foreign workers in the Gulf States, Indian shopkeepers in Britain, all believed in the soundness of Mr. Abedi.'[6] A sum of $20 billion in deposits was fraudulently mobilised from these one million depositors. When the BCCI collapsed in July 1991, $9.5 billion was missing. Reviewing two books on the BCCI affair (*BCCI* by Peter Truell and Larry Gurwin and *A Full Service Bank* by James Ring Adams and Douglas Frantz), *The Economist* (February 20, 1993) wrote: "In hour-long addresses at its lavish international conferences, Mr. Abedi would waffle on about BCCI's mission to serve as the developing world's own financial organisation. But the bank's main purpose was to siphon billions out of the poor countries for their rich, corrupt ruling classes. Hundreds of millions were lost in speculation; Third-World rulers were bribed to place currency reserves in BCCI; there were pay-offs, whores, limos at the airport, free shopping at Harrods and fictional annual reports."

The operation of the bank seemed to be quite efficient and the staff was very well-behaved towards the customers, which was a novel but pleasant experience for those hailing from the Third World. It needs to be noted that the BCCI had lured away a substantial number of bankers of proven calibre from various commercial banks of the Indian sub-continent and elsewhere and they were well paid.

The bank gave special attention to the needs and problems of small business persons and entrepreneurs in developing countries and advanced loans on terms on which no national or international bank was willing to lend.

Besides, it funded quite a number of charitable organisations and socio-cultural causes which normally no bank does. This was the reason that when it became quite clear that all this concern for the Third World in general and poor Muslims in particular was just a facade, many refused to believe it. *Time* staffer John Greenwald wrote: "From Buenos Aires to United Nations headquarters in New York City, the political heat soared amid a new wave of revelations and signs of impending prosecutions of BCCI. Yet, from London to Bangladesh, the bank's depositors, who may have been bilked of $10 billion in deposits, protested BCCI's closure as a Western plot to subjugate the Muslim world."[7]

BCCI: Danger to Society

The BCCI's operations did not arouse any suspicion till the early years of the 1980s because most of the deals and operations remained well camouflaged. Only from then onwards, all scruples and caution were thrown to the winds and the result was that the BCCI sank into one crisis after another. Its greed led it to involve itself in narcotics trade, money laundering, legal and illegal arms deal brokering, clandestine operations on behalf of the US intelligence agency CIA (Central Intelligence Agency) and the Pakistani espionage organisation ISI (Inter Services Intelligence) and liaison with terrorists of various types.

The undercover agents of the BCCI offered money-laundering services to drug dealers. When the offer was accepted, these agents helped move huge sums of money to Colombia via Panama. The bank arranged for laundering of millions of narco-dollars through banking channels and fake businesses and converted them into Colombian currency. It handled narco-dollar accounts and money-laundering needs of the Panamian dictator, Manuel Noriega.

To begin with, the BCCI and two of its subsidiaries

and nine of its officers were indicted for laundering $14 million of drug profits. About four months later, the two subsidiaries pleaded guilty.

It is interesting to note that the CIA had not only an intimate knowledge of both covert and overt functioning of the bank but it kept mum. Nay, it was deeply involved with it.[8] The CIA kept substantial amounts of money at bank's various branches and used its Pakistan office as a conduit for providing millions of dollars in secret US aid to Mujahedin fighting the Soviet-backed government in Afghanistan.[9]

A substantial portion of this aid was stolen by corrupt Pakistani military and civilian officers using their BCCI accounts, with active connivance of the bank. It is said that there was a bank within the bank consisting of secret 'managers' accounts' used to help favourite clients to move funds without evoking the suspicion of international banking authorities. The CIA's excuse was: 'The opportunity to collect intelligence outweighed (the risks of) any dealing with unsavoury characters.' And 'when you're pursuing scoundrels, you can't be a boy scout.'[10] According to Jack Blum, a former US Senate investigator, the BCCI served as some sort of "Federal Express Service" for weapons, drugs, gold and currency for smugglers all over the world. The CIA was aware of the fact that Pakistani officers were using the bank to launder their drug money. To quote Blum, "People who are very close to the Mujahedin have said many of the Pakistani military officials... were stealing our foreign assistance money and using this bank both to hide and market American weapons... that they stole and to market and manage the funds that came from the selling of heroin that was apparently engineered by one of the Mujahedin groups."[11] The CIA was all through aware of the nature and character of the bank. In 1986, the CIA had prepared a five-page report, summarising what it knew about it. *The Economist* (August 3, 1991) has this to say, referring to this report: "This is evidence... that Robert Gates, George Bush's nominee for director of the CIA, knew about the bank's corruption, yet did nothing. In the spring of 1986, Mr. Gates moved from being deputy director in charge of intelligence analysis to number two at the CIA. In the first of those jobs, the report would have been drawn up by staff members for whom he was responsible. A former Commissioner of Customs, Mr. William von Raab, who says he was shown the report in 1988, told the *Financial Times* that Mr. Gates was being "less than candid" about the CIA's involvement with the bank. He has accused Mr. Gates of stonewalling." Even the British counter-espionage agency MI5 was aware of the corrupt practices of the BCCI and its close links with terrorists. Nobody knows whether it reported on the activities of the bank to the government. In fact, the US government was alleged to be aware of the CIA-BCCI link-up. The Senate sub-committee on terrorism charged the government with covering up this relationship because repeated requests could not bring a single document for it from the Justice Department, except one unwanted court transcript. The following report which appeared when the government's connivance was being hotly discussed in the USA is quite revealing: 'The administration plainly has some charges to answer:

• 'After BCCI, five bank officials were indicted in 1988 in Tampa, Florida, on money-laundering charges, two former senior executives told the Tampa prosecutors that the bank falsified loans, invented shareholdings and in essence lacked capital. Nothing was done'.

• 'An informer of the American Drug Enforcement Administration turned up in mid-1988 at the Embassy of Panama with documents relating to President Noriega's involvement with the BCCI. He was flown to Florida. So should have been a box containing the documents. It arrived—without them. The man was told to go back to Panama, where (he said) his life was in danger'.

• 'In the Tampa indictment, "truckloads" of potentially incriminating BCCI documents were impounded. Some investigators say that the plea bargain which BCCI struck last year with the Justice Department prevents the use of many of these documents in future cases against it.'[12]

The US bank, the First American, was alleged to be deeply involved with the BCCI. As far back as 1987, it paid a substantial amount—$255m for National Bank of Georgia which was in reality controlled by the BCCI though fronted by somebody else.

The BCCI helped the ISI and the Pakistan Government in many ways. It tried to get nuclear bomb technology and materials from various sources clandestinely. This came to light when a retired Pakistani General, Inam-ul-Haq, was arrested in Germany. He was financially backed by the bank in his endeavour of purchasing nuclear weapons-grade steel for Pak Bomb-Development Programme. According to an international arms broker, 'You can't draw a line separating the bank's black operatives and Pakistan's intelligence services.'[13]

BCCI: Used Islam as a Mask

The bank brokered arms deals and supplied weapons to all and sundry without any scruples involved. It helped both Iran and Iraq and did business on behalf of the allied forces trying to restore Kuwait. It was friendly with Libya, Iran, Saudi Arabia, Syria and the manufacturers of Mirage 2000. It drew towards it terrorists of all hues and helped them finance their activities. Evidence shows that as many as 11 terrorist outfits were doing business with its London branches alone.

To sum up, the bank had links with terrorists, arms dealers, drug runners, the CIA, the ISI and many corrupt rulers from different parts of the world. It used Islam as a mask. It is said that from Khashoggi to Noriega to the CIA, everyone was impressed with its efficiency. Noriega had deposited at least $33 million and recommended its facilities to a US narcotics ring desperate to launder the ill-begotten money. Alan Garcia, a former President of Peru, used its Panama branch to siphon away funds from the national treasury. And the BCCI itself plundered innocent small depositors of the Third World, from sub-Saharan Africa to Bangladesh. Even the central banks of Nigeria and Zambia were induced to keep their money with it and the result was huge losses for them when the bank had collapsed.

The bank manipulated its account books so cleverly that even a reputed firm of auditors like Price Waterhouse could not detect anything fishy in the first attempt. It was given tons of bogus data to write its audit reports. It is said that as many as 6,500 individual customers' files were kept by Abedi himself under his own personal custody and auditors were not allowed any access to them. Manipulations were mind-boggling. Key bank officials received payoffs to keep mum. During 1987-88 alone, they were paid $53.1 million. According to Price Waterhouse, the BCCI concealed each fraud behind another one. Ian Brindle, a top official of Price Waterhouse said: "We satisfied ourselves with a whole pile of evidence that the incomes we queried were all right, because you can't go on the basis that everything you see and touch is a lie."[14] It could succeed in unravelling the mystery only when a former top executive of the bank agreed to help it.

When the bubble burst, depositors realised that they were ruined and among them, the Muslims had a sizeable proportion. It became clear that frauds, thieves and robbers whether sporting blue collars or white collars do not make any discrimination on the basis of religion. Even the American Express lost around $30m and so did the Peruvian Central Bank, because it too had put in substantial amount of money at the instance of two of its officers who were bribed by the BCCI.

According to a report: "When holes appeared in the balance sheet, the secret bank plugged them by raising deposits without recording these in the books. While native depositors put their money in, managers and others close to the bank were cleverly pulling it out. Deposits rose from $3.3 billion in 1989, to $22.1 billion; deposits from "related parties" dropped by $481 m to $336 m.

"To keep regulators guessing, BCCI shuttled assets and liabilities among its many subsidiaries. Bad loans on the banks' books would disappear into offshore accounts when regulators came calling; good assets would conveniently emerge. In 1988 alone, subsidiaries and affiliates paid $152m of fee income to one another. All this was incidental to other seamy sidelines: laundering money for drug dealers and helping clients evade taxes and exchange controls."

Soon the BCCI came to be described as "Bank of Crooks and Criminals International" or as Bank of Criminal and Conmen International". Robin Leigh-Pemberton, the Governor of the Bank thought, the culture of the bank was criminal. Some others regarded it as a "global rogue". Summing up the activities of the Bank, *Time* (as quoted in *The Economist* of July 27, 1991) asserted: "BCCI operated on an international network of criminals—called the black squad or the black network—which smuggled arms and drugs, bribed officials and kidnapped, even murdered the bank's enemies."

Many influential people around the globe unsuccessfully tried to save it from exposure and collapse. It was found that as much as $17 billion was unaccounted for.

Its collapse came as a rude shock to many people in the Third World. They thought that its closure and the sentencing of Abedi to a jail term of 8 years by a court in the United Arab Emirates and his being wanted in the USA to stand trial as the mastermind of "the largest bank fraud in world financial history" were regarded as a Western conspiracy to destroy a dynamic enterpreneur from the Third World. He was so popular in his own country that the Pakistan Government refused to extradite him. He had given millions of dollars from the coffers of the bank to hospitals and schools in Pakistan. He died a natural death in his home country on August 5, 1995. His obituary in *The Economist* (19 August, 1995) said: "All truly great swindles," said O. Henry, an American writing about a 19th century sting, are "beautiful and simple." But defenders of Mr. Abedi say this is a distorted western way of looking at his career. They see him, not as a crook but as a man, destined for greatness, who allowed his empire to get out of control. BCCI was, it is said, run along the lines of Mahmudabad, a princely state in northern India where Mr. Abedi's father was an aid to the Rajah. Mr. Abedi lived as part of Rajah's court until he was 25. When the Indian subcontinent was divided in 1947, he moved to the part that became Pakistan. He had rapid promotion in the two banks he worked for in Pakistan before founding BCCI. His generosity or extravagance, during the 25 years of the bank's existence supported the picture of "Rajah" Abedi. His first benefactor, the ruler of Abu Dhabi and his 14 wives, had the use of a palace with a staff of servants in Pakistan. Any sizable depositor could expect a royal welcome, a limo at the airport and whores if he needed them. Loans were freely given, often without security. Employees were well paid and even a humble depositor could expect a better return than at a rival bank. In the end, even with the dirty money from the launderers, the bank was insolvent. It is surprising that BCCI lasted as long as it did, particularly as millions were lost in poor speculations. Mr. Abedi was compared to Charles Ponzi, an Italian-American banker who, in the 1920s; paid investors, using the money that came in from new investors".

Gokal: 'Crook of the Century'

More startling things about the BCCI have surfaced recently during the trial of the UK-based Pakistani, Abbas Kassimali Gokal, in a London Court. To quote a report: 'Gokal is the biggest single fraudster to stand trail anywhere on earth. At $1.2 billion, his swindles dwarf those of Robert Maxwell, Bernie Cornfeld or any of the other giants of fraud. Three years before 2000, we have our "crook of the century" and his name is Abbas Kassimali Gokal. Thief, forger, smuggler of nuclear-weapons components, bed-mate of the cocaine barons' favourite bank... the rap sheet exhausts several typewriter ribbons.[15]

Gokal was a shipping magnate in Karachi before he went to UK. During the 1970s he made huge profits because of the commodity boom. He became a close confidant of Pakistani military dictator, General Zia, (his brother Mustapha was made the Minister of Shipping by General Zia even though he was, technically, a British citizen.

Mustapha was also a financial adviser to Ayatollah Khomeini. And during the Iran-Iraq war, Gokal's ships carried both military and non-military supplies for Iran) and, through his lavish dinners he could befriend the influential people of various countries. He endeared himself to a number of rulers of Asian and African countries as, just like Abedi, a champion of the cause of the Third World. But, in reality, he was a cheat. His Gulf Transport group and Abedi's BCCI were the two sides of the same counterfeit coin. 'Neither had any money of its own, indeed both were insolvent many times over. But in the hall of mirrors that is banking, Gulf was just what BCCI needed. These two bankrupt shells maintained each other's illusion of solvency.'

"It worked like this: BCCI was able to show all its dud loans to Gulf front companies as solid assets, while Gulf was fraudulently kept afloat by the injection of cash, some real, some illusory, from BCCI."[16]

In 1991, *The Guardian* reported that the BCCI tried to help a consortium of Pakistan, Libya and Argentina formed in order to help it in assembling atomic weapons and Gokal undertook to transport necessary materials. It is said that the Americans wanted to enter into a deal with him in 1994 and they invited him to the USA by providing him and his wife with air tickets and the promise of hospitality, but, as ill-luck would have it, he was arrested by the British during his plane's stop-over in Frankfurt. During his trial which ended in his conviction, it came out that Gokal's group of companies received from the BCCI as big as three times the latter's total capital and 30 times of the accepted ratio. $122.5 million of $185 million was lent to it by the bank and it was in the category of bad debts.

REFERENCES

1. *The Economist*, August 3, 1991.
2. Robert Emmet Long (ed.), *Banking Scandals: The S&LS and BCCI*, The Reference Shelf, volume 65, No. 3, New York, 1993, p. 72.
3. *Ibid.*, p. 83.

4. *The Economist*, August 19, 1995.
5. Robert Emmet Long (ed.), *op. cit.*, p. 83.
6. *The Economist*, August 19, 1995.
7. Quoted in Robert Emmet Long, *op. cit.*, p. 75.
8. According to *The Economist*, August 3, 1991: 'Although everyone, whether he approves of the idea or not, expects intelligence agencies to run clandestine operations, many people appear to be surprised that they open bank accounts in order to finance those operations. It is not only agents who need to be paid; so do the governments or resistance groups that the agency wants to assist. BCCI, with operations in some of the world's nastiest corners, was well suited to the CIA's needs. It provided the agency (as well as, probably the Defence Department and the Drug Enforcement Administration) with a form of one-stop financial shopping more secure from prying eyes than the alternative of passing money through a longer chain of banks and front companies.' It goes on to add that the CIA used the BCCI as a conduit for passing money to the Afghan rebels and the right-wing Nicaraguan rebels. Further, 'Manuel Noriega, the now-imprisoned strongman of Panama, was told by the CIA to open BCCI accounts through which money for the contras was destined to pass.'
9. For details see *The Newsweek*, 12 August, 1991.
10. Robert Emmet Long, *op. cit.*, p. 84.
11. *Ibid.*
12. *The Economist*, July 27, 1991.
13. *Ibid.*, p. 83.
14. *Ibid.*, p. 84.
15. *Guardian Weekly*, April 13, 1997.
16. *Ibid.*

4

White-Collar Theft

Theft is one of the oldest crimes. We find numerous references to it even in the *Rig Veda*, one of the oldest books of the world. It pertained to stealing material possessions such as food and drinks, water for irrigation, animals and even women. In ancient Indian scriptures, we find frequent references of milch cows and sturdy horses stealing.

Theft: One of the Oldest Crimes

Sita was abducted by Ravana and the result was a war between Rama and Ravana. Nectar was stolen by Asuras which led to a long-drawn battle with Suras. When the Aryans came and the non-Aryans retreated in the face of their superior military power, the latter went on harassing the former by stealing their possessions during the night. This was one of the reasons for the Aryans dreading darkness and worshipping the moon, the sun and the dawn. The *Rig Veda* is full of hymns in praise of them.

In Dandin's *Daskumarcharitam* (Tales of Ten Princes), we find a reference to Karnisuta who was supposed to be an exponent of "the science of theft". He was also known by three other names such as Kalankur, Mulbhadra and Muldeva. It is said that he had written treatises and laid-down precepts for those wishing to enter the profession of crime and achieve great success. Unfortunately, none of his works have till now been discovered. Had they been available, they could surely have been of great help for white-collar thieves all over the world. What we are driving at is this that our ancient land was the first to throw 'scientific light' on the profession of theft.

In Amarsimha's *Amarkosa*, there are ten kinds of thieves (2/10/5), four kinds of thefts (2/10/6), but only one name for stolen goods (2/10/7) has been mentioned. In other words, while the players in the game may be various, their strategies and tactics may vary, yet the outcome is the same!

In Sanskrit literature, we find the use of theft to outwit one's political rivals. To give an instance, Vishnugupta Chanakya got the seal of his rival, Rakshasa, stolen and, with its help, he indulged in forgery to put him in a tight corner where he had no alternative but to surrender to him and cross over to the side of Chandragupta Maurya, giving up the efforts to restore the defeated Nanda dynasty to the throne. Visakhdatta in his famous play *Mudrarakshasa* has vividly portrayed the entire incident. Thus, theft was used not only for material gains but also as an instrument to realise political and business ends. In recent times, two examples easily come to mind. First, the Watergate scandal in the USA, in which the Republicans had organised a break-in in the office of the Democrats to steal certain valuable documents. When the incident came to light, the former suffered a great loss in their prestige and Nixon had to resign his presidency and his successor had to pardon him in order to save him from going to jail.

Second, not many years ago, a rival of the Birlas got certain documents and incriminating materials stolen from the latter's offices and placed them in the hands of a certain gentleman who attacked the Birlas in the Rajya Sabha and was projected by the print media owned by his patron as a great radical!

Karl Marx: Came Face to Face with Theft

The nature and character of theft underwent a big change after the institution of private property was to be firmly established and widely extended, drastically curtailing communal ownership and traditional rights and privileges of common people. Karl Marx came face to face with this problem when he dealt with the issue of forest products being appropriated by peasants in violation of private property rights. His editorials in *The Rheinische Zeitung* so infuriated the Prussian Government that it closed down the paper. Incidentally, the problem of grazing rights and freely taking timber and fuel figured in most of peasant agitations in Champaran from the one led by Gandhi onwards. While peasants asserted them, zamindars and indigo planters who exercised zamindari rights termed them as theft.

Since the days of Marx, the nature and character of theft has undergone a sea change. There are a large number of thefts which are not committed by the poor, half starving people and lowly blue-collar workers, but by the rich and influential. Carl P. Simon and Ann D. Witte have rightly stated that: "The theft industry... can be broken into two sectors—traditional and non-traditional".[1]

The Traditional and Non-traditional Sectors of Theft

The traditional sector of the theft industry includes mostly offences concerning property, which find a place in the records of the police department, such as robbery, burglary, shoplooting, etc. The attention of the society is focused most of the time on this sector. An outstanding work on this sector is exemplified by Edwin H. Sutherland in *The Professional Thief*, published in 1937. There has been no dearth of research work on this sector since then and we find ample light on traditional thieves and their various categories and *modus operandi*, besides the role of a section of the police in aiding and abetting their activities. We also know of the factors that lie behind the traditional categories of theft.

But the non-traditional sector of theft constitutes a penumbra because our knowledge of the current happening is very insignificant. It has been government stationery being regularly stolen by employees to be used by their wards, studying in schools and colleges or to be sold clandestinely to supplement their legal earnings. Similarly, we find workers pilfering goods either from factories or in transit. Such thefts also occur from the shops and godowns. It is an open secret that there is quite often an organised network for taking out the stolen goods safely and get them distributed. Quite often union leaders and corrupt superiors help and abet such theft being committed by workers.

Railway goods wagons stolen by organised gangs are sold openly. These organised gangs have the connivance of railway employees and the police.

Sometimes when organised gangs realise that they may get caught, they resort to arson. They may burn warehouses or trucks carrying goods. In the USA, the value of goods stolen from factories and warehouses in the course of transportation is estimated at $5.4 billion to $8.9 billion.

We, The People of India

In India, players in the non-traditional sector of theft industry do include "very respectable" people. To give an instance, during the early 1960s, it was alleged that S. Mulgaonkar, a front-ranking editor, was involved in an act of theft. It was said that he was given a substantial amount of money by some Indian freedom fighter, living in Paris, to be passed-on to Jawaharlal Nehru for Prime Minister's Fund. During those days, the country was facing difficulties as a fall-out of the Chinese aggression. It was alleged that Mulgaonkar did not hand-over the money to Nehru, but appropriated it for his personal use. This was exposed by *Blitz, New Age* and H.D. Malviya's *Socialist Congressman*. S. Mulgaonkar filed a defamation suit against them, but promptly withdrew it in the face of cross examination and arguments by the advocate A.S.R. Chari.

It is well-known fact that the relief materials do not reach the intended beneficiaries in their entirety. A substantial portion is stolen in 'transit' by organisers. Thus, a number of people and organisations profit by the sufferings of the victims of the earthquakes, cyclones, floods, landslides, droughts, epidemics and other natural calamities. Blankets, sarees, food, medicines, building materials, etc. are misappropriated. Similarly, in normal times, all the hand pumps meant for dalits and tribals may not go to them, a significant number of them may go to others for pecuniary considerations.

The owners of fair price shops steal a sizeable proportion of essential goods to be sold in the open market and the gain is shared with officials of civil supplies department and political bosses.

Few years back, a Minister of Transport in Bihar was found taking a few litres of diesel every day from the State transport depot to run his personal generator for lighting his house in his home town where there was regular load-shedding. He was not a poor person and could have easily afforded a few litres of diesel every day. Perhaps he thought it would lower his dignity to do so when he was the unquestioned boss of the transport department. This betrays a particular kind of attitude widely prevalent in the non-traditional sector of theft industry. This particular person could not draw any distinction between State property and his personal property.

Thieves operating in non-traditional sector are generally dehumanised and are no better than beasts otherwise how could hospital authorities and jail authorities steal a substantial part of the money meant for feeding, clothing and medicating of the sick and the hapless inmates of hospitals and jails.

During the 1950s and 1960s, the American aid organisation, CARE, sent powder milk, butter oil and *dalia* for school children. Most of these materials were sold in the open market by officials in-charge of their distribution. As long as the CARE programme was in operation, it has been found a large number of vendors hawking *pedas* at railway stations and bus stops in Bihar. They were made with powder milk, meant for undernourished children.

One more example comes to mind. In Bihar and various other parts of the country, the money and materials meant for national literacy mission was siphoned away by the officials and workers in quite a substantial number of cases. Once some Japanese organisation had provided mopeds for teachers connected with this campaign, but these vehicles came to be used more for purely personal and private work rather than for the purpose for which they were meant. Kerosene oil was utilised for lighting their own homes and houses rather than helping the literacy campaign.

The Government of India has instituted pensions and other facilities for freedom fighters and for the old destitutes. If one makes a scrutiny in Bihar and the Telengana region of Andhra Pradesh, one is sure to find a significant number of "freedom fighters" who were either not born or were too young to have participated in the Quit India movement. Besides, some recipients of freedom fighter's pension were on the side of the British, opposing freedom movement. Similarly, in Bihar a number of recipients of old age pension, meant for the destitutes are from well-off families. Thus, the benefits meant for others are stolen.

Years ago, a friend told us a very interesting story as to how the furniture and crockery of the canteen, attached to the Patna Old Secretariat were "stolen". According to him, every year the government bought new furniture and crockery for the canteen but within six months or so they got replaced with old and broken ones. How?

Whenever there was a marriage ceremony or some other function at the place of some official, the entire furniture, crockery and cutley were taken from the canteen, but at the time of returning good and new ones were replaced with used and old ones by the family of the official concerned. We are told that this mode of stealing still continues.

Idols, paintings and other pieces of antiques are regularly stolen and smuggled out of the country and in this racket quite a number of bigwigs are involved. This is a multi-million-rupee racket. Besides, the country is deprived of valuable pieces of its heritage.

Mahapandit Rahul Sankrityan had brought manuscript materials from Tibet and deposited them in the Patna Museum. A substantial part of them is said to have been subsequently stolen and the thieves have not been poverty-stricken, illiterate or semi-literate people.

Khushwant Singh in his widely-circulated column during the first half of 1997 mentioned an incident of stealing costly items from a hotel in a foreign country by an official attached to an Indian delegation sent by the government.

Rajiv Gandhi: Told the Naked Truth

The late Rajiv Gandhi, as Prime Minister, stated that out of every rupee allocated by the Central Government for poverty Alleviation Programmes, as much as 85 paise was stolen and only 15 paise could reach the intended beneficiaires. In this respect, we do not think there are many rivals to India.

Even in Indonesia where Suharto regime exercises absolute power without any real democratic check, the pilferage is only up to 30 per cent. According to Jeffrey A. Winters of the Northwestern University: "The World Bank resident office in Jakarta, for example, admits that 30 per cent of the money lent to Indonesia routinely disappears somewhere inside the government. Since current and future generations of ordinary Indonesians will have to repay the loans amount to a particularly nasty form of regressive taxation."[2]

Different Kinds of Thefts

Embezzlement is a special form of theft under which an employee steals money from his employer. When the employee is very high up in the bureaucratic set-up, the act has widespread ramifications. The nature and modus operandi of embezzlement have undergone a sea change in India ever since Independence. It is no longer a lowly clerk manipulating the records to embezzle provident fund money or bank deposits. We now find scores of top politicians, bureaucrats and businessmen hatching conspiracies to embezzle crores and crores of rupees.

There are two consequences of theft. First, an individual or a collector finds its resources stolen or snatched away. Second, the society has to spend money on investigation and criminal justice. In a large number of cases there is seldom any success in catching up thieves and getting them punished. The plain and simple reason for this is that the thieves involved in them are no ordinary people, they are rich and influential. Take, for example, fodder scam of Bihar. Not only the State has been deprived of thousands of crores of rupees, but, in addition, it has also to foot the bill of investigation and prosecution of the alleged criminals and even then one has to keep one's fingers crossed about the outcome.

There is another kind of theft that has been plaguing almost all countries of the world. It is plagiarism and piracy of intellectual works from books, documents, paintings, audio and video cassettes, technology and so forth and the result is that the original authors are deprived of their rightful credit and monetary incomes. Some years ago forged diaries of Adolf Hitler were published as genuine and the forgers earned huge amounts of money from the gullible buyers. In 1991, a master forger of paintings by world famous master painters, Eric Hebborn, published his autobiography *Drawn to Trouble: Forging of an Artist*, in which he detailed his modus-operandi. He was patronised and trained by none other than the master deceiver Sir Anthony Blunt. Blunt authenticated Hebborn's forged paintings as genuine and minted money by selling his works.

While generally it is held that crime is bad, morally and ethically both for the person indulging in it and for the society in which he lives and moreover, it has disastrous consequences for them economically two US economists, Daniel Nagin and Joel Waldfogel, think otherwise. In a paper "*The Effect of Conviction on Income through the Life Cycle*" (National Bureau of Economic Research Working Paper No. 4551, November 1993), they have presented a study of the incomes of 1,700 first-time offenders who were convicted of fraud in the USA in 1984.

Most of the cheats, after being caught and convicted, lost their jobs and those who retained their jobs found their earnings reduced. But there were people under 25 who found their post-conviction incomes almost 25 per cent higher than their pre-conviction earnings. Since they do casual jobs, employers do not have spend on their training and they can afford to pay more to them. Their conclusion, however, applies to young people who indulge in fraud rather than to the old and normal criminals.

REFERENCES

1. Carl P. Simon and Ann D. Witte, *Beating the System*, Boston, Mass., 1982, p. 82.
2. Jeffrey A. Winters, "Down with the World Bank" in *Far Eastern Economic Review*, February 13, 1997.

5

The World of Media

The world of media claims itself as the guardian of public morality and crusader against all sorts of crime, be they blue-collar or white-collar. They claim to be impartial, free and frank without the influence of fear or favour. They claim to be great sticklers to truth and care for nothing but the truth.

Truthfulness of the Media

Alas! these claims are easier to make than sustain. Let us begin with their truthfulness. During the early months of 1997, after years of thaw, one saw a warfare between two groups of newspapers, owned by two big business houses of India. While Sahu Jains' *The Times of India* claimed that it "has captured Delhi", meaning thereby that it had occupied number one position as regards circulation, displacing its rival *The Hindustan Times*, owned and controlled by the Birlas, the latter declared that this claim was nothing but a lie, plain and simple and the fact, according to it, was that its circulation had crossed half-a-million-mark, i.e. it was far, far ahead of its challenger. This fact, as the impression was given, was supposed to have been certified by the ABC (Audit Bureau of Circulation).

Notwithstanding the stature of these two newspapers and the great prestige enjoyed by the ABC about whose methodology of certification, not only little is known, but a great deal of doubt persists. Logic casts a great deal of shadow over the claims of these newspapers. Why do we say so?

The claim of *The Times of India* is so vague and subjective that it cannot be quantified because "capturing the heart" or "captivating" may be interpreted in many ways, hence, this claim cannot be fruitfully and unambiguously scrutinised to prove it true or false.

Thus, let us take up the claim of *The Hindustan Times*. We assume that what it means is that the total number of copies sold by it on any day is more than 5 lakh. We ignore the number of complimentary copies distributed free because it is assumed to be a very insignificant proportion of the total turnover. We also assume that this newspaper is sold mainly in Delhi and Bihar (from these two States it is simultaneously published), besides U.P., Haryana, Punjab and Rajasthan. It needs to be noted that it is the number one English paper only in Delhi. In Bihar, it is far behind its rival. In Chotanagpur area of Bihar, Calcutta-based dailies also have sizeable circulation.

In U.P., Punjab and Haryana, it is not in the top position because it has to compete with *The Tribune, The Indian Express, The Pioneer* and *The Northern Indian Patrika* which are published from there. In U.P., Rajasthan, M.P., Himachal Pradesh, Haryana and Bihar people generally read Hindi papers. The total population of these States is around 38 crores and the proportion of people literate in English is less than two per cent. On this basis, the number of people who are literate in English, i.e., those who can sign their names in English is 76 lakhs. Out of them, the number of people who can read and understand English newspapers cannot be more than 15 lakhs.

To verify the authenticity of what we say, one should undertake a survey of the capacity of comprehension of graduates and post-graduates, coming out of numerous universities of the Hindi heartland.

Being university teachers of more than three decades' standing, we can stand by our statement. If somebody doubts our statement, we invite him to meet us and we shall help arrange his meeting with graduate and post-graduate students whom he can interview on newspaper reading habit.

If there are 15 lakh people, capable of reading and understanding English newspapers, it means there are not more than 3 lakh households who can subscribe to an English newspaper. But all of them do not do so because, generally, a household buys such a newspaper which can meet needs of all the members of the family, both young and old, male and female. We have found in U.P., Bihar, M.P., Rajasthan, Haryana and Himachal Pradesh most families prefer to buy a Hindi daily. If some family wants to subscribe to an English daily, the preference is for local or regional English dailies rather than a paper coming from Delhi and giving very meagre coverage to local happenings and problems. There must be some special reason for a person living in Chandigarh or Simla or Lucknow or Allahabad to go in for an English newspaper coming from outside and also hours after locally published newspapers are distributed. Then there are very few families which go in for more than one daily.

With the advent of multi-channel TV programmes and the easy availability of audio and video cassettes, there is very little time available for most middle class families to read newspapers. They obtain most of the information from TV. Our personal observation indicates that the fascination for newspapers in general and for English ones in particular has been going down. The closure of a number of English and Hindi newspapers in recent times testifies to it.

On the basis of what we have said above, the claim of the management of *The Hindustan Times* falls through. But, then, one may say that, qualitatively, it is so superior that its circulation has been leaping forward while the circulation of all other newspapers have been going down. This claim cannot sustain itself if a comparison is made with *The Hindu* and *The Telegraph*. Its language has no respect for grammar and no care is taken to correct spelling mistakes and factual errors which abound while articles on the editorial page are without much substance.

What we have been driving at is that the same sort of lies, frauds, deceptions and cheatings are resorted in the world of media to boost the sale of its products (journals) as in the corporate business arena. The late V.K. Krishna Menon was perfectly right when he stated that the newspaper Press and the jute press were inter-changeable for the tycoons who owned them. Their main aim has always been to make profits directly or indirectly.

Inflated figures of circulation bring more newsprint quota, a significant portion of which may be sold in the blackmarket to bring in revenues which need not be accounted for in income-tax returns. Besides, they help secure higher rates of advertisement tariff.

Quite often, even though newspapers run in a loss, yet, in the ultimate analysis, they help their owners to influence governmental policy decisions, support convenient politicians and bureaucrats, and blackmail inconvenient ones. They suppress uncomfortable facts but propagate falsehoods to harm rivals in business and opponents in politics and bureaucracy. Let us quote a few instances.

The Times of India: Let us Know the Truth

During the early months of 1997, the premises of Ashok Jain, the head of the family controlling the Bennett, Coleman and Company, the publishers of *The Times of India* group of papers were searched by the personnel of the Enforcement Directorate (ED) in connection with some alleged violation of foreign exchange regulations. The readers of this group's newspapers were for weeks ignorant about this happening and when they came to read about the court proceedings in connection with the ED action, they could not make out what the charges were. All the time, readers were informed that the ED was the villain against whom Jain and his lawyers were fighting and scoring successes! Incidentally, Ashok Jain's father Sahu Shanti Prasad Jain was also caught at the Palam airport during Nehru's regime for illegally bringing in foreign currency and then also, the event was blacked out though other newspapers carried a report on it. His grandfather Seth Ram Krishna Dalmia was arrested, convicted and made to serve a jail term, but the newspaper of this group did not find all these things newsworthy.

Justice Vivian Bose wrote a voluminous report on the murky happenings in the business house of Dalmia-Jain, but no reporting was done in this group's newspapers and none of the learned editors thought it worthwhile to comment on it. H.K. Dua wrote a thundering front-page signed editorial condemning Laloo Yadav's refusal to resign from Chief Ministership even after being chargesheeted, but ignored the FERA violation case against Ashok Jain, his paymaster. In fact, under his stewardship; the main aim of the *Times of India* appears to be the defence of Ashok Jain by vilifying and blackmailing the ED. One may also find a serious attempt to put a communal colour on the entire episode. To substantiate, we invite the readers to see just a few issues of the newspaper of the last week of January, 1998. The newspaper reports that the efforts to prosecute Ashok Jain are regarded as directed against the entire Jain community which has been called-upon to launch a non-cooperation movement against the government. This stand leads to several things. First, the newspaper questions implicitly the impartiality and efficacy of our legal system. Second, the newspaper which is a public institution and owned by numerous shareholders including financial institutions, has been converted into an instrument for the defence of the alleged act of theft of country's foreign exchange, which if proved will amount to a crime against the nation. Will not the editor then become guilty of abetting this crime? Third, the employees' union has demanded the arrest and prosecution of Ashok Jain and not a word on this has appeared in the paper. Is it ethical on the part of editor? Does the freedom of press mean freedom to purvey lies and untruths to defend the business interests and cover up crimes of persons controlling the companies publishing newspapers? Obviously, there is a dual standard of morality and an editor in a tycoon-owned press is nothing but a mercenary mouthpiece of his master's voice.

This reminds one of what John Swinton, then Chief of the Staff of *New York Times* said at New York Press Club in 1953 when a toast was proposed in his honour: 'There is no such thing, at this date of the world's history, in America, as an independent Press. You know it and I know it. There is not one of you who dares to write your honest opinions, and if you did, you know beforehand that it would never appear in print. I am paid weekly for keeping my honest opinion out of the paper I am connected with. Others of you are paid similar salaries for similar things and any of you who would be so foolish as to write honest opinions would be out on the streets looking for another job. If I allowed my honest opinions to appear in one issue of my paper, before twenty-four hours my occupation would be gone.

'The business of the journalists is to destroy the truth, to lie outright, to prevent, to vilify, to fawn at the feet of mammon, and to sell his country and his race for his daily bread. You know it and I know it, and what folly is this toasting an independent Press?

'We are the tools and vassals of rich men behind the scenes. We are jumping jacks, they pull the strings and we dance. Our talents, our possibilities and our lives are all the property of other men. We are intellectual prostitutes.'

Similarly, Birla-owned newspapers never bothered to inform their readers of the enquiry conducted by the late Justice A.K. Sarkar in the affairs of the Birla house nor did they report sufficiently the Rajya Sabha proceedings when Chandra Shekhar exposed gross irregularities committed by it.

The Aaj, a well-known Hindi daily, all of a sudden during the 1960s started blacking out all the news items concerning Raghunath Singh, a prominent MP, representing Varanasi because he had refused to bail out its then proprietor, Mr. Satyen Gupta, who was also a prominent grain dealer. Gupta cared a damn for the ideals of his maternal grandfather, Shiva Prasad Gupta, a great philanthropist and nationalist who was its founder.

Before Independence the Maharaja of Darbhanga uncermoniously removed the then editor of *The Indian Nation* because he had dared to write some unpleasant things about the British Viceroy. It needs to be noted that throughout, the newspapers of the Maharaja opposed peasant movements and worked for the perpetuation of zamindari system and the British Raj. They attacked the Congress and supported the Hindu Mahasabha because these were the ideological moorings of the Maharaja.

R. Goenka: Presented One-sided Picture

In recent times Ramnath Goenka used *Indian Express* to support Nusli Wadia in his intercorporate warfare against Dhirubhai Ambani and presented a one-sided picture and distorted facts. Did not the readers have a right to know what the other side had to say? No, because the proprietor did not like the truth to prevail. It is widely known that he always treated his journalists as bedsheets. Once he took fancy to some obscurantist and adopted him as his guru and for months went on inflicting rubbish as his great thoughts on readers. We remember Goenka claiming that, at times, he himself wrote editorials instead to Frank Moraes because he was not sure whether the latter would carry out his diktats the way he wanted.

Thus, all the talk of editorial freedom or the freedom of the Press is a humbug. In plain and simple terms it means the freedom for the proprietor to publish and propagate what he likes and suppress what he does not. If it goes to the head of somebody that he can be independent of proprietor as editor, he is shown the door just like Pran Chopra who was ousted from *The Statesman*, notwithstanding all the opposition from M.C. Setalvad, the eminent jurist who was on the Board of Trustees. Setalvad and other trustees rejected the charge of a Communist bias on the part of the editor, as levelled by J.R.D. Tata and N.A. Palkhivala who represented the owners. They held that the policy pursued by the editor was in no way a deviation from the policy prescribed by the relevant article of the Company's Articles of Association. Having failed to persuade the trustees to fall in line, they were unceremoniously removed and a new Board of Trustees, headed by Palkhivala was appointed.

The newspaper was taken over by a co-operative but the co-operative was finally turned into, along with its intents and purposes; the property of C.R. Irani under whom, no self-respecting editor would ever like to serve. He has solved the problem by putting his own name as the Editor-in-Chief as many other proprietors of newspapers have begun doing.

N.J. Nanporia: A Thick-skinned Editor

There are very few people like the late Girilal Jain who could walk out as editor-in-chief of *The Times of India* when faced with an arrogant youngster of the Jain family owning the Bennett, Coleman and Company, but his successor was so thick-skinned that he endured all the insults and stuck to the job so long as he could. During Nehru's regime, N.J. Nanporia, who had been intimately connected with *The Times of India* in various capacities on the editorial side and had risen to become its editor wrote a confidential letter to Nehru which is quite revealing. To quote: "I would like to say generally that Shri Shanti Prasad Jain has been functioning for all practical purposes as the General Manager. His lack of sophistication, his inability to develop an intelligent interest in many affairs of the day and his total incomprehension of what "*The Times of India*" is, have fortunately imposed some limits on his interference. Nevertheless, within these limits on matters ranging from recruitment, the organisation of the library, certain aspects of coverage and directives to correspondents, to more fundamental affairs of policy, he has not hesitated to interfere and issue directives. In the latter category can be included such examples of unhealthy influence as the Krishna Menon election, reporting the Prime Minister's speeches, the paper's attitude towards certain Ministers and the Bose Inquiry Report. Equally irksome has been a system under which even details relating to the most insignificant administrative decisions could not be implemented without the approval of the Chairman through the General Manager. There have been innumerable instances of news items and interviews submitted for publication for purposes known only to the management and the Chairman".

'I have been in "*The Times of India*" as Assistant Editor and Editor for approximately 17 years, that is to say, since the days when this paper was under British management. The gradual deterioration in standards and the adoption of procedures and policies that have threatened to reduce the paper to an instrument of a single individual thoroughly incapable of appreciating the highest ideals of responsible journalism have been extremely painful to those few of us who have survived in "*The Times of India*" since the old days. Despite nerve-shattering difficulties and frustrations, we have continued to serve the paper in the conviction that it was quite essential to remain and help to preserve such standards as could be maintained against very serious odds. I would like, most sincerely, tc declare—and here, I am sure my views are shared by all my senior colleagues—that this attachment to "*The Times of India*" equally with considerations of our livelihood, have impelled us hopefully to wait for the day when the standards and editorial independence usually associated with "*The Times India*" could finally be restored. Wherever possible, we have modified the management's directives or ignored them and sometimes have even succeeded in opposing them fully. The strain of doing this in addition to running the paper has been considerable...'

He went on to talk of 'the mismanagement, the unscrupulous exploitation of so significant an institution as "*The Times of India*", the indifference to any kind of standards and interference of a kind that cannot be considered as other than thoroughly illiterate'. Now it is the third generation of Shanti Prasad Jain running the paper without any change in the approach towards what the management thinks a humbug called editorial freedom.[1]

In fact, all the so-called opinion-makers are nothing but mercenaries working for those who are in a position to pay for their services. All the talk of so-called high ideals is nothing but deception. Had this not been the case, the approach and thrust of individual journalists would not have changed after going from one newspaper to the other of differing policies. In India, a person editing a pro-Congress paper can very comfortably run a pro-BJP newspaper without any difficulty or trouble to his conscience. He does not have any pin-pricks of conscience when he switches-off from propagating ideals of secularism to disseminating the virtues of Hindu communalism! We can cite several examples to illustrate this point. These journalists easily adapt themselves to be changed, nay, mutually opposing and totally incompatible ideological and political moorings and situations. Most of the so-called leading journalists' writings abound in, to borrow a phrase from *The Economist* 'overwrought prose used to disguise underwrought thought'.

Balzac: Termed Journalistic World as 'Mental Brothel'

During the last century Balzac looked very closely at the journalistic world which he termed as "mental brothel".[2] He found it very corrupt where bribery was the order of the day and it was abounding in hired assassins of ideas, truths and industrial and dramatic reputations. He presents the self-confession by a journalist-character in the following words: 'Newspaper-proprietors are contractors; we're their masons. And so, the more mediocre a man is, the sooner he arrives at success, he can swallow insults, put up with anything, flatter the mean and petty passions...'[3] Though journalists talked of conscience, it was the insistent tickling of the money pendulum that throbbed their heart, 'conscience, my dear, is a kind of stick that everyone picks up to thrash his neighbour with, but one he never uses against himself.'[4]

He was perfectly right when he commented: 'Instead of being a priestly function, the newspaper has become a political party weapon; now it is becoming merely a trade; and like all traders, it has neither faith nor principles. Every newspaper is a shop which sells to public whatever shades of opinion it wants. A journal is no longer concerned to enlighten. Consequently, in due course, all journals will be treacherous, hypocritical, infamous, mendacious, murderous; they'll kill ideas, systems and men, and thrive on it. They'll be in the happy position of all abstract creations: wrong will be done without anybody being guilty. Napoleon gave the explanation of this phenomenon—moral or immoral, whichever you like in the superb aphorism dictated to him by the study of the convention: *In corporate crimes no one is implicated.* A newspaper can behave in the most atrocious manner and no one on the staff considers that his own hands are soiled.[5]

To him a journalist appeared as "an acrobat."[6] And 'Journalism is an inferno, a bottomless pit of iniquity, falsehood and treachery: one can only pass through it and emerge from it insullied if one is shielded as Dante was by the divine laurels of Virgil.[7]

India is roughly at the same stage of capitalist development as France was during the days of Balzac. Today India has completed half-a-century of its independent existence and Balzac dwelt on the journalistic world roughly half-a-century after the French Revolution which heralded the development of modern capitalism in France. Hence, the economic basis of the society being more or less similar, there is bound to be general resemblance between the superstructure here and the superstructure there. The world of media constituted then as now an important part of the superstructure.

We know of a journalist who has got several intellectual fans. While he was editing his own weekly, he was after the blood of Indira Gandhi, so much so that he appeared to testify before the Shah Commission, constituted by the Janata Party government to investigate the "misdeeds" of the previous Indira Gandhi-led Congress government. But, lo and behold! he changed his tune and made a round-about-turn after Mrs. Gandhi came back to power with a thumping majority in January 1980 and became a supporter of her till she was alive! Recently, he was seen running down the Jain Commission report on the ground that no judge was competent to judge historical events!

What we are driving at is the lack of any morality or intellectual honesty on the part of the so-called public opinion-makers. They are mercenaries on the payroll of tycoons whose overriding aim is to maximise their profits.

Those were the Days!

In the olden days, we had people like M. Chalapathi Rau, Edatata Narayanan, Girilal Jain and others whose writings showed their professional honesty, national commitment, socio-political awareness and learning. They were great sticklers to facts. One may find this vanishing tribe still lingering in a paper like *The Hindu*.

In the recent past, we had Tushar Kanti Ghosh who never wrote even a single sentence though he "edited" *The Amrita Bazar Patrika* for several decades till his death. Now we find it a fashion for proprietors to get their own names inserted as editors so that they can formally and legally dictate their policies.

In India, most of the journalists are purchasable commodities and their prices vary from cash to foreign trips via liquor bottles, gas and telephone connections. Not many years ago, Mr Mulayam Singh Yadav, the then U.P. Chief Minister, saw to it that a number of prominent journalists, including some in national news agencies were materially so propitiated that they fell in line with him. It is an open secret that a number of journalists accredited to ministries and government departments act as informal liaison men for private sector and also gather intelligence on policy matters for it. The daring ones among them work for foreign intelligence networks.

There are very few papers which take the trouble of checking the authenticity and veracity of news items before they are carried into print. One instance which easily comes to mind is the forged letter carried by Calcutta and Patna newspapers on the eve of the second general election to mar the prospect of our late friend, the CPI candidate, Ramavatar Shastri, for Patna Lok Sabha constituency.

Internationally, the case of the Zinoviev letter is quite well known. News items and stories are manufactured intentionally to harm certain people and parties. One may refer to the writings and cartoons in *The Hindustan Times* at the time of the Chinese aggression in 1962 or to the issues of *The Indian Express* after the failure of Ram Nath Goenka to win over Rajiv Gandhi to his side.

Some newspapers intentionally spread obscurantism by manufacturing and publishing news items and stories to the effect. To give a concrete example, a front-page story in *Hindustan*, the daily of the Birlas, on 12th July, 1997, asserted that the Pathfinder mission sent by the NASA was not able to yield any new results as were not known to ancient Indian astronomers. It added that the planet Mars was born in Ujjain, a town of Madhya Pradesh and everything from its origin and distance from Earth to the colour and composition of its surface had been known to Indians for thousands of years! Can there be anything more crass than this? Is it not a crime to mislead the gullible and propagate irrational and obscurantist ideas? Nobody in the management or the editorial department bothers because it boosts the sale of the paper.

Years ago like Jhumri Talaiya (Bihar) which had emerged as the main centre of Hindi film song lovers when the Radio Ceylon was the rage, Ghoghardiha (Bihar) was made by the newspapers of Maharajadhiraj of Darbhanga as the place where all sorts of unbelievable happenings took place. At least a miracle a day seemed to be the rate. To give a sample, one day a she-goat gave birth to a lion cub, another day a bull with three heads appeared, third day a Brahmin had a newly-born baby reciting Vedic hymns from the very moment of his arrival on this earth! Obviously, the owner of these papers did not bother whether these led to the spread of superstition, what mattered most for him was increasing their saleability among the ignorant rural masses.

Blitz's Double-think

The same thing can be said of the *Blitz*. It quite often, under R.K. Karanjia dispensation indulged in the glorification of black magic in order to create sensation so that its circulation could increase. Thus, while on the one hand Karanjia talked of socialism, secularism, non-alignment and so on, on the other, he promoted and patronised a Hathayogi. Almost all newspapers and journals which talk of scientific temper and high-tech carry daily/ weekly/monthly astrological columns to keep the readers in the grip of superstition and obscurantism. Thus, all the talk of rationalism turns out to be a sham.

Most of the tycoons who own and control the media in India are big swindlers. They have no compunction in cheating contributors of their promised remunerations, workers of their dues and the government of its tax revenues. Some indulge in grabbing public land and violating building bye-laws. Not only these tycoons but even journalists freely encroach upon public land. We know of one prominent journalist whose wife has grabbed a part of the public park. The authorities concerned are blackmailed into silence.

Lately, in India a number of people who have made money through unfair means have begun launching new or taking over existing newspapers and journals. Some have gone into electronic media too. It is just like Russia where the mafia has acquired control over newspapers and a TV channel. It does not require much intelligence to guess why this has been happening. With criminals coming to have a decisive say in the world of media, the consequences will be, to say the least, disastrous for both polity and economy. Here one should turn one's attention to the-still-not-stale story of Robert Maxwell.

Robert Maxwell: A Big Tycoon or Swindler

Robert Maxwell was a big tycoon of Britain. He had a variety of interests[8] spread over both Europe and America and one of them was newspaper publishing. "Chaos and bluster" were supposed to be his "forte". His Maxwell Communication Corporation (MCC), the publishing corporate which controlled newspapers and the prestigious publishing firm Macmillan, besides other business activities. He had declared several times that he was not interested in a company where he would hold less than 50 per cent of the shares. In 1990 he was supposed to have suffered losses and 1991 did not seem to be any better. This put the MCC in a precarious position. The situation became so grave that he committed suicide. His dead body was found floating in the sea off the Canary Islands in November 1991. And with this discovery the Maxwell group of companies collapsed. Then it came out that he had eaten up anything between 400 million pound sterling and 606 million pound sterling from the pension funds of his companies and he left behind few assets. The result was that as many as 32,000 people could not get their pensions. Among them there were not less than 12,000 from the *Mirror* Group.

When the Maxwell scandal came to light, there was shock and outrage all around. To begin with, many did not believe that he was a swindler. He was known to be suave and cultured. It came out that he had cheated from top financial establishments like N.M. Rothschild, Smith New Court, Goldman Sachs, National Westminster and Coopers & Lybrand Deloitte to middle class journalists of *The Daily Mirror* and other publications. *The Economist* editorially commented: “Many journalists knew for years that Maxwell was up to no good. They were prevented from warning their readers of this, because Maxwell wielded libel writs as a weapon against any publication that dared to contemplate criticising him or his businesses.”[9]

What happened after Maxwell's departure from this world is no less curious. Britain's Serious Fraud Office filed a case against his sons Kevin and Ian. On the last day of May in 1995, i.e., four years after the scandal came to light, their trial began. They were accused of conspiracy to defraud and misuse the Maxwell pension funds. They were charged of fraudulently using the resources of the pension funds for securing loans to prop-up the Maxwell group of companies which were ailing. Since Kevin had been declared bankrupt, the government had to give 5 million pounds sterling in legal aid to him and other defendants and it was estimated that the total aid might came to 10 million pounds sterling when final accounts were prepared. Thus, the British tax-payers had to bear the burden of providing legal defence to the cheats. Both of them were acquitted and the cost of the case came to $ 17m or 11 million pound sterling. It needs to be noted that the annual budget allocation for Serious Fraud Office was only 20 million pound sterling.

This underlines two things: First, the media owners include among them quite a number of swindlers and criminals not only here but in a country like Britain too. And bringing them to book is quite an uphill task. Second, so-called fearless and investigative journalists fight shy of exposing them everywhere. In this connection one may refer to the comment made by the late Peter Jenkins when he stopped writing his popular political column in the *Sunday Times* (London). He said, "he had seen how good newspapers, and once independent spirits, withered in (Murdoch's) presence—or at 3,000 miles removed.'"[10]

As in developed countries so in India, a handful of business groups control most of the largely circulated newspapers and magazines. And this ownership pattern dictates what kinds of articles and news and views are to be served to the readers. The small and medium newspapers and magazines run by non-business groups do not altogether account for much circulation and their number has been dwindling with fast changes in technology. It is no longer possible as it was 40-50 years ago for a few people to come together and start daily, weekly or monthly journals. Except for the journals of political parties, there remain no papers of any consequence in terms of circulation to reflect independent thinking in political, social and economic arena. Diversity of views and content in journals can be achieved only when the newcomers enter the media market and compete with the established ones. But it is more easily said than done. Since advertisements constitute the biggest source of revenue and this source is controlled by business groups and the government, both of whom seldom support any kind of independence of views beyond a particular point. With coming into existence of electronic media, advertisements have downgraded the print media in their priority list. Advertisers generally go in for newspapers and journals with larger circulation than for those with independence of views but with very poor circulation. Moreover, most of the advertisements are routed through advertising firms which are, in turn, controlled by big business groups.

Business houses with a single or multi-publications can afford to incur losses for quite some time because they use them to protect their interests, but an individual or a group of individuals cannot do so because of the paucity of funds available. The result is that there is seldom any possibility of hundred flowers to survive and spread their fragrance, even if they bloom.

Investigative Journalism

In recent times, many scams have surfaced in the country, while the media have been full of all kinds of stories about these scams involving politicians, bureaucrats, business tycoons and the mafiosi, yet they have not played any significant role in unearthing even a single scam. We do not have an I.F. Stone or a Walter Lippman. We once had a band of so-called investigative journalists, led by Arun Shourie, who used to dish out concocted stories most of the time and when the people realised this, their attraction declined and they faded out. They failed to appreciate that investigative journalism requires a great deal of intelligence, pains-taking and skilful analysis than mere sensation-mongering. Lately, what we have seen is reporting on investigations rather than investigative journalism. "In India, some journalists complain that their employers are discouraging them from probing too deeply into the scandals that may involve powerful figures. Some media magnates fear libel suits and retaliatory tax raids, other simply baulk at the often high costs of investigative reporting."[11]

The media magnates are wise people; they want to minimise the costs of production and keep themselves on the right side of politicians whose future is unknown in this period of coalitions and instability. A person who is nobody today may become a powerful person in the government tomorrow. It is cheaper and safer to report on the trial proceedings and government investigative agencies' findings.

REFERENCES

1. N.J. Nanporia's letter to Jawaharlal Nehru dated September 17, 1963.
2. Honoré de Balzac, *Lost Illusions*, Harmondsworth, 1981, p. 316.
3. *Ibid.*, p. 249.
4. *Ibid.*, p. 289.
5. *Ibid.*, p. 314.
6. *Ibid.*, p. 356.
7. *Ibid.*, p. 229.
8. *The Economist*, December 14, 1991.
9. *Ibid.*
10. *Ibid.*, August 13, 1994.
11. *Far Eastern Economic Review*, March 20, 1997.

6

Criminal Godmen

A criminal, masquerading as a holyman or godman, has not been a rare sight in an ancient country like India. In fact, it has an unbroken chain of such criminals from Rahu, Ravana and Kalnemi of the mythological era to the present day.

In old Indian literature, there is a great deal of discussion on such characters and the way they operate and swindle. In *Panchatantra* and elsewhere, we find a number of stories about impostors, which yield only one lesson that one must not be taken in by just outward appearance otherwise one is bound to meet the same fate as that of the greedy Brahmin who landed in the trap of an old tiger which posed itself as a reformed, non-violent and vegetarian being, out to do penance for its past sins![1]

Tulsi: Illustrates the True Picture of Bogus Holymen

Tulsi Das, a very perceptive observer of human beings and their affairs, warned of impostors and their trickery in the very initial pages of his magnum opus, *Ramcharitamanas*:

"An impostor of fair and outward show may be honoured on account of his garb, but in the end, he is exposed and does not succeed, like Kalnemi or Ravana or Rahu."[2]

Rahu was a demon but posed as a god and infiltrated the ranks of gods in order to steal nectar. Ravana in the garb of a hermit deceived Sita and induced her to cross the safety zone in order to abduct her. Kalnemi, a friend of Ravana, unsuccessfully tried to poison Hanuman while he was on his way to the Himalayas to bring the prescribed herb to revive unconscious Lakshmana.

According to Tulsi Das, in the present age, "anyone with unkempt hair and nails" is "celebrated... as a model of mortification." Further, "to be dressed in the loathsome rags and ghastly adornments of a mendicant and feed indiscriminately on any kind of food" is "to be an ascetic, a saint, an object of veneration in that age of iniquity. All kinds of evildoers" are "held in high honour and respect, and the idlest babblers" are "accepted as preachers" in these "miserable days". In this age "ascetics amass wealth" and "make Brahmans bow down to their feet."[3]

He narrated the story of an impostor in the very first chapter of his epic to underline this point. He ended it by saying that it was not easy to avoid falling into the clutches of these impostors because 'not merely fools but even clever men are taken in by a fair appearance; look at the beautiful peacock; though its notes are sweet and ambrosial, it feeds on snakes.'[4]

He stressed that such holymen or godmen 'are outwardly swans, but inwardly as black as crows; walking in evil ways, abandoning the *Veda*, embodiments of falsehood, vessels of impurity, hypocrites, professing devotion to Rama, but slaves of gold, of passion and of lust.'[5] They are so fair without and foul within as if they were a golden jar full of poison.'

He was very harsh on the so-called mystic philosophers who abound here. Exposing them, he wrote: "Lecherous after their neighbour's wives, surpassingly clever only in trickery, clasped about with ignorance, violence and selfishness, these are the men who are reckoned as mystic philosophers."[6]

Criminality and Spiritualism

Even a brief visit to any city or town of India will show how *ashrams, maths* and temples having huge wealth and property are being used. One will find there, these holymen with their innumerable underlings, eating good food, dressing well and enjoying life. With their spurious spiritualism and their magic tricks, they deceive the gullible, the frustrated and all others who are in need of false solace and extort money on various counts. A newspaper report said that one Swami Premananda, a 45-year-old Sri Lanka born "holyman" was sentenced to double life imprisonment and fined Rs. 66.40 lakhs by a sessions court in Padukottai (Tamil Nadu) for raping 13 of his female disciples and murdering one inmate of his ashram and added he would not be entitled to any remission nor would he avail himself of any amnesty announced by the government in the future. If he failed to pay up the fine, he would have to serve a further jail-term of 32 years. The swami through trickery had built a large following.

We find holymen having no hesitation of any kind in encroaching upon valuable public property and, at times, creating hazards and impediments in the way of free flow and safety of road traffic. A look at the Lodhi colony temple complex on any Thursday illustrates this point perfectly well. Both the civic authorities and the police are so fearful of deities that they dare not take any action even though accidents may take place, taking a toll on human lives. In recent years, the Supreme Court has come down with a heavy hand on those encroaching upon the Ridge in Delhi. Many of the encroachers have been made to vacate the Ridge area. In spite of strict injunction, one Asa Ram Ashram has come-up on the Ridge near the Springdales School, Pusa Road, New Delhi. The enforcement agencies have not done anything, may be, because they are enamoured of the divine power of this vendor of bogus spiritualism called Asa Ram Bapuji. Thus, criminality and this kind of spiritualism seem to be symbiotically related.

In Bihar, the provisions of zamindari abolition were evaded with the help of gods, huge amounts of rent-free land were settled in the names of deities like Ram, Janaki, Krishna, Hanuman and so on and the effective occupation remained with the zamindars who went on appropriating the produce.

In fact, religion is a very lucrative business if one has necessary tact and cunning. One has to organise public relations and propaganda work carefully and in a planned manner. The so-called divine powers of the projected holyman have to be carefully and convincingly advertised in order to attract devotees. Each holyman has to choose his target and on the nature of target, depends the approach and publicity campaign. The holyman has to have his agents, financiers and patrons to begin with. He must adopt requisite mannerism, accent and the mode of speech. Once the gestation period is over, there is nothing to stop the onward march except some very big scandal.

Palmistry-Astrology and Semi-literate Holymen

Palmistry and astrology are the two important instruments to captivate the corrupt and frustrated politicians, bureaucrats and businessmen who have no self-confidence. The next instrument is *tantrik yajnas* to propitiate the gods and goddesses who seem to be unhappy with the client. In this process, the swami or an astrologer/palmist fleeces him and also forces him to take decisions according to his dictates. Thus, he becomes a powerbroker. A client loses his sanity and reason so much that he is not prepared to examine whether there is any scientific basis for palmistry/astrology. Every undergraduate science student knows that human hands have maximum number of joints of small bones and, as a result of constant folding and un-folding of palms, lines get formed on them. The refusal or inability to recognise this simple fact lands the gullible in the clutches of the frauds masquerading as "holy men" or astrologers/palmists.

It is a mistaken view that these holymen or godmen are well versed in scriptures and philosophy. Most of them are illiterate or semi-literate. To illustrate this point, we may have a look at some of the most successful holymen. Let us begin with Dhirendra Brahmachari. He was a semi-literate person from Mithila region of Bihar. He was ignorant of scriptures as well as *yoga*, but, with his cunning, he could worm his way into the homes and houses of people who mattered in the country and began playing the role of a powerbroker. He came to possess even his own aeroplane, house property at several places and factories.

Divine Powers or Magical Tricks

Sat Sai Baba, before whom VVIPs prostrate, is nothing but a trickster. With his magical tricks, he is able to convince the gullible that he possesses divine powers and make them propitiate him. He is not known for his erudition in theology and philosophy, but he has become a multi-millionaire. It has been demonstrated at various times by Prof. Kovoor of Sri Lanka, Prof. Narsimaiah and the magician P.C. Sorcar, Jr. that he is nothing but a fraud.

Prabhat Ranjan Sarkar, a former accountant with the Eastern Railway at Jamalpur (Bihar) one day assumed the name of Anandmurti to organise the sect of Anand Marg with its short-lived political wing Proutist Federation of India. He received foreign funds as well as foreign disciples and opened branches both inside and outside the country with great rapidity during the first half of the 1960s when India was passing through great economic and political difficulties. Anand Margis indulged in black magic and criminal activities. They are alleged to have been involved in the murder of L.N. Mishra, a Central Minister and close confidante of Mrs. Indira Gandhi, the recent case of arms dropping in Purulia (West Bengal) and numerous incidents of killings and bombings. Anand Marg has great resemblance with certain sects of Japan and the USA which also indulge in violence and function like secret societies.

Maharshi Mahesh Yogi of transcendental meditation (TM) fame has an empire of commercial enterprises at Noida, a suburb of Delhi where workers are exploited as much as possible. He is an ordinary graduate from the Allahabad University with no contributions of any significance to philosophy and the practice of *yoga*. For a while, he had powerful patrons with whose help he succeeded in popularising TM so much so that it was to be introduced in schools and colleges in India and abroad.

His downfall as a hi-fi *guru* began when it came to light that he was alleged to be an instrument in the hands of the CIA for placing some device in the Himalayas in order to gather intelligence. It is an open secret that quite a significant number of these *babas* and *yogis* are used by foreign agencies for activities ranging from smuggling to intelligence gathering.

Chandra Swami: Holyman Behind Bars

One may take, for example, Chandra Swami. It is a matter to be studied by sociologists and psychologists as to how a school drop-out, having fled from Hyderabad, after evading a warrant of arrest in a cheating case, could influence such powerful people as Margaret Thatcher, actress Elizabeth Taylor who was supposed to have shed weight as per his spiritual guidance, the Sultan of Brunei, Mobuto of Zaire, Marcos of the Philippines, the Prince of Monaco, the Prince of Liechtenstein, the King of Jordan, the President of Egypt, Lee Kwan Yew, Romesh Bhandari, Devi Lal, Chandra Shekhar, Kedar Pandey, P.V. Narasimha Rao, Dr. Pratap Reddy of the Apollo group of hospitals and so on.

The international arms peddler, Adnan Khashogi, of Saudi Arabia hosted several parties in honour of Chandra Swami. Steven Martindale, an American who was his close associate and also had CIA connections, described his activities in a book *By Hook or By Crook*, published in 1989. The book has detailed Chandra Swami's business deals abroad, running into millions of dollars. His business relationship with Lakhubhai G. Pathak, the pickleman of Wagan, Lancashire is also touched upon. Pathak is said to have given $100,000 by cheque, payable to the Canadian Imperial Bank of Commerce by way of a commission to secure a contract for him from the Government of India on the condition that the money was to be refunded if the contract was not secured by the stipulated date. To impress his audience, Chandra Swami used to claim that he practised *tantra* under some Nepali *guru* and, as a result of penance, secured the blessings of the presiding deity of Tirupati and emerged "as a swami and tantrik yogi at the age of 21." He performed a *yajna* in 1984 in llinois which was attended by a number of big businessmen. The author could not meet Mrs. Indira Gandhi through the Swami, though he could have very cordial meetings with Romesh Bhandari and P.V. Narasimha Rao. About his meeting with Rao, the author writes: "The Minister of Defence at that time was P.V. Narasimha Rao, an impressive little man with a long history in government... The Swami had befriended Rao years ago in Hyderabad. There was more than mutual respect between them and they conducted themselves as long time friends. The Minister received me both in his office and later at his residence exactly as he would have welcomed a visiting Secretary of State. This was heady stuff. In the course of our conversation which covered the high points and low points of Indo-US relations, he pointed out the stumbling blocks that prevented closer ties between our two countries and suggested ways to put them aside. 'Please convey this message to your friends in Washington', he implored.' He then goes on to describe Chandra Swami's financial relationship with the Sultan of Brunei and business deals with the ITC (India Tobacco Company) which was induced to enter into some joint venture with US firms. In this venture were also involved some American doctors of Indian origin.

Chandra Swami's interests were not confined only to business and financial deals but to international political relations too. To quote the author: "Soon after I met the Swami, we had discussed the formation of the Council on Indo-US Relations... Founding members were Sen. Charles Percy, Zubin Mehta, Se. William Cohen, Zbigniew Brzenzinski, Don Riegel, Paige Rense, Amb. Robert Goheen. Publisher of magazine *India*. Festival of India exhibition in US worked with it.' About the fortune accumulated by the Swami, he says: "A major part of the Swami's fortune came directly from the grateful President of Zaire (Mobuto) at least $18 million in cash and 26.5 kilos of uncut diamonds."[7]

Most of his business and financial deals, detailed by Martindale, were in violation of various provisions of Indian law. Hence, they were in the category of criminal acts. Some of these and subsequent deals are at present being investigated by law courts and agencies of the government.

Chandra Swami is a big ignoramus so far as theology and philosophy are concerned. He is incapable of performing even *yogic* exercises, not to speak of delivering impressive spiritual discourses like the late J. Krishnamurty to bring solace to the frustrated and unhappy souls. Then what is it that has attracted the powerful to him? Obviously, his activities as a powerbroker and money launderer. A report in an Indian financial newspaper is quite revealing. "The CBI and other investigating agencies are of the opinion that unusually large amount of foreign contributions to Chandra Swami and his Vishwa Dharmayatan Trust is a well organised money laundering racket in which there may be other beneficiaries". His hand is suspected not only in smuggling, currency racketeering, forgery, brokering deals and even in murders. More will be known when Babloo Srivastava deposes in the court and the Jain Commission, looking into certain aspects of Rajiv Gandhi's assassination submits its report. According to a report in an international journal: "Babloo Srivastava, recently extradited from Singapore, claimed the guru sheltered him at the ashram for nine months in 1993 when police wanted him for murder. Srivastava also told Indian interrogators that Chandra Swami had met the most-wanted Dawood Ibrahim, suspected of masterminding the 1993 serial bomb attacks in Bombay and abetted the kidnapping of two Hindu holy men who criticized the guru."[8]

During the Narasimha Rao dispensation, Chandra Swami was so powerful that he used to intervene in the distribution of Congress tickets for elections to Assemblies and Parliament and the appointment of Ministers. Powerful people used to prostrate before him. When his mother died during the first half of the 1990s, powerful politicians from a number of parties and businessmen and industrialists rushed to his village in Alwar district of Rajasthan.

The fact that the Swami is a fraud came to light when he told the Jain Commission that he was a *sannyasi* and his conduct was governed by the *Sannyas Upanishad* which ordains that, after being initiated into asceticism, one must forget one's past and obliterate all previous memories and happenings. He, thus, expressed his inability to answer the questions about his past. He knew that this particular kind of book was not easily available and he would be able to bluff.

The *Sannyas Upanishad* is one the twenty-nine minor *Upanishads*, attached to the *Atharva Veda*. Incidentally, this particular book does not have much of sanctity among the Hindu scriptures. Besides, the preliminaries, this book consists of 123 *slokas* which deal-with the conduct of a *sannyasi* or ascetic, but nowhere is there any mention or even a faint hint of what Chandra Swami stated before the Jain Commission. It nowhere mandates a *sannyasi* to forget his past. What it mandates is that an ascetic must not involve himself in any *yajna* (*sloka* 75) or with *samsarik prapanch* (101-110). Judged against these stipulations, he does not appear to be an ascetic.

The surge in the number and growing proximity of a crop of godmen and astrologers of dubious character and criminal tendency is a post-Nehru era phenomenon in India. They have come to play the role of power-broker between business and industry on the one hand and politicians on the other. These people have no responsibility and accountability to anyone. With their grip over people in power, they indulge in all sorts of orgy which can put even a Rasputin to shame.

This phenomenon has arisen because there has been a lot of discretion left to politicians in power in the matter of decisions concerning business and industry. And this has led to a scope for all sorts of middlemen and brokers to come in and godmen and astrologers have been among them. These people have an advantage over other brokers. They can make corrupt politicians rest assured that they will neither be caught by ordinary mortals nor will incur the wrath of the divine. This may well be illustrated with the example of Shivaji Singh Margdarshi alias *Satellite Baba*. This semi-literate former newspaper hawker of Patna seemed to have convinced Laloo Yadav that, through his *yajnas*, he would frustrate the attempts of the CBI and his political rivals to involve him in fodder scam and get him out of power politics for ever. He would, ultimately, get acquitted in all the cases and would bounce back with greater strength and mass base to rise so high as to occupy the highest executive position in the country open to a politician.

He claims that he, through his spiritual power, could get Dr. Jagannath Mishra and Daroga Prasad Rai, two former Chief Ministers out of the urban land scandal and the pipe purchase scandal respectively without any harm. He claims to have a direct access to nine planets, revered by the Hindus, who are supposed to make or mar the fortune of human beings. Even a sample survey will confirm that a growing number of politicians are in the clutches of criminal gods and their demon devotees. The gods that condone criminal activities on the recommendations of Chandra Swami, Margdarshi and the like of them cannot be described in any other way. In the post-Nehru era, not only rationalism and scientific temper have considerably weakened but greed and criminal tendencies have grown considerably among politicians and this has weakened their moral fibre which is being exploited by godmen. There is one more aspect which needs to be mentioned, that the frustrated and corrupt politicians use these godmen to carry on their *benami* business activities.

Illegal Activities in the Name of God

Religion and God are used to defraud and dupe those who, in their turn, cheat and exploit the people at large. In any metro city of India, we have at any time of the year more than a dozen spiritual *Bapus* (fathers) and *Maas* (mothers) making discourses in posh colonies from well decorated and beautifully lighted platforms. They tell black marketeers, currency racketeers, adulterators, smugglers and corrupt bureaucrats and politicians who constitute the bulk of the gatherings not to hanker after *Maya* though their own sole purpose is to gather as much black money as possible. An investigation into the sources of their revenues and the mode of expenditure will reveal how deeply these holymen and women have been involved in various nefarious and criminal activities. Take, for example, Chandra Swami's palatial *ashram* in South Delhi. It is the symbol of violating all sorts of building bye-laws, safety regulations and the rules framed by the Delhi Vidyut Board. These godmen and women do not declare their revenues to taxation authorities and, thus, evade taxes, produce nothing tangible and survive on the fruits of the labour of the working people. Thus, these parasites are venerated by the rich and the mighty!

In actual practice they are no different from ordinary mortals. Whenever the question of succession to the head of a monastery or the head priest of a rich temple comes up, these people fight like dogs and indulge in all kinds of intrigues. They even resort to murder. Many people still remember the family feud arising out of the decision of Bal Yogeshwar's decision to marry an American girl and settle down in the USA. His elder brother Satyapal (Rawat) Maharaj, later a Minister in the United Front government at the Centre, deposed him and grabbed the headship of the sect, floated by his semi-literate father. The sect has enormous wealth, used mainly for personal ends without much concern for the sad plight of the fellow poor people of the U.P. hills. This pattern of utilisation of wealth and property is not uncommon to other such sects. Moveable and immovable property and wealth amassed at the expense of the public are used for purely private ends.

Tonnes of milk, milk-products and grains are burnt in the name of performing various kinds of *yajnas* and ceremonies in a country where a large number of people do not get enough grains to fill their bellies and most children do not get milk to drink. Against this background, is it not a criminal act perpetrated in the name of religion and God?

But more than the above, the criminal acts are to divide people and pit one section against the other in the name of religion by destroying some dilapidated structure in order to revive the glory of Ram or Krishna. Those who indulge in such acts, try to disrupt the unity and harmony of the people and divide them into two groups: one supposedly superior and the other inferior, giving the former the right to annihilate the latter. The rioting and acts of vandalism that followed in the wake of the disputed mosque at Ayodhya inflicted incalculable damages on the economy.

The happenings in Japan and California in recent times underline that criminal activities in the name of God are not confined only to a backward country like India. Industrially advanced countries are no less prone to criminal gods and their demon devotees. A look at Japan's Aum Shinrikyo sect is not only quite revealing but helpful in understanding sects like Anand Marg in India.

It was founded in 1987 by Chizuro Matsumoto, a 32-year-old almost blind owner of a chemist's shop. Like Nemi Chand Jain, who became Chandra Swami after attaining the knowledge of the ultimate reality in the Himalayas or Prabhat Ranjan Sarkar who became Anand Murti after the same process, supposedly having attained *nirvana* in the Himalayas reappeared as Shoko Asahara. He too attracted a large number of followers through his *yoga* classes. His sect spread not only far and wide in Japan but also to Russia, the USA and Western Europe. During 1987-1995, its membership increased to 10,000 in Japan and 30,000 in Russia. Two years later, it was registered as a religious organisation which got it out of the tax net. This facilitated the acquisition of property on a large scale, beginning with the purchase of land in Kamikuishiki village at the foothills of Mt. Fuji. And with this, began its criminal activities clearing the impediments in the way of its acquisitive spree, starting with the elimination of a lawyer Tsutsumi Sakamoto and his wife and child.

In 1990, like Anand Marg's political front, Proutist Federation, in 1967 general election in India, Asahara with his 24 followers unsuccessfully contested parliamentary election. On June 27, 1994, it first tested its sarin gas on people in the city of Matsumoto. Less than a year later, the release of sarin gas[9] in Tokyo subway system killed 12 people and injured more than 5,000. Country-wide simultaneous raids on its establishments by the police resulted in unearthing huge amounts of lethal chemicals.

Ten days later, the chief of Japan's National Police Agency, Takaji Kunimatsu, was shot by a masked gunman just outside his home. The finger was raised towards the Aum sect which had specialised in kidnapping and murders for quite some time and the attack on Kunimatsu was to terrorise the police which had been investigating them.

The crackdown by the police created mutual suspicion and dissension in the sect, leading to fatally stabbing Hideo Murai, "Minister of Science and Technology" of the sect and desertion by as many as two-thirds of the 1,500 followers. A deserter Masato Inose revealed that, as a member of the sect, he 'habitually wore a headset that Aum members said would transmit Asahara's brain waves to the wearer through electrodes attached to the skull.'[10]

The police arrested the sect's "intelligence minister" and the head after conducting raids at 100 places and arraigned them before a court of law on various criminal counts. It came-out that 'Aum's criminal aspirations—and its weird collection of apocalyptic beliefs, which include the conviction that nuclear conflict will destroy most of the human race in 1997—mark it out as an oddity by the standards of the mass of esoteric religions that have mushroomed in Japan during the past few years.

'But the group stands out most significantly for its ability to recruit from the upper reaches of Japanese society. While Asahara himself began life as the fourth child of an impoverished tatami mat-maker in Kumamoto prefecture, many of the aides... came to Aum with degrees from prestigious universities such as Tokyo, Keio or Waseda.'[11]

A debate ensued whether the sect had connections with Japan's organised criminal gangs and whether it really had any Buddhist background. Police investigations revealed: "Its chief deity is a Hindu god, Siva, the consort of Kali. The two are best-known as deities of destruction. They were the chief idols of the Thugs, Indian cultists who murdered travellers as a holy ritual. The friends and relatives of ten dead travellers on the Tokyo subway may see a familiar pattern".[12]

As we have referred to above, the fashion to consult and seek guidance and help to advance one's career and tide over existing or impending difficulties, calamities and misfortunes from astrologers, *tantriks* and holymen and women has been on the increase in the post-Nehru era. On the basis of one's mentor's advice, money and time are spent to perform a variety of sacrifices and *yajnas* with all seriousness and devotion. Most of the people going in for these expensive rituals are fairly rich and educated as a superficial survey reveals. Why have they been doing so?

There are a variety of reasons. One of them is ignorance and incapability to understand certain natural or social phenomena, notwithstanding formal educational degrees and diplomas. This has been a major factor, prompting the belief in certain supernatural entities and fashioning out explanations accordingly.

Another one is uncertainty and insecurity which have tremendously increased ever since the advent of capitalism. The decline of village community and the break-up of joint family system have rendered an ordinary Indian more lonely. His fortunes are no longer influenced only by natural factors, but by the ups and downs in the market both here and abroad, swindling and corruption. Many people have only recently been ruined by non-banking financial companies, growing accidents while travelling and deadly viruses quickly spreading from the one part of the globe to the other. Then there are corrupt bureaucrats and politicians besides swindlers in the world of business, finance and industry, always fearful of raids and searches by the CBI, vigilance department, ED and so on and so forth. Politicians are afraid of exposures leading to defeat in the election. These people regularly consult astrologers to know of impending dangers in advance so that they can be taken care of through various kinds of elaborate rituals.

Here astrologers and practitioners of occult science act as intermediaries between the client and gods/ goddesses. Nobody bothers about one of the basic tenets of Hinduism that there is no scope for any intermediary between a man and his god/goddess. *Atman* is nothing but a part of *Brahman* from which it gets separated and its ultimate destiny is to merge with it.

It is only in Judaism, Christianity and Islam that God is totally separate from human beings and never incarnates in the form of a human being. In these religions, a prophet is an intermediary.

Thus, the concept of an intermediary is an alien one to Hinduism and came to be interpolated much later by the vested interests. Thus, the very basis of the operation of Sat Sai Babas, the Chandra Swamis, the Satellite Babas and so on is spurious and they are nothing but frauds and criminals out to deceive and rob the people going to them.

Corrupt Society and Babas

Yet the politicians who are unsure of their prospects at coming elections or the reshuffle of the government have to get the gods to take care of their interests and the intermediaries from the practitioners of occult science to Bajrangbali Hanumanji are appeased so that they recommend their cases strongly and push up their files in the divine court as speedily as possible.

Corrupt politicians, bribe-taking bureaucrats, dishonest shopkeepers, smugglers, unscrupulous industrialists and traders, tax evaders, thieves, pick-pockets, robbers and professional murderers are all great devotees of the *babas* and the *mahatmas*. And these are the people who are in a great need of the services of astrologers. One seldom finds a landless agricultural labourer or an urban hawker queuing for their services nor do these intermediaries of gods care for the poor clients.

These intermediaries of gods operate generally near hospitals and law courts because there, they can find their prey in plenty. A patient or his relations who are unsure of his survival and the litigants doubtful of winning their law suits until and unless some miracle takes place seek the help of these intermediaries who, in turn, assure them of the sought-after miracle taking place if the gods are propitiated through them. Thus, these frauds dupe the people and relieve them of their money in a non-violently pious way. And this crime is condoned by the society and the law.

Astrology infringes on human dignity by declaring that human beings are subjected to the elaborate influence of the planets millions of kilometres away from them, travelling on their predestined courses. In fact, these intermediaries of gods rob those who, in turn, rob the people at large. Thus, it is the case of one set of criminals exploiting another set of criminals or sharing in the loot brought by the latter.

REFERENCES

1. Sitaram Shastri (ed.), *Hitopadeshah*, Banaras, 1955, pp. 30-40.
2. R.C. Prasad (ed.), *The Ramayana of Tulsidas*, translated by F.S. Growse, Delhi, 1989, p. 9.
3. *Ibid.*, p. 689.
4. *Ibid.*, p. 105.
5. *Ibid.*, pp. 13-14.
6. *Ibid.*, p. 690.
7. Steven Martindale, *By Hook or By Crook*, see extracts from pp. 163-164 re-produced in *New Wave*, March 23, 1997.
8. *Far Eastern Economic Review*, October 12, 1995.
9. For information on sarin gas and how it works, see, *The Economist*, March 25, 1995.
10. *Far Eastern Economic Review*, June 27, 1996.
11. *Ibid.*, May 25, 1995 and also see, David E. Kaplan and Andrew Marshall, *The Cult of the End of the World*, London, 1996.
12. *The Economist*, April 1, 1995.

7

Crimes in the World of Education

Prof. John Kenneth Galbraith thinks that an important requirement for economic development in any country is an educated and therefore, a competent and socially and economically motivated population. The importance of education was fully recognized during the initial years of industrial revolution in the present-day developed industrial countries. Free and compulsory education came to be regarded as a basic requisite for modern economic growth. To quote: "In the last century, nothing occupied a more prominent place among the requirements for economic and social advance than public education and popular enlightenment..... Popular education releases the energies not of the few but of the many, and it opens the way to technical knowledge. Literate people will see the need for getting machines. It is not so clear that machines will see the need for getting literate people. So under some circumstances, at least popular education will have a priority over the dam, factories and other furniture of capital development."[1] Similarly, 'All over the world, it is taken for granted that educational achievement and economic success are closely linked—that the struggle to raise a nation's living standards is fought first and foremost in the classroom.'[2]

It was realised by a Lenin or a Mao or a Ho Chi

Minh, but not by Indian leaders though they themselves were highly educated and well travelled that "nothing enfranchises like education". The result was an utterly disproportionate emphasis on institutes of higher learning or, what is called in the jargon of educationists, the tertiary sector in the field of education. There also, the emphasis came to be placed on humanities and social sciences and natural sciences without any link with the sphere of production and technological development.

Illiteracy: Biggest Crime Against the People

Consequently, India has roughly half of its population illiterate. In the States like Arunachal Pradesh, Bihar, Rajasthan, Uttar Pradesh, Madhya Pradesh more than 60 per cent of the population is completely illiterate even after 50 years of Independence.

Can there be a greater crime than this against the people of this country? And the perpetrators of this crime have been among the most influential. All the talk of empowering the people, lifting them out of age-old darkness and fighting for their cause turns out to be nothing but utterly bogus. Even a State like West Bengal, ruled by the venerable Jyoti Basu and his friends on the Left, has 43 per cent of the total population as illiterate while 53 per cent of women there can neither read nor write at all.

Dharma Kumar, a distinguished scholar of India's economic history, says: "Public expenditure on education in India was a miserable 0.2 per cent of national income in the nineteenth century and never much above 0.5 per cent in the twentieth. Further, even those small amounts were not spent in the most useful way. As is still the case, too small a share was spent on primary education—Bengal, for example, spent more on university, than on primary education. And much of the expenditure on primary education was said to be wasteful, particularly in the countryside."[3]

In a nutshell, the alien government did not care for human resource development, but the governments at

Delhi and in the States, irrespective of their ideological and political complexion, too, after Independence; have not cared to attempt a change in the situation.

What is the result? In the words of Jean Dreze: "The rhetoric of every Indian government—without exception—has included handsome tribute to the importance of basic education. The real issue is not rhetoric acceptability, but the willingness to put actual—not imagined—emphasis on this particular requirement for the transformation of the Indian economy. This simply has not happened. While India has a highly developed—if overextended—higher education sector (sending nearly six times as many people to the universities and institutions of higher learning as China does, compared with its population), it remains one of the most backward countries in the world in terms of elementary education. For instance, literacy rates in India are much lower than in China, lower than literacy rates in many east and south-east Asian countries at the time of their economic take-off 30 years or so ago, lower than the average literacy rates for "low-income countries" other than China and India and also lower than estimated literacy rates in sub-Saharan Africa.

'With nearly half the people—and close to two-thirds of the women illiterate, the transformation of the Indian economy is no easy task. Even an efficient utilization of the world market requires production to specification, needs quality control and depends on an informed consciousness of the economic tasks involved. The success of the East Asian "tigers"' and more recently of China, has been based on a much higher level of literacy and basic education than India has. The persistence of endemic illiteracy in India, even in the younger age groups, is one of the basic social failures that shackle the Indian economy and society.'[4]

In view of what has been stated above, the failure of Indian States becomes glaring and it turns out to be guilty of not fulfilling one of the most basic needs of the people and the pre-requisites of economic development.

True Picture of Our Educational System

The recent crop of leaders like Laloo Yadav and Mulayam Singh Yadav who talk of social justice and empowering the hitherto downtrodden people seems to be expert in deceiving people. Laloo has used the slogan of Charwaha Vidyalayas to allow backward castes in general and his own castemen in particular to grab the valuable farm lands belonging to the Bihar Agro-industries Development Corporation rather than any genuine concern for giving them light of literacy and education. Under his seven year dispensation, the entire education system in the state collapsed. There are very few government schools which have any furniture left. Even door and window frames have been stolen. School buildings need urgent repairs but the government does not have money to spend. Teachers seldom come to schools because they share a part of their salary and allowances with those who are supposed to see that they regularly and punctually attend to their duties. A substantial number of teachers have engaged unemployed youth to teach in their place on subsistence wages while they are busy with something more lucrative. This informal kind of sub-contracting is an open secret. In this situation, students are not at all wrong in their thinking that it is futile and waste of time to journey to schools where classes are rarely held.

Education bureaucracy of Bihar is happy because it gets discounts and commissions. Politicians are no less happy as they get some of their workers and supporters jobs in non-functioning schools. Laloo in his zeal to break the CPI's hold on the legislative council constituencies among secondary teachers resorted to mass transfers and the result was that many schools in the crime-infested areas of West Champaran went without adequate number of teachers for months because fearful outsiders, on some pretext or the other, refused to take-up their new assignments.

It needs to be noted that the Chief Minister and his fellow politicians do not send their wards to government-run schools because they know they are defunct. They send them to public school in and outside the State. Laloo's children have gone to a public school run by the missionaries near Ranchi and to the Mayo College, Ajmer, which was setup originally for the wards of native princes.

Neither educational bureaucracy nor are the politicians interested in making the government-run schools work effectively because this will make private teaching shops that go by the name of "public schools" redundant. It is an open secret that a sizable number of such teaching shops are directly or indirectly run by private businessmen in collaboration with education bureaucracy and politicians and they share in the extortions from parents and the teachers who are seldom paid the amount which they "formally receive". The RSS-clan has opened Sarswati Shishu Mandir groups of schools in many parts of the country to inculcate their ideological orientation in the minds of children from a very young age, besides providing a regular revenue.

In the U.P., the blame for bringing chaos in the sphere of school education goes to Mulayam Singh Yadav, himself a former school teacher. He, by condoning the use of unfair means, destroyed the sanctity of examinations and ushered in an era of indiscipline.

Not only in Bihar but elsewhere too, a number of people who have set-up chains of so-called public schools are businessmen out to make money by hook or by crook. This may be illustrated by citing a few examples. In one of the posh colonies of New Delhi, we find the management of two schools encroaching upon the public park. When the resident welfare society complained to the local police, the management of one of them immediately contacted the then police commissioner and his wife to be chief guests at the annual day function! Not only this, the plot on which it has come-up was originally earmarked for a primary schools, but during the "social justice" dispensation, it was given to an NRI society to build a senior secondary school. Incidentally, the chief of the NRI society belongs to the same caste as messiah of "social justice". Local residents say that the school has not cared to abide by the building bye-laws laid down by the Municipal Corporation of Delhi. There is a serious doubt whether the building is all right from safety and security angles. Notwithstanding high fees charged from students, there is neither a proper playground nor facilities for sports.

'Public' Schools are Looting the Public

The education directorate of the Delhi government found during 1997, 16 private "public" schools, selected at random for inspection, indulging in extortions from students on various counts. They included, among others, Delhi Public School, R.K. Puram; Modern School, Vasant Vihar; Springdales School, Dhaula Kuan and Pusa Road; Bal Bharati Public School, Ganga Ram Hospital Marg; Mont Fort School, Ashok Vihar; and Apeejay Public School, Peetampura. According to *The Times of India* (August 20, 1997): 'Some of the major findings of the inspection are:

*Schools are collecting money in the name of pupil's fund, excursion fund, magazine fund and so on and the funds collected under these heads are manipulated for other purposes by the schools authorities;

*The Delhi Public School Society is opening schools even outside Delhi with the money collected from the Delhi students. The DAV School Society is doing the same. Some schools are charging money for issuing school-leaving certificates—this is illegal;

*Some schools have mortgaged school land and building to public and private enterprises and banks to generate money for their respective societies. The interest on the loans taken by the individual society from these enterprises and banks is being paid by the school;

*Some societies and trusts managing schools have given loans to the schools at an interest rate of 21 per cent. The managing committee of a school is not a separate legal entity and hence, the loaner and the loanee cannot be the same person;

*Most schools are collecting huge sums by selling thousands of admission forms, the price of these ranges from Rs. 50 to Rs. 250. They shouldn't be more than Rs. 10 each.

*Collection of huge amounts in the name of admission fee, ranging from Rs. 1,000 to Rs. 5,000. The admission fee should not be more than Rs. 200. Some schools are "capitalising" on the money collecting at admission fee.

*Huge amounts are being collected in the name of security or caution money at admission time, ranging from Rs. 1,000 to Rs. 8,000. It shouldn't be more than Rs. 500. This money is either not refunded or if it is refunded then it is returned without any interest. Similar amounts are also collected as loans from parents at admission time.

*Schools collect science fee every month from all students. However, in most schools, there are no separate laboratories for middle classes and secondary classes. Science is one of the subjects in the syllabus and hence, there is no question of a separate science fee.

*In some schools, a building fund is being collected even though the building is complete in every respect.

*Many schools are transferring surplus funds to their respective societies, which if retained in school, would enable the managing committee to lower the fee structure and to provide better facilities and staff.'

Mafia and Education

A mafia has emerged in the field of education and culture of India since Independence. It sets up and controls schools and colleges and staffs them with its near and dear ones besides and with those who are able to pay for securing appointments. This is widely prevalent in Delhi, U.P. and Bihar. There is a nexus of businessmen, mafia, bureaucracy and politicians in the field of education. Businessmen treat opening and running schools as nothing but profit-making activities. The Ansals, well-known colonisers and builders have opened a number of schools in Delhi, U.P. and Haryana, they also own a number of cinema halls and other business activities. They do not make any distinction among them so far as maximisation of profits is concerned. They flout all norms and rules and regulations which hinder profit maximisation. It is alleged that the Uphaar Cinema tragedy on June 13, 1997 which cost 59 lives was the result of this kind of attitude, leading to the neglect of basic safety procedures.

About Bihar, Nageshwar Sharma who was, for a number of years, Director, Higher Education in the State, has written at length about how top politicians and bureaucrats combined to loot the resources of education department and extort bribes from job seekers. According to him, since 1965, excepting two (Dr. George Jacob and Sachindra Nath Datta), the rest of the appointments to Vice-Chancellorship of the Patna and other universities have been, not on the basis of academic stature and administrative skills but, as a result of political-connections, sycophancy, mortgaging oneself mentally to the powers-that-be or the capacity to buy.[5] Consequently, indiscipline, anarchy and chaos have come to prevail on the university and college campuses. This may be illustrated with only one instance. In 1972, two senior professors of the Patna University, namely, Anirudha Jha of Philosophy Department and V.P. Verma of Political Science Department fought a physical duel in the meeting of the Syndicate while the Vice-Chancellor, Mahendra Pratap, seemed to act as umpire. The situation went on deteriorating. One Vice-Chancellor, bypassing the objections of the head of the department, appointed Ranjan Yadav, merit-wise not to be much spoken of, as demonstrator in the Geology Department. This gentleman quickly rose to Lecturership, Readership and Professorship without any creditable teaching experience, publication or research work to his credit, thanks to his proximity to Laloo Yadav. So much so that the Bihar Grantha Academy, a government body, came out with his biography with his picture on every page, written by Dr. Amar Kumar Singh, sycophant *par excellence*! Since 1990, he has been the extra-constitutional authority running Bihar's universities.

Sharma has given concrete instances how doctoral research work became a mockery. Plagiarism became the order of the day.[6] Frivolous topics such as "A scientific study of the binding of Sant Tulsi Das's Ramcharit Manas" were approved for doctoral dissertations! There opened "factories" for churning out doctoral theses. From the production of a synopsis to the dissertation and arranging for pliable examiners could be arranged for a fee by certain teachers-turned-contractors.[7]

There were Vice-Chancellors like P.L. Srivastava and Shyam Nandan Kishore under whose dispensation, the Bihar University (now known as the Babasaheb Bhim Rao Ambedkar Bihar University) reached its nadir. A mafia took over its administration. Question papers were sold in advance and examinations became a farce. A one-man committee, headed by a high-ranking officer, appointed by the government, levelled charges of casteism, corruption (which included the sale of 1000 bags cement in the black market) and a number of financial irregularities. Shyam Nandan Kishore continued the regime of corruption further. He, as Nageshwar Sharma has alleged, used to take bribes for everything from admission of students, appointment and transfer of teachers to the purchase of materials. Nepotism had a free play.

K.K. Mandal set up a new record as Vice-Chancellor of the Magadh University. So much so that a Hindi weekly from Calcutta, belonging to the *Ananda Bazar Patrika* group, in a signed article in December, 1981 claimed that every position in the Magadh University was being auctioned off to the highest bidder. He had fixed the rates for different posts (for a peon's job Rs 3,000, for a clerk's post Rs 5,000, and for a teacher's position from Rs. 10,000 to Rs 50,000 depending on the rank and place of posting), though he was always ready to be flexible according to the degree of political pressure and the demand of the circumstances. His wife played a key role in the transactions. He seldom made any distinction between university's assets and his own. There were a number of agents and middlemen between the Vice-Chancellor and favour-seekers and it is needless to add that they also had their share in the extortions.[8]

Sharma's book abounds in concrete instances based on documentary proofs as to how corrupt and pliable Vice-

Chancellors with no academic credentials like A.K. Dhan were always on the beck and call of political bosses and flouted all rules and regulations to gift away jobs to their nominees. Dr. Jagannath Mishra used Vice-Chancellors like Shyam Nandan Kishore and A.K. Dhan for his personal and political interests. Even the level of corruption went so low that during Dhan's stewardship of the Ranchi University, every application for seeking permission to do research had to be accompanied with a bribe of Rs 200 and it had to be submitted to clerk Kullu.[9]

During the early 1980s, the V.S. Jha Committee, having a number of eminent educationists of the country as its members, which was appointed to look into the affairs of the universities of Bihar, detailed how they were being treated by politicians and their hirelings, masquerading as Vice-Chancellors. To quote: "More than 7,000 teachers of the constituent and affiliated colleges are inducted into the university service as teachers. The inevitable casualty is the quality of work in the colleges and the university teaching departments. Several generations of the eager students are, thus, robbed of opportunity to learn from clean and competent teachers. And it is sad to realise that these teachers will produce the next generation of teachers, if the damage is unchecked and the various multiplying process will continue. Provisions of acts and statutes cannot be held responsible for this kind of situation created by small minds for small gains unconscious and unheedful of the damage caused.'[10] It added that "the goondas and politicians" alone dominated the field of education in Bihar.

Known criminals too came to dominate the affairs of higher education. To give a concrete instance, Ramchandra Prasad Singh who was found to be involved in the acts of embezzlement of funds and frauds and had been imprisoned in the Beur Central Jail was appointed as the Chairman of the Bihar State University Service Commission during the early 1980s, thanks to political backing. The situation has not changed but gone from bad to worse under the Laloo Yadav—Ranjan Yadav dispensation, indiscriminate creation of universities without any regard to infrastructure and the appointment of all and sundry as Vice-Chancellors have made higher education a matter of ridicule.

Education-Corruption and Criminality

A substantial part of the explanation of corruption and criminality in the sphere of education in the State lies in the nature and state of its economic development. Bihar has not seen any industrialisation of consequence since Independence anywhere except Chotanagpur's tribal belt though an oil refinery and a fertiliser factory came up in Barauni in North Bihar of which the latter has ceased functioning while former has not been able to make much of a dent in the problem of growing educated unemployment. In fact, this problem has worsened with the closure of old industrial units. On balance, there has been deindustrialisation. The entire Dalmia Nagar complex has been closed for decades, many sugar factories and cement units have gone out of commission. Mica mining business is no longer lucrative after the disintegration of the Soviet Union. Cycle and cotton factories which were in existence on the eve of Independence have since long closed their business. No new investment has been coming or can come in the future for a lack of infrastructure and non-existence of even a semblance of law and order.

In this situation, setting up educational institutions has turned out to be a very profitable proposition both financially and politically. More than 200 former and present legislators and parliamentarians are associated with colleges and universities to further their political interests besides minting money. Some years ago, a report in a newspaper said. "Mr. Ram Lakhan Singh Yadav, a veteran Congress MLA, has got more than 80 colleges in his name and he is associated with more than 150 colleges in various capacities. The BPCC chief, Dr. Jagannath Mishra, has more than seven colleges in his name. The prestigious L.N. Mishra Institute of Economic Development and Social Change is his creation. Mr. R.P. Sharma, MLA, has got a number of educational institutions in his name.

Besides, scores of colleges, located in different parts of the State are named after politicians like Anugrah Narayan Sinha, Mahesh Prasad Sinha, Shree Krishna Sinha, Satyendra Narayan Sinha and Karpoori Thakur".[11]

Since the publication of this report, the situation has reached the nadir. In this intervening of eight years, more and more colleges have been opened in the names of politicians, contractors, mahanths and erstwhile zamindars. The joke goes that you put up a sign board on a telephone or electric pole or a tree, it becomes a college and with the help of some politician, it can be secured affiliation by the university concerned. People have lost count of educational institutions named after Ram Lakhan Singh Yadav, Satyendra Narayan Sinha and his father, wife and father-in-law, Jagannath Mishra and L.P. Shahi.

Some have even opened institutes of management in which seats and degrees/diplomas are purchased by the moneyed class for their wards. They are veritable money-minting factories in view of the growing craze for an MBA degree.

There are other purposes also behind opening colleges. We know for certain one instance where a college was founded to evade the provisions of land ceiling legislation in a very covert manner. This case needs some detailing. A gentleman, lawyer by profession, with political pulls, had quite a substantial amount of land in his village, which had to be surrendered after all the feasible manipulations to retain as much land as possible.

He hit upon the idea of founding a college in his district town which is not more than 16 kilometres from his village. He founded the college and named it after himself and had a managing committee controlled by himself. He got people mostly from his own caste and the families aligned with him. He took money from them for handing over appointment letters. For years, these people received much less than what they signed for. He had some land in the town which he gave on lease to the college and the college to which he had donated all the land in his village, which was over and above the limit of ceiling, gave, in turn, the village land to him on lease. Before the college came to be taken over and made a constituent unit of the concerned university, he received money for construction of buildings, etc. from which he grabbed a substantial portion. Thus, he killed many birds with one stone!

An investigation into the history of colleges founded and then turned into constituent units of various universities since the 1960s is sure to reveal criminal aspects clearly.

To give just one typical example, any newly-founded college before being turned into a constituent unit usually ran mainly on fees and other revenues collected from students who could be attracted only when results were impressive and they, in turn, could be had only by resorting to copying and manipulations.

Many parents usually fell for these short-cuts to good results for their wards. Gangsters came forward to lend their helping hand to this business. If invigilators and university representatives tried to go by rule books, they were assaulted. A number of them connived and allowed the answer books to be taken out, filled in or dictated for a prescribed fee usually called *suvidha shulk* (convenience fee).

Nobody bothered to see whether a college to be made a constituent unit fulfilled the requisite conditions, laid down by the ordinances and statutes of the university concerned. What mattered was political pulls or hush money which was shared from Vice-Chancellors to political bosses.

It is no longer a secret that Satyendra Narayan Sinha as Education Minister had brought people like C.P. Sinha and P.L. Srivastava to head the Secondary School Examination Board and the Bihar University respectively and these two bodies got themselves drowned in innumerable scandals. In the former as many as 40,000 certificates were found to be missing or sold to those who had either failed or had not appeared at all at the examination. In the latter, the question papers for various examinations were sold through selected outlets before their commencement. To quote from a write-up in a weekly, 'Under his patronage, the Rajputs captured key posts and control of educational life. It will be interesting to note the increasing number of Rajputs appointed as papersetters, examiners and collators in the Board examinations.'[12]

At present, the education system in the State has completely collapsed. Certificates and degrees are sold and examinations have become a farce. A Ph.D in Hindi becomes a reader in physics while a philosophy man may be appointed to teach a subject like mathematics. A student studying engineering in far away Moscow can simultaneously do Post-Graduation in Ancient History and culture acquiring a first division as a regular student without visiting Bihar even once.

In the Name of Nehru

Many of the institutes of higher learning have nothing tangible to show as their achievements though huge resources have been spent on them. Take, for example, the Jawaharlal Nehru University. Till today, we have not been able to understand the rationale of its coming into being. Nehru does not need roads, bridges and institutes to perpetuate his memory.

In fact, Nehru's name and the sentiments, it aroused were used to create a fiefdom by certain people who also paraded their fake Leftism to serve their own ends. They brought their friends and disciples to fill up the university. Posts, centres and divisions were created to adjust them and not the other way round. Only a small percentage of them was qualified and did produce works of excellence, but not so the rest. A person having just a post-graduate degree in geography was elevated to higher and higher positions without having a look at his competence and qualifications. At the time of his death, he headed one of the premier funding agencies. The chief patron of the mafia was such a learned man that his published contribution in his field of specialisation was almost nil. If one has a closer look at the contributions made by this so-called centre of excellence by keeping in view the huge resources spent on it year after year, the inescapable conclusion will be nothing but criminal waste of scarce resources which could have been better utilised by allocating them to elementary education.

Similarly, a stock-taking of the achievements of numerous institutions, funded by the ICSSR and the UGC are warranted. In most cases, the so-called research work done by them are repetitive and irrelevant, hence worthless. They have no purpose other than strengthening the hold of the mafia by giving it huge patronage in the form of jobs and funds. They can be safely closed down to use the resources more fruitfully.

Prof. J.V. Narlikar, a renowned scientist, has recently talked of 'a steady erosion of academic life in our campuses' and added: "Barring very few notable exceptions, students see no inspiring examples of brilliant scholars lecturing to them or of international quality research going on in their campuses. What they see are universities which have tied themselves in knots in litigation, internal politics and a downward spiral in maintaining academic standards. The students have been to colleges where adequate infrastructure for training does not exist, where staff appointed is not on merit and many manifestly are ill equipped to lecture properly, where terminal examinations are held but answer scripts are not even marked".

'In this environment, if a few faculty members are engaged in good research this is an embarrassment to their colleagues and every attempt is made to hamper their work.'[13]

Education Bureaucracy

In the course of time a veritable education bureaucracy has grown, which has developed a vested interest in perpetuation and proliferation of its empire. This well-entrenched education bureaucracy operates more or less on the same pattern as the Sicilian mafia. It runs through a network of "friends" and "friends-of-friends". The head of this network may be termed as an entrepreneur if the term don looks derogatory. This education entrepreneur manipulates two distinct types of resources. The first includes jobs, establishments of institutes and centres of study and research, setting up of funding agencies, scholarship and fellowships, foreign assignments, grant and so on. The second comprises 'strategic contacts with other people who control such resources directly or who have access to such persons.' Jeremy Boissevain has termed the former as the *first order resources* while the latter as the *second order resources*. 'Persons who dispense first order resources may be called *patrons*. Those who dispense second order resources are *brokers*. A broker is thus a special type of entrepreneur: one who controls *second order resources* and manipulates these for his own profit. Brokers are, thus, highly expert network specialists'.[14]

An academic broker places people who need help in touch with the patron for profit which may be tangible or intangible. To have a control over the distribution of the *first order resources* through an access to the patron increases the power and dominance of the broker. To give an example, the ever-lengthening queue before the residence of an academic broker in Patna's Churi Bazaar denoted his control over the first order resources through his proximity to the patron during the State's first "social justice regime". Whenever there was a piece of news that the patron was distancing himself from this broker, the queue became shorter and shorter.

There are sub-brokers too particularly in countries like India and a sub-broker always tries to establish his direct access to the patron so that he can have a greater control over the first order resources and he does not have to go through a broker. Sometimes, one finds coalitions under which people enter into temporary alliances to achieve specified goals like getting somebody out of Vice-Chancellor's office or destabilising an existing arrangement of things or getting somebody appointed in order to prevent someone else from securing it. Years ago, a self-proclaimed Marxist teacher ganged up with a whole range of elements to destabilise the incumbent Vice-

Chancellor who was renowned economist, sincere teacher, honest to the core and with an unimpeachable record of service to the university. Once the Vice-Chancellor quit, the various members got their rewards. Ideologically, politically and otherwise the coalition was heterogeneous, the only binding thread was the common goal of getting rid of the incumbent Vice-Chancellor.

There are other types of formations too. For example, sometimes we find a clique where mutual affection and appreciation is the basic factor for bringing a group of people together. Helping one another in matter of jobs, promotions, special assignments, projects, writing work, publication and praising one another's academic achievements by the word of mouth and/or arranging favourable reviews.

Over the years, the appointments to academic and administrative posts in Indian universities have been manipulated to an utter disregard of academic worth. One may investigate the background of such appointees to realise what we are saying. In a premier university of India three senior professors were dismissed from service in 1996. What were the charges? One of them had manipulated the admission of his son to a prized course, another had misappropriated public funds and the third one had misbehaved with a woman colleague. One of the college principals of the university was allegedly involved in the murder of a lecturer, but could be suspended reluctantly by the university because he had powerful protectors.

Virus of Casteism and Regionalism

Casteism and regionalism are rampant. To give a concrete example which is in no way an exceptional case, in one of the topmost colleges of this particular university, out of the five principals till date, four have been from one region and three from the one caste. Academic qualifications and administrative skills have never mattered in their selection. Once these people were appointed, each one of them brought their caste and region kith and kin to fill-up the posts at lower levels so that a strong protective wall is erected around their acts of manipulations.

It is needless to add that once appointments are made on the basis of caste, region and group loyalties, the universities, colleges and institutes are bound to go down the drain and give rise to intrigues and all sorts of nefarious activities.

If one looks at the Banaras Hindu University, the Kurukshetra University and the Patna University one may find how non-academic considerations in appointments are available on the basis of emoluments and facilities suited to it. A university requires a Madan Mohan Malaviya or a V.K.R.V. Rao to push aside bureaucratic and other hurdles to bring outstanding scholars to teach and research.

The P.B. Gajendragadkar Committee, appointed to look into the plight of the Banaras Hindu University, wrote in its report: "The atmosphere on the university campus is surcharged with suspicion and fear, division runs through all the sections of the university community; the teachers appear to be divided; the students are divided and even the Class IV employees are divided." And it went on to add: "As our report will show, some of the causes which, in our view, have led to the recent unrest consist of incidents which partake of a criminal character".[15]

As far back as in 1957, the Mudaliar Committee was appointed to look into the malaise that had gripped. It suggested certain drastic steps and the government did go in for them but the situation did not improve, instead, it deteriorated. A decade or so after that, the Gajendragadkar Committee found caste and region playing a dominant role in the life of the university and despite a formal organisation like the Teacher's Association 'the spirit of groupism based on castes persists amongst the teachers and the existence of this spirit is undoubtedly a source of infirmity in the academic life of the university'.[16] The committee found that the university which earlier had an all India character where teachers and students from all over the country were welcome was reduced to a regional entity meant mostly for eastern U.P. and western Bihar. The result was a fast deterioration in the standards of teaching and research. This was the finding of the Mudaliar Committee too. In fact, the Mudaliar Committee had given specific instances to substantiate this. According to it, Ph.D. theses in a number of cases were written not by candidates but by hired scholars. There was such a moral degradation that a professor of the stature of B.L. Atrey who was decorated by the President of India was caught for taking a marriage party on railways without tickets.

By the time, the Gajendragadkar Committee was appointed, communal virus had also penetrated the university and the RSS had established its presence on the campus by securing accommodation, courtesy the then Vice-Chancellor.

Even after almost three decades of the Gajendragadkar Committee report the situation has not improved a bit. In fact, it has reached a point of no return. As compared to the Universities of Bihar, it seems to be in no better position.

In India there are more "seminarists" than serious scholars doing teaching and research in so-called institutes and centres of excellence, whom Arthur Koestler aptly termed as "call girls". They hop from seminar to seminar and committee to committee with hardly any time for reading, writing and reflection. These people are nothing but parasites on the society and after they retire, there is nothing left behind to remind that they once existed. Since they manipulate to grab the resources belonging to the society without any *quid pro quo*, they are nothing but thieves and criminals.

Thorstein Veblen's Revolutionary Views

Thorstein Veblen who shook the American social science establishment by his writings, to quote the Japanese economist Shigeto Tsuru, 'thought that even a good and honest scholar, once in the President's (Vice-Chancellor's) seat would soon become as corrupt a salesman of 'ponderous vendible intangibles' as any small town banker, delegated by the board of trustees to give the institution an 'efficient, business like management'. In fact, Veblen recognized here the unfortunate role of the scholar-president, 'caught on the margin between God and mammon, between science as a collective heritage and the business culture as a growing nastiness'.

'Veblen apparently felt that the universities could run themselves, once outside interference was removed... Thus, he listed university presidents as one of the superfluities of American society, along with prostitutes, advertising, hotelmen, the services of porters and retailers.'[17] With only slight modification, this view will apply to Indian universities and institutes.

We know of one institute which conducts training programmes for bureaucrats. A retired civil servant who is a member of Parliament, belonging to a particular political party, generally believed to be Hindu communal in character, has grabbed the chairmanship of the editorial board of its Research Journal notwithstanding the fact that he has neither academic nor scholarly depth and achievements like a Dr. K.S. Singh or a B.R. Nanda. The result is that the standard and prestige of the journal have been fast declining. Similarly, two IAS officers have grabbed the Archaeological Survey of India, without possessing the requisite technical qualifications and expertise needed for running this body. There has been a strong protest lodged by the Indian History Congress, but nobody bothers?

Then there are pseudo-professors and academicans who plagiarise the published works of others and publish them or submit them as their theses in order to secure Ph.D. degrees. To give a specific instance, S.K. Mittal of Chaudhry Charan Singh College of the Meerut University published a book in 1978, which is nothing but largely copied from two already published works[18] A former Chief-Minister of a state in order to secure a doctorate degree submitted a thesis, copied largely from a popular textbook which shows the extent of criminality.

REFERENCES

1. John Kenneth Galbraith, *Economic Development in Perspective*, Cambridge, Mass., 1962, pp. 8-9.
2. *The Economist*, March 29, 1997.
3. Dharma Kumar (ed.), *The Cambridge Economic History of India*, Vol. II, CUP, 1982, p. 937.
4. Jean Dreze and Amartya Kumar Sen, *India: Economic Development and Social Opportunity*, Delhi, 1995, concluding chapter (we have taken the quotation from the concluding chapter distributed by Dreze at a seminar in New Delhi, organised by the Observer Foundation in the first half of 1995).
5. Nageshwar Prasad Sharma, *Bihar ke Dhahate Vishwavidyalay*, Patna, 1997, p. 29.
6. *Ibid.*, p. 41.
7. *Ibid.*, p. 106.
8. *Ibid.*, p. 115-17.
9. *Ibid.*, p. 127-30.
10. Quoted in *Ibid.*, p. 135.
11. *The Times of India*, Patna, May 1, 1989.
12. *Mainstream*, June 14, 1969.
13. J.V. Narlikar, "Attacking Achievement: The Declining Image of Academia", *The Times of India*, July 17, 1997.
14. Jeremy Boissevain, *Friends of Friends: Networks, Manipulators and Coalitions*, Oxford, 1974, pp. 147-48.
15. *Report of the Banaras Hindu University Inquiry Committee*, New Delhi, July 1969, p. 13.
16. *Ibid.*, p. 16.
17. Shigeto Tsuru, *Institutional Economics Revisited*, Cambridge, 1993, p. 66.
18. S.K. Mittal, *Peasant Uprisings and Mahatma Gandhi in North Bihar*, Meerut, 1978 has been plagiarisation of Ram Narayan Sinha, *Bihar Tenantry (1783-1833)*, Bombay, 1968 and Girish Mishra, *Agrarian Problems of Permanent Settlement: A Case Study of Champaran*, New Delhi, January 1978.

REFERENCES

8

Corruption and Bureaucracy

After half-a-century of Independence, there has been lots of changes in India's economy, polity, society and culture. Some have been good while others have been quite harmful. Among the latter, there has been all-pervasive corruption. It has assumed such alarming proportions that it has become a veritable threat to India's democracy and socio-economic advance.

Though corruption in public life has been witnessed ever since the beginning of human civilization, it has become an all-pervasive phenomenon only in recent years. Its linkages and interconnections, quite often cross local boundaries and, at times, involve a number of nations, their citizens, governments and business concerns. Whether one recalls Iran-Contra Scandal or the Lockheed pay-off or the Bofors case or more recent Harshad Mehta Bank scam, sugar scandal, Jain Hawala, JMM MPs' bribery case, urea-non-import scam, Lakhubhai cheating case, the Bihar animal husbandry scam, Government accommodation (out of turn) allotment scam, allotments of gas agencies and petrol pumps from the discretionary quota of petroleum minister, other and scams, they have not been confined strictly to the four corners of one nation. With globalisation of economic and financial relations, the ramifications of corruption have become more complex and deeper. There is hardly any country in the world untouched by the virus of corruption and not even the most stringent punishment of execution (as in China) has been able to curb the disease.

Such a phenomenon needs to be studied quite carefully in all its aspects, but, unfortunately, in India while media have been writing at length and, at times, mixing with substantial sensationalism about individual instances and the cases of corruption at all levels and politicians have been shouting loudly (though in quite a number of cases hypocritically), there has been an utter lack of any generalised theoretical discussion. For example, very few people are at all clear about the connotation of the term "corruption" and how it emerges and affects the functioning of a democratic polity and the development of the economy.

Different Forms of Corruption

It is not very easy to define corruption because it does not always involve monetary considerations. It may be taken as an illicit form of influence to get or prevent certain decisions or actions which are otherwise impossible under the existing laws, rules and practices. There are diverse forms of corruption.

A political scientist, Mr. J. Nye, in the paper "Corruption and Political Development: a cost-benefit analysis" in *American Political Science Review*, [61(2), June 1967] defined corruption as a 'behaviour which deviates from the formal duties of a public role (elective or appointive) because of private—regarding (personal, close family, private clique) wealth or status gains (which) violates rules against the exercise of certain types of private—or regarding influence.' The French scholar, Y. Mény, has given four characteristics of corruption, namely:

'1. The violation of rules and norms associated with what is perceived to be the general interest (or public ethics) in a political society at a given time;
2. In the course of a secret exchange among political, social and economic markets;

3. With the (anticipated) consequence of providing individuals or groups with resources of access and influence in the process of political and administrative decision-making that are superior to those available in the (normal) course of open dealings;
4. Eventually resulting in tangible benefits, material or otherwise, for the party or parties involved in the transaction.'[1]

In view of these four characteristics, a proper definition of corruption should be taken into account considering the relationship between wealth, power and the consideration of legitimacy.

One finds corruption at all levels and in various degrees. One sees Lowly government or private sector employees demanding *bakhashees* when some work is accomplished or some favourable decision is made and conveyed is encountered. One quite often comes across postmen, telephone linesmen or sweepers of municipal bodies visiting the people of localities they have been serving, on some specific occasions for gratification.

A postman delivering a passport or a telegraph employee bringing greeting cards on the occasion of marriage or birth of a son or excellent performance at examination or election may ask for some monetary tips or sweets. They are seen as "grass eaters" as against the highly-placed officers and politicians who have a say in the decision-making process and work towards getting kickbacks who are regarded as "meat eaters".

A traffic constable may extort some money to let you off rather than booking you for not displaying the number plate of your vehicle or not having proper lighting system. Or you may bribe a policeman to allow you to disregard some traffic rules in order to take a very sick man to a hospital without delay. Such types of corruption do not cause much harm nor are they severely condemnable. To cite a well-known instance given by Susan Rose-Ackerman. "One does not condemn a Jew for bribing his way out of a concentration camp."

But corruption at lower levels is not always worth ignoring because, at times, it may be greatly harmful. To give a typical example, if a sweeper or sentry allows some foreign agency to bug the room of a highly placed government official, dealing with matters of national security, it can be ignored only at great peril. Similarly, if a typist or personal assistant of an important minister or secretary passes on confidential papers, it a serious matter which may adversely affect national security and interests. Thus, it must be dealt with ruthlessly.

Corruption at higher levels, with which we are concerned in this study, generally involves matters where stakes are much greater and, quite often, national or regional interests are involved. Decisions influenced by considerations other than those of established rules, regulations, procedures and norms are bound to be harmful and may result in a heavy loss to the exchequer and damage social interests.

There is a lack of agreement among scholars who have made a special study of the phenomenon of corruption as regards its impact on or consequences for development. Some have suggested that corruption may be functional in certain circumstances when it may make the system work. It may push up the rate of economic growth through two types of mechanisms. First, corrupt practices such as "speed money" may enable individuals to cut short bureaucratic tangles and delays. Thus, they can reduce the cost over-runs and other difficulties. Second, government employees who extort bribes generally try to work harder, especially where bribes act as piece rates.

While the first mechanism may increase the chances of corruption being beneficial to economic growth only in countries where bureaucratic regulations are cumbersome, the second one may operate irrespective of the level of red tape. It has been seen that tips to waiters or peons invariably improve the services and lead to saving of valuable time of tip-givers. It is needless to add that for many people time is money.

There are, however, economists who reject this

viewpoint. They assert that corruption tends to lower economic growth. Thus, hush money acts as a lubricant to the giant and complex administrative machinery in order to promote economic growth and induce bureaucrats to work hard only to a limited extent. In fact, it increases the costs of production for an investor who wants speedy clearance of his project and proposal and the higher costs of production are realised from people at large who have to buy the commodity at higher prices.

Corruption influences the distribution of wealth, power and privileges both at the primary as well as the secondary levels. It not only perpetuates but widens the disparities. It leads to a chunk of money being withdrawn from the legal economy into the illegal or underground one. To that extent, monetary and financial regulators become ineffective. In addition, the scope for indulging in corrupt practices in order to make money in certain bureaucratic and political positions, enhances their value and induces people to grab them by hook or by crook. It is because of this in many countries "transfers" and "postings" become a money-minting activity for ministers and highly-placed officials. According to Michael Johnston: "Corruption can help preserve objective inequalities in two ways: by facilitating the unequal appropriation of wealth and privileges and by inhibiting changes which could threaten existing advantages".[2]

Corruption involves two sides, a person with power to influence the decision-making process and another person, willing to corrupt him by offering material or non-material inducement so that the decision is favourable to him. Both sides are indispensable to each other in accomplishing an act of corruption, therefore, both are equally guilty.

Corruption has far-reaching influence on almost all aspects of the society—economic, political, cultural and moral. Susan Rose-Ackerman who has earned great fame for her study of the phenomenon of corruption writes: "Corruption is never more than a second-best solution. Its very illegality produces inefficiencies since resources are wasted in keeping transactions secret and in enforcing arbitrary status. Moreover, a corrupt system of government services has the distributional disadvantage of benefiting unscrupulous people at the expense of law-abiding citizens who would be willing to purchase the services legally. Corruption may also be impossible to limit to "desirable" situations. A system which overlooks corruption in areas where it is "economically justifiable" may find in time that corruption has spread to all aspects of the government structure. If trust, honesty and altruism are valuable traits in some areas of life, they may be impossible to preserve if dishonesty is openly tolerated elsewhere".[3]

Corruption accentuates and widens existing inequalities. At the stage of secondary distribution of national income, a substantial part goes into the pockets of those who do not participate in the process of production in any useful way. In other words, corruption strengthens a stratum of parasites and bloodsuckers, since ill-begotten incomes and wealth cannot legally be invested in the names of persons who possess them and the members of their families. Consequently, they are invested either *benami* or in illegal activities like smuggling, hoarding of essential items of consumption or goods for which the demand exceeds supply, black-marketing, manufacture and peddling of narcotics and so on. Most people with huge amounts of black incomes and wealth indulge in extravagant and vulgar display. Real estates are acquired by paying large sums under the table, cheating the state exchequer of stamp duties and other dues. Since ill-begotten incomes and wealth are not shown in income and wealth tax returns, the government loses income and wealth tax revenues.

Corruption: A Powerful Barrier to Investment

Peter Eugen, Chairman, Transparency International, regards corruption as a powerful barrier to investment because it reduces the profitability and economic growth. Some time back, he told Beta Gomez of the US Information Agency that 'Corruption has a direct cost in terms of siphoning-off resources—and it can be considerable. The payments required to get a large contract used to be about two to five per cent of the total; practitioners tell us that it is now in the order of 10, 15, even 20 per cent. If you look at the public sector investment programme of a poor country, which might build a few power dams, a few roads, a port and a few hospitals, an additional 10 per cent or so for bribes is a direct cost to that economy and to the people whom these projects are supposed to serve.'

"Bribonomics" or economics of bribery shows that in a country where the incidences of corruption is quite high and where bureaucrats (and politicians) sell government properties, including production licences, passports, building contracts and so on for personal gain, most often efficient firms are excluded and those in a position to pay the highest hush money succeed in getting production licences and building contracts are seldom the most qualified for the job. People and firms are discouraged from putting premium on hard work and efficiency.

Andrei Shleifer and Robert Vishny in their paper "Corruption" (*Quarterly Journal of Economics*, Autumn, 1993), have underlined that not only the level but the form of corruption also matters a great deal. For example, there was corruption during the Soviet regime, but it was benign, not oppressive, hence, it did not retard the economic growth. Japan and Malaysia too have corruption but the record of their economic growth is quite impressive. In Russia, corruption exists but in an oppressive form. Even if some enterpreneur bribes, he cannot be sure of having no difficulty in the pursuit of his activities. Earlier, the official who was bribed did enjoy monopoly control over a service and could ensure its smooth flow to the bribe-giver. Today, this monopoly in Russia does not exist. There are several agencies in place of the official. They include officers of different concerned departments, political bosses and the mafia. And there is no co-ordination among them and each one of them has to be propitiated. Each one of them charges as much as possible without taking into account the fact that others have also to be paid. Their conclusion is that an organised and disciplined system of corruption is likely to be less damaging to economic growth and this discipline could be imposed by the Communist Party during the Soviet era and can still be imposed by a gang of power-brokers or the mafia. This kind of discipline existed under Liberal Democratic Party rule in Japan. Where there is one monolithic party rule, corruption is likely to be less oppressive and more disciplined.

Recipients of black incomes and wealth distort the pattern of demand and, thus; the pattern of investment and production by their spending. They also influence political processes by bringing politicians and the formations to which they belong under their sway. Politicians and political parties depend on these people for resources to support their election campaigns and day-to-day political activities. In India, this mutual dependence of politicians and the people, who operate and sustain the dirty or underground economy has been rising more and more. To borrow a simile from Balzac, these licenced thieves are "wells" while politicians have become "buckets."

Corruption: Awareness of the Western and Eastern Scholars

Balzac in one of his novels says that there are only two ways by which a man can "acquire a fortune rapidly" and "make his way here" where in every corner vested interests squat. It is 'by brilliant genius or by skilful corruption. You must either cut your way through these masses of men like a cannon ball or steal among them like a plague. Honesty is nothing to the purpose. Men bow before the power of genius. They hate it and try to slander it, because genius does not divide the spoil, but if genius persists, they bow before it. To sum it all up in a phrase, if they fail to smother genius in the mud, they fall on their knees and worship it. Corruption is a great power in the world and talent is scarce. So corruption is the weapon of superfluous mediocrity—you will be made to feel the point of it everywhere.'[4]

These days we hear of the detection of "assets disproportionate to the known sources of income" being the ground for booking officials of the government and semi-government departments under the law to prevent corruption. More than one-and-a-half centuries ago, this phenomenon was widespread in France. Balzac, thus, writes of the 'women who spend more than ten thousand francs a year on dress while their husband's salary (his whole income) is six thousand francs. You will see officials buying estates on twelve hundred francs a year.'[5]

Much before Balzac, our Vishnugupta Chanakya was aware of this phenomenon. That is why *Kautilya Arthashastra* devoted substantial space to its prevention. It advised the ruler to have a system of regular shifting and transfer of officials so that they did not develop any vested interest in any particular place or group of people. It wanted regular and thorough auditing of accounts and prescribed stringent punishment for any defalcation. Further, high officials were required to render full accounts of their activities and it was the duty of the ruler to see that there was no contradiction in them. Thus, accountability was introduced.

The king was advised to follow a 'carrot and stick policy' whereby sincere and honest officials were rewarded and promoted while the negligent and dishonest were to be severely punished. Kautilya stated: "It is possible to know even the path of birds flying in the sky but not the ways of government servants who hide their (dishonest) incomes". (2-9-84)

Consequently, 'those officials who have amassed money (wrongfully) shall be made to pay it back; they shall (then) be transferred to other jobs where they will not be tempted to misappropriate and be made to disgorge again what they had eaten.' (2-9-85). Kautilya had anticipated the situation which has led to the fodder scam in Bihar in whose capital city, he composed his *Arthashastra*, centuries ago. He had laid down that no work, consequently, no withdrawal of funds should take place without proper authorisation except, of course, in the case of emergencies.

Writing much later, Kalhan in his chronicle of Kashmir *Rajtarangini*, narrated several instances where high handedness and corruption of officials, including ministers led to the downfall of rulers and warned that those who did not want to meet this fate must draw proper lessons and keep a watch on bureaucracy.

With the rise of capitalism, whose impact was described by Marx and Engels in the *Communist Manifesto* one-and-a-half centuries ago, administrative apparatus became more and more complex. Discovery of the hitherto unknown lands and the development of productive forces, leading to vast expansion of both national and international trade and financial relations and the rise of modern forms of organisation of both production and exchange had unprecedented consequences for economy as well as society. Revolution in the sphere of transport and communication made the movement of men and material and the transmission of ideas and information much faster. All these had an impact on the role of the government and the size, powers and influence of bureaucracy fast expanded and came to touch or affect the lives of the people staying even in the remotest areas.

The old situation where the fight between rulers or the intrigues in the royal family did not touch the tillers of land living in India's remote villages has changed. Now they are dependent on the government and its bureaucracy for inputs, marketing of their products, supply of goods and services consumed by them and for protection from natural calamities and criminals. It is the government which has been re-organising production relations through various land laws.

Thus, the complexion and quality of bureaucracy is a matter of concern for the people living even in far-flung areas of the country and one can easily grasp the significance of what we say by looking at the root cause of the turmoil in the North-east and the hilly regions of the U.P. The demand for reservations of jobs in government services for certain sections of the society is, *inter-alia*, informed by this consideration also. A feeling has now entered in the minds of the people that they no longer control their destiny. To quote Henry Jacoby: "the term bureaucracy refers to the fact that man's existence is directed and controlled by central agencies, not only is he unable to escape from the regulation and manipulation, he seems to depend on it. The overpowering anonymity of the control and the impenetrability of large powerful administrative machines produce fear and discontent. In spite of universal education and increasing use of the printed word and electronic media, the individual finds it increasingly difficult to understand the machinery. He has less influence now than before, because he lacks the means of making his will known. Man's alienation from his own world is expressed in his dissatisfaction with bureaucracy.'[6]

British historian, George Robb, has traced the real origins of white-collar crime to about two centuries ago in the past when the Industrial Revolution began, which saw tremendous growth of financial sector and the proliferation of the activities of the government and bureaucracy. "The Industrial Revolution called into being a complex economy increasingly dependent on finance and investment. This new economy was characterized by a vast banking network, a burgeoning commercial nexus of insurance, stocks and credit and an increasingly complicated legal system. These phenomena as well as concomitant increase of lawyers, brokers and financiers greatly expanded the potential for white-collar crime.'[7]

Rapid expansion of bureaucracy as a result of the growth in the activities of the State led to the alienation of the governed from the government. Karl Marx summed-up the situation in the following words: "The bureaucracy has in its possession, the affairs of the State, spiritual being of society; it belongs to it as private property. The general spirit of bureaucracy is the official secret, the mystery... Conducting the affairs of State in public, even political consciousness, thus, appear to the bureaucracy as high treason against its mystery. Authority is, thus, the principle of its knowledge and the deification of authoritarianism is its credo. But within itself, this spiritualism turns into a coarse materialism, the materialism of dumb obedience... As far as the individual bureaucrat is concerned, the goals of the State become his private goals, i.e. hunting for higher jobs and the making of a career... possible. Hence, the bureaucrat must always behave towards the real state in a Jesuitical fashion, be it consciously or unconsciously. The bureaucrat sees the world as a mere object to be managed alongside the real state, it is the spiritualism of the state. Everything has, therefore, a double meaning: the real and the bureaucratic one.'[8]

Marx's views on bureaucracy are contained mostly in his early works where his sole concern seemed to be a radical change in the society so that 'man could find his true human nature in the recognition of himself as the creator of social institutions and not as their slave.'[9] And bureaucracy was a big impediment in the way of this radical restructuring. Later, Marx talked of bureaucratization of social life and mentioned educational institutions and even local bodies coming in the grip of bureaucratization.

Complex procedures and rules and regulations increased the powers of bureaucrats and they could delay the decisions indefinitely. In a country like India with most of the ministers having no tangible experience and understanding of the procedures and rules of business of the government, it is the bureaucracy which wields the real power. If the minister concerned is corrupt, then there is nothing to stop the bureaucrat from having his way. One may take the example of Laloo Yadav, one of the most powerful Chief Ministers in the country. All these years in power, as he himself says, he had been signing on the dotted lines because of his inability to understand the rules and procedures of governance. Obviously, bureaucrats have been in a most happy position, grinding their own axe, not being perturbed at his idiosyncrasies. Bihar is not an exceptional case, the same situation obtains almost everywhere in the country.

To the argument that a person enters civil service on the basis of his ability, competence and knowledge and opportunity to enter civil service is open to every citizen means that it is bound to have a friendly attitude towards the people at large, Marx said: "It is of a very superficial and dualistic nature. Every Catholic has the opportunity to become a priest (i.e., to separate himself from the laity as from the world). Does the clergy confront the Catholic as an other-worldly power, and lessen that account? The fact that anyone has the opportunity to acquire the right of *another* sphere merely proves that in *his own* sphere this right has no reality".[10] In fact, there is a hostility between civil society and the State and its arm civil service or bureaucracy. A person joining the civil service *ipso facto* deserts his old loyalties and joins the hostile army out to repress the people. In other words, he gets the opportunity to be a member of the civil service only as a result of desertion of the old camp. Thus, Marx was of the view that, in a class society, civil service or bureaucracy could not become pro-people or friendly to the mass of citizens.

The Role of Bureaucracy

Barring a few, at present most bureaucrats hanker after, what Aristotle called "superfluities" of life. They have only one way by which they can fulfil their desire and, that is, by resorting to bribery and there is hardly any dearth of people ready to oblige them. In this process, an indispensable role is played by middlemen who are variously known. They masquerade as liaison officers, public relations officers and so on. In fact, they are power-brokers. At times, newspaper editors, correspondents, retired, bureaucrats and even serving or retired MPs also perform this role. If someone makes a survey of the national capital region to find out how many erstwhile MPs, belonging other parts of the country have been staying here without any ostensible business or engagement, it will be interesting to find out the sources from which they receive money not only to bridge the gap between their expenditures and legal incomes but to add to their assets. It may come out that most of them act as power-brokers and secure permits and quotas and arrange suitable transfers and postings for their clients.

Long ago, we were told by a common friend, at that time working in the government secretariat at Patna, of the power of even a lowly clerk. He told us that if this clerk was not propitiated, he could block any decision, notwithstanding a favourable decision desired by the minister or the Secretary. Take, for example, a proposal to set up a factory somewhere. Let us say, the proposal was first rate, but the clerk was not properly "tackled", in that case he would just make a noting that it should secure the clearance from the Department of Environment and, in this process, the sanction of the proposal would easily be delayed for months and the party concerned would incur losses and face cost escalation. Even if the proposal was cleared by the Department of Environment, the concerned file might be "lost" or "misplaced" in transit and it might take months to retrieve it. Marx was perfectly right when he remarked: "The bureaucracy is a circle from which no one can escape. Its hierarchy is a *hierarchy of knowledge.* The top entrusts the understanding of detail to the lower levels, whilst the lower levels credit the top with understanding of the general and so all are mutually deceived".[11]

Taking another example, a Delhi-based trader once supplied carpets to the Raj Bhawan of a particular State. For years he could not realise payment for them even though he met a number of successive Chief Ministers and spoke to one ADC after another of the Governor. His only fault was that he did not go through "proper channel", propitiating both small and big deities in the bureaucracy dealing with this issue.

It is a matter of common knowledge that outside booksellers, do not supply books to institutions in Bihar because they cannot afford to pay cuts and commissions at every step and even then it takes many months to get their bills paid.

In such a situation, "interference income," both accounted for and unaccounted is bound to be quite sizeable. This term was first used by Joseph Schumpeter who, in his efforts to secure US citizenship, came face to face with redtapism and had to rely on lawyers who had to be paid even though they did not perform any function in-dispensable to the running of socio-economic life. This, he jokingly termed it as "interference income" in the course of a cocktail party. Prof. Shigeto Tsuru has defined it 'as the generation of income by otherwise dispensable services, which are made indispensable through built-in institutional arrangements in the society concerned. There is usually a historical background explaining why a particular service acquires built-in indispensably in a particular society, and there is, of course, no opprobrium implied in singling out a particular profession of 'income-interfering.' As a matter of fact, an 'income-interfering' profession in a particular society draws very often the best of brains in the society and its members distinguish themselves as outstanding citizens of the community.'[12]

Though some part of "interference income" is included while computing the GNP (Gross National Product), the rest cannot be because it is not declared and is illegal. For example, while the incomes of lawyers, various types of consultants and advisers are legal incomes and are included the GNP, the receipts of unauthorised agents who procure reserved bookings on trains, the middlemen through whom bribes are paid to officers and ministers and so on cannot be included.

Even if "interference income" is included in the GNP, its welfare significance is questionable. *The Economist* (October 10, 1992) in a special article "America's Parasite Economy" discussed 'how lawyers, lobbyists and assorted non-criminals, (including government) legally steal Joe Public's money and why he lets them do it.' It presented few figures which were really astounding. For example, in 1960, there were only 365 paid lobbyists registered with the US Senate, but in 1992 the number reached 40,111 which worked out to 400 per senator. During 1960-1990 the number of lawyer rose from 260,000 to 756,000. This raises a big question mark before the concept of GNP employed all over the world. Let us not go into this because this may lead us astray.

That part of "interference income" which is illegal, forms a significant part of the underground or parallel economy and the greater its size, the bigger is the difficulty created in the way of the smooth functioning and regulation of the economy. According to one estimate, the GNP of the underground economy of the USA accounts for no less than 10 per cent of the official GNP. For India, there are various estimates, yet, one thing is clear that moonshining and unreported income of the self-employed do not constitute a big proportion of unreported GNP. The major portion of the GNP of the underground economy is accounted for by bribery, non-traditional theft, smuggling and so on.

One of the greatest sociologists of modern times, Max Weber, thought bureaucracy to be a rational form of government. To him, its characteristics included responsibility, devotion to duty, well-defined functions and requisite authority for enforcement of rules and regulations and discretion and a sense of timing as to the use of force. He was impressed by bureaucracy's precision, methodical approach and seeming efficiency. In practice, this has not been observed. In view of what has been happening in India and elsewhere, especially in recent times, in place of rational administration, has become irrational exercise of power, there do not seem to be, in practice; any defined limits to coercion. An arrogant behaviour on the part of bureaucracy is everywhere visible. By and large, bureaucrats do not regard themselves as "servants of people", but their masters and exploiters. They generally behave like autocrats and most of them aim at enriching themselves by hook or by crook. Their main intention is to harass the people by delaying decisions, obstructing their work by putting in irrelevant and irresponsible objections.

Max Weber held that though society's bureaucratization was undesirable, it could not be avoided. It stood in the way of real democracy and prevented the emergence of self-responsible and socially active citizens.

In the nineteenth century itself, Balzac with his keen insight wrote a play *Les Employés (La Femme Supérieure)* which touched upon the role of bureaucracy. Its English translation *Bureaucracy*; or *a Civil Service Reformer*, translated by Katherine Prescott Wormeley and published from Boston in as far back as 1889, is not available. Hence for his views, expressed in it, we have no alternative but to depend on his biographer the late Andre Maurois.

According to Maurois: "Balzac could never touch a subject without deepening it. Under Napoleon, the imperial despotism had restricted the power of the bureaucracy, 'that ponderous curtain set between the good that needs to be done and the man who can command it'. Under a constitutional government, ministers being of uncertain duration and mainly concerned with safeguarding their existence before Parliament, officialdom reigns supreme and creates a device of inertia known as the Report, which delays effective action. "Every kind of lobbying springs to life... The best thing in France have been accomplished when there was no Report and decisions were spontaneous". Wholly composed of narrow minds, bureaucracy obstructs the prosperity of the country, keeps a canal project... in its files for seven years, eternally drags out abuses and, thus, perpetuates itself.'[13] Balzac proposed a drastic reduction in the number of ministries and the size of bureaucracy to economise on resources and curtail the scope for delays and inefficiency in decision-making and implementation.

For England in the same period, the valuable descriptions of Charles Dickens are still relevant. Talking of the Circumlocution Office which was supposed to be "containing the whole science of a government," Dickens wrote: "No public business of any kind could possibly be done at any time, without the acquiescence of the Circumlocution Office. Its finger was in the largest public pie and in the smallest public tart. It was equally impossible to do the plainest right and to undo the plainest wrong, without the express authority of the Circumlocution Office. If another Gunpowder Plot had been discovered half-an-hour before the lighting of the match, nobody would have been justified in saving the Parliament until there had been half-a-score of boards, half-a-bushel of minutes, several sacks of official memoranda and a family-vault full of ungrammatical correspondence, on the part of the Circumlocution Office'.

'This glorious establishment had been early in the field, when the one sublime principle, involving the difficult art of governing a country, was first distinctly revealed to statesmen. It had been foremost to study that bright revelation and to carry its shining influence through the whole of the official proceedings. Whatever was required to be done, the Circumlocution Office was beforehand with all the public departments in the art of perceiving—HOW NOT TO DO IT.'[14]

'It is true that 'How not to do' was the great study and object of all public departments and professional politicians all round the Circumlocution Office. It is true that every new Premier and every new government, coming in because they had upheld a certain thing as necessary to be done, were no sooner come in than they applied their utmost faculties to discovering How not to do it. It is true that from the moment a general election was over, every 'returned' man who had been raving on hustings because it hadn't been done and who had been asking the friends of the honourable gentleman in the opposite interest on pain of impeachment to tell him why it hadn't been done and who had been asserting that it must be done and who had been pledging himself that it should be done, began to devise: 'How it was not to be done'. It is true that the debates of both Houses of Parliament the whole session through, uniformly tended to the protracted deliberation, 'How not to do it'. It is true that the royal speech at the opening of such session virtually said: "My lords and gentlemen, you have a considerable stroke of work to do and you will please retire to your respective chambers and discuss, "How not to do it". It is true that the royal speech, at the close of such session, virtually said: "My lords and gentlemen, you have through several laborious months been considering with great loyalty and patriotism, 'How not to do it' and you have found out and with the blessing of Providence upon the harvest (natural, not political), I now dismiss you. All this is true, but the Circumlocution Office went beyond it.

Because the Circumlocution Office went on mechanically, every day, keeping this wonderful, all-sufficient wheel of statesmanship, how not to do it, in motion. Because the Circumlocution Office was down upon any ill-advised public servant who was 'going to do' it or who appeared to be by any surprising accident in remote danger of 'doing it', with a minute and a memorandum and a letter of instructions, that extinguished him. It was this spirit of natural efficiency in the Circumlocution Office that had gradually led to its having something to do with everything. Mechanicians, natural philosophers, soldiers, sailors, petitioners, memorialists, people with grievances, people who wanted to prevent grievances, people who wanted to redress grievances, jobbed people, people who couldn't get rewarded for merit and people who couldn't get punished for demerit, were all indiscriminately tucked up under the foolscape paper of the Circumlocution Office.

'Numbers of people were lost in the Circumlocution Office. Unfortunate with wrongs or with projects for the general welfare (and they had better have had wrongs at first, than have taken that bitter English recipe for certainly getting them), who in slow lapse of time and agony had passed safely through other public departments; who, according to rule, had been bullied in this over-reached by that and evaded by the other; got referred at last to the Circumlocution Office and never reappeared in the light of day. Boards sat upon them, secretaries minuted upon them, commissioners gabbled about them, clerks registered, entered and ticked them off and they melted away. In short, all the business of the country went through the Circumlocution Office, except the business that never came out of it and its name was Legion.

Sometimes, angry spirits attacked the Circumlocution Office. Sometimes, parliamentary questions were asked about it and even parliamentary motions made or threatened about it, by demagogues so low and ignorant as to hold that the real recipe of government was, 'How to do it'. Then would the noble lord or the right honourable gentleman, in whose department it was to defend the Circumlocution Office, put an orange in his pocket and make a regular field-day of the occasion. Then would he come down to that House with a slap upon the table and meet the honourable gentleman foot to foot. Then would he be there to tell that honourable gentleman that the Circumlocution Office not only was blameless in this matter, but was commendable in this matter, was extollable to the skies in this matter. Then would he be there to tell that honourable gentleman, that, although the Circumlocution Office was invariably right and wholly right, it never was so right as in this matter. Then would he be there to tell that honourable gentleman that it would have been more to his honour, more to his credit, more to his good taste, more to his good sense, more to half the dictionary of commonplaces, if he had left the Circumlocution Office alone and never approached this matter. Then would he keep one eye upon a coach or crammer from the Circumlocution Office sitting below the bar and smash the honourable gentleman with the Circumlocution Office account of this matter. And although one of two things always happened; namely, either that the Circumlocution Office had nothing to say and said it, or that it had something to say of which the noble lord or right honourable gentleman, blundered one half and forgot the other; the Circumlocution Office was always voted immaculate, by an accommodating majority.'[15]

The essence of what Balzac and Dickens wrote about bureaucracy during the nineteenth century when industrial capitalism emerged as the dominant mode of production has not been contradicted anywhere in the world. Even in the Soviet Union and elsewhere too where capitalism was overthrown and a new system was sought to be built up, no progress was made to get rid of the stranglehold of bureaucracy. In fact, the hold of bureaucracy increased and became more pervasive and Marx's dream seemed to be chimerical. What the Yugoslav leader, Milovan Djilas, wrote in his *New Class* is well known. Talking of the process which led to a rapid growth of bureaucracy L. Kritzmann in a book published from Berlin in 1929 noted that it was not easy to organise production in a country as vast as the Soviet Union. The coordination of production, transportation, supply of raw materials and labour, distribution and so on in the face of internal sabotage and external military intervention in the early years of revolution was an extremely difficult task. Though the government came out with a number of decrees and regulations, their implementation was the key factor. For some time, workers did try to perform the task of coordination and implementation of decrees and regulations, but they did not succeed because they had neither competence nor experience and the general level of education among them was quite low. In view of this, the growth and proliferation of bureaucracy was inevitable. In the course of time, it came to control almost every aspect of socio-economic life. To what a ridiculous extent bureaucratization went was explained by the Russian novelist, Valery Tarsis, by referring to a conversation of the boss of the Housing Department with a writer working as an official in the same department. To quote: 'Krasnbryukov explained to me: "You are the lowest form of life: you make the preliminary check on applicants. As a senior inspector Rosalia Grib checks on you. Both of you are controlled by our lawyer. Then all of you are checked by me and my two assistants. I am controlled", he ticked them off on his fingers, "by the District Soviet inspector—one, by the District Party Committee inspector—two, by the Deputy Chairman of the District Soviet, Solovey—three, by the Chairman himself, Mosolkin—four and then by innumerable officials of the Moscow Housing Administration, the Moscow City Soviet, the State Control Committee, a commission of the Supreme Soviet and so on without end.'[16]

Notwithstanding so many layers of controlling mechanism, the Soviet administration was neither efficient nor free from corruption. Nikita Krushchev was so enraged that he called the Soviet bureaucrats at the twenty-first Congress of the CPSU "busy loafers".

Till now, the socialists of all types have failed to tame and make bureaucracy pro-people. Quite often, they have yielded before the machinations of bureaucracy. To give a concrete example, in the year 1923 Rudolf Hilferding, a leading light of the German Social Democratic Party and internationally renowned Marxist theoretician, learnt a bitter lesson about the role and strength of bureaucracy when he became the sixth Finance Minister of the Weimar

Republic. Bureaucrats concerned decided not to send any important documents to him because they were suspicious of him. The result was that he found himself sitting at an empty table without any work to do. He had a nervous breakdown and bureaucrats relented only when he made a promise that he would not make any radical change in the proposals submitted by them. Then the situation became normal.[17] Thus, "Hilferding learned the hard way what most of us already know: that permanent officials have political power.'[18]

It requires a great deal of tact to handle and control bureaucracy. This task cannot be performed by an impractical man. No bureaucrat would ever say "no" to his political boss but he would 'adjust the political plans to expeditiousness and would take the fundamentals off the radical proposals and reduce them to cautious experiments. The most serious case of bureaucratic sabotage arises when large portions of the civil service act in concert to cross the legitimate policy of the government.'[19] Henry Jacoby has correctly observed: "The "political master" always finds himself to be the "dilettante" when he comes face to face with the bureaucratic "expert". Every bureaucracy tries to increase the advantage of its professional administrators by *keeping secret* its expertise and its intentions. The tendency of bureaucratic administration is to exclude the public."[20]

Because of its permanent nature, superior knowledge of administrative and technical matters and no worry about any electoral compulsion, bureaucracy is stubborn in its relations with its political masters. Once it gets entrenched, it is hardest to destroy.

The virtue of neutrality on the part of bureaucracy has always been a myth. At best it may be seen only when there is no danger perceived to the existing socio-economic system. It always exhibits a conservative attitude and approach and condones all kinds of crimes and acts of corruption so long as there is no danger to the very existence of the system under which it is working.

Let us cite few concrete examples from our experience of how woodenheaded bureaucracy is. It is known that a pensioner is required to submit periodically living certificates. If a person submits living certificate for the current year, but not for the previous year, he may be paid pension for the current year but not for the previous year because the bureaucracy is not sure that he was alive last year! It is not sufficient to convince him that if he is alive now, he must not have been dead during the previous year. Thus, the bureaucracy seems to be miles away from any kind of rational thinking or logic. Take another example, a lecturer, according to the UGC norms, to be promoted to the senior grade is required to have attended two training/ refresher courses even if he has an M. Phil. or doctorate, but if he applies for readership and possesses a doctorate degree, the requirement of participation in training or refresher courses is not there. Obviously, bureaucrats framing these rules have nothing to do with any kind of rational approach.

In India, since the end of the Nehru era, the political decision-making machinery has considerably weakened for a variety of reasons. New breed of leaders is mostly incompetent and inexperienced so far as administrative affairs are concerned. A number of these leaders are from the classes and segments who have been for a long time oppressed and dominated. Consequently, they suffer from a particular complex which impels them to behave like feudal rulers and exhibit their power. Laloo Yadav is a typical example. His arrogance towards upper castes and bureaucracy, largely composed of them reflects such a complex. Most of the politicians like him have neither time nor understanding of administrative matters which are left solely in the hands of bureaucrats who, after knowing the limitations and handicaps from which their political masters suffer, use power for their own enrichment by extorting bribes and looting the government exchequer and developing a nexus with the world of business and industry and in quite a number of cases, with the underworld.

Secondly, with no single party enjoying absolute majority and the lurking danger of the collapse of the government any moment, making fresh elections. Imminent politicians and political parties want to amass wealth and financial resources to take care of their future needs—both political and personal and with this consideration in view, they develop a nexus with bureaucrats. Various scams which have been unearthed in recent times highlight the fact that corrupt politicians and corrupt bureaucrats quite often combine to loot the resources of the State and oppress the people. Unwilling bureaucrats are "insulted" and humiliated and the self-respecting ones quietly withdraw and go elsewhere.

One needs to investigate why the craze for government jobs in general and IAS, IRS, IPS, etc. in particular is very strong among the States and regions and classes in India, which are more backward. There is hardly any attraction towards these services among youngmen of Mumbai, Delhi (we exclude those who study in Delhi but are not domiciled there), Pune, Ahmedabad, Bangalore, Hyderabad and so on because they do not suffer from the complex, referred to above and they can earn more money and perks legally by going in for the private sector.

Not only the bureaucracy but the judiciary too in India has been affected by the virus of corruption. This has been admitted by no less a person than Mr. Justice J.S. Verma, soon after his retirement as Chief Justice of the Supreme Court of India. In an exclusive interview to the *Indian Express* (22 January, 1998), he said: 'There is no point in saying that there is no corruption in the judiciary. No one is going to say it, much less accept it. One cannot go on sweeping it under the carpet and not expect it to show. It is showing now'. He suggested enactment of a law to hold judges accountable because 'when moral sanction doesn't work, then legal sanction is required'. He underlined that 'traditions and conventions' were not sufficient guarantees for ensuring judicial accountability. He cited examples in support.

REFERENCES

1. John Girling, *Corruption, Capitalism and Democracy*, London, 1997, p. 10.
2. Michael Johnston's paper "Corruption, inequality and change" in Peter M. Ward (ed.), *Corruption, Development and inequality*, London, 1989, p. 20.
3. Susan Rose-Ackerman, *Corruption: A Study in Political Economy*, New York, 1978, p. 8.
4. Honoré de Balzac, *Pere Goriot*, p. 105.
5. *Ibid.*
6. Henry Jacoby, *The Bureaucratization of the World*, Berkley, 1973, p. 1.
7. George Robb, *White-collar Crime in England*, Cambridge, 1992, pp. 1-2.
8. Quoted in S. Avineri, *The Social and Political Thought of Karl Marx*, Cambridge, 1968, pp. 23-24. Also see, Karl Marx and Frederick Engels, *Collected Works*, vol. 3, Moscow, 1975, pp. 47-48.
9. Dennis Warwick, Bureaucracy, London, 1974, p. 31.
10. Karl Marx and Frederick Engels, *op. cit.*, p. 50.
11. *Ibid.*, pp. 46-47.
12. Shigeto Tsuru, *op.cit.*, p. 90.
13. Andre Maurois, *Prometheus: The Life of Balzac*, New York, 1965, p. 340.
14. Charles Dickens, *op. cit.*, p. 104.
15. *Ibid.*, pp. 104-106.
16. Valery Tarsis, *The Blue Bottle*, New York, 1963, p. 119.
17. Henry Jacoby, *op. cit.*, p. 163.
18. Edward C. Page, *Political Authority and Bureaucratic Power, A Comparative Analysis*, Brighton, Sussex, 1985, p. 1.
19. Arnold Brecht's paper "Bureaucratic Sabotage" in *The Annals of the American Academy of Political and Social Science*, January 1937, p. 53.
20. Henry Jacoby, *op. cit.*, p. 149.

9

Corruption in Political Sphere

In the last chapter we talked of the growing dependence of politicians and political parties on black economy and its operators and also referred to their relationship by invoking a simile used by Balzac, according to which the former were buckets while the latter were wells. In the pre-and post-Independent period (or Nehru era), election campaign and day-to-day running of political parties did not require much money as compared to the present scale of expenditures. Most of the political parties, barring the Bharatiya Jana Sangh were part of the national liberation struggle against the British imperialism. They had their own mass base and they had moved and worked among the people propagating their viewpoints, ideology and politics. They were known to the electorate and they seldom needed jeeps and cars to move among the people. They had grass-root workers and organisational structures. Moreover, they depended on their voters and supporters for regular subscriptions and donations to finance their activities. Since most of the candidates, barring the Rajas and Maharajas, zamindars, jagirdars, talukedars, etc. who contested mostly on the Hindu Mahasabha and the Bharatiya Jana Sangh tickets were, freedom fighters and were imbued with Gandhian or socialist or communist ideals. They lived a very simple and austere life and did not indulge in any kind of vulgar display in their election campaign.

Honest-to-Goodness

Even during those days businessmen funded political parties, but, generally, the money went to the coffers of political parties rather than to individuals. One C.B. Gupta or S.K. Patil or Atulya Ghose could raise lakhs of rupees, but not a single paisa was used for personal purposes. Personal finances were kept strictly separate from organisational accounts. There were certain norms inherited from the days of freedom struggle, which were strictly adhered to. Old timers may still recall the finance manager of the undivided CPI, Mr. S.V. Ghate, walking on foot from the Asaf Ali Road where his party headquarters were located to the Windsor Place where the CPI had its parliamentary office to attend meetings or to have his meal. Mind you, the CPI was the second largest party in the Lok Sabha during the Nehru era. Then there was another thing that reduced election expenses. Both the Lok Sabha and the Vidhan Sabha elections were held simultaneously.

All these things changed with the end of the Nehru era. The tribe of freedom fighters fast dwindled. Most parties, including those on the Left became more and more bureaucratised with less and less regular grass-root contacts, their organisational elections became less and less regular and democratic and more and more stage-managed while some did not hold elections for years, nay, decades, a number of parties appeared on the eve of elections and then disappeared soon after or came to have new incarnations, most of whom lacked distinct ideologies, programmes and policies to attract young people. The growing struggle for mere survival also acted as a damper for those who dared entertain the idea of entering politics. The dependence of political parties on mass subscriptions and donations not only declined but completely disappeared as they found domestic business and industry and/or foreign source of funding easily available.

Winning elections came to depend, to a significant

extent on mercenaries, caste, communal and regional factors, besides certain attractive slogans. To combine all these factors in such a way that the people were induced to vote required huge financial resources. With the delinking of the Vidhan Sabha and the Lok Sabha elections on the plea of separating local and provincial issues from national and international ones so that the electorate could apply its mind properly and make rational decisions. Besides, with changing class correlation of forces as a result of socio-economic development during the Nehru era, there was a change in the voting behaviour and pattern. The emergence of the neo-rich among the OBCs brought a new element of instability in State politics as evident from 1967 onwards. Frequent Vidhan Sabha elections became a normal thing.

A number of non-Congress parties and splinter groups came to share powers at the State level and India's business and industry quickly recognised their potential and usefulness in order to farther their own interests and opened their coffers to them. Foreign agencies also did not lag behind to have a leverage to realise their own ends. In most political parties, certain individuals and groups emerged, who specialised in fund-raising. The old distinction between party and personal finances disappeared. For a long time to come, there was neither proper accounting nor auditing of the funds received and spent. Generally, a distinction was made between members and workers loyal only to the party and those loyal to the party and certain individual leaders. The former received less money for electioneering than the latter. Both at the Centre and the State levels, there emerged in every party certain leaders with their own separate funds to take care of the personal and political monetary needs of workers and members who pledged their loyalty to their factions. On the basis of our personal knowledge, we can say this about K.B. Sahay of Bihar, C.B. Gupta of U.P., S.K. Patil of Mumbai and several others. We know for certain that a general secretary of a leading Left party arranging for "rest and recreation" of members belonging either to his faction or willing to cross over to it!

Influence of the Big Business Houses

Business houses and industries came forward to help the parties financially, in order to have a say in or have influence over decision-making process and corner licences, permits and government facilities at concessional rates if they were in power or whenever they came to attain it. They helped the Opposition parties even if they had no prospect of attaining power to keep them in good humour so that they did not attack them inside or outside the legislature and did not give a call for a strike by their trade union wings. They assisted certain political parties and organisations which had links with foreign countries and outfits who were profitable business partners. Certain businessmen and industrialists came to have their trusted men inside important political parties who kept them posted with various trends and development in those parties besides lobbying for them. Thus, there developed a close nexus betwen the moneybags and parties and people in power or those wanting to grab power. Both needed each other. The latter needed funds to hire workers, maintain offices, carry day to day activities and lubricate and run the election machinery. The days of austere and simple leaders of national movement were over, the safari suit clad new breed of leaders hated travelling by the lowest class of trains or on cycles or carts. Instead, they preferred airconditioned coaches or airplanes. They needed cars and jeeps where roads were not so good. Election compaigns became costlier and costlier till the former Chief Election Commissioner T.N. Seshan took steps to curb expenses.

Electoral lies and electoral bribes came to be used on larger and larger scale by political parties without any regard for their impact on national interests. One may recall how H.D. Deve Gowda during his Prime Ministership promised to reopen the fertiliser factory of Gorakhpur and create a separate hill State in the U.P. within months of Vidhan Sabha election, but conveniently forgot these promises after. There was a Common Minimum Programme to be implemented when the United Front Government came to power at the Centre. One of the important items was rebuilding the destroyed disputed mosque in Ayodhya. Neither this nor other items of Common Minimum Programme were implemented by the previous government. Obviously, these are exercises in duping the people. In this regard, political parties are no better than other frauds who lure people by making false promises of attractive returns on money invested by them in their schemes and then decamp. The *modus-operandi* is the same.

Years ago, rural loans up to Rs. 10,000 were remitted by the V.P. Singh government. Earlier governments organised loan *melas* in order to gift away the resources of nationalised banks to all and sundry, without caring to look into their end use and recoverability. Subsidies were multiplied to win over voters without caring to work out implications for the national exchequer. Free passes on roadways and railways were distributed and are still being distributed on one pretext or the other to lure voters or propitiate vote-bank managers. Lastly, free electricity has been promised by the Akali Dal-BJP government in Punjab while Laloo Yadav, soon after becoming the Chief Minister of Bihar in 1990-91, announced scrapping of the excise on toddy and the tax on fishery on the plea of helping the downtrodden sections of the society. In fact, in all these cases, the intention has been to create vote banks without paying any heed to the likely burden on the exchequer and implications on the economic growth.

In Delhi and other cities and towns, politicians have been trying to encourage new immigrants from rural areas to encroach upon the public land to construct their huts. They have secured for them electricity and water connections either legally or illegally. When the authorities wake up and try to clear these encroachments, these very politicians lead resistance movements against them in the name of getting them "justice" and protecting the poor. In this process, they create vote banks for them and ultimately, these unauthorised colonies became authorised, enhancing the prestige and popularity of the leaders concerned.

Elections and Anti-social Elements

Over the years, politicians and political parties with no record of public service or participation in freedom struggle have recognised the great potential in helping them to win elections by capturing booths, stamping the ballot papers and terrorising recalcitrant voters. These anti-social elements have to be looked after and provided with sources of income, which may not always be legal. These guys are helped in their activities ranging from smuggling and kidnapping to distillation and vending of illicit liquor, forcibly taking possession of land and house properties of others and getting permits for bus and truck operation and dealerships of cement, iron and steel, fair price shops and so on. A nexus has, thus, developed between politicians and criminals and in this matter the bureaucracy and police acquiesce.

In many parts of the country criminals specialising in encroachment upon public land, forest resources and mineral wealth have emerged. They have been operating fearlessly because they have secured the protective umbrella provided by politicians. A study of the Dhanbad mafia testifies to it. It has, over the years, specialised in illegal mining and pilferage of minerals, yet there has been no decisive action against it solely because of its political connections.

Relationship between Leaders and Businessmen

In recent times, there has been a lot of heat generated by the Jain-Hawala case. Whatever may be the legal position, the facts which have emerged from it are nothing but startling. its ramifications have within their fold diverse elements, ranging from businessmen, bureaucrats, currency racketeers, smugglers and plain and simple criminals to politicians of various hues (from the votaries of Hindutva to democratic socialists, centrists thrown in between) and a number of countries around the globe. This and other cases, including Jharkhand Mukti Morcha (JMM) MPs bribery case, Lakhubhai Pathak cheating case, St. Kitts forgery case, fodder scam, Ayurvedic medicine scam, Bitumen scam, scandalous way of allotting government accommodations and dealerships of petroleum products, urea scam and so on amply illustrate the rot that has been eaten into the vitals of the Indian polity. Politics seems to have been vastly criminalised. It is not without reason that nobody now remembers Nabakrishna Chaudhury while everybody sings hymns in the praise of Biju Patnaik, the so-called builder of Orissa.[1] Similarly nobody remembers Jaglal Chaudhury and Karpoori Thakur while floral offerings are made on the birth and death anniversaries of Jagjivan Ram and large crowds are mobilised to greet Laloo Yadav?

We have talked of the relationship between leaders whether political, spiritual or social and businessmen. This relationship has been as old as Indian history. We find them helping each other. For example, it was the men and materials of the only son of the *shreshthi* of Kashi, estranged from his father that helped Lord Buddha to put across his message far and wide. While the youngman got in return was mental peace and spiritual satisfaction and the feeling that his resources were being used for the enlightenment and welfare of humanity at large.

We also find in the Buddhist literature a story about Lord Buddha being convinced and persuaded by Vishakha, the wealthiest businesswoman of Shravasti to put in a word to King Prasenjit of Kosala to waive the duty on the merchandise imported by her from neighbouring kingdoms. It must be underlined here that the Lord did not expect nor did he get anything tangible in return from Vishakha. It was the genuineness of the case that mattered. Similarly, Mahatma Gandhi too the help of businessmen rangings from Jamnalal Bajaj and Shiva Prasad Gupta to G.D. Birla and Ambalal Sarabhai in the fight for freedom but he never allowed them to influence his thinking and decisions. Pandit Madan Mohan Malviya took the help of businessmen, native princes and the landed aristocracy to build the Banaras Hindu University, but these elements had no say in the running of the university. In both these instances there was no *quid pro quo*.

Nothing could tempt away a Buddha or a Gandhi

from his mission. Wealth and wordly comforts had no attraction. For example, when King Bimbisara of Magadh saw Lord Buddha, he told him: "Thou art both young and delicate, a lad in his first youth possessed of a fine complexion... I will ornaments the army-house and at the head of the assembly of chiefs give (thee) wealth; enjoy it.' But Buddha declined the offer and told the king that he did not have any dearth of wealth as he was the crown prince of the Sakyas 'from that family I have wandered out, not longing for sensual pleasures.' And 'seeing misery in sensual pleasures and considering the forsaking of the world as happiness, I will go and exert myself, in this my mind delights'.[2]

As against a Buddha or a Gandhi, a number of top politicians of the country have remained dependent on businessmen and industrialists for support not only in political but private life too and this link has influenced their outlook and attitude. To illustrate this, let us take the case of Jaya Prakash Narayan (JP), a founder of the socialist movement in the country, who played a very important role in breaching the uninterrupted rule by the Congress since Independence.

Unlike a Buddha or a Gandhi, he lived a life of luxury, he wore *khadi* clothes but of very expensive variety, very costly shoes and ate a very rich diet and seldom travelled on foot or in the lowest class of trains and maintained an elaborate secretariat. Who paid for all his expenses? Of course, not the poor and the middle class people of India. Nor did he have a steady flow of regular income from his books and articles as in the case of Jawaharlal Nehru then and Madhu Limaye later.

One source of regular income was the House of Birlas, where he had served as private secretary for a year or two to G.D. Birla on his return from the USA after completing his studies in the early 1930s. The Birlas were, it seems, so impressed by his work that they decided to pay him all his life salary and allowances with proper indexation for the fall in the real worth of the rupee. This he himself admitted in a signed statement in one of the issues of

Everyman's Weekly in the mid-1970s. It appears intriguing to us what had really motivated the Birlas to be so large-hearted to him, especially in view of their treatment to the employees who work in their companies and the contributors to their journals and the peasants who supply sugarcane to their mills. Throughout his political career, we have not found him uttering a single word against the Birlas even if the occasion warranted.

He had close connections not only with the Birlas but with the House of the Dalmia-Jain too. Justice Vivian Bose who was asked by the Government of India to look into the murky goings-on in the House of the Dalmia-Jain wrote a report running into more than 800 pages, bringing to light the swindling of public money, the breach of public trust and other criminal acts. Ultimately, the head of the House, Rama Krishna Dalmia, was convicted and served a term in prison. His son-in-law Sahu Shanti Prasad Jain was deprived of the control of his newspaper empire for a number of years. What is most interesting about the report is Chapter XI, entitled 'Oral Evidence: "Outside" Witnesses'. One of these was JP who told the Commission, headed by Justice Vivian Bose that he had personal knowledge that both the father-in-law and the son-in-law had parted company with each other, their business dealing were no longer joint and Dalmia had withdrawn from the management of the Rohtas Industries.

The Commission analysed the evidence and found it trustworthy and wrote: "we attach no importance to the evidence" tendered by witness no. 46 (J.P. Narayan).[3] It is not without reason that the journals, controlled by Sahu Shanti Prasad Jain were always supportive of him and his movements. Hindi journals *Dinman* and *Dharmayug* of the group appeared to be his mouthpieces. JP on his part never uttered a single word against Sahu Jain even if the journalists were victimised by him.

To continue our story, JP's financial sources and status had always been dubious. During the Total Revolution phase, it was Ram Nath Goenka who launched *Everyman's Weekly,* edited by S.H. Vatsyan to provide him with an exclusive mouthpiece. Goenka too had an axe to grind. Indira Gandhi had refused to bend before him and all his machinations through Bhartiya Jana Sangh had failed to bring her to him with folded hands. He had helped the Sangha Parivar found its daily *The Mother Land* to emit poison against her. He had himself entered the Lok Sabha on the Bharatiya Jana Sangh ticket. Yet Indira Gandhi could not be cowed-down. Thus, JP appeared to him as his last bait and Total Revolution as the last stick to beat her.

JP was very comfortable in the outfits, funded by the CIA. He helped it in its endeavour to propagate the message of anti-Communist "cultural freedom". He did not think of quitting the Congress for cultural freedom, even after its CIA-connections came to light. He founded an institute in Varanasi in the name of Gandhi, though one of its activities was training of American Peace Corps volunteers. We do not know how much money was received on this account.

About his personal honesty and integrity, let us produce some hard facts, supported by documentary evidence. The people of India are familiar with the name of Champaran, the district where Mahatma Gandhi launched his first *satyagrah* in 1917. This district is now divided into East and West Champaran. The latter has a place called Sathi.

Soon after the Congress Government was installed in Bihar, there came to light a number of scams. Among them were molasses and Sathi land scam which were interconnected and the kingpins were Rai Bahadur Ram Prasad Narayan Sahi, the Excise Commissioner (the father-in-law of Krishna Sahi, a Minister in the Narasimha Rao government) and his brother Ram Rekha Prasad Sahi. They not only belonged to the same caste of the then Chief Minister, Mr. S.K. Sinha, but were also closely related to him. Injustice was done to local peasants whose claims were ignored when lush green land amounting to more than 250 acres was settled with the Sahis who were neither cultivators nor local residents. There began a peasant agitation to get the settlement annulled. The Socialist Party (which till March 1948 functioned as Congress Socialist Party and was a part of the Congress) appointed a committee under Dr. Rammanohar Lohia to look into the matter and write a report JP regarded it as a very convenient instrument to pull down the Bihar Government and capture power in the ensuing election. On 22 May, 1950, he demanded the resignation of the government and in the Press conference, concentrated his ire on S.K. Sinha and his right hand man K.B. Sahay.

What followed is really an eye opener. It exposes the hypocrisy of a leader who has always been moralising and pontificating on a thousand-and-one matters to the outside world and has been hailed by the gullible mediamen here and abroad as an embodiment of ethics and morality. To continue our story, on 26 May, 1950 while replying to a member in the Bihar Assembly, Sahay disclosed that JP was himself not above board and his honesty and integrity were doubtful.

He stated that as much as 459 bighas of land was settled with two prominent leaders of the Socialist Party and JP was one of them. The settlement was secured by them by fraudulent means. The lands under Pratapganj Police Station of the Saharsa district of Bihar belonged to the grandsons of the late Shiva Prasad Gupta of Banaras, who was for a very long time, treasurer of the All India Congress Committee. Only after his demise, Seth Jamnalal Bajaj became the treasurer. He was a great philanthropist who had founded the Kashi Vidyapith and the daily *Aaj* and built the Bharat Mata Mandir, a temple of great secular and nationalist importance.

JP: A Controversial Politician

According to K.B. Sahay, the settlements were made with JP and his friends after 'ignoring the claims of local tenants.' No *salami* was paid and the annual rent was nominal. The net annual income amounted to Rs. 17,000. Sahay named the local peasants whose claims were ignored. Though he refrained from naming JP, nobody was left in doubt as to the identity of the lessees. K.B. Sahay couched his reply with the following words: "Let the Lohia Commission first examine these settlements and decide whether these leaders should have more than 25 bighas each and then come to Champaran. Mr. Jayaprakash Narain has issued a statement on the Sathi Lands (Restoration) Bill, in which he has stated that the notorious ministers must be turned out. He has not named the notorious ministers. I would warn him not to name them. But if he names them, I will also name the two leaders of the Socialist Party, who have taken settlement'.[5]

Three days later, JP came out with a long statement in which he lamented the ungratefulness of Mr. Sahay and reminded him how he had helped him save his ministerial berth when he was on the verge of being thrown out.

He, however, admitted that he was one of the two leaders of the Socialist Party, who had received the land settlement. In order 'to dispel the wrong impression in the public mind', he stated: "It was many years ago that, in the course of a talk with the late Babu Shiva Prasad Gupta of Banaras about the economic difficulties of wholetime workers, Shiva Prasadji, generous as he was, offered me some virgin land for cultivation in the Bhagalpur district (Saharsa was then a part of Bhagalpur)".

"It was arranged that three others would join me in taking settlement of these lands. These three friends were second cousin of mine Panna Babu and Babu Deokinandan Singh and Babu Kamala Prasad Singh of the village of Khaspur in the district of Patna".

"In due course about 250 bighas were taken and these friends started reclaiming and cultivating parts of the land. Most of the time, those being the war years, I was in prison. When I came out of prison, it did not seem right, on reconsidering the matter, that I should take any share of these lands. So I wrote to Babu Satyendra Prasad Gupta, Shiva Prasadji's grandson, who with his brother had become the proprietor of the estate after Shiva Prasadji's death, that I was no longer interested in the land. Later on, the land was settled with the gentlemen who were to be my partners".

"...Originally, the intention was that I should take a share of those lands, but as it turned, the partnership never became effective and at no stage did I have anything to do with it. I never invested a pie in it nor received a pie in return, nor a grain of corn".[6]

On 3 June, 1950 Sahay came out with a press statement that JP was lying, he never divested himself of Saharsa lands. In fact, he was in possession of 200 bighas of land. K.B. Sahay's statement was quite revealing.

"The questions that I would like to put are as follows: Did Shri J.P. Narain discuss his own case with Shri Shiva Prasad Gupta or did he discuss the case of Congressmen in general? If he discussed his own case, will he tell me, if it was in keeping with high principles of public life for a political worker of his eminence to have tried to feather his own nest in the name of the sacrifice that he had made? If he discussed the case of Congressmen in general, why did he not place the gift, the settlement at the disposal of the Congressmen or even of the Socialist Party which has in its fold many starving workers"?

"It seems that after he got the settlement, Shri J.P. Narain realized his mistake, but instead of retracing his steps he, finding the pleasures of possession irresistible, placed a cloak over the transaction. He induced his own men, namely his cousin Shri Panna Babu, Shri Deokinandan Singh and Shri Kamala Prasad Singh, who have no political status and had no claim on the lands, into the cultivation which went on flourishing for several years from 1939 to 1945, when, coming out of jail his conscience having been awakened, he wrote to Shri Satyendra Prasad Gupta... that he did not want to take any more interest in the land. But did this amount to surrender of the land in the sense in which the word has been used in the Bihar Tenancy Act"?

"Did Shri J.P. Narain return the land free from the encumbrances of Shri Panna, Shri Deokinandan Singh and Shri Kamala Prasad Singh? Did Shri J.P. Narain tell Shri Satyendra Prasad Gupta that he (Shri Satyendra Prasad Gupta) should now settle the lands with local tenants who had so long been deprived of their natural rights? Obviously, the answer to all these questions is negative".

"If Shri Satyendra Prasad Gupta had been left absolutely free to dispose of the land as he liked, he would never have settled the land with Shri Panna and Shri Deokinandan Prasad Singh and Shri Kamala Prasad Singh, who had never any *locus standi* and nor even a shadow of claim. Deny it as he will, it is clear from his own statement that Shri J.P. Narain never divested himself of these valuable lands. If in the circumstances, I had the cheek to say that Lohia Commission should examine this case also, did I commit so heinous a crime as to deserve being exorcised from public life book, bell and candle?"[7]

This statement silenced JP so much that there was no further protest from his side. It needs to be noted here that the Saharsa land episode is not alone, there were others too, including the Kudamkuan property belonging formally to the Mahila Charkha Samiti, a public trust with specified aims and objects, but used by the Loknayak for his purely personal purposes.

From the above, it appears that JP had resorted to lies and deceit to take the land settlement from a zamindar who trusted him and his words. Secondly, he deprived the local peasants who had more genuine and stronger claims to the land. Lastly, he and his friends used the land and appropriated its produce for personal benefit rather than for the welfare of needy freedom fighters. Broadly speaking, it was a multiple crime which he committed.

In this country, if encouraging the forces of disunity and disintegration is a crime, then JP was certainly guilty of it. This statement may appear very blunt and may shock some intellectuals but it is based on facts. His role in Bihar's casteist politics has been dealt at length by us elsewhere[8] and it need not be repeated here.

One may recall that it was JP who had blamed Sardar Patel for not taking stern action against the RSS (Rashtriya Swayamsevak Sangh) in order to save the life of Mahatma Gandhi. He, in a signed statement, had condemned the

RSS and other Hindu communal elements for spreading hatred and creating the situation leading to the assassination of Gandhiji. The same JP became an admirer of the RSS and its parliamentary wing, Bharatiya Jana Sangh, without any kind of change in the character and ideology of the Sangh Parivar. From 1967 onwards, when the Bharatiya Jana Sangh joined the SVD government in Bihar, he established close connections with it, involved the Sangh Parivar in the famine relief work and gave it respectability. Thus, he attacked one of the basic principles of Gandhiji that the purity of means mattered no less than the purity of ends. Thus, a self-proclaimed votary of national unity and communal harmony began patronising the forces of disunity and communal hatred.

Profiting by the discontent and difficulties of people, in the wake of strains on the Indian economy as a result of Bangladesh liberation, JP launched his Total Revolution with the help of disperate elements around him. Quite a substantial number of them had criminal tendencies, manifested in looting shops and government property and extorting money from traders, shopkeepers and assaulting ruling party leaders and legislators. The RSS technique was clearly visible when hundreds of postcards written by a handful of people addressed to sitting Congress legislators and MPs telling them to resign, were mailed from selected post offices.[9]

While JP was obsessed with his one point programme of removing Indira Gandhi-led Congress from power by hook or by crook, he had to depend on the Sangh Parivar because it was the only well-organised force among the supporters of Total Revolution. It needs to be noted that none of the present day warriors against communalism from Laloo Yadav to CPI(M) in Bihar had any hesitation in joining hands with the Sangh Parivar for striving to realise the goal of Total Revolution. Thus, retrospectively, it was JP and his Total Revolution that resurrected the forces of Hindu communalism and put them in the forefront. The representatives of these forces were given prominent position in the first non-Congress Government at the Centre, led by Morarji Desai.

Former Andhra Pradesh Chief Minister, Mr. J. Vengal Rao, is reported to have come out with the allegation in his autobiography that the Allahabad High Court judgment, unseating Indira Gandhi, was part of a grand conspiracy. This judgment gave a fresh lease of life to Total Revolution which had started petering out. Till now, this allegation has not been challenged in any court of law.

Politics of Corruption: India and Abroad

Political corruption does not exist only in India but in almost all countries of the world irrespective of the form of the government, level of education and the socio-economic system. It existed in France when Socialists were ruling, in the former Soviet Union and in China and Vietnam where the leaders who had accomplished revolution were in command. To illustrate, let us begin with France. In May 1992, Bernard Tapie was forced to resign his job as Minister of Urban Affairs as he was charged with fraud and forgery. Two months later, Henri Emmanuelli, President of the National Assembly was accused of committing financial irregularities when he was the treasurer of the Socialist Party. Besides, Laurent Fabius, a former Prime Minister and afterwards the First Secretary of the Socialist Party and two other former Socialist ministers were accused of their hand in the medical scandal. It was said that they along with four senior public health officials had allowed the transfusion of blood contaminated with the virus that causes AIDS for pecuniary considerations. As a result, more than 250 haemophiliacs died and 1200 fell sick during 1980-85. The officials admitted their guilt.

Two years earlier, another scandal came to light whose trail reached those who had been in-charge of Francois Mitterand's Presidential election campaign funds. This was connected with *fausses factures* (phoney invoices). It involved sending bills for non-existent services or inflating the cost of real ones. It was alleged that this was, in fact, the device adopted to realise the kickbacks and present them as legal. This device was resorted to by various kinds of people ranging from football club managers and real estate developers. to political parties. While a number of non-political beneficiaries were arrested, politicians seldom came into the police net. For example, Michel Mauer, a big real estate developer and Rolland Courbis, the general manager of the Toulon football club were arrested, no big political leader met this fate. To keep the politicians out, an amnesty scheme was introduced in January 1990. Since this scheme did not cover members of the National Assembly, almost all political parties made others in their set-up as fund collectors. "Until public financing of parties began in 1988, the official sources of party income in France were membership dues, levies on the party's members of Parliament and donations from individuals (but not companies). Parties found these inadequate and sought less official ways of raising money".

"One of the most popular was to set up "consultancy" services to help clients get big public contracts, normally backed up by *fausses factures*. Right and Left were equally guilty, but the Socialists seem to have developed a particularly slick system. So claims Mr. Antoine Gaudino, a police inspector, whose book, "Enquête Impossible" (Impossible Inquiry), is a best-seller in France".

"While on a big corruption case in south-east France, Mr. Gaudino claims to have found evidence that some Ffr 25m ($5m) of "dirty money, raised by corrupt practices" helped finance President Mitterand's 1988 campaign. The money was reportedly channelled through a "consultancy" company, Urba-Gracco, set up soon after Mr. Mitterand took over as leader of the newly unified Socialist party in 1971".[10]

While the managing-director and two senior officers of his consultancy company were arrested by the police, it could not lay its hands on politicians, connected with the company. The investigator was suspended from the job for trying to unearth the political connections. The Opposition leaders too were indifferent because they were fearful of skeletons coming out of their own cup-boards. Later, a new law on party financing allowed company donations to election campaigns.

By the end of October 1994, one ex-minister of France was already in jail while another serving minister was forced to quit and five more were being investigated. As many as 29 existing or former members of Parliament were already charged or convicted. Dozens of prominent businessmen faced prosecution and hundreds of lesser-known politicians, businessmen and functionaries were being investigated. *The Economist* (October 29, 1994) reported that 58 per cent of the Frenchmen believed that their politicians were corrupt. It added: "Petty graft and corruption have always been part of French public life. But the problem has grown enormous over the past decade. Decentralisation of power, a policy begun by the Socialists in 1982, has increased both the number of decision-makers and the money available to local authorities. Hence, opportunities for graft have grown".

"At the same time, the escalating costs of election campaigns have encouraged politicians to take them." As we have already mentioned, earlier membership dues, donation from individuals and levies on members of Parliament along with phoney consultancy work to help firms win public contracts in return for hefty "commissions" and advertisements in party papers at inflated rates were the main sources of revenue. All political parties irrespective of ideological orientation indulged in them.

When the new policy was introduced in 1982, it "began to exploited by individuals to line their own pockets. Payments came in various forms: cash; cut-rate home improvements; free flats; foreign trips; swimming pools and works of art.

"As a result, two laws on political-party financing were passed in 1988 and 1990. They provided for some public funding of parties, allowed business contributions up to Ffr 500,000 ($98,000) per party per year".

These measures, however, failed to stop the abuse of the policy and Antoine Gaudino, a former police inspector, whose book we have already referred to, stressed that the rot had gone very deep and "corruption has infiltrated everywhere, not just among politicians, but also in the civil service—at all levels. Corruption's main ally is that it has become commonplace. What was still unacceptable three years ago is today accepted". People feared that corruption in France might reach Italian levels.

If France was trying to catch up with Italy in political corruption, how could Britain be left behind? In October 1994, the then Prime Minister, Mr. John Major, was forced to appoint a commission, headed by Lord Justice Nolan to look into the problem and suggest ways and means. At that time, public confidence in the probity of British parliamentary politics had sunk to a very low level. Tim Smith, a junior minister for Northern Ireland and Neil Hamilton, a junior minister for trade were alleged to be involved in acts of corruption. Hamilton had spent a week at the Ritz Hotel in Paris in 1987 with his wife as the guests of Al Fayed who owns the Harrod chain of shops. The total hotel bill amounted to $6,500. The most intriguing thing was that Hamilton had not signed the hotel register. After availing himself of the hospitality of Fayed, he tabled five parliamentary questions to further the interests of his host. In addition, Fayed contributed £250,000 to the Conservative Party coffers in 1980s. As has been reported, the Nolan Commission has recommended that public servants from ministers to those holding secondary positions should be jailed, fined or disqualified for misusing their office. It has proposed 'a new criminal offence to cover abuses such as willful misconduct or unlawful spending by officials and elected members in Central and local government, the police, magistrates and judiciary and other public bodies'.[11]

In Indonesia, there is Bob Hasan who not only arbiters in the family business affairs of President Suharto after his wife, Siti Hartinah's death but keeps Suharto's sons and daughters disciplined so that they do not fight among themselves over their business and other interests. He has been called "the fix-it man". He is supposed to know Suharto's mind and conveys his wishes to the people who are eager to know. He has an access to funds from Suharto's foundations and invests them according to his judgement. In other words, he is a power-broker and frontsman for Suharto..

In Nigeria where political corruption has been rampant, a 30 per cent kickback is regarded a quite normal thing while in Pakistan Asif Ali Zardari, the husband of the former Prime Minister, Mrs. Benazir Bhutto, is nicknamed "Mr. 30 per cent". On April 24, 1997, the navy Chief Admiral Mansur-ul Haq, was dismissed on charges of corruption and misappropriation of public funds. It was alleged that he along with Asif Ali Zardari had received kickbacks from the purchase of three French-made Agosta 90-B class submarines. In January, 1997, the second in command Air Marshal Arshad Chaudhry quit in protest against the purchase of 40 second-hand Mirage-5 fighters in which huge kickbacks were supposed to have been received by politicians and military top brass. Three months later, squadron leader Farooq Ahmed was arrested in New York for trying to dispose of 2 kg. of heroin worth $160,000. He had flown it in an airforce transport plane that was supposed to pick up spare parts for F-16 fighters. On interrogation, it turned out that he belonged to a ring of drug, computer spare parts and electronic goods smugglers, having the blessings and protection of politicians in power, who received substantial protection money. Another person of this ring Major Munwar Shah who had retired from the ISI was arrested near Peshawar while trying to smuggle heroin worth $500,000 to London. Retired Vice-Admiral Akbar Khan, ex-chairman of the Karachi Port Trust was rounded up in connection with his alleged involvement in multi-million dollar land scam. A number of politicians too were an active party to these acts of corruption. Corruption in the armed forces became endemic under General Zia's dictatorial regime of 1977-88. Afghan war and massive inflow of weapons, other war materials and relief money provided the opportunity. Everybody from politicians and military people to bureaucrats seemed to be extremely happy. The unsettled conditions in Afghanistan gave a big boost to the smuggling of narcotics, the Americans looked the other way because of Cold War considerations and the BCCI helped launder the dirty money. According to a report in the *Far Eastern Economic Review* (May 15, 1997): "Pakistan is rated as the second most corrupt nation in the world behind Nigeria by Berlin-based anti-corruption Transparency International." The same journal, a year ago (June 27, 1996) had quoted the representative of an international lending agency in Islamabad as saying: "There is a gaping black hole in the economy into which money is just disappearing because of the massive leakages and widespread corruption." It went on to add: "There was the hope that the government could milk the cow of privatization of State-owned assets. But that stalled in April when the sale of 26 per cent of the country's second-largest bank, United Bank Ltd., to Basharhil, a Saudi group, exposed shady dealings within the institution. Ten bank officials were arrested following an embezzlement investigation. There were fears of a total collapse of the bank, which has some 24 billion rupees in bad debts. And there were some 3,000 ghost workers bilking the bank of pay cheques, as well."

Benazir: Power to Plunder

Though stories about corruption and extortions by the family of Benazir Bhutto had been circulating for years, till September 1997 there was no official investigation. This was for the simple reason that she headed the government. Only after her dismissal from prime ministership, leading to fresh polls resulting in her party's defeat that an official investigation could become possible. In the third week of September 1997, four Swiss bank accounts belonging to her and members of her family were frozen on the request of the Pakistan government. It was estimated that the total money deposited in these four accounts were somewhere between $50 m and $80 m and it was alleged that all this money was the result of corrupt dealing during her prime ministership. It was later alleged that the total amount stashed away in foreign accounts amounted to not less than $100 m besides movable and immovable property acquired by her and her family. It was stated by Pakistani official sources that her husband 'may have ripped the country to the tune of $1.5 billion' (*Indian*

Express, 11 January, 1998). Zardari is said to have seldom missed any opportunity of robbing the exchequer. 'Defence contracts, power plant projects, the privatisation of state-owned industries, the awarding of broadcast licenses, the granting of an export monopoly for the country's huge rice harvest, the purchase of planes for Pakistan International Airways, the assignment of textile export quotas, the granting of oil and gas permits, authorisations to build sugar mills and the sale of government lands were all game for his greed'.

It has not been an easy task for the Pakistan government to unearth foreign accounts of the Benazir Bhutto family and gather evidence to persuade the Swiss government to freeze them. It hired a private investigative agency—Jules Kroll Associates—of New York to do the job. The agency is said to have spent $1 m in cash to acquire the necessary documents from a mole. They included statements relating to accounts in Switzerland and Dubai and the details of payoffs in deals with companies registered in the Virgin Island. The largest single deal was with Abdul Razzak, a bullion trader from West Asia. It yielded not less than $10 m to Zardari. Razzak was granted the monopoly of gold import into the country to sustain its jewellery-making activity. The hush money was deposited in one of the Citibank accounts of Zardari.

According to an investigative report, 'The rip-off began in January, 1994, weeks after Bhutto began her second term, when her confidant Schlegelmilch (who developed his relationship with the Bhutto family through links between his Iranian-born wife and Bhutto's mother, who was also born in Iran) established a British Virgin Island company known as Capricorn Trading SA, with Zardari as its principal owner.

'Nine months later, on Oct. 5, 1994, an account was opened at the Dubai offices of Citibank in the name of Capricorn Trading. The same day, a Citibank deposit slip for the account shows a deposit of $5 million by Razzak's company, ARY Traders. Two weeks later, another Citibank deposit slip showed that ARY had paid a further $5million.' (*Ibid*)

A month later, Razzak was granted the monopoly over gold imports into Pakistan and he imported gold worth more than $500 m.

It is said that the most lucrative deal was with the French company Dassault Aviation for the purchase of 32 Mirage 2000-5 fighter planes worth $4 billion. Zardari and his Pakistani partner were to get $200 million by way of commission which was routed through an offshore company, controlled by Zardari. In addition to Dassault Aviation, two other French companies, namely, Snecma which manufactures aircraft engines and Thomson-CSF which produces aviation electronics also paid handsome amounts to Zardari in return for getting government orders for their wares.

It was not only foreign deals but domestic deals too yielded huge amounts to Bhutto and her husband. To illustrate their clever way, when the IMF put pressure on Pakistan to reduce its budgetary deficit by plugging leakages and increasing revenue collections; the government gave the job of pre-shipment verification of all major imports to two Swiss firms on the understanding that they would pay 9 per cent of their incomes from the contract into the accounts of three offshore companies, controlled by Zardari and his mother-in-law. It has been found that these two firms paid $11.8 million to the Bhutto family.

Now, Benazir Bhutto has come out with details of corrupt deals by Prime Minister Nawaz Sharif. She has petitioned to Ghulam Mujadid Mirza, a retired judge, who has been appointed chief accountability commissioner. She is supposed to have listed details of dubious deals from wheat contracts to bank loans which are supposed to have yielded huge pay offs to Sharif. Till now, the contents of her complaint have not been published. It is for Mirza to look into it, but as the news goes, he has refused to entertain it and sent it to Prime Minister's accountability cell for investigation.

From what has been said above, it appears that the Transparency International's listing of Pakistan among the most corrupt nations of the world is not wrong.

In Brazil, Antonio Magri, the Labour Minister, was dismissed in January 1992 for accepting $30,000 in bribe. Two of the president's assistants were linked to irregularities in business transactions. Fernando Collor de Mello, the head of the government too was indirectly implicated. In 1994, a report said. "Close to 5,000 businessmen and politicians have been arrested on corruption charges over the past two years. One-third of parliament's outgoing members face corruption or related charges.[12] Joao Alves, a senior Congressman who, for five years, headed the budget committee was found to be in possession of assets worth more than $5 m. Likewise Ibsen Pinheiro, another leader whose annual salary was less than $80,000 was found to be having a bank deposit of $1 m at the end of five years. In October, 1993, the Brazilian federal police recovered from Jose Carlos dos Santos, an economist who had recently retired from the congressional budget committee more than $1m stuffed in his mattress. On interrogation, he admitted that he had manipulated the congressional records and decisions. He made certain startling revelations about politicians connected with the budgetary committee. In the course of a congressional hearing, he alleged that politicians on the committee had pocketed millions of dollars in illegal commissions for sanctioning public works contracts, welfare assistance, and so on. In all 23 congressmen, two ministers, four former ministers, a number of Governors and mayors came under cloud.

It was the year 1988 that the scope for this kind of plunder opened. Before this year when the military Generals ran the affairs of the country, the Congress and politicians did not have much of a say. In 1988, constitutional reforms restored to the Congress its control over financial matters. As a result, all money had to pass through the budgetary committee consisting of 91 legislators from all political parties. Because of the intricacies involved in budgetary matters, it was not easy to discover manipulations and bribe-taking. A clique of seven politicians came to control the affairs of the budgetary committee. They were derisively termed as "seven dwarfs". Nobody, for certain, knows till now, how much money was stolen by committee members. Santos admitted to having taken $3.7 m himself and, mind you, he was just chief accountant of the committee. Suitcases stuffed with money were regularly delivered to committee people. Joao Alves, the chairman of the committee or "the chief dwarf' had a salary of only $7000 per month but came to possess mansions, an aircraft and business worth more than $5m in 15 years. He claimed that it was all due to his luck at lottery. He was so fortunate that he got lucky numbers 56 times in one year! But people at large believed that the lottery was the means to launder his ill-gotten money. Thus, the budget mafia plundered the State exchequer in connivance with businessmen. When raids were conducted on the offices of Odebrecht, one of the biggest construction firms of Brazil, 18 boxes of documents were seized and they revealed a list of legislators, each of whose name had a percentage figure written against his name.

In China, notwithstanding harsh and quick punishments and a great deal of vigilance, corruption has been on the increase and several political leaders have been found to be involved directly or indirectly. The incidence of corruption has increased with the process of liberalisation. While the wages and salaries have remained fixed or sluggish, the attraction of new goods and the impact of consumerism have compelled many a person to go in for "extra earnings". A policeman was reported saying: "There is a price for everything. A price for getting a thief out of prison, a price for getting out a rapist. Even a price for getting out a murderer."

At the end of 1992, a novel scheme was evolved, whereby bureaucrats who were invariably members of the Chinese Communist Party were permitted to set up businesses enterprises without giving up their government jobs. Ostensibly, the decision was aimed at both bringing down the expenses on bureaucracy and boosting up private enterprise. This was thought to be a good device of bringing down the incidence of corruption among party officials and, at the same time, having a control over a significant part of private sector through party officials-turned-businessmen. These people were supposed to give up their official pay and benefits and live on the profits of their newly set up business. This reminded one of the arrangements which existed during the feudal dispensation.

But few such officials severed their links with their parent departments. In fact, they made use of them to enrich themselves. As soon as a bureaucrat-cum-party official secured a business licence, he sent out invitations to the managers of state enterprises to celebrate the start of the new venture. According to an investigation conducted by a government-run magazine, *Fortnightly Chat*, many of these invitations had a bank account printed in the corner. Those coming to the celebration were told that they were not to bring gifts, but were expected to bring cheques. Failure to abide by this instruction meant offending the new entrepreneur's government department. It was also found that these bureaucrats-cum-party officials-turned businessmen generally dumped their shoddy products on companies terrorised by them. A tax department official-turned businessman threatened the companies refusing to buy his products with investigations.[13]

In 1996, Jiang Zemin admitted that graft was posing a major threat to the prestige and rule of the Communist Party in China. A special campaign was launched in 1995 and Wei Jianxing, the chief of the discipline committee of the Party claimed that more than 20,000 officials were disciplined during a period of 11 months. In spite of this, the battle to restore the prestige of the Party seemed to be an uphill task. Even in the countryside, the traditional stronghold of the Communists, the faith in it was declining. The following report in *The Economist* (February 3, 1996) is quite revealing: "In one typical village in Gansu province in north-west China (to identify it would be to invite reprisals), crime and corruption have become major grievances.

"The village is still reeling from its biggest crime since the Communists took power in 1949, the theft of Wang Yifei's new tractor. It cost him 8,000 yuan ($1,000), two years' income and was intended to make his labour on the land a little easier. Only two weeks after the purchase, it disappeared in the night. Thieves killed the family's guard dog with poisoned meat and broke open the shed where the tractor was stored. The dog's head was found in a ditch a few days later.

"The mood in the village is one of profound insecurity. A century ago the villagers built mud fortifications around their houses to keep out bandits, but these defences were allowed to crumble into dereliction in the peace and safety brought by the Communist victory in 1949. Now people talk darkly of replacing their wooden gateways with iron doors. One household already has an electrified wire around its courtyard walls".

"The feeling of unease is heightened by the suspicion that local officials responsible for enforcing the law are in collusion with the criminals...."[14]

The police did nothing because the thieves had bribed them. This could be possible because the party officials were corrupt and got a share in the booty. Had the local branch of the party taken a tough stand, the police could have apprehended the culprits. In fact, the theft itself had not taken place. The declining prestige of the party was due to increasing incidence of corruption, as one local leader had admitted. The corrupt party officials' comfortable houses and rising standard of living naturally raised questions about their sources of incomes.

Independent Commission Against Corruption (ICAC) was set up by Hong Kong in 1975. On its findings, *The Economist* (January 29, 1994) commented: "Corruption is more than a poison afflicting Chinese business life... The peculiar mixture of plan and market; the still pervasive bureaucracy; traditions of family, clan and locality; the huge profits to be made in an economy growing at 13 per cent a year—all contribute to a culture of gifts, kickbacks and *guanxi* (connections). An ICAC survey conducted last year of Hong Kong companies doing business in China found that an average of 5 per cent of their operating expenses there went on bribes—probably an understatement".

China has been found to be trying to influence the US presidential election in favour of Clinton by funding his campaign in 1996 and tilt the policies of the US administration towards it. In 1995, China realised that it lacked sufficient clout in the corridors of power in Washington, DC because, in spite of its opposition, the US administration granted visa to the Taiwanese President. This prompted the Chinese embassy to redouble its efforts at having better liaison with members of both Houses of the congress. It flooded cash both to Clinton's campaign funds and to selected members of the congress. On March 7, 1997, when *The Washington Post* came to know of this, one Senator immediately returned $12,000 of the contribution that might have come from the Chinese. The Democratic National Committee returned more than $3 m 'shady donations, many of which were raised with the help of Mr. Clinton or Mr. Gore. The shadiest cash came from a trio whose names feature prominently in the Senate's chart; John Huang, Charles Yah Lin Trie and Johnny Chung. Together, these men raised about $4.5 m for the DNC, half of which has had to be returned. Mr. Chuang presented one cheque for $50,000 to Hillary Clinton's chief of staff in the White House itself, defying the usual role of keeping such transactions off federal property.'[15] It needs to be remembered that Charles Yah Lin Trie had been a member of the panel that advised the President on his Asia policy. It is said that Trie, to be on the safe side, skipped most of the meetings of the panel.

Japan has been, for years, nay, decades, quite notorious for political corruption. There was time when a veteran leader and Prime Minister Tanaka was convicted in connection with the Lockheed payoff case. Since then, not a year has passed without a scandal involving top politicians. If it is not some payoff, then it is involvement with *geisha*. In 1989, the Recruit shares-for-favours scandal surfaced costing the then Prime Minister, Noboru Takeshita, his office. Then came a sex scandal sending his successor, Sosuke Uno, to packing. Uno was replaced by Toshiki Kaifu. It was during Kaifu's regime that a scandal involving four largest brokerage houses, namely, Nomura, Daiwa, Nikko and Yamaichi came to light underlining the nexus between business and politics. These "Big Four" were made to publish the list of big clients who were reimbursed, obviously, at the expense of taxpayers, for losses after the stockmarket crashes of 1988 and 1990. Later, 13 middle-ranking stockbroking firms too submitted to the government a list of their favoured clients. This prompted Kaifu to focus on the urgency of changing electoral laws in order to reduce the dependence of politicians on businessmen for campaign funds.

Yet the spate of scandals did not cease to surface nor could politics-business nexus be broken. In 1996, the Japanese Prime Minister, Mr. Ryutaro Hashimoto, seemed to be a much harassed person. As soon as he doused the flame of one scandal, another one surfaced. A bribery case, involving the Ministry of Health and Welfare, was followed by another involving the Ministry of International Trade and Industry (MITI). The former forced the Prime Minister himself to admit that he had received a sum of ¥7m ($62,000) in political donations from organisations involved in the bribery scandal. It was proved that he initially lied when he denied receiving any such sum. In the latter case, an oil wholesaleing company—Izui Sekiyu Shokai was involved whose founder, Junichi Izui, was arrested in November, 1996 for tax evasion on the money earned by him on his deals with Mitsubishi Oil during 1992-94. On the basis of papers seized from places, a link was established between MITI and Mitsubishi Oil. Sleaze money was shared by officials of MITI and top politicians. The late Michio Watanabe, the then Deputy Prime Minister and Foreign Minister was one of the main beneficiaries, followed by nine LDP members of the Diet.

Every scandal underlines the dominance of the "iron triangle" of interlocking interest—business, the bureaucracy and politics. Politicians have been angry at the media for making them the chief culprit. They claim that they get no more than one-tenth of the total slush funds. It is the bureaucracy that gets the nine-tenths of such funds. They have, thus, been clamouring for administrative reforms in order to clip the wings of bureaucrats.

In Belgium, financial sleaze plays a major role in influencing governmental decision. In 1988, an Italian firm spent millions-of-dollars to ensure that the helicopters manufactured by it were bought by the Belgian Government. A contract worth $224 m was signed under which Belgium agreed to purchase 46 military helicopters from the Italian firm, Agusta, notwithstanding the fact that when the scandal came to light, it blackened the face of the government. Three ministers quit, an air force general committed suicide and Willy Claes who was the Economics Minister, when the deal was struck, was thrown out of his job as head of the NATO (North Atlantic Treaty Organisation). "Then there was the murder in 1991 of Andre Cools, a former Deputy Minister and for many years the Socialist Party's boss in Liege... four men, including another former Socialist minister, were charged with involvement in his murder. Some of those arrested, it transpired, had links to the chief suspect in the paedophile case. As it happens, the magistrate on the Cools case was also taken off it some three years ago, apparently when close to a breakthrough.

"Political cronyism, if not corruption, reaches deep down into Belgian life. It is hard to get a job in the public service without being a member of a mainstream political party or without at least having a known penchant for one. Journalists on State-run radio and television are appointed by quotas agreed upon by the main parties. Not the best recipe, perhaps, for investigative journalism if your masters are suspected of dirty dealing. Not the best formula, either, for choosing investigative magistrates or senior policemen".[16]

In Zaire (now renamed as Congo), dictator Mobutu during his long rule bled the economy white. He plundered its people and resources so cruelly that not even the barbarians of the olden days could have dared do that. "Zaire experienced more than corruption—many countries suffer that. It saw the systematic theft of the State, from top to bottom. Politicians and officials of every rank have gobbled up the institutions of government until they resemble wooden pillars devoured by termites; the slightest push makes them collapse in a cloud of dust'.[17]

Not only Mobutu's whim was law, as it happened in the case of every middle age monarch, but his own personal bank account was indistinguishable from the national treasury. It was bedlam all round. Whenever opportunity arose, the army looted whatever remained unstolen by politicians. This happened in 1991 and 1993 for all the world to see. The economic ruin was reflected in mind boggling rate of inflation in the country. In 1996, it was around 600 per cent. In 1993, one US dollar fetched three new zaires, but in March 1997 one US dollar was being exchanged for 162,000 new zaires. The commonest note of 10,000 zaires was worth just 6.2 cents.

Mobutu was estimated in 1993 to have slashed $4 b abroad, mostly in Swiss banks. It is doubtful that the new Kabila-led government will ever be able to lay its hand on this fortune because even in the case of Marcos's deposits, amounting $15 billion, the government of Mrs. Aquino could get less than $400 million. The Swiss laws require that it should be proved that the depositors indulged in embezzlement and violated human rights. Tax evasion cannot be the ground for claiming the deposits. Moreover, only a guilty verdict is not sufficient, it must be conclusively proved that there was a direct connection between the crime and the Swiss bank deposits. Till now, Panama has not been able to lay hands on Noriega's $460,000 lying in his Swiss accounts.

In Albania, a former Communist country ruled for decades by the Stalinists, has witnessed a popular uprising in 1997 not for the restoration of Communism but against the new ruler, Sali Berisha, who had cheated the people of their meagre savings. In 1996, his Democratic Party, in order to mobilise election campaign funds, encouraged the proliferation of bogus investment schemes that were sure to collapse. When the collapse came during the winter of 1996-97, almost half the population of the country lost whatever savings they had. This led to riots, anarchy and chaos.

In Italy, when Silvio Berlusconi was the Prime Minister, he packed the State-owned television network—RAI—with his supporters. It reminds one of what happened during the Morarji Desai's Janata Party government when the All India Radio and the Doordarshan were sought to be packed with the RSS-oriented people by the then Minister of Information and Broadcasting, Mr. Lal Krishna Advani. Returning to the Berlusconi regime in Italy, when Prime Minister's brother was caught in anti-corruption operation, a vigorous attempt was made to restrict the powers of Milan's magistrate probing into the case against him in the second half of 1994.

South Korea has the distinction of handing over to two of its former Presidents the harshest punishments in its history. While Chun Doo Hawn was sentenced to death, his successor Roh Tae Woo was to serve a long prison-term of twenty-two-and-a-half years. Roh Tae Woo confessed that he had illegally amassed $650 million through political slush. He admitted on in October 1995 that he stashed 170 billion won ($221m) of the 500 b won in slush-fund donations he collected while in office from 1988 to 1993. It is interesting to note that he donated around 170 b won for the Presidential election campaign of the opposition leader, Kim Dae Jung, a self-proclaimed fighter against corruption. Like the Janata Dal leader, Mr. Sharad Yadav, who admitted to having received funds from the Hawala kingpin, Jain-brothers, but less than what the CBI alleged, Kim Dae Jung admitted that he received only 2 b won from Roh.

The cat came out of the bag in January 1992 when Chung Ju Yung, the then chairman of Hyundai business group revealed that he had paid Roh 20 b won ($26 m) in illicit political funds. Roh admitted it but stated that he had not used the funds for his own personal and political purposes. He had spent them on "various charity works helping the poor and the elderly".

He was also involved in a kickback scheme linked to a $5 b contract for F-16 fighters in 1991. In 1993, his daughters and son-in-law were convicted by a US federal court in California for violating currency laws. They had taken $190,000 in cash into the USA without proper authorisation. At that time, it was alleged by the South Korean Opposition that it was part of the kickback.

It is an open secret that in South Korea slush funds play a big role. They finance everything from the monthly budgets of legislators' district offices to the election campaigns of legislators. Like his predecessors Chun Doo Hwan and Park Chung Hee, Roh too used slush funds to bribe military commanders and senior bureaucrats to buy their loyalty and support. All three military dictators illicitly amassed political funds by taking kickbacks and bribes. It is said that Roh licensed 139 golf courses and 17 electric power plants and got 17 b won or 10 per cent of the total cost of power projects. The going price of a golf-course licence was 2 b won.

The present President Mr. Kim Young Sam, who came to power on an anti-corruption plank, seems to be in trouble. His son Kim Hyun Chul has already been arrested and facing charges of corruption. This resulted from the bankruptcy petition filed by the Hanbo Iron and Steel Company in February 1997. A bribes-for-loans scandal came to light which involved not only Presidential aides but the Oppsition parties too. The needle of suspicion points towards the direction of the President too.

The company got 5 trillion won ($5.9 b) in bank loans for a massive steel plant despite its assets being only 300 b won. The scandal is based on the accusation that the Hanbo chairman Mr. Chung Tai Soo, bribed government officials and politicians to obtain bank loans for his collapsing corporate empire. As many as 9 ruling party leaders were involved. Hong In Kil, a relation of the President and former general affairs senior secretary admitted that he had taken a bribe of $1.1 m from Chung for helping him secure a bank loan. The Chief Executive Officer of the company Kim Jong Kuk delivered the bribe money to important ruling party leaders, including Kim Deog Ryong, a former secretary to the President of the country.

On February 25, 1997, President Kim Young Sam apologised to the nation for involvement of his aides and his son. He said: "I lower my head in shame for involvement of people close to me in the scandal.' *The Far Eastern Economic Review* (May 15, 1997), however, commented: "Involving bribery, influence-peddling and political slush funds, the scandals have virtually wiped out the moral legitimacy of Kim's administration and its anti-corruption platform".

From whatever has been said above and a look at the Indian situation, political corruption seems to be quite prevalent all over the world. Politicians and businessmen need one another. The former need funds to run their party establishment and carry on election campaigns. Since the prices have been going up rapidly, the costs of running parties and fighting elections have also been mounting. All over the world, political parties have shown utter disinterestedness in going to people at large and collecting donations and subscriptions. Dipping into the public purse and depending on kickbacks, payoffs, commissions and various kinds of bribery have become quite prevalent. In the countries where private sector is not strong, the former has become the order of the day. In India, we have seen dipping into the public purse is more prevalent in backward States like Bihar, U.P., Assam and so on because the private sector, the alternative source, is not only weak but contracting also. Had there been a strong and flourishing private sector in Bihar, there would have been no need for various scams in which the target had been the public exchequer. Hence, the more backward a country or a region, the greater is the danger to the safety of the public purse.

In India, not only there is lack of severe dependence of political parties on people at large for funds, but most of the parties do not have genuine living organisational set-up at lower levels. The lower level set-up is only on paper. Arrivals and departures of members and workers continue uninterruptedly at a swift pace and we have found that in Bihar a large number of existing members of the CPI depart between the two Congresses, but the total increases because of new enrolments and a little investigation will show that most of the new recruitments are bogus. The same person may be recruited or enrolled by a number of parties of differing ideologies and he may not be aware of this. In this situation, what happens is that the person who is nominated as party candidate has to gather his friends, relations and castemen to sustain his election campaign. These people have to be well looked after and for this, the money has to come either from the political party concerned or the candidate himself. Both of them depend on businessmen for this. Businessmen also keep political parties whether in power or outside pleased so that they get licences, quotas, bank loans and other facilities. Parties with trade union wings or the mafiosi support are given special attention so that business activities are not disturbed.

After the election is over, the winner has to fix up his supporters in such a way that they get regular incomes to live a comfortable life. They are provided with licences to run fair price shops, allotted dealerships of petrol pumps, kerosene, LPG agencies, government contracts, besides "harassment" by the police, excise and customs being taken care of in case some of the supporters indulge in criminal activities from extortion to smuggling and illicit distilling of liquor. Even the candidates who lose have to give a special attention to their supporters if they entertain the ambition of continuing in electoral politics. Permits for buses and trucks have to be secured for their supporters by politicians and in case they encroach upon public or private property, they have to be protected. In some States politicians solicit the help of the gangsters for booth capturing and stamping ballot papers and sometimes murdering rivals. In many States, criminals have themselves become politicians and entered Parliament and legislatures. In the Rabri Devi Government in Bihar there are at least three new ministers (who were not in the previous Laloo Yadav Government) with criminal record. In the Deve Gowda Government, a person with criminal record was inducted in to the Ministry of Home Affairs but he had to quit because of public protest.

Soon after the first Laloo Government was formed, *The Economist* (April 6, 1991) observed: "Perhaps the most worrying trend in Bihar is the number of criminals who, having helped others to get elected are now having a go at themselves. The present State government has an absurd 74 ministers. Fourteen of them are "hardened criminals", claims a senior police officer. Brij Bihari Prasad is facing trial for six murder cases in Muzaffarpur district court. Birbahadur Singh, a member of the State's Legislative Assembly was shot last year while facing two dozen charges of murder and banditry.

"Political power gives the *goondas* control of the whole system. It enables them to transfer meddling civil servants and judges who try to do their job. It forces national politicians to court them for their support because Bihar has 54 seats in the national Parliament".

"What peace Bihar does enjoy is the peace of a mafia neighbourhood, which everyone pays for protection and disputes are settled with a gun".[18]

The Election Commissioner Mr. G.V.G. Krishnamurty, has lately released some data from a study "criminals and politics", prepared by the Commission. According to it, 40 members of Parliament and 700 MLAs out of a total of 4,027 have been involved in criminal activities. Of the 13,952 candidates in the last elections, around 1,500 had criminal record and cases of murder, dacoity, rape, theft and extortion against them.

One of the key elements in political corruption and criminality is nepotism. The word "nepotism" entered English language in the seventeenth century after a study of the medieval and Renaissance papacy. It was derived from the Latin word *nepos* which meant a nephew. There is something very interesting about how it came to acquire the present connotation. "An element of euphemism is apparent in this etymology. It was not that the Popes were exceptionally fond of their nephews. It was rather that, given the vow of celibacy which supposedly bound the Catholic clergy (and which had been revived by 11th century reformers partly as a barrier to nepotism), the church preferred gloss over questions about the Pope's children—which was what many *nipoti* (plural of Italian *nipote* which was, in turn, derived from the Latin *nepos*—GM & BKP) in fact were.

"During the papacy's most purple patch, Innocent VIII (1484-92) married off a son and two grand-daughters in the Vatican. His successor, Alexander VI, a Borgia, had three sons and left his daughter, Lucrezia, to act as a deputy in the Vatican when he was away from Rome. Julius II, Alexander's successor, had at least three daughters and was himself the *nipote* of Sixtus IV, the predecessor of Innocent VIII".

"The medieval and Renaissance papacy was absolute power corrupted absolutely. It practised nepotism: every position filled by a member of the Pope's family was one fewer for the rival families seeking to surround and extinguish him. This process, once begun, was all but unstoppable and fatal to good government".[19]

Every time a new Pope assumed office, a veritable power struggle ensued in which the new incumbent tried to replace the people who were loyal to his predecessor by his own people. Thus, there was a charge of favouritism or, better to say, nepotism laid at his door. Over the years, the term nepotism came into wide currency. Rulers relied on their own kith and kin more than others because it was said that blood was thicker than water. It happened everywhere irrespective of ideological and political orientation. The dictator Francois "Papa Doc" handed over Haiti to his son Jean-Claude "baby Doc". In Saudi Arabia and some other Arab countries ministers, army Generals and senior officers are all related to one another. The ruling Al-Saud clan has incorporated its name with that of the country it rules. King Abdul Aziz who founded Saudi Arabia had 44 sons from his 22 wives. In the current generation of rulers, Prince Sultan has fathered 17 sons and 18 daughters. The country is, thus, no better than personal property of the ruling family and its relatives. "If Saudi Arabia contrives to combine nepotism and prosperity, that is because its rulers draw their wealth from the ground without having to appropriate it from the populace".[20]

During the early months of 1994, most of the 23 Cabinet Ministers in the government of Bophuthatswana were relatives of Chief Lucas Mangope. Antigua which has a population of only 60,000 with a national debt of $400 m or so has been ruled by the Bird family for more than half-a-century. The Philippines was ruled by Marcos and his wife Imelda with the help of their relations. After the overthrow of Marcos, Mrs. Corazon Aquino's government was not much different. She as the President of the country shared power with her brother-in-law, sister-in-law, uncle and brother. During both the regimes, the economy of the country declined at the annual rate of one per cent. In North Korea, the great leader, Mr. Kim Il Sung, found none but his own progeny the dear leader Mr. Kim Il Jong, most suitable to succeed him as the President of the country. Kim Il Sung had strengthened his rule by installing as many as 30 of his relatives in key position during the 1950s and since then, he had seen to it that in key positions only such were placed. Nicolae Ceausescu made his wife the most powerful person after him in the country and used his own position to get her made member of a number of international academies and scientific societies though on no account did she deserve the honour. Had he survived, he would have certainly made his son Nicu as his successor as the President of Romania. This gave birth to the description of the Communist rule in Romania as "socialism in one family". During Todor Zhivkov's rule over Bulgaria, the most powerful person was his daughter, Ludmilla. He "continued to involve various members of his family in political affairs after his daugher's death—and on occasions may have been embarrassed by his own actions. Thus, when he visited China in May 1987, there was a discrepancy between the Chinese and Bulgarian lists of guests; the former included his 20-year-old granddaughter, Evegenia Zhivkova, while the latter made no reference to her.'[21] In Albania where Enver Hoxha ruled for 41 years continuously from 1944 to 1985 with an iron hand put his relatives in key positions. To give a concrete instance, in 1961, the fourth congress of the Albanian Communist party elected 53 to its Central Committee and almost a half of them were related among themselves and to Hoxha by blood or marriage.

In revolutionary Cuba, the most trusted person for Fidel Castro is his younger brother Raul. Leonid Brezhnev's son-in-law, Yuri Churbanov, was appointed the first Deputy Foreign Trade Minister. He and his wife made money in whatever ways they could. He made a vulgar display of his wealth when he gave a tip of $100 to a striptease, dancer at the Crazy Horse nightclub in Paris. Mind you, this sum represented two weeks' earnings of an average Soviet worker at the prevalent exchange rate. Later, after Gorbachev came to power, he was arraigned before a court of law and convicted on a number of charges of corruption and fraud and sent to jail. Earlier, when the Soviet Union was under Stalin, his son Vasily enjoyed princely comforts. According to his sister Svetlana, he 'lived in a big government dacha (with) an enormous staff, a stable and kennels, all of course at government expense... They gave him medals, higher and higher ranks. Horses, automobiles, privileges, everything.'[22] Notwithstanding his alcoholism, he was made a lieutenant-general even before the age of 30 and air commander of the Moscow military district because he was the favourite child of the dictator. Nikita Khruschev's son was appointed editor of *Izvestia*, the government-owned paper and a member of the Central Committee of the CPSU and after the ouster of Khruschev, he was promptly removed. At present Boris Yeltsin's daughter, Tatiana Dyachenko is wielding a great deal of power. Her only qualification to do this is her being the daughter of the President. She is a powerful extra-constitutional centre of authority. During Mao's life time, his wife played the same role and during Deng Xiaoping's regime, his family too wielded power without any legitimacy. His youngest son, Deng Zhifang, controlled a Hong Kong company that got lucrative contracts of building shopping centres across China, a son-in-law, He Ping, was vice-chairman of Poly group, country's largest manufacturer of arms and was on the boards of two Hong Kong-based companies, dealing in real estate and insurance business. Another son-in-law, Wu Jian Chang, managed a large State corporation handling precious metals besides being connected with two Hong Kong-based companies. While his elder daughter headed the State Commission on Science and Technology, the younger one acted as his private secretary. "If and when Communism collapses formally in China, the piling-up of fortunes within its leaders' familes will probably be seen to have played a crucial role, by persuading those leaders that life can offer pursuits even more rewarding than the struggle for socialism. If so, the notion of nepotism as a way for family to "bank" the spoils of power will have produced its logical conclusion—retirement of those in power, confident of living comfortably on the income from their deposits".[23]

"In Russia after the 1917 revolution, it was announced that all children whether of Central Committee members or of illiterate peasants would be given identical schooling. Idealists like Lunacharski thought the family would die away along with the State as Marx had foretold".

But the family soon started to be used just as it might in any non-Communist society as a means for the new ruling class to entrench itself and its gains. The separation of rulers from ruled began with education. By the late 1930s, a network of special schools had been set-up to cater exclusively for the children of the ruling caste or *nomenklatura*. Special institutions of higher education followed.

"Entry to the *nomenklatura* was not by birth alone; but a study of the children of members of the Central Committee from 1953 to 1975 indicates just how big a head-start percentage became. Of 51 known offsprings, seven were directors of national institutes; 13 had plum globetrotting jobs in journalism or foreign relations; 12 held high positions in the military establishment; seven were in academia; two were actors; two were architects; two were incapacitated by alcoholism; the positions, if any, of the other six were unknown."[24]

A 1995-case implicating Datuk Rafidah Aziz, the then Malayasian Minister for International Trade illustrated how nepotism was prevalent in Malayasia. She was accused of exerting her influence in getting the shares of a listed company allocated to her son-in-law in violation of her own ministry's guidelines. It came to light that in Malayasia politicians were using government policies in such a way that they reaped windfall gains for themselves and/or their relatives and getting lucrative contracts awarded to their business associates.

Darkness of Nepotism

In our own country, nepotism has played havoc with the standing and efficiency of even otherwise honest and competent politicians. One may take the case of the late Pratap Singh Kairon to whom goes the credit of modernising the economy of Punjab which did not have any mineral resources. It was much more backward than the part which went to Pakistan in 1947. He developed its agriculture, encouraged people to set up small industries which became a great foreign exchange earner, provided infrastructural facilities and instilled a sense of self-confidence in the Punjabis. But his image was spoilt by his son Surinder Singh Kairon who emerged as an extra-constitutional centre of authority. An enquiry commission indicted him on several counts.[25] Similarly, Morarji Desai's son Kanti Desai's activities did not bring credit to his father. Rajendra Prasad's weakness for his relation Bipin Bihari Varma lowered his prestige. Even though Varma played an ignoble role during the Quit India movement, he was given Congress ticket for Provisional Parliament, Lok Sabha, Rajya Sabha and Bihar Legislative Council, where he never opened his mouth even for once.[26] In addition, Rajendra Prasad's preference for his semi-insane sister to the legendary freedom fighter Bahuriyaji for Congress nomination to the Bihar legislature sullied his image. In recent times, we have found leaders like P.V. Narasimha Rao, H.D. Deve Gowda, Balram Jakhar, Kamal Nath, Buta Singh, Jagannath Mishra, K. Karunakaran, Laloo Yadav, M. Karunanidhi, Kamalapati Tripathi, Ram Lakhan Singh Yadav and a host of others promoting their kith and kin in politics. In our neighbouring country—Pakistan—Benazir Bhutto pushed up her husband in politics.

On the basis of even a cursory glance at the instances of nepotism in this country and elsewhere, it can be safely said that family-based politics has caused national distress, encouraged criminality and brought down efficiency. More often politicians' kith and kin have been found to be indulging in corrupt practices and anti-social behaviour. "Now, the view that nepotism is at best a bar to efficiency and at worst, an index of corruption, is well established.[27]

An important form of political corruption is the patron-client relationship which develops between a politician and his supporters. This is witnessed mostly in the countries and situations where class interests and class-based politics are not clearly developed. A politician tries to gather around himself a band of supporters who mobilise votes for him and sing hymns in his praise. In return, as we have already mentioned, the politician concerned helps them financially and get them jobs, bus route permits, fair price shops, dealerships of cement, LPG, kerosene, diesel, petrol and so on. We can cite any number of examples, but we shall confine ourselves to only the latest one. Ram Vilas Paswan, the former Railway Minister, was pulled up by the Delhi High Court on August 19, 1997 for arbitrary issuance of thousands of "cheque passes" (discretionary travel passes). The High Court questioned the validity of the April 30 order of the Railway Ministry for extending platinum pass facility to the retired Railway Board members and their families and allowing them to avail unlimited travels in the first class AC. If a scrutiny of the beneficiaries of "cheque passes" given during the

Ram Vilas Paswan dispensation is made, it will be amply clear that the Minister's aim has been to create and nourish a special constituency of supporters for himself. We can give another instance. After the split in the Janata Dal and the formation of Laloo Yadav-led Rashtriya Janata Dal, Paswan was worried about the Yadav support in his constituency. As a measure of damage control, he immediately appointed a person of the Yadav caste, who is supposed to have some influence over the Yadav voters in his Hajipur constituency, as chairman of the Railway Recruitment Board, Muzaffarpur. This person had also been a member of some railway committee. A write-up in the *Prabhat Khabar* (July 25, 1997) with his photograph contained a number of white lies about his social orientation and love for the down trodden and this we can testify on the basis of our personal knowledge of him since 1957.

Political parties and politicians in India seldom display scruples in their behaviour. This may easily be illustrated by referring to certain recent examples. Take, one of the largest parties BJP (Bharatiya Janata Party). It claims to be an adherent of value-based politics, but what has it done in recent times? It has embraced Mr. Bansi Lal and Mr. Jagmohan who were leading lights of the emergency regime of Mrs. Indira Gandhi and the Bharatiya Jana Sangh (the previous incarnation of BJP) and its leaders attacked them in season and out of season. Now Mr. Bansi Lal and his Haryana Vikas Party are allies of BJP while Mr. Jagmohan is its active member. Not only this, it has forgotten about its fight for clean, corruption-free politics when it welcomed with folded hands, the non-too-desirable defectors from the Congress in U.P. and aligned with Ms. Jayalalita, allegedly most corrupt politician in the country. It forgot about its fight against corruption in Bihar, whose symbol was supposed to be Mr. Laloo Yadav. More startling is the grant of Lok Sabha ticket to Swami Sachchidanand Sakshi who is supposed to be involved in the murder of Brahma Dutt Dwivedi, the BJP leader of Farrukhabad (U.P.). Another concrete instance is the grant of party ticket to Mr. Sanjay Singh for Lok Sabha election from Amethi. He belongs to a landlord family which was traditionally a British stooge. He has a number of scandals behind him. His wife has been fighting a case of desertion and adultery against him. In view of this, BJP's glorifying Ram seems to be nothing but hypocrisy. The alliance with the AIDMK underlines that its love for Hindi is only an eyewash.

Mr. I.K. Gujral, the JD Prime Minister forgot the so-called crusade of his UF against communalism and agreed to be sponsored by Akali-BJP combine for Jalandhar Lok Sabha seat and, barring Mr. Mulayam Singh Yadav, all other leaders of the UF indulged in white-washing this act of crass opportunism.

The Left talks of its clean record and honesty, but how far can this be sustained is a matter of investigation. To give just one example, the CPI gave put up Mr. Kamala Mishra Madhukar for Lok Sabha in Bihar in 1998 while the CBI had filed a chargesheet, accusing him of selling gas connections from his discretionary quota during 1991-96 when he was an MP. In the light of this, its fight against Laloo Yadav turns out to be a hoax. Some of its leaders in Bihar have been aligning with casteist and communalist elements to win elections.

Large-scale tampering with voters lists, booth capturing, looting of ballot boxes and adopting other methods of rigging, elections have been well-documented. Here businessmen provide funds and the mafia muscle power and arms. Bihar is one of the prominent States where gun-manufacturing has become a cottage industry. In addition to locally manufactured arms and bombs, one can have sophisticated ones from across the borders. They include a number of varieties AKs and devices operated with remote control mechanism. In many parts of Bihar, a handful of people capture booths and stamp ballot papers, keeping in mind the percentage fixed by the Election Commission, crossing which excludes the votes of a particular booth from being counted. The polling staff, in view of inadequate security, has to submit meekly to them and produce all the ballot papers for stamping. If they do not do so, they are bound to be taught "appropriate lessons" sooner or later. At times, not only the polling staff but local police force and counting staff also cooperate with powerful candidate out of fear or because of caste or communal loyalty.

REFERENCES

1. '... the former Chief Minister of Orissa, Mr. Biju Patnaik and his successor, Mr. Biren Mitra, were accused of helping their wives amass wealth by doing business with the Government which they headed at the time.' Surendranath Dwivedi and G.S. Bhargava, *Political Corruption in India*, New Delhi, 1967, pp. 109-127.
2. *The Sutta-Nipata*, (III.1. 419-423).
3. Government of India, Ministry of Commerce and Industry (Department of Company Law Administration), *Report of the Commission of Inquiry (Inquiry of the Administration of Dalmia-Jain Companies)*, Delhi, 1963, pp. 145-46.
4. *The Searchlight*, May 24, 1950.
5. *Ibid.*, May 28, 1950.
6. *Ibid.*, May 30, 1950.
7. *Ibid.*, June 5, 1950.
8. Girish Mishra and Braj Kumar Pandey, *op. cit.*, pp. 306-13.
9. We have ourselves collected and kept in our possession of a number of such postcards.
10. *The Economist*, December 15, 1990.
11. *Guardian Weekly*, July 20, 1997.
12. *The Economist*, March 26, 1994.
13. *Ibid.*, July 17, 1993.
14. *Ibid.*, February 3, 1996.
15. *Ibid.*, March 15, 1997.
16. *Ibid.*, October 26, 1996.
17. *Ibid.*, March 22, 1997.
18. Also see, Vikas Kumar Jha, *Bihar: Criminalization of Politics*, Patna, 1996.
19. *The Economist*, December 24, 1994.
20. *Ibid.*
21. Leslie Holmes, *The End of Communist Power*, Oxford, 1993, p. 97.
22. Quoted in *The Economist*, December, 24, 1994.

23. *Ibid.*
24. *Ibid.*
25. Surendranath Dwivedi and G.S. Bhargava, *op. cit.*, pp. 93-108.
26. Girish Mishra and Braj Kumar Pandey, *op. cit.*, pp. 181-83 and 188-91.
27. *The Economist*, December 24, 1994.

10

The Dawn of Mafia

Almost daily, we hear or read of mafia. In the course of our discussion we too have mentioned this term a few times especially in connection with its nexus with politicians. What do we mean by "mafia" and what are its characteristics?

Origin of Mafia

The term "mafia" originated in the remote past and over the years, its meaning and characteristics underwent many changes. In the dialect of Florence it was commonly used to denote a poor or miserable person, but in the dialect spoken in Piedmont, the word *mafiun* stood for a petty person. In Sicily, however, where mafia came to have strong roots and acquired most of its present-day connotation, the term was used in a different sense than the above.

The first mention of this term in Sicily can be found in a document dating back to 1658 symbolising boldness, ambition and arrogance. We find its use in the same sense after 250 years also. It was used in connection with a person to denote his superiority and manliness. A writer had this to say in 1889: "A *mafioso* is simply a courageous, brave fellow who won't stand any nonsense from anyone."[1]

There is a great deal of controversy as regards the origin of the term in the sense in which it is used in Sicily and till now, no consensus has been arrived at. A number of scholars think that it has an Arabic origin—'either from 'Mahias', meaning a bold man or braggart or from 'Ma afir' the name of the Saracenel tribe that ruled Palermo' (the capital of Sicily). There is yet another group of scholars who, while accepting its Arabic origin, think that it has been derived from the word '*maha*' which means a quarry or a cave in a rock and are of the view that "The 'mafie', the tuff caves in the Marsala region, served the persecuted Saracens as hiding places and later provided hide-outs for other fugitives. A slightly far-fetched variant of this theory is put forward by Loschivavo, prior to Garibaldi's landing. He suggests the rebellious Sicilians had hidden-out in the *mafie* near Marsala and had, therefore, subsequently, during their successful advance on Palermo, been called *mafiosi*, the people from the *mafie*. In the course of time, the word had come to be used as an adjective, meaning 'outstanding, manly, handsome' and had kept this meaning in popular speech.'[2]

The term gained currency during the nineteenth century and it was first used in an official communication in 1865, justifying the arrest of a person who was supposed to be part of a mafia. Gradually, he came to stand for a fence of planner of crimes rather than himself committing the crime. To quote a German scholar Henner Hess, a well-known authority on mafia and mafiosi: "Eventually the word mafia was used, above all, for organised crime, until sensation-hungry journalists confused North Italian juries and foreign authors interpreted it as the name of an organisation. The emergence of the word was linked with the emergence of a secret society and, thus, gave rise to frantastic speculations.'[3]

Let us not pursue any further this controversy about the origin of mafia, which is not only endless but, in some cases, quite unbelievable or fantastic. To illustrate this, let us mention just one version of the origin, which traces it back to as far back as 1282 and claims that mafia then was an association of nationally-minded people who were fighting out the growing influence of the French and the North Italians. Some scholars, putting this line forward, claim that mafia was the name of a secret sect, headed by Mazzini who is supposed to have authorised theft, arson and poisoning!

Towards the last quarter of the nineteenth century, the concept of mafia entered German, French and English languages. In our country, we do not come across very many references to the term mafia before the mid-1970s. It gained wide currency only after the beginning of the 1980s. Thus, the kind of mafia relevant to our discussion is not a medieval phenomenon but a modern one having its effective origin in the 19th century.

In common parlance, the term "mafia" stands for a number of things. To begin with, it denotes an attitude of defiance towards the established authority of the State and its law. Generally, a member of the mafia does not allow the State to interfere in his private quarrels. He accepts no obligation except those entailed by the code of honour or *omerta* (manliness) which forbids him from going to public authorities. Thus, mafia is 'the sort of code of behaviour which always tends to develop in societies without effective public order, or in societies in which citizens regard the authorities as wholly or partly hostile'.[4]

Generally, the mafia may mean any centrally organised society in which the power is concentrated in the hands of the man at the top. The rest of the people belonging to the mafia are his retainers. Almost all the mafia chiefs have been men of substance, belonging largely to the middle class. Among them have been prosperous farmers, contractors and professionals like lawyers. In the course of time, the mafia has ceased to be a largely rural phenomenon. "Politics made the power of the local boss; politics increased it and turned it into a big business."[5]

Another sense in which the term "mafia" is used is akin to what we have stated in the preceding para. In this, 'it is the control of the community's life by a secret—or rather an officially unrecognized—system of gangs. So far as we know, this type of *Mafia* was never a single society, centrally organized'.[6] In all the three senses, we have referred to, the mafia denotes an organisation parallel to the existing State apparatus and the areas under its influence only this parallel organisation matters.

The main characteristic of mafia, according to historian Charles Tilly, "is the private use of unlicensed violence as a means of control in the public arena.[7] In 1992, it is estimated that at least half of 1,697 murders in Italy were committed by the mafia. Looking back, one finds a big change in Italy leading to the collapse of the State's monopoly over violence. There was a change in the balance between the two parts of Italy—South and North. The number of migrants from South to North not only dwindled but the direction got reversed. Secondly, there was a change in the nature of State intervention on the economy and society of the South, which proved to be disruptive rather than unifying. "Gradually, fresh inputs of public spending lost their power to strengthen internal integration and promote market fluidity, until the situation was reversed and state intervention began to create all kinds of tensions—above all, territorial tensions".[8]

Mafiosi-Turned-Entrepreneurs

During this period of the ascendancy of the forces of disruption and disintegration, entrepreneurial mafia emerged. This brought far-reachings changes. The mafiosi "now found themselves, for the first time in their history, impelled to act and think outside the bounds of the traditional culture."[9] This new culture gave a new direction to mafia activities. The mafiosi saw in the accumulation of capital and the prosperity of their business, a new source of power to reassert themselves. Now, while the State's hold weakened because of disruptive tendencies referred to above, the mafiosi became more powerful and the latter began encroaching upon the former's monopoly of violence with impunity. According to Pino Arlacchi's study, "the collapse of the State's monopoly of force meant that violence was transformed into an economic power, a tool by which existing property and production relations could be altered. Murder, no longer a taboo enforced by the State, began to become an increasingly risk-free and inexpensive way of resolving conflicts. The mafia's power began to expand once more because economic competition and conflicts between individuals and pressure-groups of the most diverse kinds, began to involve the formerly forbidden weapons of assassination and physical violence. The crisis of the State's monopoly of force redoubled the power of the *mafiosi*, allowing them to pursue the goal of accumulation by resurrecting the whole repertory of overbearing and violent behaviour that had been the stock-in-trade of the man of honour thirty years ago. In entering on a massive scale into industrial competition, the *mafiosi* were doing something radically new, but this innovation was at the same time marked by a resurgence of many of their most archaic traits.

"To obtain the very large sums of money needed to purchase goods, machines, buildings and labour-power, old forms of violence were given new and harsher life. Kidnapping, with all its ferocious accompanying ritual, was once again employed".[10]

The mafiosi-turned-entrepreneurs began using their traditional skills for achieving new goals like restraining their competitors, acquiring capital through criminal activities, keeping the wages low by terrorising the workers, money laundering and so on. All these helped the mafiosi-controlled firms expand at a much faster rate.

As we know, an individual member is called *mafioso*, but all the individual members together are called *mafiosi* who exercise power through the systematic use of private violence. The sum total of their actions constitutes the phenomenon known as *mafia*.

Mafia must not be confused with bandits notwithstanding certain superficial similarities. There are two respects in which the mafiosi are different. First, bandits employ direct force or violence while doing most of their work but the mafiosi use force only after somebody refuses to yield or crosses the *Lakshman rekha* or the limit set by them.

Second, bandits, as against the mafiosi, do not belong to long, trustworthy and protective patron-client chains. Yet the fact remains that, sometimes, successful bandit groups metamorphose themselves into mafia. How does it happen? "When they begin to build up their own power domains, bandits threaten *mafia*, the operators of *mafia* then co-opt them or destroy them. The comparison shows mafia to be both more similar to regular government and more dependent on regular government than is banditry. In that regard, one might imagine a continuum running from anarchy to banditry to mafia to routine government. The defining feature of that continuum is the extent to which control over the use of force is concentrated in a single organization.'[11]

Likewise the mafia cannot be taken as a synonym of a violent gang. As against the mafia, a violent gang is not a permanent organisation, it has limited expectations of any responsibility on the part of its members and is all inviting to youths who are unable to fit themselves into a more integrated and defined world. "Among gang members, little is expected and little is given. Membership definition is vague. A youth can join one day and quit the next by merely stating "I no longer belong." Violent-gang organisation is ideally suited to the defective personality and limited social ability of these disturbed youths.

"A prime function of the modern gang is to provide a channel to act out hostility to satisfy the continuing and momentary emotional needs of its members. The gang is a convenient and malleable structure quickly adaptable to the needs of emotionally disturbed youths who are unable to fulfil the demands required for participation in more normal groups. They join gangs because they lack the social ability to relate to others, not because the gang gives them a "feeling of belonging".[12] The acts of violence committed by the gang are without any premeditation and, thus, are senseless. It looks for a magical shortcut of achieving its temporary dominance over and keeping in awe the society.

Operation of Mafia

Anton Blok who intensively studied the operation of mafia in a Sicilian village for 100 years from 1860 to 1960 found the realm of operation of the mafia much wider and public. Mafiosi take decisions which affect the community. They seldom attack individuals on their homes and houses to settle personal scores. The relationship between mafiosi and governmental authorities is not always clear-cut or straight forward. "On the one hand, *mafiosi* disregard formal law and are able to withstand the impact of the legal and governmental apparatus. On the other, *mafiosi* act in connivance with formal authority and validate their control through covert and pragmatic relationships with those who hold formal office. This symbiosis distinguishes them from outlaws and bandits, whose power domains are also buttressed by physical force but contrast openly with those of the State.'[13]

Another important finding of Anton Blok is this: "The *mafioso* can be considered as a variety of the political middleman or power broker, since his *raison d'etre* is predicated upon his capacity to acquire and maintain control over the paths linking the local infrastructure of the village to superstructure of the larger society.'[14] He acts as political middleman or power broker. He controls sizeable vote banks to make or mar the prospect of any candidate or political party. It is said that mafia barters votes for favours in Sicily on a regular basis. It is claimed that the mafia controls around 200000 votes in the city of Palermo which has a population of 600,000. It needs to be noted that a mafioso is seldom interested in resolving any dispute for all time to come or a long period for fear that it may render him redundant".

These two points along with the fact that both mafia and corruption go together will help us a great deal in developing our understanding of the phenomenon of mafia in the presentday Indian society as well as the nexus between mafia and politics.

It needs to be noted that the mafia cannot be taken as just a group of gangsters. "Unlike the characters in "The Godfather", Sicily's real *mafiosi* are not gangsters, even murderous gangsters, squabbling over the profits of rigged horse races and casinos."[15]

In an Italian document dating back to 1876, we find

the following formulation: "The *mafia* is the instinctive, brutal and interest-conditioned solidarity which, to the detriment of the State, the law and regular organisations, unites all those individuals and social strata which prefer to derive their means of existence and comfort not from work but from violent action, from fraud and intimidation".[16]

Though this formulation is a little imprecise, yet it will be quite helpful if it is taken into consideration along with the following statement as regards mafioso, made by Cutrera in 1900: "He knows how to achieve his rights by his own efforts and if he lacks the power, he will do so with the help of others who think and feel the same way".[17]

The term "mafia" in Sicily from where it has proliferated to various parts of the globe means not a single or special association but a complex association of a large number of groupings whose objectives are varied. In spite of differences, the objectives are such that they make the members come hard-up against the limits of the criminal law and, at times, fall foul of it. These clique-type groupings, in spite of being independent of one another, maintain ties among them and come to one another's aid.

Usually a mafioso is an ambitious person who wants to rise vertically in the society by wielding both economic and political power. He is also conscious of the need to refurbish his public image. He wants to whitewash has past because he generally comes from the social stratum which engenders dependence and inferiority complex.

For a *mafioso*, his rise to political power is the precondition for his economic prosperity. Later, economic advancement reinforces his political power. Hess adds: "An act of force opens a man's road to power; without having applied physical force at least once he would find it impossible to meet the other requirements necessary for the exercise of *mafioso* functions. He could not gain recognition, instil fear, or successfully confront *mafiosi* rivals.'[18]

There are four steps in the process of his vertical rise to power. First, the mafioso must create a clientage of his own. Second, he must create a network of relationships with socially and economically higher-placed persons. Third, in order to publicise these relations, he must get himself photographed (or publicly appear) with political leaders, ministers, high-ups in the bureaucracy, editors and foreign dignitaries to underline his proximity to them. Fourth, he must control the vote banks to get political leaders and their fortunes dependent on them. Likewise, he must control labour and raw materials as well as marketing network to make businessmen and industrialists beholden to him and open up new avenues of getting financial resources.

Generally, the mafioso acts as a mediator in people's affairs and holds court and settles their disputes behaving like a benevolent prince of olden days. This gets him social respect and base. Mafia is generally called *Cosa Nostra* (our affair) by its members and has been described by a high-ranking law officer of Italy 'as a State within the State, "with its own territory, population and laws".'[19] It has its own armed forces too and has been at war with the legally constituted State in Italy and elsewhere if the latter does not fall in line with it.

A mafioso without any payment appropriates public property and facilities for himself and his followers and supporters. In the second half of 1990, it was reported that the public procurement was the largest source of income, bigger than either racketeering or the drugs trade, for the 426 mafia families supposed to be operating in the three southern regions worstly-affected by organised crime. He, in exchange, realises protection money from the propertied and well-to-do and assures them undisturbed peace.

The mafia is no longer confined to national boundaries as it has become international in its operation. This internationalisation took place after the Second World War when smuggling and blackmarketing came to have a field day. The link between the Sicilian mafia and the U.S. forces, which took its help in the fight against the Fascists, was forged. The mafiosi of the Sicilian origin in America were released and sent to Sicily to mobilise support. Two decades following the War afforded immense new opportunities to the mafia in the sphere of urban development, which made it economically powerful.

The mafia phenomenon is present in many countries. Despite certain basic similarities, there are national peculiarities. To cite just one example, Sicilian mafia hates brothel-running while the American mafia does not. In fact, the latter derives a substantial amount of revenue from this activity.

Historians, political scientists, sociologists, journalists, literateurs and even movie-makers have dealt with mafia phenomenon as an established area of study and research for a long time and have produced works of lasting importance, adding to our knowledge. Among them, we can easily count Eric Hobsbawm, Anton Blok, Henner Hess, P. Arlacchi, Mario Puzo and so on. The economists, however, have been very late in turning their attentions to it. It is hardly three decades ago that they started looking into the relationship between crime and economics and the first study by economists on the organised crime in general and mafia in particular came recently. It contained papers and comments by the Italian as well as the American economists and the phenomenon, while reviewing the study, was termed *Mafianomics* by *The Economist.*[20]

The delay in taking up the study of mafianomics by economists was due to the disagreement among them as regards the model to be applied. The question posed was: should one treat mafia family as a firm that turns out goods and services for which there is a demand notwithstanding the fact that they are illegal or as a parallel government with its own distinct laws, rules, regulations and procedures and enforcement agencies?

American economist, Mr Thomas Schelling, has been advocating the latter model because he thinks that the two characteristics of mafianomics make the quasi-government analogy more apt. First, the basic business of the mafia is to frame its own rules for given areas, no matter whether geographical or functional, so that it can extort money or "taxes" and force its own regulations on legal and/or illegal business activities. Second, in order to be in a position to enforce its discipline the mafia, just like the government, must have a monopoly over the use of force.[21]

It has been demonstrated that neither of the two models is adequate to the task of carrying out a proper study of the phenomenon because of its complexities and breadth. "In fact, both models of organised crime have their limitations. For a start, mafia organisations often operate in legal markets—albeit in illegal ways. Take the Sicilian mafia, for instance. A growing share of its activity lies in "allocating" the contracts provided by projects financed by subsidies from the European Union. Nor do mafia groups always have centralised government style control over the markets in which they are involved. In activities where new competitors can enter fairly easily, there is often unhealthy competition between the rival groups."[22]

Besides the problem of a suitable model to be applied, for a long time, a substantial number of economists could not be sure whether the tools of economics could be fruitfully applied to the study of mafia groups because of the involvement of large number of non-economic factors in their activities and functioning. Now, this doubt has been banished and both the Italian and the American economists have agreed that economic tools can be successfully applied and they have demonstrated this in their research papers, published as *The economics of organised crime*, edited by Gianluca Florentini and Sam Peltzman (CUP, 1995).

The model of a firm helps one analyse the internal structure of mafia groups along with their decisions about what markets to operate in. If a mafia group, for example, operates in markets which do not have formidable impediments to entry and where economies of scale are not substantial, it cannot avoid competition for long. Prostitution rackets constitute one such market.

Toward off competition and keep the monopoly intact, the mafia group must invest in weapons and hit-men who physically bar the entry of competitors, both present and potential, into the activity concerned. We have seen clashes when new groups try to enter smuggling of a particular commodity, distribution of narcotics and so on and try to dislodge or curtail the area of operation of the established ones. In a particular town of north Bihar, a few years ago, a person murdered his cousin because the latter was not allowing him to enter PWD (Public Works Department) contract business.

Nexus between Politicians and Criminals

Even a preliminary investigation into the long-standing feud between Pappu (alias Rajiv Ranjan) Yadav, the star of Mulayam Singh Yadav's Samajwadi Party in Bihar and Anand Mohan Singh will reveal what we have been driving at. These two dons have been operating in areas, bordering Nepal and their "kingdoms" overlap. These two honourable members of Parliament have a number of times clashed with each other. Both have powerful political patrons though they have been changing with the circumstances. Anand Mohan Singh belongs to George Fernandes's Samata Party, a close ally of the BJP which shouts loudly its adherence to all that is noble in Indian traditions! On the other hand, Pappu Yadav belongs to the Defence Minister, Mr Mulayam Singh Yadav's party. To begin with, Anand Mohan Singh was a protegy of Mr Chandra Shekhar, a former Prime Minister while Pappu Yadav was patronised by Mr Laloo Yadav. The former is a Rajput, i.e., upper class fellow while the latter is an Ahir (i.e., an OBC man). This caste-distinction is also reflected in the composition of their followers, supporters and well-wishers.

Certain activities like money laundering, international gun-running and drug trafficking are profitable when carried on a large extent because of the economies of scale. These activities carried on by illegal firms face impediments in the way of their expansion which legal firms, involved in lawful activities, do not face. The former cannot rely on established national and international regulations and agencies in order to enforce contracts. This, increasing scale of business leads to both economies and diseconomies. The mafia must have its own agencies to enforce contracts. In other words, it must maintain hit-men wherever this contract enforcement requires and must invest in weapons on a big scale.

Quite often, various mafia groups collude and form producers' cartels. Whenever these cartels fall through, bloody clashes among the erstwhile collaborators take place. Whenever they come together, they help one another in contract enforcement business. They corrupt law enforcement agencies, buy up politicians both in and out of power and try to subvert the rule of law. Pino Arlacchi, the celebrated authority on the Sicilian mafia, has pointed out that there is an inverse relationship between economic development and mafia activities. He has pointed out that those areas of southern Italy which have vibrant economies have lowest levels of mafia activities. In other words, backwardness and mafia activities go together. This explains, why we have mafia activities widely spread in Bihar and U.P. and not so much in Haryana, Gujarat, Karnataka, Kerala and Tamil Nadu.

In Mumbai and elsewhere the nexus between politicians and criminals has developed because the latter who operate smuggling activities, gun-running, gambling rackets, real estate grabbing and brothels need the help of the former to subvert the established law and order agencies while the politicians need large funds to carry on their political business. This reminds us of an Italian situation where 'Mafia has for years enjoyed links with local and national politicians and other sources of power.'[23] Gulio Andreotti who served as Prime Minister not once but seven times has been found to have close links with the mafia. Both are said to have been helping each other. To quote Ms Annelise Anderson: "the essential characteristic of a mafia that differentiates it from other groups engaged in violent or criminal activity is corruption or substantial influence in at least some agencies and bureaux of the legitimate government."[24] The attempt of the mafia to establish a State within the State is what makes it unique.

History underlines three conditions that encourage the emergence and growth of mafia groups: (a) an abdication (possibly combined with rejection) of legitimate government power, (b) excessive bureaucratic power and, (c) the potential of illegal markets. "These conditions may interact each providing growth opportunities to a mafia originating for another reason.'[25]

Reflecting the rise of mafia in its classic home of Sicily, the validity of (a) becomes quite apparent. During the second half of the nineteenth century, after the unification of Italy, there arose a vacuum of power in Sicily. The State was either unable or unwilling to ensure public order. Various groups came into being to exercise power and law and order maintenance functions at local levels. Estate owners hired their own private musclemen to protect their property and enforce discipline among peasants and agricultural labourers. Diego Gambetta in his book (translated into English as *The Sicilian Mafia*, Harvard University Press, 1995) shows that the mafia seldom flourishes so long as feudalism is the dominant mode of production, its heydays begin when feudalism starts collapsing and the development of capitalism is stunted or aborted. Under feudalism land is concentrated into the hands of a small number of people who also have the monopoly over the use of force. After the collapse of feudalism, the number of property owners increases, but these new property owners do not inherit the monopoly over force. The exercise of force vests absolutely in the State.

The validity of (a) has been demonstrated by recent developments in Russia, Italy and Eastern Europe. In Russia, the State seems to have vacated its legitimate space which the mafia has come to occupy. It seems to dominate in a number of areas and does not tolerate anyone crossing its path. In October, 1994; a journalist Dmitry Kholodov was blown to pieces because he had undertaken to write a series of articles exposing large-scale thefts by the officers of the Soviet forces, stationed in Germany. On March 1, 1995; Vladislav Listyev, Russia's one of the best known television journalists was shot dead. He was soon to become chief of the Russian Public Television that was to take over from the State-owned broadcasting service which reached 200 m people in the territories comprising former USSR.

He had announced his intention to suspend all advertisements till new regulations were being drawn up to ensure that the station received all that was due to it by selling airtime. This was not to the liking of the mafia that controlled access to airtime which yielded several hundred-million-dollars. These events exposed the impotence of the State to protect the lives of even prominent people. Boris Yeltsin himself had admitted this when he praised the Government of Uzbekistan which went in for summary trials and execution of six groups of mafiosi. He went to add: "The merging of the mafia with commercial structures, administrative agencies, interior-ministry bodies, city authorities—nowhere else in Russia do the authorities turn a blind eye to these things as they do in Moscow.'[26]

In Italy, during the post-Second World War period, the State seemed to have abdicated its powers to the mafia. Giulio Andreotti, seven times Prime Minister, was as good as a mafioso. In fact, a Palermo court remanded him to judicial custody pending his trial as an alleged member of the mafia. The chargesheet against him was based on the evidence of 17 witnesses, all members of the Sicilian mafia and its allied organisations on the mainland, the Neapolitan Camorra and the Calabrian Ndrangheta. "They say Mr Andreotti had acted, for at least 14 years, as the Mafia's protector in Rome. In exchange, the Mafia ensured fat electoral majorities for Mr Andreotti's political proteges in Sicily—all members, like himself, of the once-dominant Christian Democratic Party. Another Prime Minister Benito Craxi, too, was charged with corruption and links with the mafia, but he fled to Tunisia. "If organised crime in Italy has had so much clout, this was largely a result of its close ties to politics. The links between Sicilian politics and *Cosa Nostra* date back at least to the last war, when local mafiosi worked hand in hand with British and American troops occupying the island. But it was not until the late 1970s, according to Mr Arlacchi, that Cosa Nostra became the dominant partner. By the late 1980s, public-sector contracts were the Sicilian Mafia's main source of revenue—one more important than either the once vastly profitable heroin trade or racketeering.'[27]

In Eastern European countries in the post-Communist period, the State has been not only weak, but, in many cases, directionless too. The disintegration of once well-knit economy of the CMEA has brought chaos, unemployment and scarcity of a number of goods. As in the case of Russia, so in the case of these countries too, a large number of the functionaries of the CPs have been without any function or role in socio-economic life in spite of their skills and expertise and most of them have engaged themselves in organised crime in order to appropriate public resources. It was reported that a person wanting to secure speedy connection of telephone, had to pay more than $500 and a contract killing in Sofia could be had for $10,000. In Hungary everybody knew the exact price of a minister or an official to get something done.

Police and Mafia

In most of the countries of Eastern Europe, the police was poorly paid and ill-equipped to fight the new types of crimes and criminals with international connections. Most of the police families living below the poverty line easily fell victim to hush money. In Poland, a number of policemen were arrested because they used official computers to trace cars whose insurance cover had expired and passed this information to the mafia who stole these cars and released them after extorting money from their owners. Of course, the police informers were suitably rewarded by the mafia. In one Polish town, the mafia was found to be using police cars for distributing stolen whisky bottles. "In Hungary (population 10 m), 1 m., companies have been registered, many of them set up as tax dodgers. Throughout Eastern Europe, the authorities have been overwhelmed by the soaring rate of white-collar chicanery.

"Crime in the new East often has an international flavour. Many gangs in Eastern Europe are Russian, Ukrainian or the former Yugoslav republics. In the Hungarian town of Szeged, sometimes known as Mafia City, Hungarians act as middlemen for Russians selling oil to sanctions-strapped Serbia, which lies across the border to the south. Polish crooks steal cars in Germany, then sell them back home or drive them to markets farther east or south. Even poverty-stricken Albania, where private cars were banned under Communism, is a popular new destination for stolen vehicles. Gangs of ethnic Albanians, especially from Serbia's Kosovo region, are prominent in drug smuggling. Whereas five years ago drugs usually flowed through the Balkans-en-route to the West, domestic addiction is now catching on—nourishing still more crime at home.

'Everywhere, criminals seem increasingly able to make deals with leading businessmen, officials and politicians. In Bulgaria and Romania, criminals tentacles reach close to the top. In the Czech Republic and Slovakia, politicians have been less biddable, but businessmen frequently bribe bank officials to give them licences and credit.'[28]

What is being witnessed in Bihar at present seems to be a re-enactment of what happened more than a century ago in Sicily. The state in Bihar has abdicated its duty to enforce law and order and protect lives and property of people. After the sunset, there is a virtual self-imposed curfew in large parts of the State. The propertied, especially in rural areas, have formed their own *senas* (private armies) while petty peasants and agricultural labourers have found shelter with various factions of the CPI (ML).

In a number of areas the youth without access to any employment opportunities, but under great influence of consumerism has organised itself in mafia groups of various kinds and has taken to smuggling, kidnapping, looting, extortions and so on. The State is not in a position to curb its activities because in the situation of declining economy, it cannot promise anything tangible to young men and women. Abdication of the exercise of its power and functions by the State has repelled potential investors. Its inability to protect train travellers shows its impotence. Those who continue in business have to seek the protection of mafia groups and pay for it. This reminds one of what happens in Sicily where, as Gambetta has argued, mafia emerged in response to a specific situation. There was market failure and the State was too weak. It means there was no legitimate institution to enforce business contracts and property rights. To give an example, suppose somebody mortgages his land, the mortgagee may not be sure that the mortgagor actually has the right to do so (as it happened in Bihar during the 1970s when the Gandhi Maidan and the Patna Railway Junction were mortgaged to the State Co-operative Bank and huge amounts of money were taken by some racketeers). In such a situation mutual trust is lacking and without this no economy, based on market can run. This situation provides a scope for the mafia to emerge and function because it provides protection to the mortgagee. He cites what a cattle breeder of Sicily told him: "When the butcher comes to me to buy an animal, he knows that I want to cheat him. But I know, he wants to cheat me. Thus, we both need, say, Peppe (that is, a third party) to make us agree. And we both pay Peppe a percentage of the deal."[29] Peppe is nothing but the mafioso taking his cut for providing the missing element of trust.

In the above example, both the cattle-breeder and the cattle-buyer paid to the mafioso willingly because, without his help, the transaction would not have taken place. In Patna and other places, the Dularchand Yadavas perform the same function by bringing landlords and tenants of houses or the buyers and the sellers of the real estate together and guaranteeing the transaction. Reviewing Gambetta's book *The Economist*, made the following comments: "During his interrogation by the Italian magistrate, Tommaso Buscetta, a *mafioso* who turned State's evidence, argued that this is common. He told the magistrate that "around the Mafia families and the men of honour, there is an incredible number of people who, even though they are not themselves *mafiosi*, co-operate, sometimes even unconsciously, with the Mafia. With regard to the nature of these relationships, I must stress that they cannot be explained as the result of coercion. It is like courting a woman: if a relationship gets started, it is because the woman has co-operated in being chosen; she has agreed to be chosen". This is what has given the Mafia its staying-power in Italy. It has become an economic-enforcement agency similar to the State. And this means it is sometimes regarded, in the absence of anything else, as legitimate. It has turned from being a hunter, who kills his prey and moves on, into a rancher—someone who not only lives off his herd, but also "protects" it.[30]

Russian Economy and Mafia

From this, it follows that the mafia is not merely extortionist, but performs an indispensable function when the State and market forces are too weak and this happens during the transition period ranging from the disappearance of the pre-capitalist mode of production to the establishment of a dynamic capitalist mode of production. This may be illustrated by referring to what has been happening in the sovereign states that have arisen over the ashes of the Soviet Union. In the Soviet Union, there was no private property and there were no private owners of the property. After its collapse and disintegration, Russia gave its citizens right to property and the former state assets were privatised and went to anyone who was in a position to buy them. By 1995, Russia came to have 40 million private property owners. Along with this, the Communist Party and the various organs of the state like the KGB, the police and the army which were its creation; lost their monopoly over the use of force. The result was the space for the emergence and operation of the mafia. Gambetta holds that in both Russia and Sicily, "The consequence is a phenomenal increase in the fear of losing property and of being cheated and, correspondingly, in the demand for trust; trust in other people and trust in whoever has the power to enforce property rights".[31] Stephen Handelman in his first full length study on Russian mafia *Comrade Criminal* (Yale University Press, 1995); confirms Gambetta's assertion. In Moscow or St. Petersburg, even if you have money to pay, you cannot get the desired goods without the help of the mafia. He is an indispensable link joining the two sides of the transaction. It arranges all kinds of services and provides protection to business and property and guarantees the validity of transactions. As in Sicily, after the collapse of feudalism, the state was too weak to enforce law and order in Russia and there was an all-round mistrust of the state and its different organs. Till the beginning of 1995, there were no clear-cut laws to operate the rule of law. In this situation, a handful of people combined together and grabbed most of the former USSR's assets and set themselves up as "entrepreneurs". It is widely believed that seven of these control half of the Russian economy. Whether this is correct or not, they have got strong mafia-connections. It is a fact that these new tycoons forcibly grabbed the state assets during the process of transfer, which was 'a ferocious, unregulated affair in which bombs, shotguns and even toxin on teacups seem to have played as big a part as bids, offers and due-diligence searches. To this day, doing business in Moscow may mean passing through metal detectors and meeting behind bullet-proof glass. Foreign banks may operate from anonymous offices in seedy buildings lest they draw the attention of those who would offer unwelcome protection. A visitor to a tycoon's home may find him lurking in a sumptuous apartment with folded packing cases taped across the windows: the cardboard diffuses human body heat and, thus, foils the infra-red sights of potential snipers.' But it does not mean that ordinary Russians are untouched. In fact, 'ordinary Russians are frequently affected by mafias of one kind or another, who may control anything from the supply of food in the market, to the sale of video cassettes, to the production of minerals. They see the limousines sweep by, often followed by jeeps packed with bodyguards. They see the opulent *kottedzhi* go up-country retreats that outdo the mere *dachas* of the not-so rich with the exuberance of their turrets and the grandeur of their gatehouses. They read of contract killings which almost serve as an index of business activity: 28 bankers (never mind anyone else) murdered in 1994, 41 in 1995, 49 in the first eight months of 1996. ... The International Institute of Strategic Studies in London, reckons that four-fifths of Russian enterprises pay, on average, 10-20 per cent of their profits as protection money.'[32] It is said that the mafia spent huge sums of money (some estimate it at $3 m) to ensure the victory of Yeltsin or, better to say, the defeat of the Communists. The two TV channels and radio stations, controlled by it worked tirelessly to this end. Today, it is widely believed that it has got one of its trusted men as an important functionary of Russia's Security Council. The mafia arranges *propiska* (residence permit), essential for one who wants to reside in Moscow for $20,000. "With a corrupt and underpaid judiciary, anyone in business, whatever his ethnic origins, may sooner or later need the services of a *krysha*—a fixer, either in or outside officialdom, who will sort out disputes, if necessary by striking deals with other *kryshas*. Resorting to such extra-legal intermediaries is just one of the ways to survive in a society where rules count for little. Indeed, it has become almost impossible to do business honestly, as criminals increasingly invest their ill-gotten gains in legitimate operations, making offers that wise men cannot refuse. According to the Interior Ministry, criminal gangs now control 40,000 enterprises in Russia, including 500 banks.'[33]

During the first half of 1992, the murder rate in Moscow was 9.6 per 100,000 people which rose to 15.5 per 10000 people during the first half of 1993. Thus, an average Muscovite was ten times more likely to be murdered than an average Londoner. A substantial part of these murders were carried out by the mafiosi. Alexander Gurov, director of research at the ministry of security, was of the view that the real crime rate was six times higher than the above figures doled out officially.

As soon as somebody sets up a business, he is visited by the mafiosi asking for 500 m roubles. If the businessman pleads helplessness in meeting the demand for shortage of ready cash, the mafiosi then arrange a loan of, say, a billion roubles from a bank controlled by them and they take away half of this amount. Their next visit takes place when the repayment of the loan is delayed. In its issue of February 19, 1994 *The Economist* carried the following report: "An American businessmen, recently arrived in Moscow to open an office, was met at his hotel by five men with gold watches, pistols and a print-out of his firm's net worth. They demanded 7 per cent of the future earnings.

He took the first flight back to New York, where muggers are less sophisticated."

A report, prepared by the Analytical Centre for Social and Economic Policies at the instance of President Boris Yeltsin, revealed that as many as 75 per cent of private enterprises were made to pay 10-20 per cent of their earnings to various groups of mafiosi and 150 of these groups controlled around 40,000 private and state-run companies, including most of the country's 1,800 commercial banks. Protection money was paid as regularly as taxes were evaded. The result was that the mafia grabbed the money and the state exchequer was starved of funds, leading to greater and greater budgetary deficits.

The emergence and growth of the mafia was due to the peculiarities of the transition period, which we have already touched upon. Rules and regulations governing the transition were either non-existent or quite vague. Public servants were irregularly paid and their salaries were constantly falling in their real worth. They, thus, resorted to bribe-taking. There was no shortage of weapons which were being sold by the disillusioned and unpaid soldiers and ex-soldiers. In 1992, 3,923 cases and in 1993, 6,430 cases of weapons were stolen from military depots. Most of them went to the mafia. Many companies have employed their own private security men. One business establishment which had 300 employees had assigned security duty to as many as 100 of them. The collapse of the old regime with no viable replacement for it created a vacuum. The new laws and regulations remained unimplemented. The demoralised security forces left the borders inadequately guarded, creating ample scope for the mafia to indulge in drug smuggling.

When the Soviet Union disintegrated and Russia began its transition to market-economy and privatisation of the means of production, the criminal gangs were among the few who possessed large amounts of money. "They were presented with an opportunity not merely to subvert an existing structure, as the mafia did to the state in southern Italy, but to buy a state in the process of being rebuilt.'[34]

An important change witnessed during the transition period was many an old thief-in-law going out of business and its place being taken by a new one. A tussle started among the mafia gangs of different ethnic origins. Chechens gradually acquired an upper hand among them. The liquidation of the Kvantrishvili family, a Georgian clan, by the Chechens is a typical example.

In Russia, the term mafia applies to a variety of operators. At the bottom come small businessmen who sell smuggled goods. They charge high prices and are also subject to extortion by criminal gangs who take away a portion of their loot. Then come the gangsters who wear sport track suits and gold chains and move about in cars. They collect protection money, supply girls and peddle drugs and arms. Above them are big operators who may be placed between Al Capone and the robber-barons of the early days of America. They are estimated to pay 30 per cent to 50 per cent of their earnings to politicians and bureaucrats who constitute the fourth category "the State mafia". The people in the last category are no less wealthy as can be inferred from their spending. In July 1992, the then head of the Security Ministry (the successor to the KGB) went to Zurich where he was reported to have spent $300,000 on his shopping. Obviously, bribe-taking was the source of his income.

It was extremely risky to resist or protest against extortions by the mafia. In 1993, alone as many as 94 businessmen were murdered for this kind of impunity. Sometimes mafiosi donned the police uniform to stop the cars of businessmen and then to rob. Economist Pyotr Filippov who headed the Analytical Centre admitted that there was hardly any real resistance to the mafia. Consequently, his report told the president: "An entire generation is growing up for whom the situation is normal and who in such circumstances will not turn to official authorities, but to unofficial ones. These people are more likely to hire a murderer to punish a guilty or even an unpleasant partner than to go to Court for arbitration."[35]

In 1996, the government itself admitted that two-thirds of the crimes went unrecorded in Russia. According to Mr Anatoly Kulikov who was the then Interior Minister, there were 560 contract killings in 1995 and 450 during the first ten months of 1996. In the first five months of 1994, in Moscow alone, 664 incidents of crimes took place in which fire arms or explosives were used. As compared to 16 during the entire period of 1993, 118 kidnappings took place only between January and May, 1994. During the first quarter of 1994, on an average, 84 murders took place in Russia. Most of these were contract killings as a result of conflicts in the sphere of commercial and financial conflicts. He candidly stated that there was "an almost complete criminalisation" of the gold and diamond mining industries and the mafia gangs "were waging open war" for control of the energy sector.

In February, 1993, itself Boris Yeltsin had admitted the existence of organised crime which was threatening its national security and strategic interests. He appointed Pyotr Filippov, one of his advisers to prepare a report on organised crime. The report was submitted to Yeltsin in January, 1994. It termed the Russian society as one of lawlessness where every businessman whether big or small had to pay protection money. No one had any trust in the police and faith in the implementation of laws passed by parliament.

The mafia has been a very old phenomenon in Russia. During the pre-Brezhnev era, it generally operated underground and its links with official agencies were not quite visible. Michael Waller in a book has described that some of the functions of the present day mafia were performed by the KGB itself. "The KGB procured contraband for the ruling elites, laundered Communist Party funds through investments in the West, smuggled narcotics from Central Asia to Europe, trafficked in weapons, rubbed out opponents around the world and engaged in bribery, blackmail and extortion at home."[36] During the Brezhnev regime, the mafia had a suitable environment to prosper. Incompetent people were promoted to man senior positions and then KGB was handsomely bribed to look the other way while the mafia ran a black market. "The Brezhnev era's other contribution to the development of a criminal culture was to allow the return in force of a class of Russian godfathers known as *vory-v-zakone*, or "thieves-in-law". "Theirs is an old and traditional profession, which predates the Revolution," says General Gennedy Chebotaryev, number two at the interior ministry's directorate for organised crime. But it was in the Soviet gulag that the profession renewed its rank and rites. A true thief-in-law is "opposed to laws in the most fundamental way," explains the General. "He will never do an honest day's work, never serve in the army, not own anything or have a family. When arrested, he will never co-operate with the police. He will serve as a judge in disputes between criminals and is responsible after the pooled money of the criminal group he guides."[37]

He estimated that there were 289 thieves-in-law operating in Russia. At any point of time, half of them were in jail but this seldom made any difference to their gangs' activities. There was a division of labour among them. Their operations extended to the USA too. At one stage, the Russian Government was agreeable to the FBI stationing two of its agents in Moscow.

The Russian mafia has extended its operations to other parts of the world too. In particular, it has found a very fertile ground in the USA. The US Drug Enforcement Administration, after a three-year investigation, found during early 1997, a trafficking network that shipped cocaine from Ecuador to St. Petersburg, packed in cargoes of iced shrimps and then re-exported it to the USA. Those who ran this network met regularly in the backroom of a pink-neon strip club known as Porky's near the Miami International Airport. They dealt also in Russian helicopters, smuggling of cigarettes, liquors and counterfeit currencies, besides arranging prostitutes for Russian gangsters. Thus, the Russian mafiosi or "Redfellas" as the police call them have also set up their headquarters in Miami where the Jamaican, Colombian and Italian mafiosi have their establishments for quite some time. It is said that the Russian mafiosi have entered into working arrangements with their counterparts from other countries already operating from Florida. According to a report in *The Economist* (March 15, 1997): "When the FBI opened an office in Moscow three years ago, the FBI's director, Louis Freech, estimated that there were 5,600 organised crime groups, with 100,000 active members, in the former Soviet Union. By official estimates, some 300 Soviet gangs had moved abroad and at least 24 of them had turned up in various American cities. Kenneth Rijock, a Miami-based financial crimes consultant, has been monitoring Russian organised crime for some time. "They've got more money than God," Mr Rijock said, "and they are more ruthless than the 1920s Prohibition gangsters."

In addition to drug-trafficking, brothel-running and extortion, the Russian mafiosi in the USA are supposed to be involved in clandestine arms sales, money-laundering and complex bank and financial frauds. Though they initially started their work in New York in collaboration with their counterparts from other countries, they later moved to Miami not only for climatic reasons but also for its strategic location via-a-vis Latin America. In Sunny Isles a "Little Moscow" has emerged.

In Sicily, the armed retainers of feudal lords' private armies became the mafiosi and in Russia the demobilised armymen, policemen and KGB people besides the former functionaries of the CPSU apparatus at various levels turned themselves into the mafiosi. They had lost their moorings after the collapse of the old regime. Since they were the only people with skill and expertise who could provide trust and protection during the period of transition when there sprang up a market for them. It is, this is both Sicily and Russia that earns the goodwill of people for mafia and explains its durability. It does not, however, mean that there are no other activities of the mafia. In fact, the mafia all over the world engages itself in drug-trafficking, extortions, gun-running, forgery and various other kinds of crimes.

Growth of Mafia and Bureaucracy

Excessive hold by bureaucracy also contributes to

the growth of mafia. It is quite clearly demonstrated by the happenings in the sovereign states which have emerged out of the ashes of the Soviet Union. It is obvious from their experiences that excessive bureaucratic power and its exercise on an unclear basis and without any check, provide a fertile ground for corruption and extortions. These, phenomena are obtained in some degree or the other in various parts of the world, but 'It takes on the character of a mafia when access to bureaucratic decisions is used to exclude competitors through violence or threats of violence and, thus, to control entry or access to contracts. At this point, the efficiency benefits sometimes attributed to bribing government officials to do faster or better what they ought to do anyway collapse bureaucratic corruption in collusion with criminal gang violence—'the mafia'—becomes means to monopolising industries, awarding inflated contracts and operating outside public safety standards. The activity may be extraordinarily persistent, defying repeated investigation and prosecution.'[38] It is not only in India but also throughout the world where the mafia operates, it gets a big slice of the government and other public sector contracts. We have seen it happening in Bihar and have been told by engineers that they dare not go against the wishes of mafia groups which have links with influential politicians. The fear is two-fold—physical as well as political victimisation through inconvenient postings and transfers. It was also pointed out that a former don-cum-contractor had himself become a minister! The pattern is the same in the original land of the mafia: 'Mafia-linked business... have a huge advantage over their competitors. Only those companies willing to bow to gangsters' conditions are allowed in on the deals. Besides establishing the price, the mafia imposes its own sub-contractors, its own "security men" and its own candidates for employment. To ensure compliance, it resorts to arson, dynamite attacks or even murder.'[39]

The opportunities to operate in illegal markets give rise to new or strengthen existing mafia groups. In the USA, prohibition gave birth to and strengthened mafia groups. In the present-day Haryana too the same thing has been happening. An illegal market for alcohol was created then in the USA and is flourishing now in Haryana. Operation in illegal markets generate huge amounts of cash with which the police, bureaucracy and politicians are bribed.

It has been established that by the early 1980s, the various Sicilian mafia groups or families were supplying around 80 per cent of the total heroin demand of the New York market, 'using morphine base from Asia treated in clandestine laboratories in and around Palermo. Pino Arlacchi, an authority on the Mafia, reckons, on the basis of documents produced in subsequent trails, that in the single year of 1982, four Palermo families between them sold around $750m worth of heroin,' to quote *The Economist* (April 24, 1993). Another important activity of the mafia is running Italy's pirated-goods industry which is supposed to be next only to that of Thailand in terms of total output. Early 1996, the Centro Studi sul Falso at the University of Salerno estimated that the counterfeit business produces 1.3 trillion—1.6 trillion lire ($800 m—$1 billion) of goods annually. Some put the real figure much higher and claim that 44 per cent of the total fake goods produced in the European Union come from mafia-controlled enterprises in Italy.

It is a well-known tactic, tried and tested for more than a century, that the mafia must terrorise and demoralise law-enforcement agencies. When in May, 1992 it eliminated Sicily's the most celebrated mafia-fighter, Magistrate Giovanni Falcone, just outside Palermo, with a bomb, it sent shock waves. The mafia is very protective of its loyal members. It sees to it that even those who are arrested and put behind the bars get as much comforts as possible. It procures and produces bogus medical certificates to get them transferred to private clinics, hospitals or their own homes. In case a doctor refuses to oblige, it does not have any hesitation in eliminating him just like Paolo Giacone in 1985.

It is not very easy to fight out the mafia, especially in prevailing conditions in our country. In a situation where the State has abdicated its power and the courts are so overburdened that justice has not only become expensive but very difficult to get without long delays. In places like Patna, people have no alternative but to go to a Dularchand Yadav to get their illegally occupied houses and land vacated. Such Dularchand Yadavs have sprung up in various parts of the country, discharging both executive and judicial functions and sometimes legislating too.

When one does not get correct and timely decisions from bureaucrats, one has to seek the help of the mafia. In fact, our experience shows that in a state like Bihar nothing moves without the help of the mafia. Even a small thing like getting marks sheets from university offices or school examination board, the mafia connection is a must. Getting votes through booth-capturing and mass stamping of ballot papers is a mafia speciality and no political party can and does, in practice, keep it at a distance. The mafia organises copying at examinations and ensures seats in medical and engineering colleges in Bihar and through Bihar government quotas outside the state. It organises kidnapping and stealing of cars through its own men, then the dons get the kidnapped people and stolen vehicles released and illegally occupied houses and lands vacated after they are approached and financially propitiated. They get themselves credit for helping the troubled and harassed people. Recently, the car of a lady professor of philosophy of the Magadh University was snatched away during broad daylight at gunpoint. It was released as a result of the intervention of the don who had to be paid. At the car-release "ceremony", the don got himself photographed with the professor in order to make a big propaganda about his helpfulness. The don who was an MLA at that time has now become a minister in the Rabri Devi government and is given charge of an important economic department.

The Economist has rightly suggested: "Combating this kind of mafia activity first means preventing collusion between mafiosi and politicians. It also means reducing the opportunities for organised crime to provide public services. If the State is weak and official property rights are ill-defined (as they are, say, in Russia), mafia groups are arguably filling a demand for stability and effective rule of law. Controlling their influence requires more effective government."[40]

This is easier said than done. The enormity of the task is illustrated by the situation in Cambodia where, whatever may be the facade, the mafia-led by Theng Bunma, a 56-year-old ethnic Chinese enjoys the greatest leverage. His phenomenal rise from a *khalasi* (driver's assistant) on a rural bus line to the richest businessman of the country shows profitability of forming and successfully operating a mafia group. Caming from the eastern Cambodian province of Kompong Cham, he now heads the giant Thai Boon Romg Company and the Cambodian Chamber of Commerce and is a respectable man whose company is sought by not only the high and mighty in the country but foreign missions because he alone can effectively guarantee safety and security and help establish business links. His connections cut across political and ideological differences. Politicians of all hues are beholden to him for financial assistance and he does not discriminate on the basis of politics and ideology. The unsettled conditions in Indo-China provided him excellent opportunities to further his business interests because there was hardly any State power to check his activities. "It was a tumultuous time to be trading with Vietnam, where the south had just fallen to the Communists. *The Voice of Khmer Youth* report said that Burma used boats to smuggle everything from palm oil to tobacco into the country, returning with Vietnamese girls and well-off Sino-Vietnamese refugees.'[41] He is a man of his words, apparently very dignified, homely and spartan in his habits.

His political clout is obvious from the following facts. He holds a Cambodian diplomatic passport and is special adviser to the National Assembly President, Chea Sim. "He's a benefactor of both prime ministers: He paid $1.8 million in August 1993 for Ranariddh's Kingair-200 plane and gave Second Prime Minister Hun Sen the Mercedes limousine that ferries him to official functions. He even helped underwrite the 1994 state budget with interest-free loans of several million dollars—effectively funding the dry-season offensive against the Khmer Rouge'.[42] He has given gifts to the Cambodian government of the world's two largest Russian-made Mi-26 helicopters, limousines and an aircraft.

In Cambodia, the mafia is said to have an unrestrained access to government planes, helicopters, army transportation facilities, navy boats and even soldiers to smuggle out heroin and 'some of the same military units involved in drug-trafficking have been implicated in political violence, pointing to dangerously close links between crime syndicates and political figures.'[43]

Three things in Cambodia help the mafia because they allow it unrestrained operations. They are: (a) absence of an effective legal system, (b) paucity of resources to combat mafia activities even if the state has the will to do so, and—(c) official corruption. The result is that Cambodia has been reduced, in reality, to a mafia state where there is 'a group of businessmen who consider themselves above the law, who have in-filtrated all spheres, all aspects of government, the judiciary, the parliament.'[44]

The Cambodian mafia's association is solicited by its international counterparts because of the ease with which money can be laundered in Pnom Penh. As recently as 1995, a confidential report to Cambodian Interior Ministry stated that as many as 19 out of 29 banks located in the capital were suspected to be engaged in the business of cleaning tainted cash. Cash in dirty American dollars could be easily unloaded at restaurants, casinos, night clubs and such other places owned and controlled by the mafia. And nobody has the guts to raise a finger for fear of being physically eliminated. The mafia does not want peace and stability to return to Cambodia because a strong state and the rule of law are perceived to be inimical to its interests.

In Thailand, the mafia is very much entrenched. In 1991, there were seven *jao pho* or big brothers who controlled most of the organised crime in the country. They derived enormous incomes from gambling, prostitution, heroin and logging. An important feature of the mafia in Thailand is its close links with the police. In fact, a number of policemen are a part of it and they not only protect it, but themselves participate in its activities. A typical example was Chalor Kerdted, called "uncle" in the mafia world. He was sacked in September 1994 as the lieutenant-general of the police for his involvement in the biggest scandal: the theft of the jewellery worth $20 million from the Saudi royal family in 1989. Besides him, there were a dozen or so top policemen charged with stealing or protecting those engaged in stealing. Chalor had masterminded the abduction and murder of the wife of a key witness in July 1994. In 1994 itself, a gang of police officers were nabbed for robbing and murdering Taiwanese businessmen. Besides, Somchai Khumpluen alias Kamnam Poh, believed to be the most powerful *chao por* or "godfather" too was arrested. His arrest evoked loud protests from 16 members of parliament.

Before we end this chapter, a few changes in the mafia, not only in Sicily, but all over the world need to be noted. To begin with, as we have already noted, the culture and activities of the mafia have undergone a big change. It is no longer confined to a rural milieu but has adapted itself to urban environment and taken to modern business activities. It runs big corporations and cartels of international dimensions. It has adopted its old skills like kidnapping, extortion, terrorising, etc. to new needs of capital accumulation and profit-maximisation. Before the Second World War, the mafia operating in rural areas had no need of transforming and taking to capitalist farming. It had no incentive or urge to change its economic activities and way of life. "The crucial change in the mafia in the years after 1945 was the gradual but definite detachment of mafia power from its society of origin. The old mechanism of social integration by the mafia gradually snapped during the 1950s and 1960s. In the 1970s we saw a spectacular escalation of the new entrepreneurial mafia in all the principal sectors of economic development."[45]

Unlike the traditional mafiosi who did not believe in

showing off their wealth through ostentatious living, their present-day counterparts indulge in the display of their wealth and newly-acquired status through conspicuous consumption and luxurious living because they think, they can get respectability in the society through them. A look at the Mumbai mafiosi or the animal husbandry or the Dhanbad mafiosi of Bihar, shows they live in mansions, travel in luxury cars, stay in posh hotels, fly by air or travel in the AC coach, get film actresses to entertain them and they do not desist from displaying their wealth. Obviously, they have given up their traditional culture because they have themselves undergone a metamorphosis and now they have to cater to and live in a much wider society than during the earlier times. Their ideology, outlook, values, attitude and life-style have changed as a result of their interaction with market forces. They have to take into account political situation and changes not only in their own countries but in others too. For example, a Mumbai mafioso has to keep an eye on the situation in the Gulf countries, Pakistan, Nepal, Singapore, Thailand, Burma, Afghanistan and elsewhere for their personal safty as well as smooth running of their business activities.

The present-day mafioso has a different kind of relations with his peers as well as the State apparatus and judicial system. He is in a state of continuous conflict with his peers and the judiciary because the former are his competitors while the latter tries to restrain his illegal activities. So far as the State apparatus is concerned, he tries to worm his way into it through political connections in order to influence it to his advantage. He develops friendship with important political leaders, funds the activities of political parties and pliable politicians and, at times, himself enters and occupies important positions in political parties. How the Italian mafia came to "conquer" the Christian Democratic Party[46] is quite instructive and may help us to understand the growing influence of the mafia on certain political parties in India.

REFERENCES

1. By Pitre in 1889, quoted in Henner Hess, *Mafia and Mafiosi: The Structure of Power*, Hants, 1973, p. 1.
2. *Ibid.*
3. *Ibid.*, p. 2.
4. E.J. Hobsbawm, *Primitive Rebels*, Manchester, 1959, p. 32.
5. *Ibid.*, p. 43.
6. *Ibid.*, p. 33.
7. Charles Tilly's "Foreword" to Anton Blok, *The Mafia of a Sicilian Village, 1860-1960: A Study of Violent Peasant Entrepreneurs*, New York, 1974, p. XIV.
8. Pino Arlachhi, *Mafia Business: The Mafia Ethic and the Spirit of Capitalism*, London, 1986, p. 83.
9. *Ibid.*, p. 84.
10. *Ibid.*, p. 87.
11. Charles Tilly's "Foreword", Anton Blok, *op. cit.*, p. XX.
12. Lewis Yablonsky, *The Violent Gang*, New York, 1962, pp. 1-2.
13. Anton Blok, *op. cit.*, p. 6.
14. *Ibid.*, p. 7.
15. *The Economist*, April 24, 1993.
16. Quoted in Henner Hess, *op. cit.*, p. 10.
17. Quoted in *Ibid.*
18. *Ibid.*, p. 46.
19. *The Economist*, April 24, 1993.
20. *Ibid.*, February 10, 1996.
21. *Ibid.*
22. *Ibid.*
23. *Ibid.*, April 24, 1993.
24. Annelise Anderson's paper "Organised crime, mafia and governments" in Gianluca Fiorentini and Sam Peltzman (ed.), *The economics of organised crime*, Cambridge, 1995, p. 35.
25. *Ibid.*
26. *The Economist*, March 11, 1995.
27. *Ibid.*
28. *Ibid.*
29. Quoted in *Ibid.*, July 8, 1995.
30. *Ibid.*
31. Quoted in *Ibid.*
32. *Ibid.*, July 12, 1997.

33. *Ibid.*
34. *Ibid.*, July 9, 1994.
35. Quoted in *Ibid.*, February 19, 1994.
36. Quoted in *Ibid.*, July 9, 1994.
37. *Ibid.*
38. Gianluca Fiorentini and Sam Peltzman (ed.) *op. cit.*, p. 37.
39. *The Economist*, April 24, 1993.
40. *Ibid.*, February 10, 1996.
41. Quoted in *Far Eastern Economic Review*, November 23, 1995.
42. *Ibid.*
43. *Ibid.*
44. *Ibid.*
45. Pino Arlacchi, *Mafia, peasants and great estates: society in traditional Calabria*, Cambridge. 1983, p. 205.
46. Michele Pantaleone, *The Mafia and Politics*, London, 1966, pp. 195-225.

11

Scams or the Deadly Nexus

The nexus among politicians, bureaucrats, businessmen and criminals is not only very powerful but quite deadly. Most of the time it is almost invincible. This can wreak havoc. Its power has been demonstrated quite convincingly in Italy, the USA, Russia, Japan and Pakistan, to name just a few countries. In India this nexus, as we have already mentioned, became visible soon after the end of the Nehru era and since then, it has been going from strength to strength. Its existence and power has been acknowledged even in official documents and by official institutions like the Election Commission. In quite a number of cases, the roles of a politician, a businessman, a criminal or mafiosi get merged in one and is represented by one individual. The late Haji Mastan was one such person in whom the three roles got fused in his later days of life. He had started taking a keen interest in the affairs of his religious community. Arun Gawli with his Akhil Bhartiya Sena (after his break with the Shiv Sena) is the latest example.

The Vohra Committee Report

The Vohra Committee in the very first meeting was told that the Government had established the Committee after seeing the reports of intelligence and investigation agencies on the activities/linkages of the Dawood Ibrahim gang, consequent to the bomb blasts in Bombay in March, 1993. From these various reports, it was apparent that the activities of Memon Brothers and Dawood Ibrahim had progressed over the years, leading to the establishment of a powerful network. This could not have happened without these elements having been protected by the functionaries of the concerned Government departments, specially Customs, Income-tax, police and others. It was, therefore, necessary to identify the linkages and to also determine how such information could be timely colleted and acted upon in future.'[1]

It turned out that the government lacked full information on this nexus. The secretary of R&AW emphasised: "The creation of a nodal agency to collect information regarding the activities of mafia organisation is very essential. All the existing information/data available with R&AW, IB and CBI, could be made available to this nodal agency."[2]

The Director of CBI explained the genesis of the nexus: "An organised crime syndicate/mafia generally commences its activities by indulging in petty crime at the local level, mostly relating to illicit distillation, gambling, organised 'satta' and prostitution in the larger towns. In port towns, their activities involve smuggling and sale of imported goods and progressively graduate to narcotics and drug-trafficking. In the bigger cities, the main source of income relates to real estate-forcibly occupying lands and buildings, procuring such properties at cheap rates by forcing out the existing occupants and tenants, etc. Over time, the money power, thus acquired is used for building up contacts with bureaucrats and politicians and expansion of activities with impunity. The money power is used to develop a network of muscle-power which is also used by the politicians during elections.

"All over India syndicates have become a law unto themselves. Even in the smaller towns and rural areas, muscle-men have become the order of the day. Hired assassins have become a part of these organisations. The nexus between the criminal gangs, police, bureaucracy and politicians has come out clearly in various parts of the country. The existing criminal justice system, which was essentially designed to deal with individual offences and crimes, is unable to deal with the activities of the mafia; the provisions of law in regard to economic offences are weak; there are insurmountable legal difficulties in attaching confiscation of the property acquired through mafia activities.'[3]

He illustrated his contention with the example of Iqbal Mirchi of Bombay who was, till the 1980s, just a small vendor of smuggled liquors and cigarettes, but during 1989-93, he acquired real estate worth crores of rupees, opened multiple bank accounts and established a network of smuggling, paying lakhs of rupees to his agents. Either he was ignored or patronised by the concerned enforcement agency, facilitating his flowering into a full-fledged mafia don. At present, there are numerous Mirchis all over the country. If any one of these dons is investigated, the entire patronage enjoyed by him and his linkages will come to light.

The main mode of communications and contacts of the mafia both inside and outside the country is through telephone. With cellular telephones, e-mail, fax and so many other things coming into existence, the communication is not only faster but difficult to be kept track by intelligence agencies.

The Director of Intelligence Bureau was more candid in what he told the Vohra Committee: "There has been a rapid spread and growth of criminal gangs, armed senas, drug mafias, smuggling gangs, drug-peddlers and economic lobbies in the country which have, over the years, developed an extensive network of contacts with the bureaucrats/ Government functionaries at the local levels, politicians, media persons and strategically located individuals in the non-State sector. Some of these syndicates also have international linkages, including the foreign intelligence agencies.'[4] Then he went on to give the following concrete examples: '(i) In certain States, like Bihar, Haryana and UP, these gangs enjoy the patronage of local level politicians, cutting across party lines and the protection of Government functionaries. Some political leaders become the leaders of these gangs and armed senas and, over the years, get themselves elected to local bodies, State Assemblies and the Parliament. Resultantly, such elements have acquired considerable political clout seriously jeopardising the smooth functioning of the administration and the safety of life and property of the commonman, causing a sense of despair and alienation among the people.

(ii) "The big smuggling syndicates, having international linkages, have spread into and infected the various economic and financial activities, including hawala transactions, circulation of black money and operations of a vicious parallel economy causing serious damage to the economic fibre of the country. These syndicates have acquired substantial financial and muscle power and social respectability and have successfully corrupted the Government machinery at all levels and yield enough influence to make the task of investigating and prosecuting agencies extremely difficult; even the members of the judicial system have not escaped the embrace of the mafia.

(iii) "Certain elements of the mafia have shifted to narcotics, drugs and weapon smuggling and established narco-terrorism networks, especially in the States of J&K, Punjab, Gujarat and Maharashtra. The cost of contesting elections has thrown the politician into the lap of these elements and led to a grave compromise by officials of the preventive/detective systems. The virus has spread to almost all the centres in the country; the coastal and the border States have been particularly affected.

(iv) "The Bombay bomb blast case and the communal riots in Surat and Ahmedabad have demonstrated how the Indian underworld has been exploited by the Pakistan ISI and the latter's network in UAE to cause sabotage, subversion and communal tension in various parts of the country. The investigations into the Bombay bomb blast cases have revealed extensive linkages of the underworld in the various governmental agencies, political circles, business sector and the film world".[5]

A Parallel Government of Mafia

He also emphasised that the mafia was running a parallel government in the country and constitutional state apparatus was losing its relevance or becoming impotent. The Vohra Committee noted that the mafia had enormous muscle power and financial resources which were continuously increasing because of the inflow, resulting from its criminal activities. It shared a significant portion of its financial revenue with bureaucracy and politicians who protected them and with businessmen and foreign currency dealers who laundered their black incomes. Some of mafia dons, like their counterparts in Italy (about whose metamorphosis, we have already said something in the preceding chapter) and elsewhere, have started their own business outfits which are formed strictly in accordance with the existing company law and which seem to operate according to various provisions of law. For example, East-West Airlines and East-West TV are supposed to be owned and controlled by Dawood Ibrahim. Similarly, Haji Mastan owned a number of business establishments in Mumbai and elsewhere. One of his buildings was once rented out to the income-tax department! In fact, these legal outfits are used for washing the dirty money just as agricultural farms on the outskirts of cities and towns are used to. These mafia dons render valuable help to politicians by bringing back and laundering their kickbacks collected in foreign currency outside the country. The Jain-Hawala case shows the mechanism quite clearly, notwithstanding, the fact that it is just the tip of an iceberg. But, before we come to it, let us have a look into the mechanism of laundering black money and growing difficulties in catching the launderers because of the revolution in the sphere of information technology and also its implications for country's economy. Quite often politicians are presented with huge amounts of money at their public meetings, rallies and *rath yatras*. In fact, this is a convenient device to convert their black money into white. The mafiosi play a significant role in the organisation of this *nautanki* (drama).

Money Laundering: A Big Business

What is money laundering or the infernal washing machine? In short it is 'disguising the origin of criminals' cash and then transforming it into apparently legitimate investments'.[6] This has always been a big business carried on a large scale. How big it is cannot be said with any kind of certainty as there is no agreement on the size of black or underground economy in any country. "To prove that money laundering is significant for the macro economy, it is necessary to show that it involves large sums relative to overall economic activity. Attempts by macro economists—mainly in the 1980s—to measure the underground economy had actually been measuring money laundering (although this was not specifically stated) because they looked at the displacements in time series for currency demand associated with, for example, higher taxes and, thus, tax evasion. Another approach to estimation, used by the law-enforcement community rather than by economists, was to build up estimates by crime category (a "micro economic" approach), based on street knowledge; sampling and detailed medical, social and financial/tax records. The result of these efforts is a very wide range of estimates of the size of underground economies, as a percentage of GDP—for example, for Australia, 4-12 per cent; Germany 2-11 per cent; Italy 10-33 per cent; Japan 4-15 per cent; the United Kingdom 1-15 per cent and the United States 4-33 per cent.

"The large variations in estimates have led to reliance on "consensus" numbers. For example, on October 18, 1994, the *Financial Times* reported that, according to recent estimates by UK and US officials, the amount of money laundered annually in the financial system worldwide was roughly $500 billion—some 2 per cent of global GDP. The basis of this estimate was not given; it may have been derived from an informal updating and generalization of FATF micro-based estimates".[7]

Peter J. Quirk who works for the IMF in his IMF Working Paper 96/66 "Macro economic Implications of Money Laundering", based his analysis on cross-sectional data from 19 industrial countries and the crime data and data on labour participation as proxies for non-criminal informal markets, besides the tax evasion variables. He reached a number of significant conclusions. For example, he pointed out that crime had a major role in the extent of money laundering. According to him 'a 10 per cent increase in crime is associated with a 10 per cent *reduction* in currency demand and a 6 per cent *reduction* in overall demand. Secondly, "the relationship between crime and currency demand changed direction between the early 1980s and early 1990s. An upswing in crime once led to increased demand for currency; now increases in crime lead to decreases in currency demand. In other words, money laundering methods have changed, moving away from the banking system and cash and towards parallel financial markets, sophisticated non-monetary instruments (such as derivatives) and possibly barter (such as an exchange of boats and guns for drugs). If money laundering has moved to the parallel market—that is, debits and credits booked by organized criminal quasi-banks, say, over the Internet—there could be important implications for anti-laundering efforts, which have typically focussed on criminal activity at the point at which the proceeds enter the above ground economy".[8]

There is no agreement on the extent of the size of the black economy in India as compared to the white economy among the experts, though some put it at 50 per cent. So far as money laundering is concerned, it concerns only the black-marketeers, smugglers, receivers of big kickbacks, fat bribe-takers and so on. It does not concern petty bribe takers, small time black-merketeers and so on because they find not much difficulty in converting their ill-gotten incomes and wealth in white ones. There are perfectly legal routes like showing them as agricultural incomes, the devices like Voluntary Disclosure Schemes and special bearer bonds provided by the government from time to time and going in for *benami* asset-holding, *Hawala* transactions and all kinds of trust formations. Internationally, smurfing, misinvoicing, barter, parallel credit transactions, interbank wire transfers and derivatives are the common ways of washing the dirty money. What do they mean?

"*Smurfing* involves the use of multiple cash deposits, each smaller than the minimum cash reporting requirement.

"*Misinvoicing* of exports and falsification of import letters of credit and customs declarations can conceal cross-border transfers of, say, the proceeds of drug trafficking.

"*Barter*: stolen property (e.g., antiques or automobiles) can be exchanged, across national borders or domestically, for illegal substances.

"*Parallel credit transactions* can be used to avoid the formal economy, except for the final use made of the net proceeds of illegal activity to purchase legally marked goods or services.

"*Interbank wire transfers* may not be subject to reporting or money laundering; bribery of bank officials can, thus, make it easier to conceal large illegal transfers between accounts.

"*Derivatives* that replicate insider trading opportunities (e.g., a synthetic version of a company stock subject to merger or takeover) can be used to avoid detection of an unusual change in a listed stock price".[9]

Continuing revolutionary changes in the sphere of information technology are likely to give great advantages and relief to money launderers while creating enormous difficulties for those who are engaged in its detection. Physically moving huge amounts of cash and wads of banknotes has always caused headache to money launderers. They face grave risks of interception and detection by legally constituted authority and at the same time, from pirates and other kinds of robbers ready to loot them. These difficulties are removed by electronic money and global banking. Laundering and transferring money is much quicker and safer. As a result, both law enforcement authorities as well as pirates and robbers are at a loss. Their old ways of working have become obsolete.

There are three forms in which electronic money systems operate. "There are stored-value cards, which allow customers to load money onto a microchip-bearing piece of plastic. This can be carried around like a credit card. There are computer-based systems, for example, those involving payments over the Internet. And there is talk of hybrid systems, which allow smart cards and network-based payments to work together."[10]

This problem of electronic money has been recently considered by the officials from the Group of Ten (G-10) countries comprising the USA, France, Germany, Japan, the UK, Canada, Switzerland, Sweden, the Netherlands and Belgium. They have recommended that while the development of electronics must be closely watched, there is no need immediately to formulate rules to govern those who can produce electronic money. At the same time they do accept that the growth and proliferation of electronic money does pose grave dangers as it may become a means of defrauding consumers, of undesirable extensions of credit, of invading privacy and so on. If the issuers of such money are insolvent, acceptors will be saddled with worthless assets. They hold, however, that it is not right to stop completely the growth of electronic money because it has great potential of reducing the costs of business transactions 90 per cent of which are at present conducted with cheques. It has been estimated that the business cost of going into a bank and using a teller is between $1.26 and $4.40 per transaction. This cost goes down to 54 cents if a telephone is used, drops to 10 cents when a credit card is employed and to just one cent when an electronic device like the Internet is made use of.

The Economist (July 26, 1997) has made a rough calculation of the total amount of dirty money being generated every year in the world: "Annual turnover from the global trade in illicit drugs alone has reached $400 billion, according to a recent United Nations report. Add to this, the proceeds from financial fraud, prostitution and other crimes and the amount flowing into criminals' pockets each year (GCP, some call it, or "gross criminal product") is even bigger. An IMF working paper published in 1996, put the figure at perhaps $ 500 billion. Most of this is probably laundered, putting the annual amount of dirty money flowing through the world economy at several hundred-billion-dollars.

"The stock of crooked cash already invested in financial and other assets must be far larger than that. Indeed, some experts think that it is now so big that it could pose a threat to national economies and even to the stability of the international financial system. And they worry that international efforts to combat the problem are being undermined by a new generation of professional laundrymen and the rise of new on-shore and off-shore laundromats."

Mafia in Japan

In 1992, the Japanese government woke up to the problem of money laundering by the mafia. It brought into existence a law authorising district authorities to identify and declare those persons as shady characters who used to hang out together as *boryoku-dan* (violence groups). Certain identifying features were spelled out. They included their threatening behaviour, past criminal records and membership of a hierarchical organisation. What intrigued outsiders was that once such people were identified and registered, they were allowed to go on doing their individual business provided they did not break the law.

"Being a *yakuza* (gangster) is a legitimate profession in Japan. The gangs have their headquarters with their names on polished brass plates. Like other enterprises, they advertise for recruits and go about their business openly. Between them, the gangs now boast some 90,000 members—with the three biggest syndicates (Yamaguchi-gumi, Inagawakai and Sumiyoshi-rengo-kai) accounting for half the membership. Their main source of revenue is from trafficking in stimulants, especially crystal methamphetamine (known as ice). American narcotics agents reckon that 90 per cent of the ice on the streets of Hawaii is smuggled-in by the Japanese gangsters. As a business, organised crime in Japan is thought to make around ¥1.5 trillion ($11 billion) a year. And that excludes the gangs' new interests in property development and golf clubs."[11]

The interest of the gangs in property was aroused in 1980s by the rising of land prices. Anyone having a piece of land needed by them to enlarge the vacant plot in their possession was made to part with it. They developed the area and built a big office block (In India we have seen more or less the same goal being achieved but through a different route. In Mumbai and elsewhere, communal/ casteist and other riots are engineered by the mafia to get the existing huts razed to the ground and make the inhabitants flee so that large housing/office complexes are built to earn huge profits.)

The new law is the result of the inability of the Japanese police and other law enforcement agencies to check the activities of the mafia. They have failed to prevent it from laundering its illicit earnings by investing in property and other legitimate businesses. It has not succeeded in stopping it from collecting protection money or force businessmen to deal with suppliers affiliated to it. "A profitable new sideline is collecting damages on behalf of motorists involved in traffic accidents. Often the motorists are the gangsters themselves and the incidents are not so accidental. The gangsters stop just short of breaking the law on blackmail or coercion by using insinuation rather than violence to get results".[12]

The *yakuza*, with their tattooed bodies and strict rituals, have their origins in the remote past and many a romantic myth is associated with them. They were supposed to have valiantly defended local interests and helped the poor and needy, i.e., they had some sort of a Robin Hood-type role. But now they are pure and simple mafiosi. There are inter-mafiosi tussles, leading to violence, for supremacy. The Yamaguchi-gumi mafia with around 30,000 members has spread-out from its provincial base in Kobe and the neighbouring areas of the commercial city of Osaka. Its attempt to penetrate into the Tokyo region brought it into conflict with the Sumiyoshi-rengo-kai mafia.

The mafia in Japan has close links with business, politics and bureaucracy and this nexus is quite powerful. The new law was aimed at driving most of the mafiosi into business after giving up illegal activities. As soon as the law came into effect, Yamaguchigumi ordered 117 of its affiliated gangs to register as boards and local bosses were ordered to get themselves "elected" as heads with their competented lieutenants as directors and each board was to have a capital ¥ 10 m. It was reported that the new law made the mafiosi to put up new signboards on their office buildings. One mafia group tried to convert itself into a co-operative, but the government did not allow its application. A number of gangs converted themselves into political organisations with rightist leanings. One gang metamorphosed itself into a religious order and the don became the spiritual head. "Judging from the wealth pouring into many Japanese temples, organised religion could well be more profitable than even organised crime."[13]

Australia's Financial Intelligence organisation (AUSTRAC) in its report published in 1995 said that every year that between $740 m and $3.3 billion was washed through Australia. According to a report by Bangkok's Chulalongkorn University, every year $28.5 billion is washed through Thailand and it comes to 15 per cent of the country's GDP. Other high-priority laundering centres are Aruba, Canada, Cayman Islands, Colombia, Cyprus, Germany, Hong Kong, Italy, Mexico, Netherlands, Netherlands Antilles, Nigeria, Panama, Russia, Singapore, Switzerland, Thailand, Turkey, Britain, the USA and Venezuela. Switzerland no longer remains the safest heaven for dirty money. Washing money which was for a long time a Swiss speciality was made a crime in 1990 and Swiss Federal Banking Commission in 1992, came-out with some guidelines for bankers in order to identify dirty money on the move when they see it. A banker should immediately entertain suspicion if a dormant account suddenly becomes active; cash is withdrawn immediately after it is deposited; dealings outside the known pattern; transactions without recognisable economic motive and a customer's refusal to provide information, or provision of false information. Bankers were told to check with care if somebody wanted to open account of more than Sfr 100,000-worth ($67,800) of cash or precious metals. Subsequent large transactions were made subject to mandatory scrutiny. Concerned bankmen were asked to question people, coming with suitcases stuffed with money to be changed into other currencies. These legal steps were taken when the scandal relating to two Lebanese brothers, Jean and Barkev Magharian who were involved in some shady business came to light and Credit Suisse took no action. In 1990, they were sent to jail for laundering millions of drug-dollars. With the growing risks involved in laundering dirty money, washing charges have also gone-up from 6 per cent in the early 1980s to 25-28 per cent at present.

Banking secrecy guaranteed by law in a number of countries comes into the way of attacking money laundering. In fact, a number of countries have been trying to attract ill-gotten money by providing the facility of safe-keeping and secrecy. For long, Singapore has been an important heaven for such money in South-east Asia, but, now, Thailand and Malaysia have also entered this area of activity. In March 1993, Thailand granted offshore banking licences to 47 Thai and foreign banks. In 1990, Malaysia declared the island of Lebuan, off the coast of Borneo as an offshore banking centre.

Money laundering has serious economic consequences. Since the money demand shifts from one country to another, it has harmful consequences for interest and exchange rate. They become more volatile. There are income distribution effects too. Since criminal activity shifts income from people with a high propensity to save those having low propensity to save, there is an adverse impact on economic growth. It has been found in the USA that money accruing as a result of tax evasion, fraud, embezzlement and insider trading goes into risky and undesirable but high profit-yielding investments. These criminal activities along with the possibility of money laundering lure people engaged in legal activities towards them and, thus, undermine the efficacy of the legal system, confidence in markets and in the efficiency-signalling role of profits. "Accumulated balances of laundered assets are likely to be larger than annual flows, increasing the potential for destabilizing, the economically efficient movements, either across borders or domestically. These balances could be used to corner markets—or even small economies."[14]

Underground Illegal Banking Network

As is well known, India has an underground illegal banking network which washes the dirty money. It is generally managed and operated by members of family, relations and friends. It operates through a particular kind of mechanism called *Hawala* which literally means reference. It is a mechanism through which one can convert and remit both white and black money and launder dirty money. When smugglers and money launderers need foreign currencies, they offer higher amount of Indian currency for each unit of a foreign currency. Both wage and salary earners in foreign lands, get attracted towards them and deposit whatever amount they want to remit back home along with the address of the payees. *Hawala* dealers promptly deliver the agreed amounts of Indian currency to the payees. This also helps remit money from India for maintenance of students studying abroad, for treatment of patients, for supporting foreign tours and shopping, for financing smuggling business and so on. This appears to be more convenient than the official route though the sender has to pay more Indian money per dollar. Suppose somebody disposes his house in Delhi and he wants to migrate to the USA, the *Hawala* route for remitting money is less cumbersome and he does not have to declare the exact amount of sale proceeds and he does not have to bother about paying stamp duties and other taxes. This route is also preferred by those who indulge in over-and under-invoicing in foreign trade transactions. The dealer lend the foreign exchange gathered by them to those who need to buy gold, electronic goods, expensive watches, cameras, narcotics and so on for which there is a profitable market in India. It is also used for buying arms and ammunitions for supply to criminals and political terrorists. From here, antiques, ivory, skins of animals, sandalwood, etc. are bought and smuggled out. Criminals and certain business houses fund the activities of politicians favourable to them and bribe the bureaucrats who are willing to help them. Thus, *Hawala's* sweep and implications are manifold though a glimpse can be had by looking into, what has come to be widely known as, the Jain-*Hawala* case. But, before going into it, let us state it explicitly that we are not concerned with nor interested in whether particular politicians and bureaucrats whose names or initials occur in the Jain brothers' diary did really receive the money. Similarly, it is not relevant to our discussion whether the diary is admissible as a piece of evidence in a court of law. These are the matters for competent judicial authorities to decide. Here we shall refer to this case to illustrate how the process of money laundering operates and it benefits the deadly nexus of politicians, bureaucrats, businessmen and criminals and its ramifications are global.

Let us first narrate the bare facts of the case. Its origin dates back to March 25, 1991 when the police arrested Ashfaq Hussain Lone who was supposed to be the deputy head of Hizbul Mujahedeen's intelligence wing. This is a terrorist outfit operating in Kashmir. He was nabbed from the office of Jamaat-e-Islami at Chitali Kabar of Old Delhi. Cash and bank drafts were seized from him. The source of money was somebody called Dr Mohammad Ayub based in London. As a result of the interrogation of Lone, the police came to know of the connection of Shahabuddin Ghauri, a Kashmiri student of Jawaharlal Nehru University and a number of *Hawala* dealers through whom the money had come. Ghauri and seven *Hawala* dealers were rounded up within a period of 10-12 weeks. On interrogation of the arrested student and dealers, not only more but startling facts came to light. Consequently, on May 3, 1991 raids were simultaneously conducted at 20 places, including the business' and residential premises of J.K. Jain and residential premises and the farm house of his employer S.K. Jain. According to the CBI: "The unaccounted cash in a sum of Rs. 93,52,755, foreign exchange worth Rs. 3,69,307, Indira Vikas Patra worth Rs. 10,50,000 and gold bars weighing 4,430 kgs were recovered from five different places during the said searches. Unaccounted cash in a sum of Rs. 58,09,100, Indira Vikas Patra for Rs. 10,50,100 and foreign exchange—namely, 593 US dollars, 300 UK pounds, 2,700 Deutche Marks, 50 Hong Kong dollars, 300 francs and 50 unknown currencies—were also recovered from the house of the said J.K. Jain".[15]

Afterwards, the investigation was terminated and a case was filed only against Lone and Ghauri without any reference to above searches and seizures. It seemed the CBI was in no mood to pursue the matter further and put the ramifications on which it had tumbled under a tight lid. Why did it do so seemed not only mysterious but created suspicion in the minds of those who had come to know some details. Perhaps it did not want to antagonise the deadly nexus. According to Madhu Limaye: "From the notings of the CBI officers concerned, it appeared that between April, 1988 to (sic) March, 1991, vast sums, received from sources abroad, were disbursed by the *Hawala* racketeers. The beneficiaries were Kashmiri terrorists, politicians, bureaucrats and others whose identity could be easily established through "custodial investigation to which any accused in the situation of the four Jains could normally be subjected". Every case of non-enforcement of law in matters of corruption is an act of "discrimination and arbitrariness" and violative of Article 14 of the Constitution".[16]

Hawala Scam

In fact, the CBI had recovered a diary from the premises of the Jains, which contained the names and initials of a number of important leaders of almost all political parties except the two Communist Parties and a few smaller ones and a number of top bureaucrats and public sector functionaries. Thus, the beneficiaries of the *Hawala* through which the dirty money was washed included top politicians, bureaucrats, criminals and businessmen. Madhu Limaye once commented: "The ramifications of the *Hawala* financiers from the Kashmiri terrorists to leading Indian politicians and bureaucrats make one freeze with amazement. The Executive of this country—its political arm (ministers), bureaucracy (a serving Secretary is implicated and its intelligence wing are devoid of all conscience and wallow in corruption". And he went on to add: "*It has become a common practice to blame Pakistan for our ills. Pakistan is without doubt doing everything in its power to destabilise the Indian State. But the enemy is within*".[17] The CBI sat tight over the case till some newspapers like *Indian Express* and *The Statesman* and a person like Madhu Limaye took it up and two journalists beseeched Supreme Court's intervention through public interest litigation. Because of intervention by the Supreme Court and time and again, scolding and reprimand of the CBI, some progress seemed to have been made and charge-sheets were filed against a number of people, but the way most of the accused have been acquitted, there has appeared a big question mark against the working of the CBI. Only Sharad Yadav is to be proceeded against because he was honest (or dishonest?) enough to admit that he did receive money from the Jains. Most of the other accused have been let off on technical ground of non-admissibility of Jain brothers' diary as evidence.

Film Industry and Underworld Dons

A spate of attacks on film producers and directors in Mumbai, which have resulted in the deaths of Mukesh Duggal and Gulshan Kumar has underlined the power of the mafia. It is said that with *Hawala*, real estate and certain kinds of smuggling business becoming less profitable, the mafia has been investing their money in film production but collapse of one film after another at box office has infuriated the mafia dons. They have started extorting money from producers, directors and top actors and actresses on a regular basis. The refusal to pay means physical elimination. Gulshan Kumar's murder has made it clear that 'armed gangsters are increasingly targetting the cash cows of the entertainment industry. The industry's close nexus with the underworld has come home to roost and the attacks and blackmail have assumed alarming proportions.[18]

If the film industry has to keep itself out of the clutches of the underworld, it has to shun glamour, extravagance and seek alternative sources of not only money but untainted money. It is an open secret that, for years, the film industry in Mumbai has been financed by the underworld, particularly with its command offices based in the Gulf countries. It is obvious from the following report, appearing in a national daily: "The sleaze connection of the film industry, which was never really hidden, came-out into the open with the arrest of Magnum video producers, Samir Hingora and Hanif Karwala, for complicity in the serial bomb blasts at Bombay which claimed about 350 lives in a single day in March, 1993.[19]

Sometimes, the film people are caught in the inter-gang rivalry. For example, Mukesh Duggal who was close to Chhota Rajan gang was supposed to have been gunned-down by the Chhota Shakeel gang, allied to Dawood Ibrahim. The report then goes on to add certain startling facts: "It is a well known fact that the industry has lapped-up finances provided by Sheikhs and the underworld dons. Dawood Ibrahim's younger brother Anis Ibrahim Kaskar showed a particular interest in the films for the glamour and girls. Films also became an avenue for investing extortion money. The financing by the underworld and the west Asian sources picked up in the eighties, especially after Anis Kaskar took a fancy to films."

"The casting couch with respect to the success of several heroines is not a myth, thanks to this nexus. It led to a situation where Raj Kapoor's heroine Mandakini gave birth to a son, reportedly from Dawood Ibrahim. She was later provided with a farmhouse at Bangalore." Several other heroines have had to travel to Dubai as and when required. There is ample evidence of these visits in CBI records.

The clout of the underworld was demonstrated to telling effect when a leading starlet was dropped from four movies after she declined an invitation to Dubai. She relented after her boyfriend was severely beaten up by gangsters.

"It is also well known that a popular Bollywood hero was made to dance at a party thrown by Dawood and his men in Dubai. When this Janta hero returned to Mumbai, the hapless star was literally intercepted at the airport by a rival gang, who made him dance for them too just because he had danced for Dawood. The hero was detained for 17 hours, and literally made to dance to the tune of the dons for most of this time."[20]

It is reported that Gulshan Kumar was asked for a sum of Rs. 2 crores by Abu Salem, a lieutenant of Dawood Ibrahim. He is supposed to have paid Rs. 50 lakhs and requested for some time to arrange for the rest. This angered the don who took it as refusal and he had to pay for this with his life. There are as many as 40 film stars who have to pay regular protection money to Abu Salem. They include Amitabh Bachchan, Subhash Ghai, Rajiv Rai, Mamata Kulkarani, Manisha Koirala, Bobby Deol and so on.[21]

The link between fraudsters and top politicians in India hogged the headlines of newspapers in 1993 when Harshad Mehta, widely known as "the big bull", came out with a statement in June, 1993 that he had paid one crore rupees ($3,90,000) stuffed in a suitcase to P.V. Narasimha Rao, the then Prime Minister of India. The credibility of politicians including Rao was so low that, as *The Economist* (July 3, 1993) reported: "The public seems just as doubtful of Mr Rao's word: a recent poll showed that 43 per cent believed what Mr Mehta said." It went on to add: 'Politicians of all parties have destroyed the integrity of the police in order to protect their own tribe and the lethargic, corrupt courts take up to a decade to deliver verdicts. So, in the court of public opinion, politicians accused of corruption are guilty until proved otherwise. In passing sentence, people ask only for plausibility not proof beyond reasonable doubt."

Mehta claimed that his meeting with Rao in 1991 was arranged by a businessman Sunil Mittal whose father Satpal Mittal was a nominated by a member of Rajya Sabha (till now it is not clear in which of the four areas he had been widely acknowledged to have distinguished himself) . Mehta released tape-recording of this telephonic conversation with Mittal, which made a reference to the meeting and handing over the money, notwithstanding a denial by

Mittal. Mehta also alleged that he had told the police when he was interrogated in connection with financial sector scam, but the police did not pass on this bit of information to the parliamentary committee looking into scam. In fact, he was trying to assert that a part of the money earned by him in his fraudulent deals went into making political payoffs and by implication, he alleged that politicians were not ignorant of what he was doing.

Though Rao denied the payoff, he did not dare to take any legal action against Mehta for defamation. The defence advanced in favour of Rao included the plausible excuse that he was meeting some Pakistani delegation and then the Governor of Jammu and Kashmir when Mehta was supposed to be with him and the size of the suitcase in which the money was delivered was not big enough to hold currency notes worth Rs one crore. Mehta was declared to be an agent of certain opposition parties. Rao's refusal to take Mehta to a court of law and a joint parliamentary committee finding a possible link between one of his sons and the scam of which Mehta was the principal author did create some ground to suspect that there was something fishy. One of the bankers involved in the scam had lent two crore rupees to a company of which Rao's son was a director. There was, thus, sufficient ground for suspicion if one also remembered what Steven Martindale had written long ago in his book *By Hook or By Crook* about Rao (we have already made several references to it in an earlier chapter).

Harshad Mehta Bank Scam

Now, let us turn our attention to financial sector scam or bank scam of which Harshad Mehta was the hero (or villain?) and a number of politicians also found their names directly or indirectly linked-up with this. P. Chidambaram, however, was the only politician to quit his ministership though it was never proved that he was involved in any *quid-pro-quo*.

K.N. Kabra in a pamphlet[22] has made a brief but cogent analysis of the genesis and implications of this scam by taking into account the various reports of the

Janakiraman Committee, set-up by the RBI. It emerges from his analysis that 'through share market operations financed by means of illegal transfer of banks' funds via the subterfuge of deals in securities represented by bogus BRs and other devices, the brokers would have by means of the sale of the PSUs shares booked enough profits to be able to square up their accounts with the banks and organisations like NHB. That such stock exchange deals were financed by banks' funds would have remained buried in the account books of the banks. It may be noted that the banks had an interest in rising share prices. The banks and the mutual funds floated by them were to offload the cheaply obtained PSUs shares. Thus, the funding of brokers by them seems related to the manner in which PSUs disinvestment took place.[23]

It was also possible that the banks might have promised placement of the shares of PSUs (Public Sector Undertakings) at the disposal of the brokers. These PSUs were said to have sold their shares at very low rates. "Had the brokers received the delivery of PSUs shares, their sale would have yielded to the brokers enough resources to square up their accounts. After the sale of the PSUs shares, no problem amounts would have remained outstanding against them."[24] Unfortunately, this did not happen and the stock market crashed and brought a crisis situation. Many gullible investors, especially small ones, lost most of their savings and some sank deeper in indebtedness. The size of the scam has been a matter of controversy, but it is certain that a sum of Rs. 4 billion was lost for ever. Most of this belonged to banks and public sector financial institutions. One person estimated that the size of scam was "larger than the total value of all the property stolen during the last 27 years which amounts, according to police data, to Rs 3,626.23 crores."[25]

The Janakiraman Committee, appointed by the RBI found that there was a systematic diversion of funds from the banking system to personal accounts of certain bankers. This involved 58,000 transactions involving a total sum of Rs 12.25 lakh crores.

Kabra suspected that the scam would not have been possible if there had been no 'close and informal political backing) a manifestation of bourgeoning symbiotic relationship between lumpenised businessmen and politicians on the one hand and the subversion of the relative autonomy of the state by means of informal financing of politicians by business houses, on the other) enjoyed by the brokers and the top bureaucrats-managers of the banks and financial institutions."[26] Thus, here too the nexus was active.

Soon after the scam came to light there was a flurry of activities. The government entrusted the charge of investigating and bringing the scamsters to book to the CBI which arrested a number of people, including Harshad Mehta, a few other brokers and officials of banks and financial institutions and their premises were raided and, as usual; the CBI claimed to have recovered "incriminating materials", their bank accounts were frozen and assets were attached. The RBI set up the Janakiraman Committee and a Joint Parliamentary Committee also came into being. For some time, it was the government seemed keen to get the culprits punished. But as of now more than five years have elapsed and nothing concrete has happened. People have started forgetting about the scam and nobody seems to be worried about the loss to public sector banks and other financial institutions. Sucheta Dalal, to whom the credit of unearthing this scam goes, writes: "The absence of any pressure on CBI and other investigative agencies to frame charges within a limited time-frame leads to a bizarre travesty of justice. It leads to a situation where the biggest scam accused, Harshad Mehta, has turned into a columnist and launched his own web site on the Internet, offering investment advice even before a single case filed against him has concluded."

"Harshad's advisory service follows persistent market reports that he was back as a big player in the capital market. And there are no prizes for guessing that the first scrips recommended by him are the very ones in which he was rumoured to be a big operator. Of course nobody has any proof, because nobody is investigating—least of all CBI which is prosecuting him, or the State Government which protects him by providing him with an armed security jeep."[27]

As *Far Eastern Economic Review* (October 3, 1996) has reported, there are as many as 1,600 charges against Mehta. The Income-tax Department wants him to clear his tax arrears with interest, amounting to $1.6 billion. Mehta has now been allowed to earn his living. Before this ruling by the Supreme Court, he had seek the permission of the court for even a small pocket money. Whatever he earned had to be attached. His house, his cars, bank accounts and investments were all attached. He claimed he was surviving on loans from friends. On this, the journal comments: "Judging by his lavish lifestyle, those friends must be very generous indeed. Mehta retains 25 servants, 12 drivers and 10 bodyguards in his 10,000-square-foot duplex (complete with indoor garden and putting green) on Bombay's swanky Worli Seaface. His beloved Lexus has been seized, but he still has a fleet of cars. When he travels to Delhi to sort-out his legal affairs, he checks into the Hilton."

Mehta's name is never entered in the register of guests and he does not respond directly to phone calls because he fears they may be tapped. He talks to them from somewhere on a phone which is supposed to be safe. When he is in Mumbai, he does not allow his guests to arrive at his place in their cars, but arranges them to be picked-up by his most trusted man in his own car. He, thus, protects himself from both the law-enforcement agencies and the mafia. He is sure that, in view of the waning interest of the CBI and the Income-Tax Department in pursuing charges against him and starting prosecution with vigour, he is going to re-establish himself as one of the biggest players in the bourse because "there is one thing they cannot attach, and that's my ability". It is needless to say that he does not lack powerful, well-wishers who once were beholden to him. *Far Eastern Economic Review's* C.P.Kuruvilla writes: 'The odds are stacked against him.

But he seems to have taken to heart a verse inscribed on a wall in his home.

There is a glamour left to cheer,
The luminescent sun ascends again,
The man—a phoenix,
Rises in spite of knocks and friction.
And by his light, mark my words,
Will build the perfect ship.

Mehta doesn't know who wrote those words—he says an interior decorator picked them—but he is determined to make their message his own."

Already the CBI has quietly let off two industrialists, deeply involved in the scam, for "lack of evidence" and have "failed to nail scores of foreign bank officials who have since been transferred, sacked and sometimes sent away with hefty severance packages by the banks."[28]

This and the way the Jain-*Hawala* case has been pursued by the CBI have given rise to cynicism among the people that the nexus is so powerful that it will not allow the CBI to go beyond the *nautanki* stage and no scamster or fraudster will ever be punished. People ask about Krishnamurty who once headed Maruti Udyog and later became a member of Planning Commission. He and a son of his were arrested in connection with some scam. What happened to that? The way the CBI has been going about various scams does not arouse any hope of bringing the culprits to justice.

It seems that we have come a long way from the Nehru-era when the fraudster H.D. Mundhra deals were investigated and the culprits were made to stand trial. Mundhra whom M.C. Chagla described as 'flamboyant personality and a financial adventurer whose only ambition is to build up an industrial empire by dubious means' was sent to jail to serve a term there and the then Finance Minister T.T. Krishnamachari, had to quite. Certain highly placed civil servants were also indicted. But Harshad Mehta is treated with a great leniency and this raises lots of questions about those who run the government.

Whatever the politicians in power may say about "law taking its own course" and waging a non-compromising battle against corruption for public consumption, nothing concrete seems to be turning up. The accused are so powerful that even our sovereign state is hesitant to proceed against them. A newspaper report says that Satish Sharma, Sheila Kaul, Sukh Ram, P.K. Thungon and a number of former and serving civil servants could have been standing trial in courts but for the reluctance of the government to grant necessary sanction to the CBI to prosecute them. 'One-hundred-and-forty-nine cases, already processed and investigated, remain pending due to the Union and State governments' unwillingness to process requests for giving CBI a green signal for prosecution. These requests, some of which have been pending for several years, are a prerequisite before the CBI files charge-sheets against the government servants concerned.

'In certain cases being monitored by the Supreme Court, such as the sanction of petrol pumps by Satish Sharma and the shop allotments by Sheila Kaul, requests for government sanction have been pending for about three months. Besides adding to the backlog of arrears in the CBI the governments' recalcitrance to provide the required sanction makes matters all the more difficult for the investigating agency in these cases which are referred by the highest court of the land.'[29] In a number of cases, reminders are sent to the concerned authorities for according sanctions every fortnight but without any result. The classic example is Czech Pistol case of the early 1990s. Since 1993, every fortnight the government was being requested to accord its sanction to prosecute an additional secretary and a joint secretary of the Ministry of Home Affairs and it took four years to refuse to give the sanction.

The CBI has made repeated requests to get section 19 of the Prevention of Corruption Act and section 197 of the Criminal Procedure Code to fix a time-frame within which such requests are disposed of. Notwithstanding all the loud talk of fighting corruption, politicians in power have not heeded nor have those sitting on opposition benches in Parliament pressed for it. How the government condones the acts of corruption is clear from two instances. First, recently a law was enacted to legalise the allotments of government quarters alleged to be secured with corrupt means. It means that those who indulge in or promote corruption could be let off unscathed on "compassionate or humanitarian" grounds. Second, those who illegally encroach upon or occupy public land and build huts and shops to get them legalised or authorised on the same grounds. This attitude of the government has promoted power-brokers and the land mafia in cities like Delhi.

Mafia: A Major Force in the USA

The power of the mafia has been demonstrated again and again in the USA. Its hand in the physical elimination of President John F. Kennedy and, later, his younger brother, Robert Kennedy, has been established and this shows that it does not tolerate inconvenient politicians while helps and promotes helpful ones. Everybody now acknowledges that the mafia is a major force in American life and no politician can afford to ignore this. It was officially admitted more than three decades ago that the mafia operated in most parts of the century. Its gross revenues amounted to anything ranging from $7 b to $50 b per annum while net profits came to $6-$7 b.[30] This was possible because of its nexus with politicians. The way they helped each other has been quite vividly described in Mario Puzo's novel *The Godfather*. He has also touched upon its connection with entertainment business of Hollywood, gambling and hotel industry. It finances and runs them through frontsmen. This is possible only with the patronage extended by politicians, police and bureaucracy. It is an open secret that the US administration entered into an unwritten pact with the members of the Sicilian mafia based in America to help each other. The mafiosi who were in US jails were released and through them, the Sicilian mafia dons were persuaded to help the American Army carry on its operation against Mussolini's forces. For a long time, they were promoted against the Italian Communists.

'John A. Gardiner carried out a micro study of an American town—Wincanton to see how the problem of corruption in the law-enforcement process involved law-enforcement policy-making and urban politics.[31] He examined how this kind of corruption was organised with reference to just one activity, namely, gambling and wanted to know how the pay-offs were distributed among the police, the local bureaucracy and the politicians. He also looked into the question as to what extent the state police, the FBI, and the Internal Revenue Service were propitiated. In other words, the mafia's nexus with them was also probed into. He posed the question: 'whether there are certain types of social or political systems in which crime syndicates are more likely to succeed in capturing control of law-enforcement agencies? Are some types of social groupings, political power structures, or formal governmental arrangements more susceptible than others to pressure from organised crime?"[32]

He took up the study of gambling in Wincanton. Before coming to Gardiner's study let us say something about gambling which has been one of the important activities of the US mafia. As the opposition to gambling grew in certain parts of the USA, a new type of casino evolved. It is gambling on riverboats which float in the middle of rivers. It does not disturb law and order and annoy non-gambling local populace. "At the same time, local politicians see riverboat casinos as a way, of attracting new money into run-down places. That is why, the first boats appeared in Iowa and Illinois, whereas towns like Davenport were desperately searching in the late 1980s for ways to fill the hole left by the collapse of farming. Davesport's casinoes produces about $3 m a year for the town and a pot of gold for a non-profit licensing body to spend on other ways of brightening-up the place.'[33]

Most of these casinos are run by the mafia who are backed by politicians. The riverboat casino is a very lucrative business, it pays back its capital investment within a year or two and its shares are hotly sought after on the Wall Street.

Now let us return to Gardiner's study. From the early 1930s, the story of gambling and attendant corruption centred on the activities of Irving Stern. He was a typical mafia don and it is interesting to have a look at his career. He was born in Russia in 1889 and came to the USA at the age of six and settled down in Wincanton. He worked for some time in fruit vending business of the family, but when prohibition was imposed by the US administration, he became a bootlegger and worked for a big operator who controlled a big area. He was once attacked by a rival gang when he tried to hijack a shipment of illicit alcohol belonging to rival gang. He filed a case after he identified the assailants, but at the trial, he expressed his inability to identify them and was sent to jail for perjury. After coming out of jail, he got a rival gang leader killed and seized control of his business and continued liquor smuggling and distribution till 1933 when prohibition was repealed. Then he extended his activities and gambling became one of them. The family fruit business became the cover. In 1951, he derived a net profit of $40,000 per week. During 1952-55, the new Republican mayor came down with a heavy hand on his gambling business and he had to pass through a very bad time. When this mayor went out of office, his business revived and with the help of the East Coast mafia, brought about changes in the organisation of his activities. He had to ensure that law-enforcement agencies were immobilised. "To this end, Stern worked to put cooperative men in office, to buy off those who occupied strategic enforcement positions and to implicate most city officials in various forms of corruption so completely that they would be unable to turn upon him. Just as businessmen facing restrictions on their rates or operating practices will seek to control the choice of men who will serve on regulatory boards or commissions, so Irv Stern was interested in the men who would set law-enforcement policy in Wincanton. To gain access to those elected officials involved with enforcement agencies, Stern early became active (if secretly) in Wincanton politics. Most Wincanton election contests are decided in the Democratic primaries and that endorsements from organisations are usually less important than support from ethnic and neighbourhood blocs. Candidates devote much of their campaign time to visiting clubs and ward bars, buying drinks for all those present (an expensive proposition if the visit has been well advertised) and leaving funds with the bartender or club steward to secure a good turnout of voters and poll-watchers on election day.

"Success in this kind of electioneering requires either an exceptionally well known name or endorsements from most of the organisations with Democratic members—or a lot of money. Expenses for Wincanton primary candidates probably average around $5,000; the general election costs another $10,000 per man. In the chaos of the primaries, with three to five men seeking the mayoral nomination and five or ten vying for the two seats on the council, few candidates can line up for big legitimate money for media advertising or visits to the clubs. Knowing this well, Irv Stern often helped out men he felt would be tolerant if elected. In some years, he helped several candidates, not caring who won but wanting to guarantee access to all. In other years, when one candidate was particularly promising (or another particularly threatening), Stern concentrated his financial support on one man."[34]

His participation in primary and general election campaigns brought him in touch with a number of important bureaucrats with whom he had built some kind of rapport. With his access to politicians, he got pliable officers posted in local police and civil administration and regularly rewarded them. "Two basic strategies were used—to pay top personnel as much as necessary to keep them happy (and quiet) and to pay *something* to as many as possible, thus, implicating them in the system and keeping them from talking. The range of payoffs, thus, went from a weekly salary for the mayor to liquor and a Christmas turkey for many patrolmen. Records seized in a raid on the central members bank indicated payments totalling $2,400 each week to the mayor, police chief and other city and county officials."[35]

Thus, contributions to political leaders, regular

payments to officials, holiday and birthday gifts were used to buy protection and in the course of time, a powerful nexus came into existence, which put Stern beyond the arms of law-enforcing agencies.

One disastrous long-term result was the spread of cynicism among the people at large. They lost trust in politicians and bureaucrats and they believed, it was furtile to expect anyting good from them.

A report on Mexico's drug mafia says that at least 30 per cent of the magistrates at lower levels, who try drug traffickers have been corrupted while others are frightened with the threat of their physical liquidation and hesitate to follow the law.[36]

In Peru, even a curiouser thing than this came to light during the second half of 1996. Demetrio Chavez Peñaherrera, alias "El Vaticano", a top drug-trafficker of the early 1990s, was convicted and jailed in 1994 for collaborating with the Shining Path terrorists. He was held at naval base in a top-security cell. In August, 1996, he was made to stand trial for drug-trafficking and during the course of his trial, he revealed that in 1991-92, he was paying $50,000 a month to Valdimiro Montesinos, a top intelligence adviser of the government in order to have trouble-free drug-carrying flights into Colombia. Montesinos had been very close to President Alberto Fujimori and helped him disband the Congress and suspend the Constitution in 1992 in what came to be known as "self-coup". It needs to be underlined that the Peruvian Congress in which the ruling party had the majority, rejected the demand for an investigation in the bribery by the drug-trafficker. In this context, it needs to be remembered that 174 kg of coca paste was discovered from a former Presidential plane, followed by the discovery of 100 kg of coca paste on board of two navy ships, one of them in the Canadian port of the Vancouver. It came to light that there was a nexus between drug-traffickers and the army. Between 1990 and 1996 around 300 army men were investigated or charged with helping drug-trafficking. The poorly paid army men and impoverished peasantry depend on coca-trafficking for supplementing their incomes. The peasantry finds coca cultivation more profitable than other crops because of bad roads and difficulties in marketing crops other than coca. The involvement of politicians is also there to protect and facilitate drug-trafficking.

In Italy, there erupted a big controversy relating to handling of financial crimes. Francesco Greco, a Milan-based prosecuting magistrate who has specialised in financial crimes along with his colleagues is concerned with three proposals being discussed by a parliamentary commission, called the *bicamerale*. "The first is that the roles of Italy's prosecuting magistrates and the judges should be separated. The second is that massaging company accounts (which has led to many convictions) should become a civil rather than criminal offence. The third is to modify Article 513 of the criminal procedure code, so that a statement will not be allowed as evidence if the witness refuses to repeat it in court. Magistrates say that changing the rules now would slow down trials and, because of a statute of limitations, hundreds of defendants in corruption cases would not be prosecuted."[37]

Greco has been supported by a number of prosecutors in Milan and Palermo. It is widely believed that the growing pressure of the mafia on politicians has led to these three proposals which will bring a great deal of relief to the mafiosi. It is not surprising that both the government and the opposition are in agreement on these proposals.

How the nexus of corrupt and fraudulent businessmen with politicians protects the former is illustrated by the example of Asil Nadir, the former boss of Polly Peck International, a textile-to-foods group operating from Britain. In 1990 when this London-based conglomerate collapsed, Britain's Serious Fraud Office began looking into it and found Nadir responsible for it. It charged him with theft and false accounting to the tune of $71 m. He was arrested and then released on bail. On May 4, 1993, Nadir jumped bail, took a chartered flight and fled to Cyprus, his home country. This Turkish-Cypriot faudster enjoys the patronage of the Turkish-Cypriot leader, Mr Rauf Denktash, whom he has been useful in many ways, including as the biggest employer of Turkish-Cypriots. Since Britain did not recognise Turkish Cyprus and did not have any extradition treaty, Nadir could not be brought back to stand trial in Britain. It is said that Nadir had well-wishers in the British bureaucracy, who allowed him to get-out of Britain without much difficulty. Here in India, the government has been facing difficulties in bringing back mafia dons from Dawood Ibrahim to Amir Bhai and scamsters like Win Chadha to stand trial on various charges. In fact, the mafia dons have been operating and directing the activities of their mafiosi in India from their safe heavens in the Gulf and elsewhere. Had they not enjoyed political patronage there, it would have been quite hot for them to stay and work from there.

Take another example, this time from far off Mexico. In September, 1994 Carlos Cabal, a businessman-cum-banker whose business empire was once valued at more than $1 billion fled with huge amounts of money to Europe. The government accused him of pilfering $200 m-$700 m through fraudulent loans.

His spectacular rise within a decade from an obscure shrimp and banana farmer to the owner of country's largest agri-business was not without his nexus with bureaucracy and politics. In 1992, he took over the control of Fresh Del Monte Produce, a fruit company, from the liquidators of Polly Peck International, a bankrupt British company, once owned by Asil Nadir, mentioned above. Cabal became some sort of national celebrity when he used his financial resources and contacts acquired in the course of his agri-business to the privatisation of banks. 'With help from prominent members of Mexico's ruling political party, the PRI, he brought what became Banco Union in 1991... he merged it with Banca Cremi to form a bank that controls about 5 per cent of Mexican bank assets.'[38] Cabal proved to be a "worthy" successor to Asil Nadir!

In Thailand, the close relationship among the mafia, the police and politicians has been known for years. In the previous chapter, we referred to the cooperative relationship between the mafia and the police. As early as 1994, some important politicians were suspected to be having close connections with the mafia which financed their election campaign. In Thailand, vote-buying has been a widespread practice and it requires substantial amount of money. In 1994, itself, three Opposition legislators were denied visa by the USA because of their alleged involvement with narcotics trafficking which was supposed to yield money.

Towards the end of 1994 the Prime Minister of Thailand Chuan Leekpai told a journalist: "I can certainly say that vote-buying is on the increase. That was because there were no businessmen running for elections. They were lawyers, teachers and other professionals. I think that businessmen are used to spending money and politics provides a channel by which they can use money to obtain positions in government and, therefore, be able to protect their interests."[39]

Far Eastern Economic Review (December 1, 1994) is of the view that 'One way to cut the godfathers down to size is to reduce their role in politics. Gangland connections are often the key to raising the vast sums of money needed to buy votes in general elections. Local godfathers have the funds and connections to help politicians get elected. In turn, they want protection and legitimacy."

Mafiosi in Politics and Business

Till now, we have given instances of the nexus among the mafia, business, bureaucracy and politics while they retain their more or less separate identity or existence. We shall now turn our attention to the cases in which the mafia, business and politics lose their separate identity or existence and get fused in one person. This phenomenon has been widely witnessed in India in recent times. Many mafiosi have entered State legislatures and Parliament. Earlier, they were helping their politician-patrons by capturing booths, stamping ballot papers, rigging elections in other ways and providing funds. When they realised their strength and capacity, they themselves began entering politics. Bihar about which we have some intimate knowledge, sent in 1996 at least five known mafiosi to the

Lok Sabha. One of them was appointed a junior minister in the Ministry of Home Affairs by H.D. Deve Gowda, but had to resign when there was a big noise. In the Rabri Devi ministry in Bihar, there are at least three known mafiosi, looking after economic departments where the possibility of minting money is present in plenty. There are some mafiosi who operate both in business and politics. The term "business" has to be interpreted liberally to include provision of services like education. In Bihar, politicians like Dr. Jagannath Mishra, Ram Lakhan Singh Yadav, Satyendra Narayan Sinha, L.P. Shahi, R.P. Sharma and others have opened colleges and institutes which are, in many cases, shops arranging degrees for monetary payment. These are the people who had considerable influence over the agencies giving affiliation and financial grants to newly-set up colleges and institutions. Sometimes, they set them up not for pecuniary but political considerations. People from their own castes were employed who made financial contributions to election funds and physically participated in mobilising votes and rigging elections.

Setting-up medical and engineering colleges in Maharashtra, Karnataka and elsewhere provides a big clout both financially and politically to the mafiosi-cum-politicians. Huge capitation fees are charged and patronage in the form of admissions on account of management's discretionary quota provide ample scope to oblige the influential. One can come across scores of such instances and scandals if one looks at relevant newspaper files for the last twenty-five years. In Bihar, the Nalanda Medical College, Patna, the M.G.M. Medical College, Jamshedpur and private medical colleges at Darbhanga and Katihar were once epitomes of corruption. The refusal of Laloo Yadav to get recognition for the Katihar-based medical college led a number of Muslim leaders such as Md. Yunus Saleem, Syed Shahabuddin, Abdul Ghafoor and others to part company with him politically.

Ram Lakhan Singh Yadav epitomises the breed of politicians who combine the triple role. He was investigated by the T.L. Venkatarama Aiyar Commission in connection with corruption charges during 1967-68. In 1969, he joined the Congress (O) and captured the Sadaquat Ashram, the office of the Bihar Pradesh Congress Committee with the help of his musclemen. Later-on, he rejoined Indira Gandhi-led Congress. His son, Prakash Yadav alias Bobby, became a prominent Youth Congress leader and was made a member of the Lok Sabha. He earned notoriety as a result of an ugly incidence in the course of one of his many visits to the red light area of Calcutta. When he was denied re-nomination by the Congress, he was lapped up by the Janata Dal and made a member of the Bihar Legislative Council. Ram Lakhan Singh Yadav who headed the Disciplinary Committee of the Bihar Congress went over to the Janata Dal in 1991 and was elected to the Lok Sabha on its ticket. After a year or so, he defected to the Congress, he alleged that he was paid a hefty sum and made a minister by P.V. Narasimha Rao. The case of bribery is being investigated by the designated CBI court.

Whenever he was minister whether in Bihar looking after the PWD or at the Centre holding charge of Chemicals and Fertilisers, charges of graft were levelled against him. During his tenure as a minister at the Centre, the 133-crore urea scam was born. The National Fertilisers Ltd. (NFL), a public sector undertaking, looked after by his ministry contracted for the supply of urea by the Turkish firm Karsan Ltd. No urea arrived and, later on, it turned out that the Turkish company had its main interest in tourism not in fertilisers. The CBI investigated the scam and arrested officials of the NFL, Karsan's Indian agent, Mr Sambasiva Rao, Sanjeeva Rao, a relation of P.V. Narasimha Rao and Prakash Chandra Yadav, the son of Ram Lakhan Singh Yadav. Narasimha Rao's son Prabhakar Rao is also alleged to be a recipient of the kickbacks.

Ram Lakhan Singh Yadav is alleged to have forcibly taken possession of a piece of land in Patna, belonging to the Postal Department and built a multi-storeyed office complex which is rented out to Bihar government's Intermediate Council. In New Delhi, he has built a house in an authorised colony called the Swatantrata Senani Vihar.

The Assam Chief Minister, Mr P.K. Mahanta is involved in the Rs 400-crore Letter of Credit scam. This scam connected with the veterinary department involves unauthorised and excessive withdrawals of money from the treasury. Besides the Chief Minister, three former ministers and leaders of the ruling A.G.P. party and a number of senior civil servants are also involved in it. "According to sources, the main accused in the case, Rajib Bora—a businessman turned politician of sorts—is alleged to be close to several members of the AGP, including the Chief Minister. Mr Bora, who has already been chargesheeted and named as the kingpin of the nexus operating, is alleged to have siphoned-off crores of rupees through fake Letters of Credit with the withdrawals being made solely from the State veterinary department.

"Mr Bora is alleged to have paid money as kickback to politicians and government officials. The CBI has alleged that some of the AGP leaders used the money to obtain property in Mumbai and other cities. Agency sleuths are investigating into assets owned by Dilip Saikia (a former AGP minister), who is alleged to own two flats and an icecream parlour in Mumbai, where his wife is based.'[40] The son and the daughter-in-law of a former Chief Minister, Mr Hiteshwar Saikia, are alleged to have received as kickbacks a sum of Rs 12 crores.

Animal Husbandry Scam of Bihar

The biggest scam of post-Independence India has been the fodder or animal husbandry scam of Bihar, but before we come to it, let us refer to a few more scams involving the members of the Rao government (1991-96).

To begin with, there was a scam concerning the allotment of telecom licences for cellular and basic telephone services in 1995. The allotment was challenged in the Supreme Court which ruled that it was in order and there did not seem to be any mala fide involved. This pronouncement was flaunted by the then Minister, Mr Sukh

Ram, as the conclusive proof of his honesty. But, the situation underwent a sea-change in 1996, when the Rao Government went out of office and a Deve Gowda-led, United Front government, assumed office. In August, when Mr Sukh Ram was away to Britain, his house in New Delhi was raided by the CBI which found bundles of currency notes stuffed in sacks lying in the house. It took the CBI almost two days to count and repack them. They totalled around Rs 3.66 crores (more than $1 m). In addition, it also recovered diaries full of jottings, allegedly throwing light on the kickbacks taken from the allottees of the licences. Mr Sukh Ram as Minister of Communications had presided over tenders for more than $25 billion-worth telecom licences.

Seemingly, the entire procedure of inviting sealed tenders and then allotting the licences seem to be perfect, without any scope for the kickbacks. "Innocents may wonder how bribes could win deals that were meant to go to the highest bidder in a sealed-tender competition. There is no knowing what, if anything, happened in the cases dealt with by Mr Ram. But as it happens, greedy ministers have come up with several techniques to deal with the supposedly corruption-proof system of sealed bids. One is simply to sit on the file of winning bidder till he pays "speed money". Another is to lay down (or threaten to lay down) new conditions after the bids are in. Yet another is to accept bribes from losing companies to reject all tenders as inadequate and then to call for a fresh round of bidding. Indian politicians can be inventive, as well as rapacious.'[41]

The CBI arrested Mr Sukh Ram and an official Runu Ghose, interrogated them for days during which newspapers carried many sensational details, but afterwards nothing much has been heard about the case and its trial and in the, meanwhile, Sukh Ram floated a political party in his home State of Himachal Pradesh, ostensibly to fight out corruption!

Then there were two scams which came to light as a result of public interest litigation petitions. One concerned the out-of-turn allotment of residential quarters to government employees and the shops without prescribed procedure. It was alleged by the CBI, after investigation, that the then concerned-minister, Mrs Sheila Kaul and her deputy, Mr. P.K. Thungon had taken huge amounts of money as bribes for making these allotments. Mrs Sheila Kaul who became the Governor was forced to quit. The court imposed heavy fines on them and ordered the out-of-turn allottees to surrender their residential quarters, but the government came to their rescue and passed a law regularising the mala-fide allotments. Thus, one of the two parties involved in the act to bribing was let off with the gain. Obviously, this step of the government will not discourage bribe-givers who want to jump the queue, notwithstanding Mr I.K. Gujral's call for staging *satyagrah* against corruption.

There was yet another scam concerning the allotment of dealerships of LPG and petrol pumps by the then minister, Mr Satish Sharma. It was alleged that the minister had indulged in favouritism and taken huge amounts of money as bribes in collaboration with oil selection boards. The allottees included the wife of Mr Ram Vilas Paswan, a Janata Dal leader and later a minister in the United Front Government, a daughter-in-law of Mr Deve Gowda, the wife of a Secretary to Government of India and others. It was also alleged that politicians were given petrol pumps and LPG dealerships in order to buy their support for the Rao Government. The Supreme Court imposed a heavy fine amounting to many millions of rupees on Mr Sharma and ordered the CBI to start his prosecution.

The fodder or animal husbandry scam in which as many as 55 persons are involved is a perfect example of the deadly nexus we have referred to. Among them are two former Chief Ministers, Laloo Yadav and Jagannath Mishra, three former Ministers, Mr Bhola Ram Toofani, Mr Vidysagar Nishad and Mr Chandradeo Prasad Verma, a number of senior members of the Indian Administrative Service, one Commissioner of Income-tax, three MLAs, a number of serving and retired officers of the State Animal Husbandry Department and businessmen-cum-gangsters. All of them constitute, what is popularly known, the animal husbandry mafia. The politicians involved belong to the ruling Rashtriya Janata Dal (which has broken away with the Janata Dal), the Congress and the BJP. They cut across the barriers of caste and religion. It is said that, at one point or another, the Left was also favourably inclined towards continuing the services of certain scamsters after their superannuation.

Though the scam originated many years ago, it began coming into the public view from 1995-96 onwards. The case in the nutshell pertains to unauthorised and excess withdrawals of money from the government treasury and its account in the State Bank of India for payment of bogus bills of the purchase of the cattle feed and certain kinds of animals and poultry and of their transportation. It needs to be noted that scamsters had become so daring that they used cars and motor bikes for transporting cattle-feed, animals and poultry as the bills and vouchers submitted by them reveal.[42] The money, thus taken out of the government was allegedly shared by the scamsters. A number of scamsters invested the ill-gotten money into the real estate in Mumbai, Delhi, Bangalore and elsewhere and in gold, securities, etc. Some are alleged to have tried to launder it through the *hawala* route.

Many of the firms supplying cattle-feed, animals and poultry have turned out to be fake and owned *benami* by officials involved in the scam. The CBI, for example, is said to have detected seven fake firms in the name of the kingpin of the scam, Shyam Bihari Sinha and his relations in Calcutta. It is also said to have detected three financial companies, namely, Narang Distributors, Ramon Commercial and Troymark Consultancy through which Sinha made huge investments in the share market. These companies also provided loans to private firms as well as individuals. Sinha's wife, Rama Sinha, was a director of all these three companies. "It has been learnt that many top politicians of the State have made investments in the share market in the name of their wards through these three companies."[43]

The State exchequer is estimated to have been

defrauded to the extent of around Rs 2,000 crores and if one takes into account various other scams in the State during the Laloo regime, the loss may touch even Rs 10,000 crores.

Even though the fodder scam had been going on for a long time, it could be detected only during the mid-1990s. There were concerted attempts to ignore or suppress all demands for a thorough investigation in the affairs of the Animal Husbandry Department (AHD) and the allegations of fake bills and excess withdrawals. Questions put up in the legislature were either scuttled or given vague replies. The Public Accounts Committee too seemed to be interested in suppressing the entire affair. Mr Laloo Yadav tried to get it inquired into by a retired judge of the High Court, who was connected with one of his allied parties before being elevated to the Bench. The CBI inquiry was forced on the government by the High Court before which came a public interest litigation. Thanks to the monitoring of the progress of investigation by the High Court, the attempts to sabotage it could not succeed though all kinds of hurdles were put forth in it. After a long delay, the scamsters have been arraigned before the designated court and a comprehensive chargesheet has been filed. The CBI's "Investigation has unravelled a well-knit conspiracy, pursuant to which astronomical sums were siphoned off from the Government Exchequer over the years, in a very systematic and concerted fashion by AHD officials, in connivance with the suppliers, Government officials, politicians of different political parties, Ministers and the Chief Minister of the State of Bihar.

"Sri Laloo Prasad (A-20) was the member of Lok Sabha from 1977 to 1980, member of Legislative Assembly from 1981 to 1985 and member of Lok Sabha in the beginning of 1990. He was sworn in as the Chief Minister of Bihar on 10-3-90 and retained charge of the Finance Department and continues as such. The Finance Minister and the Finance Commissioner of the State play pivotal roles in managing public finance. The State Finance Minister and Commissioner/Secretary of the Finance Department have the responsibility to manage Finances of the State keeping in mind the provisions laid down under the rules of the Executive Business, the provisions of Bihar Financial Rules, Bihar Budget Manual and Bihar Treasury Code, etc. Investigations revealed the then Finance Minister, Shri Laloo Prasad (A-20) and the Finance Commissioner, Sri P.C. Singh (A-14), wilfully to discharge their duty to enforce discipline in managing the finances of the State. Thorough their connivance and deliberate inaction allowed their co-conspirators in AHD and other to commit embezzlement of huge amounts of money during the period of the incumbency, resulting in unprecedented loss to the exchequer.'[44]

Mr Laloo Yadav was, according to the CBI, fully aware from 1993 onwards about various facets of the scam which had been going on since 1988-89. In spite of 229 per cent excess withdrawals over and above the budgeted amount, he did not bother to initiate any action. He did it deliberately. Mr Ramjivan Singh who was the AHD Minister in 1990, had brought the ongoing scam to the notice of Mr Yadav through a note and asked for CBI inquiry which was scoffed at. Dr. Jagannath Mishra was also against a CBI inquiry and he also supported Yadav's move to scuttle. He was concerned with the plight of Mr K.N. Jha, a prominent scamster and his close relative, if the CBI inquiry was ordered. Incidently, the eldest son-in-law of Ram Lakhan Singh Yadav is also among the scamsters.

It is alleged that the proprietor of Pataliputra Travels, Mr J.P. Verma, whose wife and son were suppliers to the AHD, time to time, provided air tickets for Laloo Yadav and other members of his family. On October 21, 1995, when Mr Laloo Yadav returned from the USA, Mr Verma arranged for the air journey of his 9 children to New Delhi so that they could receive him. Scamsters financed the school education of Laloo Yadav's children at Namkum (Ranchi) and Ajmer.

The scamsters are so powerful and resourceful that those who are lodged in the Beur Central Jail in the suburb of Patna have all the comforts and access to all the modern gadgets, including cellular telephones with which they keep themselves in touch with the rest of the world including the then Chief Minister and one of the scamsters, Mr Laloo Yadav. It was an officer of an intelligence agency who incidentally found that legislators kept in judicial custody at the Beur Central Jail were carrying on conversation with the outside world on their cellular telephones. They used to ask the members of their families to pick them up in cars from the jail gate. They used to go out and then return before being locked-up. They treated the jail as if it was a hotel. A raid conducted recovered six mobile phones, foreign liquor, expensive cigarettes and as the grapevine had it, even blue films from the possession of three jailed legislators. Besides, a sum of Rs 200,000 was recovered from the BJP legislator, Mr Dhruv Bhagat.[45] In an earlier raid, foreign currency, television sets, liquors, narcotics and rifles were recovered from the same prison.

Jain Commission and Negligence of Rao

The deadliness of the nexus of mafia, bureaucracy and politicians can very well be illustrated by drawing attention to the assassination of Rajiv Gandhi, a former Prime Minister of India on 21 May, 1991 at Sriperumbudur in Tamil Nadu. The Interim Report of the Commission of Inquiry, headed by Justice M.C. Jain, a former chief justice of Delhi High Court has brought to light several startling facts, pointing towards a deep seated conspiracy to eliminate Rajiv Gandhi and then protect the conspirators.

Soon after the Jain Commission was appointed to probe whether there was a conspiracy to assassinate Rajiv Gandhi, a Congress government headed by P.V. Narasimha Rao assumed power at the Centre and it was expected that it would accord all facilities needed by Jain Commission for its smooth working and speedy completion of its assignment, but, for months, the Commission had neither proper office space nor adequate staff. Not only this, the Rao government initiated steps to disband the Commission as redundant on the plea that already there was J.S. Verma Commission looking into the issues relating to lapses in the security of the late Mr. Gandhi.

This baffles one's understanding because without going into the question of conspiracy and its various dimensions including the motives, the organisation and the personnel involved, no rational assessment of the security lapses could be possible. In fact, the Jain Commission's findings should have provided the starting point for the Verma Commission. Mr Rao's Home Minister, Mr S.B. Chavan was kept aside and was not taken into confidence by Mr Rao who himself in consultation with officials of security agencies handled matters relating to the Jain Commission. Mr Chavan told the Commission that no sensitive documents were shown to him. In addition, Mr Rao initiated a move to scrap the Commission and the then Attorney General Mr G. Ramaswamy in his very first submission underlined the government's view that the Commission had no jurisdiction to probe into the areas of the conspiracy left unattended and un-investigated by the Special Investigation Team. These areas primarily involved LTTE's top operatives like Kittu and KP who had close links with various Indian and foreign terrorist groups and intelligence agencies. The PLO chief Yasser Arafat had warned both Mr Gandhi and Mr Chandra Shekar of likelihood of an international conspiracy to eliminate the former. In view of this warning which had been a matter of public knowledge, it was all the more necessary to facilitate the speedy completion of the work of the Jain Commission. Yet it took more than six years to submit its interim report and it needed as many as 12 extensions.

For as long as two years, the Rao government did not supply documents and information on the ground of their sensitive nature. The Commission had no alternative but to begin its work on the basis of newspaper reports. Then Mr Rao initiated a formal proposal in 1994 to wind up the Commission, but it was not accepted by his cabinet. Refusing to give in, the opponents of the Jain Commission 'In March 1994, one private advocate Mushtaq Ahmed was propped up by the government... He filed a PIL (public interest litigation) urging that the commission be winded-up and obtained a stay on the commission.' (Jain Commission Report quoted in *Times of India*, 17 November

1997). This delayed the work of investigation. Even after this PIL was dismissed, the Rao government moved two special leave petitions (SLPs) in the Supreme Court, challenging the dismissal of the PIL. In January 1996, the Supreme Court dismissed both the SLPs and then only, i.e. more than four and a half years after its appointment, the Commission could resume its work. Not prepared to give in easily, the Rao government brought a proposal before the Cabinet for scrapping the Jain Commission but the move could not succeed because the Cabinet was divided. Thus, it was only in May, 1996, five years after its appointment; that the Commission could get some documents. *Times of India* (17 November, 1997) reported quoting a reliable source: 'The report makes it clear that the Rao government was all the time trying to dis-credit the Commission and wind it up. At the same time, it made sure that the commission had few staff and fewer documents. As a matter of fact, this interim report is based on the actual inquiry which started in May, 1996 to August, 1997.'

The Commission requested the government several times to fill up the post of adviser to facilitate its smooth functioning, but it was only as late as June, 1996 that Amit Verma, IPS, of the Tamil Nadu cadre was appointed.

A number of files of crucial importance were not supplied in original because they had 'disappeared' or 'declared missing' or could not be shown in view of their sensitive nature. Consequently, a host of files were submitted in doctored or reconstructed form. To give a few examples: (a) file no. 8-1-WR/JSS/90/Vol. III, containing notings of officers regarding security arrangements of Rajiv Gandhi from November, 1989 was lost by the PMO (Prime Minister's Office) in 1991. Later, it was doctored and reconstructed by the Rao government and submitted to the Commission; (b) file no. 1/12014/5/91-IAS/DIII, pertaining to the terms of reference of the Verma and Jain Commissions was not traceable from 1995; (c) file containing intercepted messages from foreign intelligence agencies, said to be addressed to Chandraswami and Janata Party chief, Dr Subramaniam Swami was destroyed by senior officials of the PMO; (d) file on Intelligence Bureau's assessment of the role played by the late, Mr Zail Singh and Chandraswami in 1987 to topple Rajiv Gandhi was missing; (e) file with records of official briefings given to Mr S.B. Chavan by intelligence agencies on the assassination of Rajiv Gandhi was not traceable; (f) the April 20,1991 wireless message asking whether Rajiv Gandhi should be killed in Delhi or Madras was found missing; and-(g) file relating to Rao's attempt to wind-up the Jain Commission was not supplied.

From the above, it is obvious that there were powerful forces preventing crucial files and information coming before the Commission or becoming public. Who were these forces and what was the role of Mr Rao and his advisers? This aspect still remains shrouded in mystery. It is said that, throughout, the Rao government showed an attitude of non-cooperation with the Commission and there is a strong suspicion that it was interested in shielding certain persons.

The fact that the Rao government had actually doctored files came to light when Mr Vinod Pandey, cabinet secretary during the V.P. Singh regime told the Commission that file no. 8-1-WR/JSS/90/Vol. III in which he had made notings on Rajiv Gandhi's security had been tampered with. In his own words: 'The file which has been placed in my hands does not contain an office copy of my note dated January 30, 1990. The first five paras of the draft are not mine.' (*New Wave*, 14 December, 1997).

The Jain Commission found that V.P. Singh who succeeded Rajiv Gandhi as Prime Minister failed to take appropriate measures to combat the growing activities of the LTTE which had active support of the DMK government of Tamil Nadu, headed by M. Karunanidhi. In the words of Justice Jain, the 'spurt in LTTE activity after taking over by DMK government in January, 1989 till the promulgation of President's rule on January, 30, 1991 clearly goes to point out that such a spurt in LTTE activity could only be with the connivance of the state government and its machinery. It cannot be found that only at the official level, action was wanting and not at the political leadership level, as stated by Mr Singh.' He went on to add: 'DMK's rhetoric against IPKF (Indian Peace Keeping Force, that was sent to implement the Indo-Sri Lanka Accord in 1987) operations against the LTTE in Sri Lanka beginning from October, 1987 must have come to the knowledge of Mr Singh through Press or otherwise and after coming into power in Tamil Nadu in January, 1989, its continued support was also reported in the Press.' In view of this 'Can it be believed that Mr. Singh was not in the know of such support. In any case, its likelihood must have put him to caution to be vigilant and he could have gathered information about such support from Intelligence and other sources. Inferences are obvious.' (*as reported in Ibid*).

Justice Jain found that the V.P. Singh-led National Front government in New Delhi winked at growing connivance between the LTTE and the DMK government in Tamil Nadu. Both V.P. Singh and Chandra Shekhar did not seriously take into account the growing threat to the life of Rajiv Gandhi. The Commission found that LTTE's activities of arms smuggling, abduction of Indian officers and citizens and so on were tolerated by then DMK government and the V.P. Singh government. The murder of the EPRLF leader K. Padmanabha also failed to awaken the then Tamil Nadu as well as the Central government. In fact, LTTE's free access to Karunanidhi and his officials got most of its workers involved in clandestine activities released from detention.

The LTTE connections with West Asian terrorist organisations was an open secret. Former Indian foreign secretary J.N. Dixit who also served as High Commissioner in Sri Lanka has this to say in his book *Assignment Colombo*: 'We had information about LTTE having sent their cadres for training with "Hamas" and other Palestinian militant groups in Libya, Lebanon and Syria. To cap it all, the LTTE even sent its cadres for training with Mossad in Israel, the details of which are available in the book *By Way of Deception* by Victor Ostrovsky and Claire Hoy.' (quoted by *K. Subrahmanyam in his article "The Jain*

Commission Report", Economic Times, 27 November, 1997). In view of this, the warning by Arafat should have been taken seriously, but obviously, it was ignored by the power that was. Why it did so is bound to raise serious doubts about the people who wielded power in New Delhi and in Madras.

The judgement in the Rajiv Gandhi assassination case leaves in doubt about the LTTE's hand, but what is yet to be fully uncovered is the conspiracy behind it. One hopes the final report of the Jain Commission will unmask the people and forces not only actively involved in its planning and execution but sheltering and protecting the conspirators.

REFERENCES

1. Govenment of India (Ministry of Home Affairs), *Vohra Committee Report*, New Delhi, 1995, p. 2 (hereafter referred to only as *Vohra Committee Report*).
2. *Ibid.*, p. 3.
3. *Ibid.*
4. *Ibid.*, p. 4.
5. *Ibid.*, pp. 4-5.
6. *The Economist*, July 26, 1997.
7. Peter J. Quirk's paper "Money Laundering:Muddying the Macro Economy", *Finance & Development*, March 1997.
8. *Ibid.*
9. *Ibid.*
10. *The Economist*, July 26, 1997.
11. *Ibid.*, February 29, 1992.
12. *Ibid.*
13. *Ibid.*
14. Peter J. Quirk's paper in *Finance and Development*, March 1997.
15. Quoted in Madhu Limaye's article "Political System is Hostage to Racketeers" in *Mainstream*, November 12, 1994.
16. *Ibid.*
17. *Ibid.*
18. *The Hindustan Times*, August 14, 1997.
19. *Ibid.*
20. *Ibid.*

21. *The Economic Times*, August 13, 1997; *The Times of India*, August 14, 1997; *Jana Satta*, August 14, 1997.
22. Kamal Nayan Kabra, *Financial Sector Scam: Fruits of Liberalisation*, New Delhi, 1992.
23. *Ibid.*, p. 3.
24. *Ibid.*, pp. 3-4.
25. *Ibid.*, p. 6.
26. *Ibid.*, pp. 14-15.
27. Sucheta Dalal's column "Money & Banking: End Trial by Humiliation", *The Times of India*, July 7, 1997.
28. *Ibid.*
29. *Ibid.*, August 9, 1997.
30. President's Commission on Law Enforcement and Administration of Justice, *The Challenge of Crime in a Free Society*, Washington DC, 1967, p. 189.
31. John A. Gardiner, *The Politics of Corruption: Organized Crime in an American City*, New York, 1970.
32. *Ibid.*, pp. 4-5.
33. *The Economist*, March 13, 1993.
34. John A. Gardiner, *op. cit.*, pp. 22-23.
35. *Ibid.*, p. 24.
36. Quoted in *The Economist*, April 26, 1997.
37. *Ibid.*, May 24, 1997.
38. *Ibid.*, September 10, 1994.
39. *Far Eastern Economic Review*, December 1, 1994.
40. *The Economic Times*, July 23, 1997.
41. *The Economist*, August 24, 1996.
42. *The Hindustan Times* (Patna ed.), February 6, 1996.
43. *The Hindustan Times*, October 29, 1996.
44. Extracts from the charge sheets filed by the CBI, *The Sunday Times of India, Patna*, August 10, 1997.
45. *Prabhat Khabar*, June 30, 1997.

12

Epilogue

Our survey makes it amply clear that the crimes variously known as non-conventional or non-traditional or white-collar crimes are a worldwide phenomenon. Corruption is a major constituent of these crimes. Notwithstanding what some uninformed people may say, the late Prime Minister Indira Gandhi was absolutely correct when she asserted that corruption was a world-wide phenomenon.[1] This is because the white-collar crimes are synbiotically connected with capitalism (which may have some elements of socialism mixed with it and go by some other name). Before the rise of capitalism as the dominant socio-economic formation, such crimes were seldom seen. With capitalism becoming a global system, these crimes have proliferated and their ramifications have assumed international proportions. There is seldom an aspect of socio-economic life untouched by them. Everything in the society, be it media, education, religion, politics, bureaucracy and so on is sought to be used by capitalists for earning maximum profits. In this process, criminality enters into all of them.

As the countries modernise or advance on the path of, what Simon Kuznets said, modern economic growth, these crimes of which corruption is the most important constituent do not disappear, but assume new dimensions and bigger proportions. There are reasons for this. As the father of modern capitalism, Adam Smith, said that individuals do not act with any sense or consideration of benevolence but solely on the basis of their self-interest. They do their utmost to further their self-interest without caring for its impact on the society at large. Thus, a white-collar crime can be justifiably used to further one's self-interest without caring for its implications for fellow beings and the nation. Likewise "corruption is the illegitimate reminder of the values of the market place (everything can be bought and sold) that in the age of capitalism increasingly, even legitimately, permeate formerly autonomous political and social spheres.'[2] There is a basic contradiction between capitalism and democracy. In capitalism, it is the logic of the marketplace that matters and only those who have money at their disposal matter and enjoy sovereignty. Those who do not have purchasing power to back their desires do not count. Under democracy, the people irrespective of the purchasing power at their disposal are regarded as sovereign and they are equal because every adult, whether rich or poor, has only one vote. Thus, there is equality, at least, in the formal sense while capitalism is a socio-economic formations where people can never be equal. Consequently, equality-oriented modern democracy always conflicts with inequitous capitalist socio-economic formation and those who have greater command over economic resources try to bend democracy and its various institutions to subserve their own ends which most often conflict with social interests and goals. It has been demonstrated umpteen times that the pursuit of self-interest does not pass through even competition in the marketplace, prove advantageous to the society as a whole. It is, therefore, wrong to say that curb on the growth of monopolies will eliminate corruption and other white-collar crimes.

The onward march of capitalism has aggravated the problem of white-collar crimes. Scientific and technological revolution, especially in the field of information, has, as we have demonstrated, made them more sophisticated and intricate and reduced the capacity of any State to detect them and catch their perpetrators. Electronic money has put central banks in a quandary. They cannot stop money laundering and the transfer of money from one part of the globe to the other, undetected. The conventional weapons in their armoury are no longer equal to the task. It is no easy job to accommodate both economic and political freedom or private and public power. Quite often white-collar crimes accomplish this task. Sometimes, when they come into the open, there is a great deal of popular anger against those perpetrating them and they are arraigned before courts of law to answer charges against them. If found guilty, they are fined or made to serve jail-terms. Though this regular ritual temporarily calms public anger, it does not solve the problem on any lasting basis, precisely because the fountainhead of such crimes, capitalist system, remains. Thus, white-collar crimes are symptoms not the disease. In a country like India, 'The 'disease' is...the frustrated popular yearning for 'the good society', to be achieved by democratic means, yet confronting an economic system that may well contribute materially but does not contribute morally (in the sense of valuing public participation and consent) to that desired social end: an economic system, moreover, that substantially escapes democratic control.'[3] And, we in India, must not forget that "Political sovereignty (in a democracy) and economic sovereignty (consumer choice in a free market) are not equivalent terms. Despite being equal political units, the millionaire, at one end of the scale, brings immense economic power to the market, which dominates social existence, as Max Weber long ago pointed out; while the worker or small farmer, at the other end, has little or no effective demand whatsoever."[4]

White-collar crimes in general and corruption in particular do not have the same impact in a growing economy and a stagnant or declining economy. We can see the difference by comparing the situation in Maharashtra and with that in Bihar. In the former they are just like froth but in the latter they lead to a grave crisis. This is because in a dynamic economy, they lead only to greater inequalities in the distribution of both economic resources and power and nobody is a net loser. But, contrary to liberal thinking, consumerism, commercialised values, self-centredness and so on come to dominate non-economic spheres. Look at the American society and see how many people even bothered about the rest of the world. In a stagnant economy inequalities increase and along with this large masses of people find their lot worsening. This poses grave dangers irrespective of the fact whether there is democracy or some other system of government.

For a multi-party democracy to function in a country like India, collusion between politics and business is inevitable. Both need each other. Politicians need economic resources to sustain their activities, including electioneering while businessmen require their services to overcome hurdles in their advance. The mafia and bureaucracy also play an important role in bringing about and sustaining this collusion. Depending on the objective situation, this collusion can be functional or malfunctional. In a dynamic economy like that which occurs in South Korea or Taiwan or Singapore or Malaysia, it is functional, but in Bangladesh it will be malfunctional. In Bihar, it is bound to be malfunctional, but not so much in Gujarat, Haryana and Karnataka.

With economic liberalisation and globalisation aided by revolutionary changes in the sphere of information technology, the incidence of white-collar criminality is bound to increase both in the extent and intensity as Kamal Nayan Kabra asserted in his pamphlet on the Harshad Mehta episode.[5] In a survey "Corruption: Reform's Dark Side", *Far Eastern Economic Review* (March 20, 1997) found that in 1996, 'From Pakistan to Japan, corruption was the year's biggest story.'

In South Korea, two former Presidents along with several business tycoons were convicted for bribery and corruption. In Pakistan, a Prime Minister was dismissed on charges of corruption and her husband arrested for corruption and collusion with the mafia and in our own country, the former Prime Minister, Mr. Narasimha Rao and several of his colleagues and other politicians were arraigned before courts of law. Bihar Chief Minister, Laloo Yadav and his three colleagues, several bureaucrats, businessmen, three M.L.A.s along with a former Chief Minister were found to be involved in the fodder scam. There were other scams in which investigation was on. In the neighbouring U.P., there surfaced Ayurvedic scam, involving a minister and several bureaucrats and businessmen. In Assam too there was a scam.

In a study entitled: "The New Corruption" by Barbara Harriss-White and Gordon White of Britain's Institute of Development Studies, it is stated that 'in some contexts... the amount of corruption has increased along with and apparently as a result of economic liberalization.' In a separate study of southern India, based on empirical surveys, Harriss-White is of the view that deregulation may be accompanied by 'mutations in relations of corruption."[6] What it amounts to is that with economic reforms based on liberalisation and globalisation, white-collar crimes have taken on new forms.

There are people who claim that increased incidence of white-collar crimes in general and graft in particular is due to incomplete or inadequate reforms. They think, once they are completed, the incidence will go down. This claim is not sustained on the basis of empirical studies of the situations in developed countries like Britain, the USA, Japan, France, Italy and so on. As we have already mentioned, these crimes result from the very nature of capitalism and its basic contradiction with democracy.

It must be stated here quite categorically that we are not among those who are opposed to economic reforms. We think, if the reforms bring in a dynamic economy in the country, bettering the lot of everybody, then corruption and other white-collar crimes will be just like a froth. But if this does not happen and in a country like India regional disparities increase and some States or regions go on stagnating or declining economically, there will be dangerous implications for the unity and polity of the country. No amount of *sátyagrah* (as wanted by Mr. I.K. Gujral) or *sadachar samitis* (*a la* Gulzari Lal Nanda) can be of any help. If someone still wants to go in for such a prescription, it means he has not drawn any lesson from

Cervantes's *Don Quixote* that with the changing situations, the mode of behaviour and attitude must change. In fact, one should read Dickens and Balzac, the best chroniclers of the days of emerging industrial capitalism. Even a person like Marx used to advise his friends to read them rather than learned tomes. What we want to underline is this that there is no use lamenting at the situation. What is required is to derive proper lessons from the forerunners and try to mitigate the evil results of modern capitalism in such a way that no harm is done to dynamism of the economy. In this context, the role of the State has to be well thought out and properly designed.

While supporting economic reforms, a note of caution needs to be sounded. There is every likelihood in view of what has been witnessed in Mumbai and elsewhere that there is a real danger of the mafia capitalist coming to occupy a significant position in the economy. If this is not checked, Indian society, polity and culture will face grave dangers. In this context, one must pay heed to what Arlacchi says in one of his well-known studies: "In order to differentiate between the capitalist, entrepreneur and the mafia entrepreneur, we must consider the relations between the two contrasting spheres of their activity. In the case of the mafia capitalist, his pursuit of rational goals interacts very differently with the extra-economic and irrational sphere of his entrepreneurial activity. Far from progressively enlarging the sway of values and conduct of a rational-capitalist type, the entrepreneurial practices of the *mafiosi* extend the domain governed by archaic and predatory attitudes.

"Mafia capital accumulation is encouraging the recrudescence of a whole range of primitive behaviour patterns. One sees this in the growing tendency for economic conflicts to become inter-family wars and for the market to be transformed into vendetta and bloody personal struggles. The entrepreneurial activity of the mafia is poisoning large stretches of territory and entire sectors of production, with heavier and heavier doses of destructive anarchy and barbarism and is proving one of the gravest threats to democracy and development."[7]

The popular pressure needs to be built to underline that white-collar crimes are, in several ways, more disastrous than traditional or conventional crimes. Since those who indulge in white-collar crimes belong to the same class that controls the State machinery or constitutes the ruling class, it has witnessed a soft or lenient attitude towards them. This is evident how various law-enforcement agencies have been proceeding in the cases involving the rich and influential. Look at any scam, there is always dilly-dallying by the CBI in spite of monitoring of investigation by a High Court or Supreme Court and then there is a delay on the part of the government in according sanction for prosecuting the accused. Take another example, the law-enforcing agencies are very harsh as regards a pick-pocket or a thief or a common murderer, but it is soft towards tax-evaders, scamsters, fraudsters, those who adulterate food, drinks and drugs or hoard essential items of consumption or disregard safety measures in factories, mines and building construction, unmindful of likely disastrous consequences. The government goes on giving one option after another to white-collar criminals to facilitate laundering of their ill-gotten wealth. This reflects the class-bias and there can be an attack on this only when other classes are organised and brought in to mount pressures on those who control State-machinery.

Our foregoing survey makes us differ with Huntington who thinks that 'low-level bureaucratic officials are more likely to be corrupt than high-level ones; State and local officials are more likely to be corrupt than national ones; the top national leadership and the national Cabinet are comparatively free from corruption, while the town council and local offices are deeply involved in it.'[8] So far as India is concerned, Huntington may be, to some extent, right for the Nehru era, but he is certainly wrong when we view his remarks in the context of the post-Nehru era. Moreover, the total damage done by highly placed white-collar criminals are many times larger than by petty politicians, bureaucrats and businessmen.

If what our survey has revealed has any validity, it makes it clear that corruption and other white-collar crimes are not indulged in by the people who find it difficult to balance their budgets. The incidence of white-collar criminality is not related inversely to a person's amount of legitimate earnings. In other words, it is wrong to say that the poorer a person, the greater is his motivation to indulge in white-collar criminality. On this basis, we can also assert that higher legitimate payments seldom go a long way towards reducing white-collar crimes.[9] In this context, it needs to be remembered, as our survey has emphasised, that 'the type of corruption that most damages economic growth is not petty bribery but rather the massive theft of State funds by venal politicians and their senior henchmen. It is hard to believe that corruption at this level is much influenced by official pay scales. And the pettier forms of corruption are anyway much harder to control when office juniors see their masters filching vast quantities of other people's money.'[10]

One of the important ways of corruption for highly placed politicians is transfer and posting mechanism. Unfortunately, there is a dearth of empirical studies on this. From our personal experience, we know that the money earned out of the exercise of this mechanism is shared by bureaucrats and politicians in power and, sometimes, politicians outside the government, who are informally given a quota of transfers and postings. The Damocles' sword of transfers to inconvenient places, disturbing the life-styles and causing hardships to the members of the family and putting impediments in the way of children's education, besides wiping out or reducing extra earnings, keeps a constant pressure on bureaucrats. In these circumstances very few refuse to be pliable.

What constitutes a corrupt practice differs from person to person. To explain this, let us take an example. If a bureaucrat accepts money or some kind of reward (like job for himself after retirement or for his son/daughter in some private sector outfit) for doing some favour, he is held to be guilty of corruption, but, if a politician promises or sanctions some project for a region or a section of population in return for votes, he is not declared corrupt. Thus, bureaucratic bribe and electoral bribe are judged from two different standards. How far this is correct is a matter of debate.

Corruption also needs to be looked at from another angle. There is parochial corruption under which seldom any money transaction takes place. Ties of caste/sub-caste, religion, region, family, friendship and so on rather than the merit of the case influence the decision-making process. And then, there is corruption where the money matters and the highest bidder, other things remaining the same, gets the decision made in his favour. At times, both of them get intermingled. In Bihar, we have seen the concessional rates of bribe available to certain castes, said to be desperately in need of "social justice". Obviously, an element of rebate enters the market-determined amount of bribe. "It is precisely in those areas of government activity involving a large number of small transactions—the issuance of drivers' licences and permits for village market stalls, the settlements of minor criminal charges, the acquisition of seats or freight space on railways cars, to mention but a few,—that 'price' corruption is common. Over time, it is also in these areas that market corruption tends to become institutionalized so that there is a widely known and rather stable price for a particular action. By contrast, the market in large transactions involving such benefits as important permits or large construction contracts is likely to show less price stability and a greater intrusion of parochial considerations".[11]

What is, thus, required is a good government based on effective representative democracy with a strong Opposition drawing its sustenance from working people, which is well-informed and does not confine itself only to rhetorics (as has been witnessed in India since Independence). This will reduce the incidence of white-collar crimes to a substantial extent. If the parties of working people, trade unions and the associations of professionals decide to draw their funds from the sections of the society, whose interests they claim to champion and stick to this decision and go in for transparency by publishing the details of their incomes and expenditures, their credibility will go-up and they will be in a position to fight white-collar crimes more vigorously. Till now no such thing seems to be happening. There is hardly any political party which does not draw large chunks of its funds from those who are white-collar criminals.

In the end, if one wants to break the deadly nexus of politics with criminals, one has no alternative but to refer to Gandhi and his insistence on purity of means. Dirty means can help achieve laudable ends, but either the ends will not be lasting or there will be, sooner or later, disastrous consequences. Let everyone remember what he said seven decades ago: "Corruption will be out one day, however much one may try to conceal it and the public can, as it is its right and duty, in every case of justifiable suspicion, call its servants to strict account, dismiss them, sue them in a law court or appoint an arbitrator or inspector to scrutinise their conduct, as it likes."[12]

REFERENCES

1. *Mainstream*, August 23, 1997, p. 2.
2. John Girling, *Corruption, Capitalism and Democracy*, London, 1997, p. vii.
3. *Ibid.*, p. viii.
4. *Ibid.*
5. Kamal Nayan Kabra, *op. cit.*
6. Quoted in *Far Eastern Economic Review*, March 20, 1997.
7. Pino Arlacchi, *Mafia Business*, London, 1986, p. xvi.
8. S. Huntington, *Political Order in Changing Societies*, New Haven, 1968, p. 68.
9. International Monetary Fund, *Corruption and the Rate of Temptation: Do Low Wages in the Civil Service Cause Corruption*, IMF working paper, May 1997.
10. *The Economist*, August 16, 1997.
11. James Scott, *Comparative Political Corruption*, Englewood Cliffs, 1972, pp. 88-89.
12. *Young India*, December 16, 1928.

Appendix-I

Vohra Committee Report

1.1 Government had (through its Order No. S/7937/SS(ISP)/93 dated 9th July '93) established a Committee, comprised as below, to take stock of all available information about the activities of crime syndicates/Mafia organisations which had developed links with and were being protected by Government functionaries and political personalities. Based on the recommendations of the Committee, Government shall determine the need, if any, to establish a special organisation/agency to regularly collect information and pursue cases against such elements:

(i)	Home Secretary	Chairman
(ii)	Secretary (R)	Member
(iii)	DIB	Member
(iv)	Director CBI	Member
(v)	JS(PP) MHA	Member Secy.

1.2 The Committee was authorised to invite senior officers of various concerned Departments to gather the required information.

1.3 Special Secretary (Internal Security & Police), MHA, was subsequently added as a Member of the Committee. The Committee was desired to submit its Report within 3 months.

2.1 In the first meeting of the Committee (held on 15th

July '93), I had explained to the Members that Government had established the Committee after seeing the reports of our Intelligence and Investigation agencies on the activities/linkages of the Dawood Ibrahim gang, consequent of the bomb blasts in Bombay in March, 1993. From these various reports, it was apparent that the activities of Memon Brothers and Dawood Ibrahim had progressed over the years, leading to the establishment of a powerful network. This could not have happened without these elements having been protected by the functionaries of the concerned Government departments, specially Customs, Income Tax, Police and others. It was, therefore, necessary to identify the linkages and to also determine how such information could be timely collected and acted upon in the future.

2.2 In the course of the discussions, I perceived that some of the Members appeared to have some hesitation in openly expressing their views and also seemed unconvinced that Government actually intended to pursue such matters. Accordingly, I addressed separate personal letters to each of the Members of the Committee seeking their well considered suggestions and recommendations. Their responses are briefly brought out below.

Secretary (R&AW)

2.3 The various offices abroad of this Agency have limited strength and are largely geared to the collection of military, economic, scientific and political intelligence. R&AW monitors the activities of certain organisations abroad only insofar as they relate to their involvement with narco-terrorist elements and smuggling arms, ammunition, explosives, etc. into the country. It does not monitor the activities of criminal elements abroad which are mainly confined to "normal smuggling without any links to terrorist elements". The present strength of the Agency's offices abroad would not permit it to enlarge its field of activities. If, however, there is evidence to suggest that these organisations have links with Intelligence agencies of other countries, particularly Pakistan and that they are being used or are likely to be used by such countries for destabilising our economy, it would become R&AW's responsibility to monitor their activities, as is being done by this Agency to collect vital information in regard to the investigations in the Bombay bomb blasts case.

2.4 The creation of a nodal agency to collect information regarding the activities of mafia organisations is very essential. All the existing information/data available with R&AW, IB and CBI could be made available to this nodal agency. R&AW will nominate an officer of suitable rank to liaise with the nodal agency on a regular basis to enable expeditious follow-up action.

Director CBI

3.1 A report on the nexus between the Bombay City Police and the Bombay underworld was prepared by CBI in 1986. It would be useful to institute a fresh study by CBI, on the basis of which appropriate administrative/legal measures could be initiated.

3.2 An organised crime syndicate/mafia generally commences its activities by indulging in petty crime at the local level, mostly relating to illicit distillation/gambling/organised satta and prostitution in the larger towns. In port towns, their activities involve smuggling and sale of imported goods and progressively graduate to narcotics and drug trafficking. In the bigger cities, the main source of income relates to real estate—forcibly occupying lands/buildings, procuring such properties at cheap rates by forcing out the existing occupants/tenants, etc. Over time, the money power thus acquired is used for building up contacts with bureaucrats and politicians and expansion of activities with impunity. The money power is used to develop a network of muscle-power which is also used by the politicians during elections.

3.3 CBI has reported that all over India crime syndicates

have become a law unto themselves. Even in the smaller towns and rural areas, muscle-men have become the order of the day. Hired assassins have become a part of these organisations. The nexus between the criminal gangs, police, bureaucracy and politicians has come out clearly in various parts of the country. The existing criminal justice system, which was essentially designed to deal with the individual offences/crimes, is unable to deal with the activities of the mafia; the provisions of law in regard to economic offences are weak; there are insurmountable legal difficulties in attaching/confiscation of the property acquired through mafia activities.

3.4 It has been suggested that the menace has first to be tackled at the local level where the agencies of the State and the concerned Central Enforcement Agencies like Customs and Excise, Income Tax, etc. would be required to take effective action. In cases where a crime syndicate has graduated to big business, it would be necessary to conduct detailed investigations into its assets, both movable and immovable. It has been stressed that when such action is not timely and effectively taken, the lower functionaries of the concerned State and Central Departments/organisations start overlooking the activities of the crime Syndicates. To elucidate this point, the Director, CBI has given the example of Iqbal Mirchi of Bombay who, till the late 80s, was merely a visitor to passenger and carrier ships to obtain liquor and cigarettes for selling the same at a profit. In the last 3-4 years, Mirchi acquired real estate valuing crores of rupees; he has many bank accounts and has been paying lakhs of rupees to his carriers. The growth of Mirchi is due to the fact that the concerned Enforcement agencies did not timely take action against him and, later, this perhaps became difficult on account of the enormous patronage that he had developed. If Mirchi is investigated, the entire patronage enjoyed by him and his linkages will come to light. Director, CBI has observed that there are many such cases, as that of Mirchi where the initial failure has led to the emergence of mafia giants who have become too big to be tackled.

3.5 Director CBI has stated that the main mode of communications/contacts of the mafias operating at the international level is through telephonic communications. Referring to the useful leads emerging from the investigations into the activities of Dawood Ibrahim, a mafia leader, the Director, CBI has stated that the effective monitoring of the telephone calls made from India/received from abroad would yield useful information and, for this being done, Government may grant sanction to monitor certain telephone connections.

3.6 The assistance of banks is an essential input. The bank managers can be placed under obligation to render reports on all heavy transactions and suspicious accounts to the Enforcement agencies. Such a practice obtains in UK.

3.7 Concluding his analysis, Director, CBI has made the following suggestions to bring under control the activities of the criminal syndicates:

(i) Identification of offences and award of deterrent punishments, including preventive detention.

(ii) Trial procedures should be simplified and hastened.

(iii) Surveillance should be carried out through finger printing, photographs and dossiers.

(iv) Monitoring mechanisms should be established at the State and Central levels.

(v) Establishment of Special Cells in the States CIDs and CBI.

(vi) Suitable amendments should be introduced in the existing laws to more effectively deal with the activities of mafia organisations, etc.; this would also include review of the existing laws.

(vii) A detailed case study of 10-15 case would provide useful information regarding the administrative/ legal measures which would be required to be taken to effectively tackle the functioning of Mafia organisations. The CBI can do this within a short period.

Director IB

6.1 DIB has reported that due to the progressive decline in the values of public life in the country "warning signals of sinister linkage between the underworld politicians and the bureaucracy have been evident with disturbing regularity, as exemplified by the exposures of the networks of the Bombay blast case". He has recommended immediate attention to:-

(i) Identification of the nexus between the criminals/ mafias and anti-national elements on the one hand and bureaucrats, politicians and other sensitively located individuals on the other.

(ii) Identification of the nature and dimensions of these linkages and the *modus-operandi* of their operations.

(iii) Assessment of the impact of these linkages on the various institutions, viz., the electoral, political, economic, law and order and the administrative apparatus.

(iv) Nexus, if any, between the domestic linkages with foreign intelligence.

(v) Necessary action to show effective action to counteract/neutralise the mafia activities.

(vi) Political and legal constraints in dealing with the covert/illegal functioning of the linkages.

6.2 Like the Director, CBI, the DIB has also stated that there has been a rapid spread and growth of criminal gangs, armed senas, drug mafias, smuggling gangs, drug peddlers and economic lobbies in the country which have, over the years, developed an extensive network of contacts with the bureaucrats/Government functionaries at the local levels, politicians, media persons and strategically located individuals in the non-State sector. Some of these syndicates also have international linkages, including the foreign intelligence agencies. In this context, the DIB has given the following examples:-

(i) In certain States, like Bihar, Haryana and UP, these gangs enjoy the patronage of local level politicians, cutting across party lines and the protection of Governmental functionaries. Some political leaders become the leaders of these gangs/arms senas and, over the years, get themselves elected to local bodies, State Assemblies and the national Parliament. Resultantly, such elements have acquired considerable political clout seriously jeopardising the smooth functioning of the administration and the safety of life and property of the common man, causing a sense of despair and alienation among the people.

(ii) The big smuggling Syndicates, having international linkages, have spread into and infected the various economic and financial activities, including hawala transactions, circulation of black money and operations of a vicious parallel economy causing serious damage to the economic fibre of the country. These Syndicates have acquired substantial financial and muscle power and social respectability and have successfully corrupted the Government machinery at all levels and yield enough influence to make the task of investigating and prosecuting agencies extremely difficult; even the members of the judicial system have not escaped the embrace of the mafia.

(iii) Certain elements of the mafia have shifted to narcotics, drugs and weapons smuggling and established narco-terrorism networks, specially in the States of J&K, Punjab, Gujarat and Maharashtra. The cost of contesting elections has thrown the politician into the lap of these elements and led to a grave compromise by officials of the preventive/detection systems. The virus has spread to almost all the centres in the country; the coastal and the border States have been particularly affected.

(iv) The Bombay bomb blast case and the communal riots in Surat and Ahmedabad have demonstrated how the Indian underworld has been exploited by the Pakistan ISI and the latter's network in UAE to cause sabotage, subversion and communal tension in varicus parts of the country. The investigations into the Bombay bomb blast cases have revealed extensive linkages of the underworld in the various governmental agencies, political circles, business sector and the film world.

6.3 DIB has stated that the network of the mafia is virtually running a parallel Government, pushing the State apparatus into irrelevance. It is thus, most immediately necessary that an institution is established to effectively deal with the menace. In this connection, the DIB has stated:-

(i) Presently, there is no system/mechanism which is specifically designated to collect and collate intelligence pertaining to the linkages developed by crime syndicates/mafias with the governmental set up. Nonetheless, the various intelligence/investigation/enforcement agencies collect, in the normal course of their functioning, information about the nexus between the bureaucracy and politicians with the mafia gangs, smugglers and the underworld. These agencies use such available inputs "only within the narrow confines of their work charter and choose not to take undue cognisance and follow-up action, leave alone sharing intelligence with any other agencies". Thus, all these agencies "function within their own cocoons, with the result that a plethora of information fails to get specific and purposeful attention needed for the exposure of the linkages". It is, therefore, necessary to immediately have an institutionalised system which "while giving total freedom to the various agencies to pursue their charter of work, would simultaneously cast on them the onus of sharing such inputs to a nodal outfit whose job will be to process this information for attention of a single designated authority". This will enable the nodal group to provide useful leads to the various agencies and, over time, a progressive data base will get generated "to facilitate periodic reviews and analysis which could then be passed to a designated body".

7.1 As would be seen from the aforestated brief discussion, specially the views expressed by Director, CBI and DIB, it is evident that the muscle power of the crime syndicates is sustained by their enormous financial power which, in turn, is secured by the mafia elements by committing economic offences with impunity. In this context, I held detailed personal discussions with Secretary (Revenue) under whose control operate the various economic intelligence/investigative/enforcement agencies.

7.2 The Department of Revenue functions through the following major agencies:-

(i) Central Board of Excise & Customs (CBEC)

(i) *Inter-alia*, CBEC is responsible for the prevention of smuggling. In this and other tasks, it is assisted by the *Director General of Revenue Intelligence* (DGRI) and the Director General of Anti-Evasion (DGAE). The DGRI deals with the evasion of customs duties; the DGAE with Excise duty evasion.

(ii) Central Board of Direct Taxes (CBDT)

Income Tax Department administers the Income Tax Act, Wealth Tax Act, etc.

(iii) Central Economic Intelligence Bureau (CEIB)

The CEIB is responsible for coordinating and strengthening the intelligence gathering activities and the investigative and enforcement actions of the various agencies responsible for investigation into economic offences and the enforcement of economic laws. The CEIB is responsible for maintaining liaison with the concerned Departments/Directorates both at the Centre and at the State levels and is expected to provide overall direction to the investigative agencies under the Department of Revenue.

The CEIB is expected, *inter alia*, to attends to the following tasks:-

(a) Identification of major sources generating black money; directing and developing intelligence about such sources; planning and coordinating action and operations against such sources.

(b) Assisting the various enforcement agencies in strengthening the intelligence gathering infrastructure and building up their capability for storage and retrieval of intelligence.

(c) Conducting investigative and analytical studies in difficult areas of black money operations and monitoring indicators thereof.

(iv) Enforcement Directorate

This Directorate is concerned with the enforcement of the investigation and penal provision of the Foreign Exchange Regulation Act; collection of intelligence relating to foreign exchange offences; enquiries into suspected violations of the provisions of FERA, etc.

(v) Narcotics Control Bureau (NCB)

The NCB is responsible for the administration of the Narcotic Drugs and Psychotropic Act. It is responsible for coordination with different Central and State

Government Departments/Ministries and the various Central and State law enforcement agencies for the implementation of the NDPS Act.

7.3 I explained to Secretary (Revenue) the broad considerations on account of which the government had set up a Committee to look into the linkages developed by the mafia elements. He informed me that he had recently held a meeting with senior representatives of the RBI, the Chairman, CBEC, Chairman, CBDT and the Economic Intelligence Council in the Department of Revenue, and readily agreed with my request to attend a meeting of the Committee along with his concerned officers for a full discussion on the issues before the Committee. Accordingly, I arranged a meeting of the Committee (30th Aug, '93) to hear the views of Secretary (Revenue), who was accompanied by Chairman, CBDT, DGRI, Member (Customs) and Director (Enforcement). During the course of the discussions with Secretary (Revenue) and his aforesaid principal officers, the following significant observations were made:-

(i) In the normal course of his work, to detect violations of Customs and Excise laws, the DGRI comes across information on linkages between crime syndicates and governmental functionaries, etc. As following up of such information is not within the charter of duties of DGRI, his officers focus primarily on the information relating to the violation of the laws relating to their charter.

(ii) As in the case of DGRI, indirect information also becomes available to the CBDT about linkages. Here again, not being directly relating to their charter of responsibilities, the CBDT do not follow up such leads.

(iii) While the NCB is specifically responsible for booking drug traffickers, with the increasing importance being given to narco-terrorism, the NCB has been asked to gather further information so that the real kingpins in the narcotics trade can be apprehended.

(iv) The Directorate of Enforcement comes across information on linkages and passes it on to the CBI and IB.

(v) Of late, currency amounting to crores of rupees is being seized, invariably packed in suitcases and gunny bags. The banks are reluctant to pass on information about account holders to CBDT and do not allow their officers to hold exploratory enquiries.

(vi) While a certain amount of information is shared between the various organisations under the Department of Revenue, and those under the MHA and Cabinet Secretariat, the exchanges are sporadic and limited. This is perhaps due to the fact that each concerned organisation/agency is anxious to protect its sources and is apprehensive that a full sharing of all information might jeopardise its operations, on account of premature leakage of information.

(vii) While DGRI, Director (Enforcement) and DG, NCB are authorised to undertake phone tapping of suspected offenders, the DGRI has not been allowed to enforce surveillance on the telephonic communications of political personalities.

(viii) Senior police officers, even in the border States, are not trained or adequately informed of the work done by the Directorate of Enforcement, specially in regard to money laundering operations.

(ix) Information about the activities of drug traffickers is passed on by DG, NCB to the concerned State Governments and their agencies. However, niggardly responses by the latter and prolonged delays in the disposal of cases before the courts seriously hampers the effective functioning of the NCB. While the NDPS Act prescribes the award of deterrent punishments to offenders, the results are to the contrary. It is necessary that the Directorates of Prosecution in the State Governments are urgently brought under the control of the State Police.

7.5 Secretary (Revenue) stated that the field officers of his various departments were faced with various problems, amongst which are:

(i) The utter inadequacy of the criminal justice system; cases are not heard timely; functioning of the Government lawyers is grossly inadequate; all this results in a low percentage of convictions and mild punishments. Unless the criminal justice system is geared up, the work of the enforcement agencies cannot be effective.

(ii) The field officers of the various agencies of the Revenue Department are often pressurised by senior government functionaries/political leaders, apparently at the behest of crime syndicates/ mafia elements. Unless the field level officers are offered effective protection, they cannot be expected to maintain interest in vigorously pursuing action against the activities of such elements.

7.6 Chairman, CBDT stated that insofar as the functioning of his officers is concerned, whenever they come into possession of any information regarding the violation of any other law, they pass it on to the concerned agency. He suggested that if the information available with other agencies is passed on to him, his officers could pursue the same.

8.1 As a result of the discussions held by the Committee with Secretary (Revenue) and his principal officers, it is evident that:

(i) While, in the course of their normal activities, information on the linkages of the crime syndicates sometimes becomes available, such information is not pursued on the score that it is not directly related to offences falling within the laws administered by these agencies;

(ii) such information is occasionally passed on by these agencies to the CBI and or IB;

(iii) the various agencies under the Department of Revenue do not specifically search out information on the linkages of crime syndicates.

9.1 Consequent to the Committee's discussion with the Secretary (Revenue) and his principal officers, I held a series of further personal discussions with the Secretary (Revenue). At my request, Secretary (Revenue) gave me a personal note indicating his views, which are given briefly as below:-

(i) The information gathered by the various agencies under the Revenue Department, while gathering intelligence on offences relating to the laws administered by them, is generally not put to any use unless it is required to be passed on to other intelligence agencies outside the Department of Revenue.

(ii) The linkages developed by crime syndicates get generally confirmed when pressure is mounted on the concerned agencies not to take action against the offenders or to go slow in the cases against them. Such pressures are mounted either immediately after a raid is conducted or at the time when prosecution is about to be initiated. Pressures are also exerted whenever corrupt and undesirable officers are shifted from sensitive assignments (Preventive Customs Divisions at the airports, sensitive Collectorates in the Central Excise, etc.).

(iii) In the narcotics arena, which includes cultivation of opium, manufacture of alkaloids, prevention of narcotics, smuggling, etc. the financial stakes are astronomically high. Consequently, the level of corruption is of a very high order in this area of functioning and enormous pressures are brought to bear even when subordinate officials are posted away, specially when the shift of an officer adversely affects the interests of those who are making easy money.

(iv) Narcotics trade has a world-wide network of smugglers who also have close links with terrorists. Terrorists indulge in narcotics trade to amass huge funds, in various foreign currencies, from which they source their procurement of weapons, etc.

9.2 While the Department of Revenue has initiated a number of steps to deal with the activities of smugglers and to plug loopholes in the system, Secretary (Revenue) has stated that a possible approach to effectively liquidating the linkages developed by the crime syndicates would be to mercilessly prosecute the offenders without succumbing to any pressure whatsoever. He is of the view that once the offenders are deterrently punished under the law, their influence and strength will start declining, as also of all those who support them, wherever located. He has emphasised that for this objective being achieved it will be extremely necessary that: the entire governmental machinery involved in taking action against the crime syndicates is allowed to perform its duties with total freedom; officers with impeccable integrity should be posted to head the various organisations which are responsible for taking action against tax offenders, smugglers, etc. Such officers should be selected with utmost care and provided sufficiently long tenures, giving them the clear mandate to ruthlessly punish the offenders; action must be taken to ensure the objective functioning of courts which deal with the trial of economic offences; all cases before the courts should be speedily concluded without the judicial officers coming under any pressure or succumbing to temptations; inefficient and corrupt elements in the various organisations must be weeded out and Government should take stringent action against officers who seek to exert political pressure for securing postings and appointments of their choice.

10.1 From the above narrated analysis, the following conclusions can be drawn:-

(i) On the basis of the extensive experience gained by our various concerned intelligence, investigative and enforcement agencies, it is apparent that crime syndicates and mafia organisations have established themselves in various parts of the country.

(ii) The various crime syndicates/mafia organisations have developed significant muscle and money power and established linkages with governmental functionaries, political leaders and others to be able to operate with impunity (as recently examplified by the activities of the Memon Brothers and Dawood Ibrahim).

(iii) While the CBI and IB and the various agencies under the Department of Revenue, in their normal course of functioning, come across information relating to the linkages of crime syndicates/mafia organisations, there is presently no system under which they are expected to pass-on such information to an identified nodal agency. Sharing of such information is presently of an occasional nature and no evidence is available of the same having been put to any operational use (the only mentionable exception perhaps relates to the recent investigations into the activities of Memon Brothers and the Dawood gang on which several of our agencies were put to work collectively).

11.1 Even where an agency comes across certain information about the linkages of crime syndicates, it has no mandate to immediately pass it on to one or more agencies. An agency which comes across information regarding linkages is also apprehensive that the sharing of such information may jeopardize its own functioning through premature leakage. In sum, the various agencies presently in the field take care to essentially focus on their respective character of duties, dealing with the infringement of laws relating to their organisations and consciously putting aside any information on linkages which they may come across.

12.1 In the discussions in the Committee, I asked each of the Members as well as the Secretary (Revenue) and his principal officers about their views regarding the establishment of a nodal agency for the collection, collation and operationalisation of all information relating to the activities of crime syndicates. Broadly, the following approaches have been mooted:

(i) The DIB has stated that while considering the establishment of any nodal mechanism "It must be appreciated that the problems has enormous impact on national security and is indeed highly political in nature". In this context, he has suggested that the nodal set-up should be under the IB, which is even otherwise engaged in monitoring various political activities having a bearing on national security. He has recommended that "an exclusive top secret cell be established in the IB to function as the nodal group for receipt of inputs from various security/ revenue agencies which reveal a politician-bureaucrat-underworld nexus. Such sharing will be through personal communications in writing, while operating difficulties could be sorted out through periodic meetings among the heads of these organisations to be chaired by the Home Secretary". The top secret cell will share all tactical and operational information with other concerned agencies on "need to know and act basis".

(ii) The other approach recommended is to set up a system under which the Heads of the various

Intelligence and Revenue agencies shall meet on a regular basis and exchange vital information, without there being any leakage.

13.1 In the background of the discussions so far, there does not appear to be need for any further debate on the vital importance of setting up of a nodal point to which all existing Intelligence and Enforcement agencies (irrespective of the department under which they are located) shall promptly pass on any information which they may come across, which relates to the activities of crime syndicates.

13.2 If the pre-position in the preceding para is sustained, a decision will need to be taken regarding the department/ministry under which the nodal set-up should be located.

14.1 Under the existing arrangements for the transaction of Government business, the Ministry of Home Affairs is responsible for all matters relating to internal security. It is for this reason that the Intelligence Bureau is a part and parcel of this Ministry (It is only by tradition that the DIB reports directly to authorities outside MHA). R&AW functions under the Cabinet Secretariat and deals with external intelligence. The various Intelligence, Investigation and Enforcement agencies dealing with the implementation of economic laws report to the Revenue Department under the Ministry of Finance. The CBI, which is the principal criminal investigation agency of the Centre, is under the Department of Personnel.

14.2 In my view, considerable care would have to be taken to ensure that the information which becomes available to the nodal cell is handled by a very senior and trust-worthy officer. Any leakage of such information would not only jeopardize potential action against the powerful criminal syndicates, but may also be suceptible to political exploitation. Under all circumstances, it will have to be ensured that the information available with the nodal set-up is used strictly and entirely for stringent action against the crime syndicates, without allowing any scope whatever of its being exploited for political gain.

14.3 In the preceding context, it would be logical if the nodal set-up is under the MHA, directly handled by the Home Secretary who can be assisted by one or more selected officers of the Ministry for the collation and compilation of all information received from IB, CBI, R&AW and the various agencies under the Department of Revenue. The manner in which such information is operationalised would need to be confidentially discussed with the concerned Heads of Organisations and, as necessary, with Secretary (Revenue). It will also need to be ensured that the nodal set-up functions with extreme secrecy. Needless to say, any leakage whatever about the linkages of crime syndicate with senior Government functionaries or political leaders in the states or at the Centre could have a destabilising effect on the functioning of Government. As such, it would not appear prudent to entrust the functioning of the nodal cell to any level below that of the Home Secretary. Further, the Government would also have to carefully consider and prescribe the authorities to whom the Home Secretary will report in regard to the sensitive information received by the nodal set-up as well as regarding the operations to be launched by one or more of the concerned agencies to apprehend, investigate and prosecute the offenders.

15.1 In the normal course, this report would have been drafted by the Member Secretary and finalised by the Committee. Considering the nature of the issues involved, I did not consider it desirable to burden the Members of the Committee with any further involvement beyond the views expressed by them. Accordingly, I decided to personally dictate this report.

15.2 I have prepared only three copies of this report. One copy each is being submitted to MOS(IS) and HM, the third copy being retained by me. After HM has persued this report, I request him to consider discussing further action with Finance Minister, MOS(IS) and myself. The emerging approach could thereafter be got approved from Prime Minister before being implementated. At that stage, other concerned senior officers would be taken into confidence.

15.3 After an initial discussion at the level of MOS(IS) and HM, I could send a copy of this report to Finance Minister, before the issues are discussed with him.

Appendix-II

CBI Chargesheet in Bihar Animal Husbandry Scam

RC. 20(A)/96-Pat. is one of the 41 cases registered under the orders of the Hon'ble High Court of Patna dated 11-3-96 in respect of fraudulent withdrawal of money from the Treasuries in Bihar on the strength of forged and fabricated allotment letters for making payments to suppliers for non-existent supplies of feed/fodder, medicines and other equipment. Hon'ble High Court Patna observed:

"I would, accordingly, direct the Central Bureau of Investigation (CBI) through its director, to enquire and scrutinise all cases of excess drawals and expenditure in the department of Animal Husbandry in the state of Bihar during the period 1977-78 to 1995-96 and lodge cases where the drawals are found to be fraudulent in character and take the investigation in those cases to the logical end as early as possible preferably, within four months. The investigation by the state police in cases already instituted shall remain suspended in the meantime."

The Hon'ble Supreme Court of India vide order dated 19-3-1996 modified and passed the following order,

"The order of the Division Bench of the High Court in paragraph 54 to the effect that investigation by the State Police in cases already instituted shall remain suspended, is modified. The entire investigation now stands entrusted to the CBI as aforesaid. The CBI is directed to takeover the

investigation already made by the State Police inclusive of the FIRs, arrest and attachments aforementioned and deal appropriately therewith."

SPE/CBI Regular Case No. 20(A)/96-PAT dated 27-3-96 under sec. 409/420/467/468/471/477/477A/201/511 r/w 120B IPC & Sec. 13(2) r/w Sec. 13 (1) (c) & (d) of P.C. Act, 1988 is a re-registered version of Chaibasa Sadar P.S. Case No. 12/96 dt. 20-02-96 instituted on the basis of a written complaint of Shri Amit Khare, IAS, the then Dy. Commissioner, Chaibasa, West Singhbhum Dist.

Allegation

The allegation in brief in the complaint is that Dr. B. N. Sharma, the then District Animal Husbandry Officer, Chaibasa, in criminal conspiracy with Dr. M.K. Srivastava, Asstt. Director (Poultry), Chaibasa, Dr. G.P. Tripathy, MVO, Chaibasa, Dr. D. Dorai, Manager, Govt. Cattle Farm, Saraikela, other officers, and officials of Animal Husbandry Deptt., West Singhbhum Distt., Shri Silas Tirkey, Treasury Officer, Distt. Treasury, Chaibasa and number of suppliers, withdrew an amount of Rs. 35,66,42,083/- during the year 1994-95 on the strength of false/fake bills of suppliers. It is alleged that such heavy withdrawals were made against a meagre amount of few lakhs of rupees actually allotted by the Finance Deptt. The complaint disclosed that the feed, fodder, medicines and instruments claimed to have been purchased were neither required nor purchased from the accused suppliers.

Result of Investigation

Investigation has revealed that during 1988-96 the accused, shown in column 1 and others unknown, had entered into a criminal conspiracy, and agreed to do or caused to be done illegal act or acts which are not legal by illegal means, at Chaibasa, Patna and other places of Bihar, and in pursuance of the said criminal conspiracy during 1994-95, an amount of Rs. 37,70,39,743/- was illegally withdrawn by the District Animal Husbandry Officer, hereinafter referred as DAHO, Chaibasa, under the major head 2403, from Chaibasa treasury, for purported purchase of feed, fodder, medicines and instruments etc. for Animal Husbandry Deptt. against the contingency bill, which were neither required nor supplied in the quantities falsely purported to have been supplied, and received. In pursuance of this criminal conspiracy, payment to the tune of Rs. 37,70,39,743/- were fraudulently made to accused suppliers, mentioned in col. 1 at sl. nos. 26 to 43 and 45 to 55, for either no supply or grossly short supply of materials and as a consequence, Govt. funds were misappropriated by the conspirators.

Investigation has further disclosed that for the financial year 1994-95, an amount of Rs. 74.40 crores, were provided to Animal Husbandry Department of the State of Bihar as Budgetary grant for the year, whereas expenses incurred during the period were to the tune of Rs. 245.01 crores, and as such, an additional amount of Rs. 170.61 crores (229%) was dishonestly withdrawn against the legislative sanction over and above the sanctioned budget allocation.

Investigation has also revealed that during 1994-95 for DAHO, West Singhbhum Distt., Chaibasa, was alloted an amount of Rs. 4,09,180 only for purchase of feed, fodder, medicines and instruments etc., and yet in furtherance of the criminal conspiracy, 78 fake allotment letters for Rs. 39 crores approximately were unauthorisedly and dishonestly got issued and introduced by the Budget and Accounts Officer, Shri B.B. Prasad (A-10) for DAHO, Chaibasa, with the active connivance of accused S.B. Sinha (A-8), Shri R.K. Das (A-25), Shri Mahendra Prasad (A-54) and others. It is also revealed that the amount of said fake allotments were fraudulently and dishonestly drawn and utilised by the accused DAHO, Chaibasa, Shri B.N. Sharma (A-1) as Drawing and Disbursing Officer for making payments to the accused suppliers against their fake supply bills for feed, fodder, medicines and instruments etc. during the financial year 1994-95.

Investigation has further disclosed that accused suppliers distributed the amount so received fraudulently and dishonestly, amongst the co-conspirators in a ratio of

20 per cent of the billed amount for the suppliers and the balance 80% for the AHD officials, Govt. Officers, Ministers, Chief Minister and other Politicians for their respective roles in the conspiracy.

Investigation has further disclosed that in order to cover up the said unlawful withdrawals out of the fake allotments the accused officials, in connivance with each other issued fictitious supply orders to accused suppliers, obtained their bills/challans and procured false acknowledgement for the receipt of suppliers of materials and thus, falsified records to show the purported procurement and receipt of supplies.

Investigation has further disclosed that in pursuance of the said criminal conspiracy, part of the defrauded amount would be utilised for extending hospitality to politicians and Govt. functionaries by way of providing free air journeys, hotel expenses and other illegal payments for protection, and patronage to conspirators.

Investigation has further revealed that Animal Husbandry Department (AHD) of Government of Bihar, is responsible for overall development of live stock in the State and is functionally responsible for breed improvement, health coverage of animals, promotion of use of specific feed and fodder, and marketing of animal and dairy products. The Animal Husbandry Department of the Govt. of Bihar has two Regional Directorates in South Bihar:-

(a) Regional Director, South Chhotanagpur Range, Ranchi having jurisdiction over the Revenue Districts of Ranchi, Gumla, Lohardaga, Palamau, West Singhbhum (Chaibasa) and East Singhbhum (Jamshedpur).

(b) Regional Director, North Chhotanagpur Range, Hazaribagh having jurisdiction over the Revenue Districts of Hazaribagh, Dhanbad and Giridih.

The status enjoyed, functions and responsibilities enjoined upon the accused public servants as revealed during investigation are given below in a tabular form:-

Name	*Status*	*Functions and Responsibilities*
Dr. B.N. Sharma (A-1)	DAHO, Chaibasa (1994-95)	He was overall incharge of District Animal Husbandry Department, Chaibasa, during the relevant period. He also functioned as Drawing & Disbursing Officer (DDO)
Dr. M.K. Srivastava (A-2)	A.D. (Poultry), Chaibasa (1994-95)	He was overall incharge of Poultry Farm Chaibasa. It was his duty to certify the receipt of all the materials consigned to Poultry Farm.
Dr. Gaya Prasad Tripathi (A-3)	Mobile Vet. Officer/Touring Vet. Officer (Mobile), Chaibasa (1994-95)	He was responsible to render necessary assistance to DAHO primarily in containing epidemics. Besides, it was also his duty to receive the consignment of medicines and instruments on behalf of DAHO and to distribute the same amongst the Field Officers of the Department as per need.
Dr. Arjun Sharma (A-4)	Asstt. Poultry officer (1994-95)	He was responsible for assisting DAHO Chaibasa in the matter relating to Poultry Development of the District. Although it was not within his job profile, he used to receive the consignments of feed, and sparingly medicines and instruments on behalf of DAHO Chaibasa.
Dr. Dubraj Dorai (A-5)	Manager, Govt. Cattle Farm Saraikela (1994-95)	He was overall incharge of Govt. Cattle Farm, Saraikela. His duty was to receive all consignment of feed, medicines and instruments meant for Govt. Cattle Farm, Saraikela.
Sri Silas Tirkey, (A-6)	Treasury Officer, Chaibasa (1994-95)	He was Treasury Officer, Chaibasa during the relevant period and as such the head of the Treasury. The duties, responsibilities and functions of the T.O. are as defined below: a) Immediate executive control over the Treasury delegated by the Collector of the District, who is answerable to AG and

Name	*Status*	*Functions and Responsibilities*
		RBI in the matter of proper observance of rules for the punctual submission of all returns. b) To refer disputable claims to AG. c) To call for requisite information from DDOs to satisfy himself about the nature of payment. d) To effect the recovery of the amount from the DDOs in case the amount paid to the DDOs is found by the AG to be wrongly/irregularly drawn. e) To ensure scrupulous observance of all the rules and norms under "Bihar Treasury Code". f) To maintain accounts as per the Accounts Code and to ensure accuracy of treasury records. g) The T.O. is essentially responsible for every amount disbursed. h) To ensure sending of various reports to the AG and other authorities by the Code. i) To initiate action as deemed fit, to eliminate delay in despatch of the prescribed accounts and returns to the AG. j) To ensure satisfaction of the AG as regard validity of the claims honoured by the Treasury.
Dr. Krishna Mohan Prasad (A-7)	Assistant Director (Planning), Regional Directorate, South	i) To render necessary assistance to the Regional Director, AHD, Ranchi, in the matter of the execution and formulation of various development schemes.

Name	*Status*	*Functions and Responsibilities*
	Chhotanagpur Region, AHD, Ranchi (1994-95)	ii) To render assistance to Regional Director AHD in the matter of assessing the actual requirement of feed, fodder, medicines instruments in the event of indents received for the same from DAHOs. iii) To render assistance to Regional Director, AHD in processing the supply orders to be placed on the suppliers.
Dr. Shyam Bihari Sinha (A-8)	Joint Regional Director, Regional Directorate, South, Chhotanagpur Region, AHD, Ranchi (1994-95) (since Retd.)	By virtue of being second-in-command of AHD Regional Directorate, Ranchi he exercised powers as Joint R.D. as well as R.D. during the absence of R.D. Being Joint R.D., he was required to perform the duties as defined hereunder: i) To render assistance to R.D. in quantifying the requirements of feed, fodder, medicines and instruments, indents placed for by different AHD units of the whole South Chhotanagpur Region. ii) To render assistance to R.D. in monitoring the distribution and consumption of feed, fodder, medicines and instruments. iii) To select the suppliers for the supply of feed, fodder, medicines and instruments and to advise the R.D. as to how much to be purchased. iv) Active assistance to R.D. in various administrative matters including staff managements.
Sri K.N. Jha (A-9)	Regional Director, AHD, Ranchi (April 1994 to Oct. 1994)	He was overall Incharge of Regional Directorate, AHD, Ranchi. Following were the duties, responsibilities and functions of the R.D. during the relevant period:

Name	Status	Functions and Responsibilities
		i) To exercise administrative control over the Region. ii) To place supply orders on the suppliers. iii) To accord sanction of the amount(s) required for honouring the bills of the suppliers, orders placed on, and to authorise the DDOs to draw the sanctioned amount and to appropriate for the purpose specified. iv) To monitor the distribution of feed, fodder, medicines and instruments. v) To Co-ordinate with AHD Head Quarters. vi) To ensure the submission of indents received from field formations before AHD Hqrs. for the preparation of budget estimates.
Sri Braj Bhushan Prasad (A-10):	Budget and Accounts Officer, AHD Directorate, Patna (1994-95)	i) To communicate the budgetary allocations to all field formations of the AHD after the approval is accorded by the Director, AHD. ii) To attend to all the works as regard budget and accounts of the department.
Dr. Ram Raj Ram (A-11):	Director, AHD, Patna (1994-95)	He was the Controlling Officer of the AHD. Duties and responsibilities enjoined upon the Director are as under: (as defined by Bihar Financial Rules) i) To enforce financial order and strict economy in the department. ii) To ensure the observance of financial rules. iii) To ensure that the expenditure of the department does not outstrip the budgetary provision to the extent possible.

Name	*Status*	*Functions and Responsibilities*
		iv) To ensure that the amount allocated is appropriated/expended in the public interest and upon objects for which the money was provided. In order to maintain proper control he should arrange to be kept informed not only of what has actually been spent from an appropriation, but also what commitments and liabilities have been and will be incurred against it. He must be in a position to assume before Govt. and the Public Accounts Committee (PAC), if necessary, complete responsibility for departmental expenditure and to explain or justify any instance of excess or financial irregularity that may be brought to notice as a result of Audit scrutiny or otherwise. v) The Controlling Officer of department and the AG will be jointly responsible for the reconciliation of figures given in the accounts maintained by the Controlling Officer of the department with those that appear in the AG's Book. vi) To ensure in May of each year that a copy of the account for April is sent to AG in F.R. Form 26. In subsequent months it is to be ensured that the extract of the expenditure under various heads of disbursements are sent to AG. The following informations are to be necessarily sent: a) Expenditure up to the end of the preceding month. b) Expenditure during the month just concluded and c) Total expenditure up-to-date, the total of (a) and (b).

Name	*Status*	*Functions and Responsibilities*
		vii) To obtain the approval of the planned and non-planned schemes. viii) To ensure the receipt of budget estimates from DDO's for compilation and preparation of integrated budget estimate for the whole of the department to be sent to the Finance Department after observing necessary formalities.
Sri Beck Julius (A-12)	Secretary, AHD, Govt. of Bihar	i) He being the Secretary (HOD) is responsible for the smooth conduct of work in the Department. ii) All the matters relating to the Department have to be routed to the Minister through Secretary. iii) Secretary has the authority to intervene in any matter concerning the Department. iv) The Secretary is primarily responsible for proper transaction of business of carrful observance and in case of any material deviation/departure from rule, he has to draw the attention of the Minister I/C and or of the Chief Secretary. v) As per Rule 472 of Bihar Financial Rules, the Head of the Department is responsible for controlling expenditure from the grant or grants at his disposal and he is to exercise his control through the Controlling Officer, if any, and disbursing officers subordinate to him. vi) As per Rule 473 of Bihar Financial Rules, it is the duty of Head of the Department to distribute the grant as voted by the Assembly or in the case of changed appropriation, as, sa-

Name	*Status*	*Functions and Responsibilities*
		nctioned by the Governor, among the various controlling and disbursing officer subordinate to him. So far as this has not been done by the Finance Department, he has to distribute any increase or deduction subsequently made in the grant or in any part of it by the competent authority. When making the distribution, he must invariably communicate to the officer concerned, the complete accounts, classi fication of each items distributed including the major, minor and detail heads of accounts, and the primary unit.
Sri Jagdish Sharma (A-13)	Chairman, P.A.C., (April, 1992 to Jan., 1995)	Bihar Budget Manual (Rule 165) defines the role of P.A.C. in the manner given below: i) The Committee should scrutinise Appropriation Accounts, Finance Accounts and CAG reports to satisfy that the money voted by the Assembly has been spent within the scope of grant by the Assembly, and to bring to the notice of Assembly in case of any deviation. ii) The Committee shall also bring the following facts to the notice of Assembly: a) Every re-appropriation from one grant b) Every re-appropriation within a grant which is not made in accordance with the rules regulating the functions of Finance Department or which has the effect of increasing the expenditure, provision for which has been specifically reduced by a vote of Assembly. c) All the expenditure which the

Name	Status	Functions and Responsibilities
		Finance Department has requested should be brought to the notice of Assembly.
		d) The Committee shall also examine Profit and Loss Accounts, Balance sheet, and Comptroller and Auditor General's Report thereon.
		e) To consider the report of A.G. cases where the Governor may have required it to conduct an Audit of any receipt or
		iii) Any report of PAC shall be presented to the Assembly by the Chairman of the Committee.
Sri Phool Chand Singh (A-14):	Finance Commissioner, Govt. of Bihar (Jan., 1992 to Feb., 1994)	The Finance Commissioner is the Head of Finance Department.
		i) He is to ensure the issuance of circular every year in the beginning of Financial Year laying down the required instruction according to which the budget estimates are required to be submitted to the Finance Department by each and every Administrative Departments.
		ii) The Finance Commissioner is responsible for preparation of the statement of estimated revenue and expenditure (as enshrined under Article 202 of Indian Constitution) to be laid before the legislature every year as well as any supplementary estimate or demand for extra grants.
		iii) The Finance Commissioner is responsible for obtaining materials and for the correctness of the estimates based on that materials.

Name	*Status*	*Functions and Responsibilities*
		iv) To ensure the examination of the estimates received from the controlling officers and also of the consolidated major head estimates received from AG and to issue budget slips where necessary, to get doubtful points clarified from the administrative department. v) To examine the schedules of the new demands before those are finally printed and forwarded to that department by Administrative Departments. All such drafts are received by the Finance Department. vi) As per Rule 132 of Bihar Budget Manual, the Administrative and Finance Departments should, in checking the estimates, apply unrelentingly the proved and well tried check of average of previous actuals which should be employed in conjunction with such known or reasonable foreseeable facts as may modify that average. Against the closed and intimate knowledge of the estimating officer must be set the wider perspective of the Administrative and Finance Department and with the proper combination of these requisites for sound budgeting, thereshould be little possibility of normal expenditure differing widely from the budget provisions. vii) Again it is laid down under Rules 125 of Bihar Budget Manual that the Finance Department makes arrangement for convening the Public Accounts Committee for dealing with their reports on the

Name	*Status*	*Functions and Responsibilities*
		Appropriation and Audit Reports.
Sri Mahesh Prasad (A-15)	Secretary, AHD, Govt. of Bihar	Same as described above in the case of Shri Beck Julius, Secy., AHD.
Sri K. Arumugam (A-56)	Formerly Secretary, AHD, Govt. of Bihar	Same as described above in the case of Shri Beck Julius Secy. AHD.
Sri Vidya Sagar Nishad (A-16)	Minister for AHD, Govt. of Bihar (1990-93)	Rule of Executive business (Rule 11) defines the role of the Minister I/C of the department and as per it, he shall be primarily responsible for the disposal of the business appertaining to the department.
Sri Bhola Ram Toofani (A-17)	Minister of State for AHD (1990-95). Presently Minister for AHD, Govt. of Bihar	Rule of Executive business (Rule 11) defines the role of the Minister I/C of the department and as per it, he shall be primarily responsible for the disposal of the business appertaining to the department.
Dr. Jagannath Mishra (A-18):	Former Chief Minister of Bihar, Former Leader of Opposition Legislative Assembly, Bihar (1990-94), presently Member of Rajya Sabha	As Leader of Opposition in Bihar Legislative Assembly, he enjoyed the status of the Cabinet Minister of the State. The Leader of Opposition is required to give constructive suggestions to the Govt., pilots cut motion in the Assembly, projects the view of his party points as regards the functioning of the Government.
Sri Chandra Deo Prasad Verma (A-19)	Minister for AHD, Govt. of Bihar (1990-93)	Rule of Executive business (Rule 11) defines the role of the Minister I/C of the department and as per it, he shall be primarily responsible for the disposal of the business appertaining to the department.
Sri Lalu Prasad Yadav (A-20)	Chief Minister & Finance Minister, Govt. of Bihar (1990-97)	The Chief Minister is the Head of the Council of Ministers and to aid and advise the Governor who is the Executive Head of the State.

Name	*Status*	*Functions and Responsibilities*
		Article 167 of Indian Constitution describes the duties of the Chief Minister as under: a) "To communicate to the Governor of the State all decisions of the Council of Ministers relating in the administration of the affairs of the State and proposals for legislation. b) To furnish such information relating to the administration of the affairs of the State and proposals for legislation the Governor may all for, and c) If the Governor so requires, to submit for the consideration of the Council of Ministers, any matter, on which a decision has been taken by a Minister but which has not been considered by the Council. **Finance Minister** i) Lays before the House the Annual Financial Statement which includes a) The sum required to meet expenditure described by the Constitution as expenditure charged upon the Consolidated Fund of the State. b) The sums required to meet the expenditure proposed to be made from the Consolidated Fund of the State. c) To make demand for grants. As per Bihar Budget Manual, the Finance Minister shall make a separate demand in respect of the grant proposed for each department of the Government, provided that the Finance Minister may, in his discretion, include in one demand, grant proposed for two or more departments, or

Name	*Status*	*Functions and Responsibilities*
		make a demand in respect of expenditure, such as famine, an interest which can not readily be classified under particular departments. Each demand shall contain first statement of total grant proposed and then a statement of the detailed estimates under each grant divided into items. It further lays down that the Budget shall be presented in such a form as the Finance Minister may consider best fitted for its consideration by the Assembly.
		d) The Finance Minister shall have a general right of reply at the end of the discussion.
		e) Provisions of Rule 126 of Bihar Budget Manual provides that the report on Audit is laid on the table of Legislative Assembly at a convenient date by the Finance Minister. Approximately, a week later, the Finance Minister moves that the report be adopted. A similar procedure is followed in case of the report on Appropriation Accounts and Audit Report.
		f) In dealing with the Appropriation Report, the PAC makes recommendation to the Legislative Assembly as to allowance or disallowance of excesses over voted grants. If allowance is recommended, the Finance Minister, when the report of PAC has been considered, presents to the Legislative Assembly a demand for an excess grant. It the PAC recommends disallowance, it is for the Government to decide whether a demand for excess

Name	*Status*	*Functions and Responsibilities*
		grant will be presented or not. If it decides in the negative, or, in any case if the Legislative Assembly rejects the demands, excess becomes leviable on the controlling officer unless he can show that it has already been covered by a similar enforcement of responsibility on his subordinate disbursing officer.
Sri Dhruv Bhagat (A-21)	MLA, (BJP), Chairman, PAC, (1995-96)	Same as described above in case of Shri Jagdish Sharma PAC Chairman.
Sri R.K. Rana (A-22)	M.L.A., Janta Dal	During the relevant period, he was member of Legislative Ass-Assembly, Bihar and represented Gopalpur (Khagaria) Assembly Segment. Besides, he was president of Bihar Veterinary Association and a Veterinary. Doctor employed by Govt. of Bihar till November, 1994.
Sri Sajal Chakraborty, (A-23):	Former D.C., Chaibasa	He functioned as Dy. Commissioner, Chaibasa during IAS the period 1992-95. i) The District Collector/Dy. Commissioner, as general incharge of the Treasury, is immediately responsible to the Govt. for its general administration and working. The appointment of a subordinate to the immediate charge of a treasury in no way releves the Collector from this responsibility. This responsibility extends not only to the security of Cash balance, stamps, opium and other govt. property and the immediate detection of any irregular practice on the part of the subordinates, but also to the correctness of prescribed accounts and returns and the

Name	*Status*	*Functions and Responsibilities*
		punctuality of their submission and to the implicit obedience of the treasury officer to the instructions issued by the A.G, the Currency Officer and other competent authority. ii) The collector/D.C. is required to send immediate notice to the AG, Finance Department, and other concerned authorities, of any defalcation or loss of public money, stamps and other property. iii) Rules 45 of Bihar Treasury Code provides that when an irregularity of any kind is brought to the notice of Collector/DC by the AG, nothing but a report on his own knowledge, after personal investigation, can be considered satisfactory. iv) Rule 46 of the Bihar Treasury Code provides that the Collector has to satisfy himself by periodical examination, at least once in every quarter, for deposits and cash and once in every six month for securities, Drafts and Cheque Forms. v) Rule 49 of the Bihar Treasury Code lays down that the Collector/D.C. must sign the accounts to be rendered to the A.G. and the Currency Officer. vi) The Collector/D.C. is required to verify the balances (Treasury balances) in person, at least once in each quarter. When the Collector does not verify the balances on the first of the month, he should depute the Senior Dy. Collector by a special order to verify the

Name	*Status*	*Functions and Responsibilities*
		balance on his behalf. The balance should be reported to the AG and the Secretary to the Govt. in the Finance Department. vii) All important communication to the A.G. are to be signed by the Collector or with his approval.
Sri Adhip Chandra Choudhary (A-24)	Commissioner Income Tax, Ranchi (1994-95)	Sri A.C. Choudhary being the Commissioner of Income Tax, Ranchi, was incharge of Dhanbad, Jamshedpur, Bokaro and Ranchi range of Income Tax U/s 263 of I.T. Act, the assessing officer has option to send a proposal to the Commissioner for reassessment mentioning therein the loss of revenue incurred in the matter of assessment already made, and the Commissioner has the opportunity to examine I.T. return files in that event. In the event of search and seizure, necessary authorisation has to be made by the Commissioner, who has to persue and consider the proproposal to his satisfaction. In case of any complaint in the matter of assessement, the Commissioner has the authority to call for any report from the Dy. Commissioner or any other subordinate officer for reviewing the matter.
Sri Raghabendra Kumar Das (A-25)	Administrative Officer, AHD Directorate (1992-95)	As Administrative Officer, he was dealing with the confidential section of the Directorate. Prior to that, Sri Das also functioned as Section Officer in the budget section.

Investigation has revealed that during the year 1994-95, accused B.N. Sharma (A-1) drew 430 nos. of contingent bills under Major Head 2403 and sent the same to District

Treasury, Chaibasa, for payment. Accused Silas Tirkey (A-6) passed the aforesaid 430 nos. of contingent bills and advised SBI, Chaibasa for making payments. SBI, Chaibasa, on the basis of said contingent bills, passed by accused B.N. Sharma and accused Silas Tirkey (A-6), Treasury Advices and Draft Purchase Application Forms submitted by accused B.N. Sharma, released payments to the tune of Rs. 37,70,39,743/- in the shape of Bank Drafts in favour of accused supplier firms. These Bank Drafts were subsequently encashed by accused supplier firms through their respective accounts maintained in various banks.

Investigation further revealed that aforesaid 430 nos. of contingent bills, passed by accused B.N. Sharma (A-1), contained bills in the form of sub-vouchers of various accused supplier firms. Accused M.K. Srivastava (A-2), G.P. Tripathi (A-3), Arjun Sharma (A-4) and Dubraj Dorai (A-5) had given false certificates showing receipt of feed, fodder, veterinary medicines, A.I. Instruments and other materials on the bills of different accused supplier firms which formed sub-vouchers of contingent bills and were the basis for releasing fraudulent payments in the name of the said accused supplier firms.

Investigation has also unfolded that the accused Dr. B.N. Sharma was required to procure feed, fodder, veterinary medicines, A.I. Instruments and other materials for consumption in the District of West Singhbhum, Chaibasa. Feed is required for maintenance of poultry birds at Reorganised Poultry Farm, Chaibasa, and the cattle maintained at Govt. Cattle Breeding Farm, Saraikela, whereas, fodder is required only for the cattle in the Govt. Cattle Breeding Farm, Saraikela. Veterinary medicines are required for treatment of sick animals and birds at Veterinary Hospitals and Dispensaries. A.I. Instruments and other related materials are required for the purpose of artificial insemination of cattle.

Investigation has further revealed that following accused supplier firms falsely shown to have supplied the following quantities of feed/fodder over and above the requirement and storage capacity and received following payments fraudulently:

Sl. No.	*Name of the accused supplier firm*	*Quantity shown to have been supplied (In Qntls.)*	*Amount received by the accused supplier firms (In Rs.)*
	Yellow Maize		
1.	Shree Badri Narayan & Co., Calcutta	158300	5,92,97,110/-
2.	Shaad & Co., Ranchi	73128	2,78,13,780/-
3.	Manas Sales Corporation, Patna	104412	3,99,14,960/-
4.	A. Traders, Patna	26400	99,52,000/-
5.	Chhotanagpur Cattle Food Supply Co., Ranchi	13200	49,89,000/-
6.	Vishal Enterprises, Ranchi	39600	1,49,54,000/-
	Total	**415040**	**15,68,90,850/-**
	Ground Nut Cake (GNC)		
1.	Shaad & Co., Ranchi	3665	1,67,39,240/-
2.	Bhagat & Co. Ranchi	19620	89,85,600/-
3.	Krishna Traders, Ranchi	11940	54,73,700/-
4.	Sanjay Sinha, Ranchi	7236	33,36,000/-
5.	Arke Enterprises, Ranchi	10840	49,74,500/-
6.	Malik Enterprises, Delhi	32410	1,49,76,000/-
	Total	**118711**	**5,44,85,040/-**
	Wheat Bran		
1.	Shaad & Co., Ranchi	23215	74,09,350/-
	Bhusa		
1.	Shaad & Co., Ranchi	10520	9,91,200/-
	Fish Meal		
1.	Shaad & Co., Ranchi	1420	9,86,800/-

Investigation has further revealed that accused person namely Dr. Arjun Sharma (A-4), Dr. M.K. Srivastava (A-2) and Dr. Dubraj Dubraj (A-5) issued fake receipts for the following quantities of materials which facilitated fraudulent drawal of aforesaid amounts:

Name of the material	*Quantities for which accused Dr. Arjun Sharma (A-4) gave fake certificate*	*Quantities for which accused Dr. M.K. Srivastava (A-2) gave fake certificate*	*Quantities for which accused Dr. Dubraj Dorai (A-5) gave fake certificate*
Yellow Maize	2,47,136 Qntls.	1,11,144 Qntls.	56,760 Qntls.
G.N.C.	42,165 Qntls.	65,756 Qntls.	10,790 Qntls.
Wheat Bran	23,215 Qntls.	—	—
Fish Meal	1,420 Qntls.	—	—
Bhusa	10,520 Qntls.	—	—

Investigation shows that following quantities of materials were actually required for maintenance of poultry birds and cattles of Reorganised Poultry Farm, Chaibasa and Govt. Cattle Breeding Farm, Saraikela respectively, during 1994-95.

Sl. No.	*Name of the material*	*Total requirement during 1994-95 in Qntls.*
1.	Yellow Maize	1539
2.	G.N.C.	746
3.	Wheat Bran	746
4.	Fish Meal	700
5.	Bhusa	3942

It is also revealed that storage facilities for storing the feed/fodder exist at: (i) Reorganised Poultry Farm, Chaibasa and (ii) Govt. Cattle Breeding Farm, Saraikela. The total storage capacity of the two stores is 3240 Qntls. approximately only.

Investigation has further revealed that following accused persons are the Proprietors/Partners of the supplier firms which purportedly supplied aforesaid quantities of feed/fodder and Dr. B.N. Sharma (A-1), wilfully and dishonestly, drew bills and thereafter the accused suppliers (A-26, A-28, A-29, A-31 to A-38, A-46, A-50 and A-51) fraudulently received payments in the shape of Bank Drafts issued by SBI, Chaibasa, on the instructions of Dr. B.N. Sharma (A-1) and on the payment orders given by accused Silas Tirkey (A-6). The bank drafts were subsequently encashed from their respective accounts in the Banks shown against each supplier:

Sl. No.	*Name of the accused persons*	*Name of the supplier firms*	*Whether Proprietor/ Partner*	*Name of the bank where the Bank Drafts were encashed*
1.	Sri Dipesh Chandak (A-26)	Sree Badri Naryan & Co., Calcutta	Proprietor	Oriental Bank of Commerce, Park Street, Calcutta
2.	Sri Ravi Kumar Sinha (A-28)	A. Traders, Patna	Proprietor	Central Bank of India, Patel Nagar, BSEB Colony Branch, Patna
3.	Sri Tripurari Mohan Prasaad (A-29)	Manas Sales Corporation, Patna	Partner	S.B.I., Main Branch, Patna
4.	Sri Sushil Kumar (A-31)	— do —	— do —	— do —
5.	Sri Pramod Kumar Jaiswal (A-32)	Bhagat & Co., Ranchi	Proprietor	1. SBI, Main Road, Ranchi. 2. Canara Bank, Ranchi 3. Oriental Bank of Commerce, Ranchi 4. Central Bank of India, Lalpur, Ranchi
6.	Md. Sayeed (A-33)	Chhotanagpur Cattle Food Supply Co. Ranchi	Partner	SBI, Doranda, Ranchi
7.	Md. Snaul Haque (A-34)	— do —	— do —	— do —
8.	Md. Ikram Hussain (A-35)	— do —	— do —	— do —
9.	Md. Hussain (A-36)	— do —	— do —	— do —

Sl. No.	*Name of the accused persons*	*Name of the supplier firms*	*Whether Proprietor/ Partner*	*Name of the bank where the Bank Drafts were encashed*
10.	Md. Tauheed (A-37)	1. Chhotanagpur Cattle Food Supply Co., Ranchi	1. Partner	SBI, Doranda, Ranchi
		2. Shaad & Co., Ranchi	2. Proprietor	SBI, Doranda, Ranchi
11.	Sri Vijay Kumar Malik (A-38)	Malik Enterprises, Delhi	Proprietor	1. Punjab National Bank, Roshanara Road Branch, New Delhi. 2. Punjab National Bank, Gokhle Market Branch, New Delhi
12.	Sri Sanjay Sinha (A-46)	Sanjay Sinha, Ranchi	Proprietor	1. Allahabad Bank, Doranda, Ranchi 2. SBI, S.N. Ganguli Road, Ranchi
13.	Sri Satyendra Kumar Mehara (A-50)	Vishal Enterprises, Ranchi	Proprietor	1. Union Bank of India, Kantatoli, Ranchi 2. Union Bank of India, Doranda, Ranchi
14.	Sri Ravindra Kumar Mehra (A-51)	Arke Enterprises, Ranchi	Proprietor	1. Union Bank of India, Kantatoli, Ranchi 2. SBI, Doranda, Ranchi

It is also revealed that none of the aforesaid accused persons while raising false and fake bills on DAHO, Chaibasa, had furnished challans and other proofs of transportation of feed/fooder and other materials to Chaibasa/Saraikela, as was required.

Investigation has further revealed that accused B.N. Sharma (A-1) in conspiracy with accused persons namely

Dr. K.M. Prasad (A-7), Dr. Shyam Bihari Sinha (A-8), Dr. K.N. Jha (A-9) and Dr. Ram Raj Ram (A-11), dishonestly and fraudulently fabricated records to show liquidation of huge quantities of feed/fodder shown to have been procured. In pursuance of the criminal conspiracy, accused Dr. B.N. Sharma (A-1) initiated a false proposal for distribution of purported excess feed/fodder free of cost, amongst beneficiaries of different Development Schemes of Govt. of Bihar. This false proposal of accused Dr. B.N. Sharma was processed and recommended dishonestly by accused Dr. K.M. Prasad (A-7), accused Dr. Shyam Bihari Sinha (A-8) and accused Dr. K.N. Jha (A-9) and finally approved by accused Dr. Ram Raj Ram (A-11). It is revealed that there was no scheme of the Govt. of Bihar during 1994-95 under which food/fodder could be distributed free of cost for the beneficiaries of Development schemes. On receipt of approval for such distribution, accused Dr. B.N. Sharma (A-1) further caused preparation of false documents showing distribution of 2,14,400 Qntls. of Yellow Maize and 74,200 Qntls. of G.N.C. amongst the beneficiaries in the District of West Singhbhum, Chaibasa. Accused B.N. Sharma (A-1), in conspiracy with aforesaid accused persons, further created false records showing transfer of 2,93,258 Qntls. of Yellow Maize and 66,598 Qntls of G.N.C. to DAHO, Ranchi. Investigation has revealed that no such supplies were distributed amongst the beneficiaries of different Development Schemes of Bihar, nor was any feed transferred to DAHO, Ranchi.

Investigation has further revealed that accused Daya Nand Prasad Kashyap (A-53) is one of the Partners of M/s Baisnav Enterprises, Ranchi and he received Rs. 24,93,500/- towards purported supply of 332500 kg of Mineral Mix without salt to DAHO, Chaibasa. Accused G.P. Tripath (A-3) issued fake receipts on the bills of M/s Baisnav Enterprises, Ranchi. The aforesaid quantity of Mineral Mix without salt was neither required nor supplied to DAHO, Chaibasa.

Investigation has further revealed that during the relevant period, the following accused persons received payments towards purported supply of veterinary medicines to DAHO, Chaibasa. The medicines claimed to have been supplied were either not manufactured at all, or manufactured in less quantity, or marked as veterinary samples, or not made available to the supplier firms for effecting supply to DAHO, Chaibasa. Accused G.P. Tripathi (A-3) gave false acknowledgment receipts on the bills submitted by these accused persons in the names of their firms, facilitating the fraudulent drawal of money. The accused persons received payments in the shape of Bank Drafts issued by SBI, Chaibasa, which were subsequently encashed by the accused persons by getting credited to their respective accounts. The details are given in the table hereunder:

Sl. No.	*Name of the accused*	*Name of the supplier firms through which supplies were shown to have been effected*	*Proprietor/ Partner/ Benami Owner*	*Amount received*
1.	Sri Tripurari Mohan Prasad (A-29)	Bihar Surgico Medico Agency, Patna	Proprietor	1,10,33,779.79
2.	Sri Sunil Kumar Sinha (A-30)	Sree Baba Chemical Works, Patna	Proprietor	40,837.07
3.	Sri Sushil Kumar (A-31)	Samarpan Veterinary Enterprises, Patna	Proprietor	60,50,295.80
4.	Harish Khandelwal (A-45)	A.B. Sales, Ranchi	Partner	1,62,583.20
5.	Smt. Bimla Sharma (A-55)	— do —	— do —	— do —
6.	Sri Paresh Chandra Kundu (A-47)	Sarveswari Drug Agency, Ranchi	Partner	21,65,500.00
7.	Sri Rajesh Verma (A-48)	J.P. Enterprises, Patna	Proprietor	4,13,867.76
8.	Smt. Shiv Kumari (A-49)	S.K. Enterprises, Patna	Proprietor	14,92,601.44
9.	Sri Sunil Gandhi (A-52)	Magadh Distributors	Proprietor	9,96,175.30
10.	Sri Mahendra Prasad (A-54)	S.R. Enterprises, Patna	Benami Owner	20,99,729.95

In pursuance to the conspiracy, accused Ajit Kumar Verma (A-27), Proprietor of M/s Little Oak Pharmaceuticals, Calcutta had raised false bills amounting to Rs. 99,81,880 for purported supply of veterinary medicines and feed supplements to DAHO, Chaibasa which were falsely certified as received by accused Dr. G.P. Tripathi (A-3) of Bank Drafts issued by SBI, Chaibasa. These Bank Drafts for these amount were encashed at Bank of Madura Ltd., Dover Lane, Calcutta and State Bank of Bikaner & Jaipur, Ballyganj Calcutta. Investigation has also revealed that accused Dr. Ajit Kumar Verma (A-27) received the aforesaid amount without supplying the medicines/feed supplements as those were neither produced by his firm M/s Little Oak Pharmaceutical or by M/s Treatment Home Products, Creek Row, Calcutta with whom M/s Little Oak Pharmaceuticals had entered into an agreement for production of veterinary medicines on behalf of M/s Little Oak Pharmaceuticals, Calcutta.

Investigation has further revealed that M/s Meeta Pharma, Patna is Benami firm of accused Gouri Shankar Prasad (A-44). While opening the Bank Accounts with Punjab National Bank, Janipur Branch, Patna and Gauriasthan Branch, Patna, in the account opening forms showed accused Ajay Kumar Sinha (A-43), brother-in-law of accused Gouri Shankar Prasad (A-44), as Proprietor of the firm. Accused Dr. Gouri Shankar Prasad (A-44) and accused Ajay Kumar Sinha (A-43) received Rs. 49,95,400/ by falsely showing supply of veterinary medicines manufactured by M/s Q-Max Laboratories, Ambad, Nasik is owned by Sri Sharad Kumar, son of accused Gouri Shankar Prasad (A-44). Investigation has further revealed that the quantity of medicines actually manufactured by M/s Q-Max Laboratories was much less than the quantity shown to have been supplied by M/s Meeta Pharma to DAHO, Chaibasa. Accused Ajay Kumar Sinha (A-43) and accused Gouri Shankar Prasad (A-44) received aforesaid payment of Rs. 49,95,400/- in Bank Drafts issued by SBI, Chaibasa drawn in favour of M/s Meeta Pharma which were subsequently deposited/encashed in the account of M/s Meeta Pharma maintained at Punjab National Bank,

Janipur Branch and Punjab National Bank, Gauriasthan Branch. After encashment of the Bank Drafts, certain portion of proceeds were transferred to the account of M/s Sanwin Pharmaceuticals, Calcutta maintained with South Indian Bank, 4, Lucas Road, Calcutta and in the account of M/s Cilson Formulations maintained at Oriental Bank of Commerce, Pitampura, New Delhi.

Investigation has further revealed that the medicines/ feed supplements were never supplied by the aforesaid accused persons to DAHO, Chaibasa and therefore not distributed to the Veterinary Surgeons/Touring Veterinary Officers for treatment of sick animals and birds. The medicines/feed supplements falsely shown to have been supplied by the accused suppliers during 94-95 to DAHO, Chaibasa are also far in excess of the actual requirements.

Investigation has also revealed that accused Mahinder Singh Bedi (A-39) who is the proprietor of M/s Semex Cryogenics, New Delhi had, in pursuance of the conspiracy, received an amount of Rs. 1,00,27,720/- in Bank Drafts issued by SBI, Chaibasa in favour of his firm. These Bank Drafts were subsequently encashed by accused Mahinder Singh Bedi (A-39) at Oriental Bank of Commerce, Pitampura, New Delhi and Oriental Bank of Commerce, East Patel Nagar, New Delhi. Accused Mahinder Singh Bedi (A-39) received aforesaid payments by raising false supply bills on DAHO, Chaibasa showing supply of 51,600 bottles of A.I.Lubricants, 3,936 pieces of Neck Plug and 12,240 pieces of stainless steel cannister.

Investigation has further revealed that accused Harish Kumar (A-41) and accused Smt. Madhu Mehta (A-40) are Partners of M/s Asian Breeders (India), Delhi. Accused Rajen Mehta (A-42), husband of accused Smt. Madhu Mehta (A-40) and brother-in-law of accused Harish Kumar (A-41) manages the affairs of the firm. In pursuance of the conspiracy, these accused persons received an amount of Rs. 49,91,400/- in the shape of Bank Drafts issued by SBI, Chaibasa in favour of M/s Asian Breeders (India), which were subsequently encashed at Punjab & Sindh Bank, Paschim Vihar, New Delhi and Canara Bank, Rajouri

Garden, New Delhi. These amounts were received by raising false bills on DAHO, Chaibasa showing supply of 36,00,000 pieces of A.I.Sheath, 8,00,000 pieces of Plastic Gloves, 1,76,00,000 pieces of Plastic Globlets and 15,480 bottles of A.I.Lubricant.

Investigation has further brought to the fore the fact that on an average 12,000 cows are artificially inseminated in the entire district of West Singhbhum, Chaibasa which require an average 12,000 A.I. Sheath and Plastic Gloves, 12,000 bottles of A.I. Lubricant of 500ml (consumable items) annually. Apart from these, Plastic Globlets, Neck Plugs and Stainless Steel Canister, meant for permanent use as equipment. Liquid Nitrogen essential for artificial insemination by Frozen Semen Method which used in the district of West Singhbhum, Chaibasa was not procured by DAHO, Chaibasa during the relevant period.

Investigation has also further revealed that the aforesaid materials shown supplied by M/s Semex Cryogenics and M/s Asian Breeders (India) are excisable items under Central Excise and Salt Act. None of the two aforesaid firms is registered with Central Excise Department and have not paid any Central Excise duty on the items purportedly supplied.

Investigation has further revealed that accused G.P. Tripathi (A-3) had issued false receipt on the fake bills of the two aforesaid firms without receiving the materials, which facilitated of aforesaid amounts from the Government Treasury and their subsequent misappropriation.

Investigation has further revealed that the drawals of the aforesaid amounts were caused by accused B.N. Sharma (A-1) on the basis of false and fabricated allotment letters. Accused Braj Bhushan Prasad (A-10) dishonestly issued the false and fabricated allotment letters with the active connivance of accused Shyam Bihari Sinha (A-8), and active participation of accused Mahendra Prasad (A-54) who had put false despatch numbers and dates of despatch on the fabricated allotment letters. Accused Shyam Bihari Sinha (A-8) handed over/caused to hand over the false and fabricated allotment letters in question to accused

B.N.Sharma (A-1) who, knowing those to be false and fabricated, used them in drawing false Contingent Bills.

Investigation has unravelled a well knit conspiracy, pursuant to which astronomical sums were siphoned-off from the Govt. Exchequer over the years, in a very systematic and concerted fashion by A.H.D. officials, in connivance with the suppliers, Government officials, politicians of different political parties, Ministers and the Chief Minister of the State of Bihar.

Sri Lalu Prasad (A-20) was the member of Lok Sabha from 1977 to 1980, member of Legislative Assembly, Bihar from 1981 to 1985 and member of Lok Sabha in the beginning of 1990. He was sworn in as the Chief Minister of Bihar on 10-3-90 and retained charge of the Finance Department and continues as such. The Finance Minister and the Finance Commissioner of the State play pivotal roles in managing public finance. The State Finance Minister and Commissioner/Secretary of the Finance Department have the responsibility to manage Finances of the State keeping in mind the provisions laid-down under the Rules of the Executive Business, the provisions of Bihar Financial Rules, Bihar Budget Manual and Bihar Treasury Code etc. Investigation revealed Finance Minister Shri Lalu Prasad (A-20) and the Finance Commissioner Shri P.C. Singh (A-14) failed wilfully to discharge their duty to enforce discipline in managing the finances of the State. Through their connivance and deliberate inaction allowed their co-conspirators in AHD and others to commit embezzelment of huge amounts of money during the period of their incumbancy, resulting in unprecedented loss to the exchequer.

Investigation has revealed that CAG reports for the year 1988-89 to 1994-95 contained details of the grant, expenditure and excess payment of AHD, were submitted to the Finance Deptt. in the year 1993, 1994 and 1995. These reports were seen by Shri Lalu Prasad (A-20) in his capacity as the Finance Minister of the State. The details of these reports are as under:

Year	*Grant (in crores)*	*Expenditure (in crores)*	*Excess (in crores)*	*%*	*Date of receipt in Fin. Deptt.*	*Date seen by FM/CM*
88-89	36.77	42.90	6.13	17	16-11-93	18-12-93
89-90	42.80	52.45	8.65	20	24-01-94	19-07-94
90-91	54.92	84.21	29.29	53	May '95	05-06-95
91-92	59.10	129.82	70.72	120	Jan '95	04-06-95
92-93	66.93	164.70	87.77	131	20-05-95	10-06-95
93-94	74.14	199.17	125.00	159	27-09-95	26-11-95
94-95	74.40	245.01	170.61	229	15-05-96	21-06-96

It is seen that Shri Lalu Prasad Yadav (A-20) was fully aware from December, 1993 onwards about the actual grants, actual expenditure and excess expenditures over and above the budget allocation of the AHD which were going on right from the year 1988-89 onwards. The CAG reports mentioned above, showed the trend of excess expenditure over the Budgeted amount which increased steadily and reached to 229% in 1994-95. Inspite of such repeated heavy excess withdrawal beyond the voted grants, no steps were deliberately taken suggesting connivance by Shri Lalu Prasad Yadav, Finance Minister/Chief Minister (A-20) and other concerned State Government Officers and politicians to enquire or stop the unprecedented and unwarranted growth of Expenditure in AHD beyond their annual budgetary allocation. Had the remedial action been taken by Shri Lalu Prasad Yadav as FM/CM and the AHD Minister or other concerned bureaucrats, the fraud, concerning excess fraudulent withdrawals over the budget allocation, would have surfaced and further loss to the Public exchequer could have been avoided.

Investigation has further disclosed knowledge of accused CM/FM (A-20) and other accused public servants in as much as that the Finance Department prepared a forecast of resources on Revenue Account for the period 1995 to 2000 for the 10th Finance Commission in May 1994, wherein Statement II-3, Non-Plan Expenditure on revenue Account under the various Major Heads were discussed. In this statement, the actual expenditures pertaining to Major Head 2403-Animal Husbandry for the last 3 years upto 1992-93 were included which were Rs. 72.79 (1990-91) crores, Rs. 117.60 (1991-92) crores, Rs. 143.25 (1992-93) crores respectively. These figures indicated excessive expenditure over and above the budget provision for respective years. Sri Lalu Prasad (A-20), the Chief Minister approved the memorandum of the Govt. on 26-5-94 showing abnormal and unprecedented expenditures, without taking any remedial measures.

Investigation has further revealed that the Deputy Accountant General (I & W), Bihar vide memo no. ECPA-1-12 dated 5-4-90 brought to the notice of the Regional Development Commissioner, Ranchi, the gross financial irregularities detected in the office of Regional Director, AHD, Ranchi during the period 1985-86 to 1988-89. In this letter, a copy of which was also endorsed to the Secretary, AHD, fraudulent payment of considerable amounts for transportation of livestock in vehicles which were found to be cars, scooters, Taxies, Tempos and jeeps etc. were pointedly mentioned to show the false nature of such payments. Dr. Ram Raj Ram (A-11), defended his co-conspirators by falsely projecting these to be inadvertant errors in reflecting correct registration nos. of the vehicles. Sri K. Arumugam (A-56) the then AHD Secretary, concurred with the report of Dr. Ram Raj Ram (A-11) to shield the other co-conspirators. However, Sri Ram Jeevan Singh, the then AHD Minister put up a detailed note on 18-8-90 to the Chief Minister on the DAG's observations and demanded a detailed probe by the CBI. The Chief Minister Sri Lalu Prasad (A-20) ignored his Minister's suggestion and ordered instead, a vigilance enquiry into the matter vide his order dated 13-11-90, Dr. Jagannath Mishra (A-18) another co-accused, in pursuance to the conspiracy and with an intention to suppress the matter forthwith, wrote to the Chief Minister (A-20), on 15-11-90 mentioning therein, inter-alia, that enquiry, be entrusted to the Regional Development Commissioner, Ranchi, as the police enquiry would cause harassment to the AHD Officials. Sri K.N. Jha (A-9) one of the then suspects in the proposed enquiry was functioning as RD, AHD, Ranchi. He is a close relative of Dr. Jagannath Mishra (A-18).

Investigation has further revealed that the said matter was kept pending till March, 1991 and Shri K. Arumugam (A-56) wilfully avoided pursuing in further. Moreover, in response to the Call Attention Motion question No. 10 dated 18-3-91 of MLCs S/Sri Kripanath Pathak and Satrughan Prasad Singh on the subject, a draft reply prepared by K. Arumugam (A-56) and approved by Sri Vidya Sagar Nishad, Minister vide his note dated 22-3-91. The Chief Minister Sri Lalu Prasad (A-20) gave a false assurance on the floor of the Legislative Council on 22-3-91 that he had no hitch in getting the matter of alleged defalcation of Rs. 30 crores in AHD Regional Directorate, Ranchi, enquired into by the CBI or by any other Agency. On 9-4-91, Sri Lalu Prasad (A-10), however, recorded note in the concerned file to await the PAC report. Sri Jagdish Sharma (A-13), PAC Chairman, being the co-conspirator, protected the interest of AHD officials and submitted report dt. 30-12-92 exonerating the AHD officials from the allegation pertaining of false transportation of live-stock as aforesaid. No police/vigilance enquiry was made into the matter further.

Investigation has further disclosed that the Vigilance Bureau case no. 34/90 dated 9-8-90 against AHD officials, including Sri R.K. Das (A-25), Dr. Ram Raj Ram (A-11) and suppliers like M/s Inter Pharmaceuticals etc. was registered, on the basis of a preliminary enquiry conducted by the Vigilance Bureau, on a petition submitted by an MLA alleging purchase of materials by the AHD officials at exorbitant rates, withdrawal of crores of rupees from the Government treasuries and indulgence in corrupt practices by AHD officials including those based at Ranchi. Soon after the registration of the case as a matter of common design, Dr. Jagannath Mishra (A-18), the Leader of Opposition wrote a letter dated 23-8-90 to the Chief Minister (A-20) with the request that the investigation of the said vigilance case should be confined to the members of Central Purchase Committee only and it should not be extended to other officials concerning AHD, Ranchi. The letter of Dr. Jagannath Mishra (A-18) was marked to the Vigilance Bureau by the Chief Minister (A-20). In the Vigilance Bureau, the letter of Dr. Jagannath Mishra (A-18) was delivered as per the direction of Sri D.P. Ojha, the then DIG (Vig.) to the investigating officer of the case under acknowledgment and thereafter no investigation was carried out against the AHD officials of Ranchi, against whom serious allegations had been made. RC-47 (A)/96-Pat. has been registered by CBI to investigate the allegations contained in Vigilance Bureau case no. 34/90 dt. 9-8-90. The amount defalcated in this case is Rs. 182 crores approximately.

Investigation has further disclosed that Sri Satrughan Singh, MLC had raised a Starred Question No. AH-2 in the 120th session of Vidhan Parishad soliciting information on the points of purchase of fodder and medicines from private shopkeepers and role of the Central Purchase Committee in purchasing medicines. The reply was to the effect that the Central Purchase Committee of AHD decided the rates of medicines and that no rates were fixed for 1994-95, as approved by Shri Lalu Prasad (A-20) is suggestive of the fact that he had indeed the knowledge about the shady deals of AHD officials in the matters of purchase of materials.

Investigation has further disclosed that the Chief Minister Sri Lalu Prasad (A-20) gave an assurance on 8-7-93 on the floor of Legislative Assembly, in response to a question raised by Sri S.K. Modi, MLA regarding alleged withdrawal of Rs. 1200 crores irrespective of the embargo, to the effect that the Government would submit the exact figure of withdrawal, nature of expenditure and the departments having incurred the expenditure. Inspite of such assurance, the Chief Minister Sri Lalu Prasad (A-20) did not disclose any reasons for heavy and excessive withdrawal of funds and his wilful inaction facilitated the fraud to continue unabated.

Investigation has further disclosed that Sri Nilambar Choudhary, MLC raised a Starred Question in the 122nd

Session of Bihar Legislative Council regarding budgetary cut in the plan in view of the tight financial position of the State and the ban on withdrawals of funds under plan and non-plan schemes from August 1994 to March 1995 and withdrawals of more than Rs. 72 crores by AHD, Ranchi during 1994-95. The reply denying excess withdrawals was mischieviously approved by AHD Director Dr. Ram Raj Ram (A-11), AHD Secretary Sri Beck Julius (A-12) and Sri Bhola Ram Toofani (A-17). Subsequently, Sri Julius (A-12) appended a note in the file recording inter-alia that there had been fraudulent withdrawals and suggested for communicating the correct position to the Legislative Council which Sri Toofani (A-17) ignored.

Investigation has further revealed that Lok Sabha Question no. 7151 was raised by Sri Lalit Oraon, M.P. sociliting thereby the information as to whether or not the Government had received complaints regarding large scale misappropriation of grants by cattle breeder mafia in Bihar and if so, the action taken by the Government against the guilty persons. The question was received in AHD Secretariate in August 1995 and seen by Sri Beck Julius, AHD Secretary (A-12), Dr. Ram Raj Ram (A-11), AHD Director. Sri Julius (A-12) sent incorrect and misleading reply on 28-9-95 duly approved by Sri Bhola Ram Toofani (A-17) to the effect that "It relates to Government of India. There is neither AH Mafia in Bihar nor has there been misappropriation of grants and hence question of taking action does not arise".

Investigation has revealed that the Chief Minister Sri Lalu Prasad (A-20) convened a meeting on 7-6-93 in which the matter of fraudulent withdrawal of Rs. 50-56 lakhs by Dr. B.N. Sharma (A-1) in one day, i.e., on 6-3-93 was raised and deliberated upon and, wherein the fact of fraudulent excess drawal was brought within the personal knowledge of the Chief Minister Sri Lalu Prasad (A-20). Investigation has further disclosed that though Dr. B.N. Sharma (A-1) was transferred on 30-6-93 from Chaibasa on administrative grounds for the above reasons, in pursuance to the conspiracy, Sri Rajo Singh's, MLA, wrote on 15-7-93 to the Chief Minister requesting him to stay the transfer order of Dr. B.N. Sharma (A-1) and accordingly, Sri Lalu Prasad (A-20) wrote an order on the same letter staying the transfer. This order of the Chief Minister Sri Lalu Prasad (A-20) staying the transfer inspite of his knowledge of irregular withdrawals made by Dr. Sharma (A-1), indicates his design to protect his co-conspirator Dr. B.N. Sharma (A-1). Dr. B.N. Sharma continued as DAHO, Chaibasa thereafter and he continued to embezzle Government funds with impunity. Investigation has revealed that during July, 93 to March 94, Dr. Sharma (A-1) had withdrawn excess fraudulent amount of Rs. 39,92,09,095 whereas during April 94 to March 95, after the stay of his transfer, a further sum of Rs. 37,70,39,743 was illegally withdrawn by him. The stay of transfer of Dr. Sharma (A-1) by the Chief Minister Shri Lalu Prasad gave a fillip to fraudulent and dishonest withdrawals of Govt. funds and its unlawful use by Dr. B.N. Sharma (A-1) and other co-conspirators. S/s Mahesh Prasad (A-15), the then Secretery, AHD, Vidya Sagar Nishad (A-16), Cabinet Minster for AHD and Bhola Ram Toofani (A-17), State Minister for AHD, being the co-conspirators never objected to the stay of Dr. B.N. Sharma's transfer and thus, they facilitated continuation of false withdrawal and misappropriation of huge amounts of Government funds.

Investigation has further disclosed that the Class-IV Employees' Union of Bihar Animal Husbandry Department submitted their charter of demands to the AHD Minister on 18-12-92 inter-alia demanding an enquiry against Dr. Sesh Muni Ram, the then Regional Director, AHD, Dumka for his alleged role in corrupt practices and murder of a Class-IV employee. A meeting of the officials of the Union with Sri Chandradeo Prasad Verma (A-19), AHD Cabinet Minister and Sri Mahesh Prasad (A-15), AHD Secretary, Dr. Ram Raj Ram (A-11), Director, AHD and others was held. It was decided that Sri Bachhu Prasad, Deputy Secretary, AHD and Sri Shiv Balak Choudhary, Joint Director, AHD would jointly conduct an enquiry into the allegations against Dr. Sesh Muni Ram. On 14-1-93, a Memorandum on the subject was also submitted by the said Union to the Chief Minister (A-20). In addition, Sri Om Prakash, Maha Mantri, Class-IV Employees Union of AHD submitted a letter dated 2-6-94 to the Chief Minister (A-20)/Chief Secretary Bihar, stating therein about the illegal fraudulent/withdrawals of Rs. 50 lakh by Dr. Sesh Muni Ram. In pursuance to the conspiracy, accused Shri Jagdish Sharma (A-13) PAC chairman, with an intention to stall the above probe, wrote to Shri Lalu Prasad, no parallel enquiry should be conducted as PAC is seized of the matter. Accused Lalu Prasad (A-20), the then CM, will his tacit support, got the matter stalled successfully thereby further aborting efforts to un-veil the truth and bringing the guilty to book.

In the meanwhile, on or about 13-06-94, the Chief Minister Shri Lalu Prasad (A-20) himself handed over six (6) photocopies of alleged forged allotment letters issued by Dr. Sesh Muni Ram, the then RD, AHD, Dumka, to Sri D.N. Sahay, Director General (Vigilance) enquiry and yet again, Sri Jagdish Sharma (A-13) PAC Chairman, invervened through his letter of 17-6-94 saying that since PAC was making enquiry on the financial irregularities of AHD Santhal Pargana Region and the PAC had already taken possession of the AHD records, parallel enquiry should not be conducted. Accused Lalu Prasad (A-20) sent the said letter to the Vigilance Bureau in his bid to stall enquiries. It has come on record that the Chief Minister (A-20) and Sri Jagdish Sharma (A-13), PAC Chairman had a meeting prior to the issuance of the said letter dated 17-6-94 of Sri Jagdish Sharma (A-13). Investigation has revealed that the concerned file which had been sent to the Chief Minister remained in the Chief Minister's Secretariat from July, 1994 to 28-3-95 without any order of the Chief Minister. The file was sent back to the Vigilance Bureau on 29-3-95. The file was again sent to the Chief Minister's Secretariat on 24-5-95 where it remained till 2-2-96 when the Chief Minister Sri Lalu Prasad ordered the vigilance department to obtain photo copies from PAC to complete the enquiry within a month. It goes to show that accused Lalu Prasad (A-20) and Jagdish Sharma (A-13), with a view to protecting and patronising the scamsters, worked in tandem to get enquiries scuttled and stalled whenever such issues were raised.

It is revealed that no enquiry was conducted either by Vigilance Bureau or the PAC with regard to the said false allotment letters, due to the communication of the PAC chairman Sri Jagdish Sharma (A-13) and the fact that Sri Lalu Prasad (A-20), Chief Minister did not pass any order on the matter for about a year. The Chief Minister (A-20) passed the order dated 2.2.96 as aforesaid when the AHD scam had already surfaced. He wilfully omitted to pass order earlier to prevent thorough enquiry. The vigilance was thwarted to protect the AHD scamster Dr. Sesh Muni Ram, the then RD, AHD, Dumka and to ensure that the matter of false and fabricated issuance of allotment letters does not come to light. It is on record that the Chief Minister Sri Lalu Prasad (A-20) has adopted a different stance in a similar matter pertaining to the Education Department of the State.

Investigation has further disclosed that on 1.8.88, Sri Lalu Prasad (A-20) who was then an MLA wrote a letter to the then Chief Minister of Bihar impressing upon him that Dr. Ram Raj Ram (A-11) was senior to Dr. Radheshyam Sharma and hence deserved the post of Additional Director. Again on 23.9.88. Sri Lalu Prasad (A-20) addressed another letter to the then Chief Minister requesting for the elevation of Dr. Ram Raj Ram to the post of Additional Director, AHD. Sri Lalu Prasad (A-20) also wrote to the Chief Secretary, Bihar pleading for the appointment of Dr. Ram (A-11) as the Director, AHD. In January, 1990, Sri Lalu Prasad (A-20) wrote a letter to the then Chief Minister, Bihar Dr. Jagannath Mishra (A-18) espousing the cause of acting Director, AHD Dr. Ram Raj Ram (A-11). Sri Lalu Prasad (A-20) made consistent efforts to ensure the seniority, elevation and confirmation of accused Ram Raj Ram and continued to protect him after his own assumption of office as the Chief Minister of Bihar.

Investigation has further disclosed that Dr. S.B. Sinha (A-8) Joint Regional Director, AHD, Ranchi was to attain superannuation on 31.12.93. Dr. S.B. Sinha (A-8) applied to the Director, AHD, Patna, Dr. Ram Raj Ram (A-11) on 4.12.93 for extension of his services by two years. Dr. Jagannath Mishra (A-18) wrote a letter dated 5.12.93 to the Chief Minister Shri. Lalu Prasad (A-20), highlighting services rendered by accused Dr. S.B. Sinha (A-8) and recommending extension of his services for two years, though by then the shady deals and corrupt practices of Dr. Sinha were well known. Shri. Lalu Prasad C.M. (A-20), AHD state Minister Shri Bhola Ram Toofani (A-17) and AHD Cabinet Minister Shri C.P. Verma (A-19) in connivance with each other did not object to the proposed extension of service of Dr. Sinha despite complaints against him, and eventually Shri Lalu Prasad, C.M. (A-20) approved the extension of service of his co-accused Dr. Sinha (A-8) for one year w.e.f. 01.01.94.

Investigation has further disclosed that though the Finance Department had strongly objected to the proposed extension of the service of Dr. Sinha (A-8), when the file was sent to the Finance Minister cum Chief Minister on 18.01.94, yet the accused Chief Minister Shri Lalu Prasad (A-20) sat over the file till 31.12.94 and over-ruled the non-concurrence of the Finance Deptt. Interestingly, he granted extension to Dr. S.B. Sinha (A-8) upto 31.12.94 i.e., the day when accused Lalu Prasad (A-20) cleared the file.

Investigation has further disclosed that the excess fradulent withdrawal in AHD during the extended service period of Dr. Sinha (A-8) went as high as 229% above the amount actually alloted i.e. Rs. 74.40 crore.

Investigation has further disclosed that Director CVC, New Delhi wrote a letter dt. 27.07.93 to the Chief Secretary, Bihar forwarding therewith the letter of complaint dt. 11.07.93, of Shri Ram Saran Yadav, MP requesting for an enquiry into the alleged corrupt practices in AHD. The said complaint of the MP revealed about I.T. raids in the premises of the officials/suppliers involved in AHD scam, recovery of Rs. 30 crores during such raids, registration of vigilance case no. 34/90, Nivedan Committee report no. 1160/85, involvement of Dr. S.B. Sinha (A-8) and Dr. K.M. Prasad

(A-7) in corrupt practices, transportation of live-stock/feed by Scooters and car etc. The said letter was dealt with by Shri Indu Bhushan Pathak, the then Additional Secretary AHD in file No. AHD/Vig cell/1-160/93 who vide his note dated 14.10.93 recommended an enquiry into the allegations by the Director, AHD and marked the file to the then Secretary AHD Shri Mahesh Prasad (A-15). Shri Mahesh Prasad (A-15) endorsed this view of the Addl. Secretary and marked the file to Shri Bhola Ram Toofani (A-17) Minister of State for AHD, who after persuing it, marked it to Shri C.P. Verma, the Cabinet Minister for AHD on 05.12.93. Shri C.P. Verma (A-19) saw the file on 11.12.93 and sent it back to Shri Mahesh Prasad (A-15). Thereafter, no action on the said complaint received from CVC, New Delhi was initiated, and aforesaid accused ministers and officials wilfully avoided pursuing the matter further.

Investigation has further disclosed that Sri R.K. Das (A-25), the then Administrative Officer, AHD, Patna was to superannuate on 28.2.94. He represented on 23.2.94 for extension of services, to Director, AHD Sri Jagdish Sharma (A-13), PAC Chairman in his letter addressed to the Chief Minister Shri. Lalu Prasad (A-20) also recommended for grant of extension of services to Sri R.K. Das (A-25). The representation of Sri R.K. Das (A-25) was processed in the file and recommended by Sri Bhola Ram Toofani (A-17), Minister of State, AHD and Sri Chandradeo Prasad Verma, (A-19) AHD Minister. The Chief Minister Shri Lalu Prasad (A-20) vide his order dated 28.2.94 extended the services of Sri R.K. Das (A-25) by one year. This extension was objected to by the finance department. Sri Lalu Prasad(A-20) in his capacity of Finance Ministery over-ruled the objection of the finance department and approved the extension of Sri R.K. Das (A-25) on 8.11.94 as was earlier done in the case of Dr. S.B. Sinha (A-8).

Investigation has further revealed that the aforesaid accused officials, bureaucrats, Ministers and the Chief Minister wilfully flouted Rules/Regulations/Instructions in the matter of extension of service to the Govt. servants with a view to patronising the officials responsible for the un-precedented financial irregularities in the AHD, Bihar.

Investigation has further revealed that on 29.1.96, the Additional Finance Commissioner initiated a detailed note concluding that the excess withdrawals over and above the budgetary allocation amounted to cheating, forgery and falsification of accounts. The note was put-up to the Finance Commissioner Sri V.S. Dubey who recommended for registration of criminal cases against AHD officials. Sri Lalu Prasad, Chief Minister (A-20), initially exhibited his reluctance to order registration of criminal cases which is manifest from the fact that Sri Lalu Prasad (A-20) in his note dated 31.1.96 desired the facts and materials to be collected first to decide future course of action. The Finance Commissioner did not consider this as sound decision and impressed upon the Chief Minister the necessity for institution of criminal cases without further loss of time. Sri Lalu Prasad (A-20) thereafter, deleted the last line of the said note and mentioned that criminal cases be registered DDO wise. By such order, the kingpins of the AHD scam Dr. S.B. Sinha, Dr. K.M. Prasad, Dr. Ram Raj Ram and others with whom the Chief Minister (A-20) had close association were kept-out of the purview of the cases contemplated to be instituted. The Chief Minister Sri Lalu Prasad (A-20), thus attempted to protect his close associates and co-conspirators up to the last.

Investigation has further revealed that Sri Lalu Prasad(A-20) in his capacity of Finance Minister, each year proposed the Budget of the State in the State Assembly. The Finance Commissioner Sri Phool Chand Singh (A-14) and AHD Secretaries and Ministers namely S/Sri Mahesh Prasad (A-15), K. Arumugam (A-56) and Beck Julius (A-12), Sri Chandradeo Prasad Verma (A-19), AHD Cabinet Minister for the period 1993-94, Sri Vidya Sagar Nishad (A-16), AHD Cabinet Minister for the period 1991-93, Sri Bhola Ram Toofani (A-17), AHD State Minister from 1991-93 (thereafter AHD Cabinet Minister) had the occasions to go through the Printed Budgets of the Government of Bihar containing information about actuals of AHD from 1992-93. But neither the Chief Minister/Finance Minister Sri Lalu Prasad (A-20) and the AHD Minister named above nor the Finance Commissioner and the AHD Secretaries referred to above initiated any action to find out the cause of such alarming excess withdrawals by AHD and thus, actively connived with each other to facilitate the fraud.

Investigation has further disclosed that the Chief Minister Sri Lalu Prasad (A-20) had close association/nexus with accused supplier Sri D.N. Kashyap (A-53) whom Sri Lalu Prasad (A-20) appointed as Vice-Chairman of 20 Point Programme and accorded him the status of a Cabinet Minister. The print outs of Telephone No. 205907 installed at the residence of accused Sri Kashyap (A-53) show that calls were made from this Phone to Telephone Nos. 222079 and 224129 which are installed at the official residence of the Chief Minister Sri Lalu Prasad (A-20).

Investigation has further revealed that Dr. S.B. Sinha (A-8) was made one of the authorised visitors to the Chief Minister's children studying in Bishop West Scott Girl's School, Namkum, Ranchi. The print outs in respect of the Telephone No. 501500 installed at the house of Dr. S.B. Sinha (A-8) show that calls were made from that Telephone No. to the Telephone no. 224129 installed in the official residence of the Chief Minister Sri Lalu Prasad (A-20).

Investigation has further disclosed that Telephone No.501500 installed at the residence of Dr. S.B. Sinha (A-8) stands in the name of Sri Ravi Mohta, cousin of accused Sri Deepesh Chandak (A-37).

Investigation has further disclosed that in the School Admission Forms of Bishop West Scott Girl's School, Ranchi in respect of two daughters of the Chief Minister Shri Lalu Prasad (A-20), the name of Shri Surya Kant alias Suraj Kumar, employee of Md. Sayeed (A-33), one of the biggest suppliers involved in AHD Scam, figures as referee and said Shri Suraj Kumar has quoted the Telephone No. of the aforesaid accused supplier Md. Sayeed (A-33) as contact number. This shows, the nexus of Sri Lalu Prasad (A-20) with the accused supplier Md. Sayeed (A-33).

Investigation has further revealed close association and nexus of Sri Lalu Prasad (A-20) with the accused suppliers like Md. Sayeed (A-44), Sri D.N. Kashyap (A-53) etc. which is evident from the group photographs collected during the investigation.

Investigation has further disclosed that Sri Dhruv Bhagat (A-21), PAC Chairman wrote to the Finance commissioner, Govt. of Bihar on 20.1.96 to stop enquiry regarding the withdrawls of funds by the AHD and to hand over all the documents to PAC without any delay. When it went un-responded, Shri Dhruv Bhagat wrote another letter dated 24.1.96 to CM Shri Lalu Prasad (A-20) for instructing the Finance Deptt. to stop the enquiry. He mis-represented the facts to show that PAC had already started the enquiry into the matter. Investigation has disclosed that Shri Dhruv Bhagat threatened the Finance Commissioner of dire consequences in case he failed to stop the enquiry.

Investigation has further disclosed that Sri Bhagat (A-21) demanded and accepted one AC Ambassador Car from Sri Rakesh Mehra, son of Sri S.K. Mehra, (A-50) and AHD supplier. The car was given to Sri Bhagat (A-21) at the instance of Dr. S.B. Sinha (A-8). The car was purchased in October 1995 in the name of one Sri Naresh Kumar Jain, an employee of Sri Rakesh Mehra. Sri Bhagat (A-21) was using the said car and subsequently when the scam broke-out, the said vehicle was transferred in the name of Sri Pramod Kumar Bhagat, relative of Sri Dhruv Bhagat (A-26).

Investigation has further revealed that accused persons Sri Jagdish Sharma (A-13) and Sri Dhruv Bhagat (A-21) in conspiracy with accused Dr. S.B. Sinha (A-8), Dr. K.N. Jha (A-9), Dr. Ram Raj Ram (A-11), Dr. K.M. Prasad (A-7), dishonestly and fraudulently created false and fabricated records to show that PAC was enquiring into the matter of excess withdrawals in AHD when in fact it was not and thereby scuttled the desired enquiry on the pretext of PAC enquiry.

Investigation has further disclosed that an amount of rupees 4,85,014/- was deposited during the material time by Sri Vidya Sagar Nishad(A-19) in his self bank A/c No. 328 maintained with SBI, Secretariate Branch, Patna. During the relevant period, Sri Vidya Sagar Nishad

(A-19) also acquired properties in his son's name on a single day i.e. 24.12.91 for a total value of Rs. 1,75,000/ approximately.

Investigation has further revealed that S/Sri Chandradeo Prasad Verma (A-23), Vidya Sagar Nishad (A-19), Bhola Ram Toofani (A-20) being the Minister for AHD were aware of excessive AHD fraudulent withdrawals of funds over the Budget allocation etc., but they intentionally ignored all these and never took any action steps to prevent flow of heavy excess AHD withdrawals which were fraudulent in nature.

Investigation has further disclosed that being the Finance Commissioner, it was enjoined upon Sri Phool Chand Singh (A-14) to ensure preparation of the statement of estimated revenue and expenditure to be laid before the Legislature by the Finance Minister every year as well as any supplementary estimate or demand for extra grant. It was further enjoined upon Sri Phool Chand Singh (A-14) to ensure proper examination of the estimates received from the Controlling Officers and the consolidated accounts pertaining to Major Heads received from the office of the Accountant General and to issue budget slips, whenever required, but Sri Phool Chand Singh (A-14) deliberatedly and wilfully omitted to perform his functions as Finance Commissioner, to facilitate the fraud.

Investigation has further revealed that Sri Phool Chand Singh (A-14) had the knowledge of the abnormal excess withdrawals made by AHD and he had seen the CAG reports for the financial year 1988-89 on 13.12.93 showing actuals to the extent of Rs. 6,12,62,065/- over and above the actual grant of Rs. 36.77 crores. The draft Appropriation Accounts for the year 1990-91 showing excess expenditure in AHD to the extent of 53% over AHD Annual Budget Provision was also seen by him but Sri Singh (A-14) wilfully did not enquire into the matter to find-out the cause of the excess cum fraudulent withdrawals made by AHD.

Investigation has further disclosed that Sri Phool Chand Singh (A-14) being the Finance Commissioner had associated himself in the matter of introduction of cash flow regulations for the financial years 1992-93 to 1993-94 to tide over the resource crunch facing the State of Bihar, but Sri Singh (A-14) did not wilfully make any attempt to introduce any meaningful and effective regulations to curb fraudulent nature of excess withdrawals in AHD.

Investigation has further disclosed that Sri Phool Chand Singh (A-14) being the Finance Commissioner dishonestly ignored the RBI statements of closing balance of the State alongwith treasury-wise cash disbursement, which could have facilitated monitoring the cash flow position of the State. Monthly Civil Accounts of the State sent by the office of the Accountant General to the Finance Department showing major headwise monthly expenditures were the input for ascertaining the actual progress of expenditures against the Budget Provisions but Sri Singh (A-14) purposefully and deliberately did not utilise these Accounts withdrawals, for investigation of excessive expenditures in AHD.

Investigation has further disclosed that although Sri Phool Chand Singh (A-14) had the specific knowledge of excess withdrawals of Rs.50.56 lakhs made by DAHO, Chaibasa (A-1) Dr. B.N. Sharma, on a single day i.e. on 6.3.93, in spite of the ban, he did not purposely take any step to enquire into it. He also had the knowledge about the excess withdrawals in AHD as he approved the reply to the Assembly question raised on 4.6.93 by Sri S.K. Modi, MLA, regarding alleged excessive AHD withdrawals.

Investigation has further disclosed that AHD under their Major Head 2043 shown surrendered some amounts every year as savings though heavy excess expenditures over and above the budget allocation were incurred. The surrender of savings on one hand and making heavy expenditures on the other hand was something very peculiar and it was the special feature which should have received the notice of all concerned especially of the Finance Commissioner Shri P.C. Singh (A-14). Inspite of such unwarranted events, no steps were taken by A-14 and others to ascertain the correct position to bring it on record.

Investigation has further revealed that on 18.2.94, the Chief Secretary of the Government of Bihar ordered in writing to Phool Chand Singh (A-14) to identify treasuries responsible for excess withdrawals and thereafter initiate departmental action against the erring officials. Sri Singh(A-14) did not carry out the orders of the Chief Secretary with a view to shield the co-conspirators of the scam and thereby the excess withdrawals continued.

Investigation has further revealed that during their assignments as AHD Secretary, S/Sri K. Arumugam (A-56), Mahesh Prasad (A-15) and Beck Julius (A-12) did not wilfully and purposely discharge their lawful duties in the matter of budgetary and expenditure control as stipulated in the Bihar Financial Rules, Bihar Budget Manual etc.

Investigation has further disclosed that Sri Arumugam (A-56) deliberately and dis-honestly did not take any steps to enquire into the alleged misappropriation of AHD funds on communication of the Accountant General, Bihar.

Investigation has further disclosed that the Draft Appropriation Accounts for the years 1990-91 and 1991-92 showing AHD excessive withdrawals to the extent of 53% and 120% respectively over AHD Annual Budget Provisions were received by Sri Mahesh Prasad (A-15) but he wilfully failed to investigate the reasons and circumstances of such excessive withdrawals. Investigation has further disclosed that though Sri Mahesh Prasad(A-15) had the knowledge of allegations pertaining to fraudulent and un-lawful activities in AHD, he knowingly failed to take any necessary step to curb the fraud.

Investigation has further revealed that the Draft Appropriation Accounts for the year 1992-93, 1993-94 and 1994-95 showing excess fraudulent withdrawals of AHD to the extent of 131%, 169% and 229% over and above Annual Budget Provisions in AHD respectively, but Sri Julius(A-12) did not enquire into the matter and thereby facilitated and encouraged the AHD scamsters to continue their corrupt and unlawful activities.

Investigation has further revealed that Sri Beck Julius (A-12) received two DO letters dated 8.6.95 and 29.12.95 from Sri Ravi Saxena, A.G., Bihar. Sri Saxena brought the excess expenditure incurred in the AHD over the last few years to his notice and he failed to take appropriate action in the matter. The Addl. Finance Commissioner (Resources), Bihar communicated to said Sri Julius (A-12) about the heavy withdrawals by AHD officials, during the period between 24.10.95 and 20.12.95 but he did not initiate any steps to ascertain out the causes of such excessive and fraudulent withdrawals even though he had the knowledge about the allegations of fraudulent and excessive withdrawals in AHD. On the contrary, Sri Julius (A-12) alongwith other co-accused provided false reply to the question pertaining to fraudulent withdrawals raised by MLC Sri Nilambar Chaudhury.

Investigation has further disclosed that Sri Beck Julius (A-12) in league with accused Sri Jagdish Sharma (A-13) and others succeeded in stalling the ongoing departmental enquiry against Dr. Sesh Muni Ram, the then RD, AHD, Dumka on the allegations of the fraudulent withdrawals. Sri Julius (A-12) received the enquiry report of Sri S.B. Choudhury, Jt. Director, AHD confirming prima facie the allegation of fraudulent withdrawals perpetrated in Deoghar treasury on the basis of the forged allotment letters issued by Dr. Sesh Muni Ram, RD, AHD, Dumka but Sri Julius (A-12) did not, wilfully and purposely, take any action in the matter.

Investigation has further disclosed that Dr. Ram Raj Ram (A-11) being the Director AHD did not wilfully discharge his lawful duties in the matter of expenditure and budgetary control as stipulated in the Bihar Financial Rules and Bihar Budget Mannual etc. Dr. Ram (A-11) deliberately and with criminal intent, furnished false information to the Finance Department in respect of budget check-slips and provided incomplete budget estimates. Dr Ram had specific knowledge about the fraudulent withdrawals in

AHD but did not wilfully take any steps to stop such fraudulent withdrawals. On the contrary, he tried to conceal fraudulent withdrawal made by AHD. Dr. Ram Raj Ram (A-11) was advised in writing by the office of the Principal Accountant General, Bihar to initiate steps for reconciliation of the figures appearing in the books of the Accountant General Dr. Ram (A-11), wilfully refrained from reconciling the figures of accounts of AHD with the books of the Accountant General, Bihar. He was also a party to the false transfer and distribution of fodder, alongwith other co-accused. He accepted hospitality from the accused supplier Dr. Ajit Kumar Verma (A-27), Proprietor of M/s Little Oak Pharmaceuticals in as much as he (Dr. A.K. Verma) settled the Hotel bills of Dr. Ram in Calcutta in February 1995.

Investigation has disclosed that Sri Sajal Chakravorty (A-23) was the Dy. Commissioner, Chaibasa, during 1992-95 and he, by various acts of ommission and commission, facilitated the perpetration of fraud at the district level of Chaibasa. Despite his knowledge about the excess fraudulent withdrawals made by DAHO, Dr. B.N. Sharma (A-1) from Chiabasa treasury, Sri Chakravorty (A-23) did not exercise control to stop mis-appropriation of Govt. funds from Chaibasa treasury. Sri Chakravorty (A-23) developed nexus with accused AHD officials and suppliers and obtained undue pecuniary benefits from them as a reward for the service rendered by him in pursuing the aims of the conspiracy.

The treasury bills/vouchers sent to the office of Sri Chakravorty had constantly been showing heavy withdrawals in AHD but Sri Chakravorty (A-23) did not take any step either to ascertain the reasons for such heavy withdrawals or to see the propriety or otherwise of the expenditure incurred by AHD. He had specific knowledge that a sum of Rs.50.56 lakhs had been withdrawn by accused Dr. B.N. Sharma (A-1), Chaibasa DAHO on 6.3.93, since he had a meeting taken by the C.M. on 7.6.93 at Patna. He purposely did not take any steps to find out the causes of such heavy withdrawals on a single day by DAHO,

Chaibasa. It has come of record that Sri Chakravorty obtained a Lap-Top Computer and two Printers from the AHD scamsters. The electronic digital diary of Sri Chakravorty (A-23) contains *inter-alia* the telephone nos. of the AHD scamsters like Dr. S.B. Sinha (A-8), Dr. R.K. Rana (A-22), and Dr. B.N. Sharma (A-1) etc. Sri Chakravorty (A-23) and Dr. B.N. Sharma (A-1) were the office bearers of the club named Blue Cross Society, Chaibasa. These facts show the close association and inter-action of said Sri Chakravorty (A-23) with the AHD scamsters.

Investigation has revealed that Sri Adhip Chandra Choudhary (A-24) who had been functioning as Commissioner of Income Tax, Ranchi during 1994-96 wilfully and with criminal intent, transferred the assessment records of AHD scam kingpin Dr. S.B. Sinha (A-8) and his wife, to Calcutta IT jurisdiction. The letter under his signature was sent by speed post and the same was also faxed to Calcutta IT office for getting the necessary no objection certificate from Calcutta IT for transferring the assessment records from Ranchi IT jurisdiction. In the petition of Dr. S.B. Sinha (A-8) and Mrs. Rama Sinha, it was wrongly averred that they had shifted their home and hearth permanently to Calcutta. Sri Choudhary (A-24) dishonestly and without checking veracity of the claim of petitioners, took prompt action with a view to help the scamster and his wife.

Investigation has also revealed that on many occasions when accused Sri Choudhury (A-24) visited Calcutta, he would utilise hired cars placed at his disposal by accused supplier Dr. Ajit Kumar Verma (A-27) proprietor of M/s Little Oak Pharmaceuticals. The said Dr. Verma (A-27) also detailed hired car for the daughter of Sri Choudhary (A-24). The rent of the hired cars used to be paid by Dr. Ajit Kumar Verma (A-27) who also bore the expenditure on the train tickets for Sri Choudhary (A-24).

Investigation has further disclosed that Sri Choudhary(A-24) showed un-due favours to the AHD scamsters by abusing his official position as a public servant.

Investigation has further revealed that in the month of October, 1995 one Sri J.P. Verma whose son and wife are involved as suppliers in the AHD cases and received payments without making any supply to AHD, purchased Air tickets for said Sri Lalu Prasad (A-20) and his children. The money for the purchase of air tickets was paid out of the income of the false supply bills raised on AHD. Total expenditure on air journey of Sri Lalu Prasad and his children borne by the accused supplier works out to Rs.44,000/- Similarly S/Sri Vidya Sagar Nishad(A-19), Beck Julius(A-12), K. Arumugam (A-56), Jagdish Sharma (A-13) and the members of his family, Dr. R.K. Rana (A-22) and the members of his family, Dr. S.B. Sinha(A-8), Dr. K.M. Prasad (A-7), Dr. B.N. Sharma (A-1), Dr. Ram Raj Ram (A-11), and others accepted the hospitality and undertook air journeys against the air tickets procured in the said manner by accused supplier of AHD.

Investigation has also revealed that illegal gratification of handsome amount was paid from time to time to said Sri Lalu Prasad (A-20) particularly by co-accused Dr. S.B. Sinha (A-8) who either paid directly or through the co-conspirator Dr. R.K. Rana (A-27). On 19.7.95, Dr. Rana (A-22) purchased bank draft for an amount of Rs.40,500/ against cash payment from Canara Bank, Diplomatic Enclave Branch, New Delhi favouring Mayo College for Girls, Ajmer to remit the fee etc. in respect of Sri Lalu Prasad's two daughters studying in the aforesaid school.

Investigation has further revealed that Sri Chandradeo Prasad Verma (A-19) received pay off from the co-conspirator Dr. S.B. Sinha (A-8) in lieu of steady and guaranteed protection and patronage extended to Dr. S.B. Sinha(A-8) and other co-conspirators from time to time.

Investigation has disclosed that Dr. Jagannath Mishra (A-18) had received an amount of Rs. 50 lakhs in 1995 from the accused supplier Sri M.S. Bedi (A-39) and further, a sum of Rs. 25 lakhs from another supplier Sri Ganesh Dubey.

Investigation has also disclosed that Dr. Jagannath Mishra (A-18) wrote a letter dated 17.1.95 to the Chief

General Manager, Bihar Circle, Department of Telecom requesting to allot a telephone connection to the daughter-in-law of Dr. S.B. Sinha (A-8) on out of turn basis against his quota for the year 1995. This shows his proximity with Dr. S.B. Sinha (A-8), the AHD scam kingpin.

Investigation has further disclosed that Sri P.C. Singh (A-14) had close association with some of the key conspirators involved in AHD scam cases particularly Dr. S.B. Sinha (A-8) as could be seen from the print outs of the telephones installed at the residential premises of Dr. S.B. Sinha (A-8).

Investigation has further disclosed that the co-accused Dr. S.B. Sinha (A-8) paid illegal gratifications to Sri V.S. Nishad (A-16) and Sri Bhola Ram Toofani (A-17) for patronising the co-accused and for not taking action on the ongoing unlawful happenings in the AHD.

Investigation has further disclosed that accused Sri Mahesh Prasad (A-15), during his tenure as Secretary, AHD, accepted illegal gratification from the accused Dr. S.B. Sinha (A-8). Likewise Sri Beck Julius (A-12) who was having close association with co-accused Dr. S.B. Sinha (A-8) and Dr. Sesh Muni Ram, received illegal gratifications from the accused. Sri Beck Julius and his family members stayed at a Hotel in Calcutta in 1995 and the entire expenditure was borne by the accused supplier Dr. A.K. Verma (A-27).

Investigation has further revealed that Dr. Ravindra Kumar Rana (A-22) (R.K. Rana) obtained undue pecuniary benefits, as an AHD officer and as well an MLA, by way of accepting hospitalities from accused suppliers. Dr. R.K. Rana (A-22) received illegal gratifications for himself as well as for Sri Lalu Prasad from the AHD scamster for patronising and protecting the accused scamsters.

The print-outs of the telephones installed at the residence of accused Dr. S.B. Sinha(A-8) shows that on a number of occasions, telephone calls were made from the telephones of Dr. S.B. Sinha to the telephone Number whose subscriber is Dr. R.K. Rana (A-22). This shows the close nexus and association of Dr. Rana (A-22) with Dr. S.B. Sinha (A-8), the kingpin of the scam. Dr. Rana (A-22) was made one of the authorised visitors to Sri Lalu Prasad's children studying in Bishop Westcott Girl's School, Ranchi and Mayo College for Girls, Ajmer.

Investigation has further disclosed that Sri A.C. Choudhury (A-24), the then Commissioner of Income Tax, Ranchi received illegal gratifications from accused suppliers with a view to protecting the AHD scamsters based in Ranchi.

Various acts of commission and omission as aforesaid, show that, in pursuance of criminal conspiracy, accused public servants viz; Dr. Braj Nandan Sharma (A-1), Dr. Mukesh Kumar Srivastava (A-2), Dr. Gaya Pd. Tripathi (A-3), Dr. Arjun Sharma (A-4), Dr. Dubraj Dorai (A-5), Shri Silas Tirkey (A-6), Dr. Krishna Mohan Prasad (A-7), Dr. Shyam Bihari Sinha (A-8), Dr. Kirti Narayan Jha (A-9), Dr. Braj Bhusan Prasad (A-10), Dr. Ram Raj Ram (A-11), Shri Beck Julius (A-12), Shri Jagdish Sharma(A-13), Shri Phool Chand Singh (A-14), Shri Mahesh Prasad(A-15), Shri Vidya Sagar Nishad (A-16), Shri Bhola Ram Toofani (A-17), Dr. Jagannath Mishra(A-18), Shri Chandradeo Prasad Verma (A-19), Shri Lalu Prasad Yadav (A-20), Shri Dhruv Bhagat (A-21), Dr. Rabindra Kumar Rana (A-22), Shri Sajal Chakravorty (A-23), Shri Adhip Chandra Chaudhuri (A-24), Shri Raghabendra Kumar Das (A-25), Dr. Gauri Shankar Prasad (A-44), Shri K. Arumugam (A-56), abused their respective official position by corrupt and illegal means and caused undue favours to accused suppliers namely Shri Deepesh Chandak (A-26), Dr. Ajit Kumar Varma (A-27), Shri Ravi Kumar Sinha (A-28), Shri Tripurari Mohan Prasad (A-29), Shri Sunil Kumar Sinha (A-30), Shri Sushil Kumar(A-31), Shri Pramod Kumar Jaiswal (A-32), Md. Sayeed (A-33), Md. Snaul Haque (A-34), Md. Ekram (A-35), Md. Hussian(A-36), Md. Touheed (A-37), Shri Vijay Kumar Malik (A-38), Shri Mahinder Singh Bedi (A-39), Smt. Madhu Mehta (A-40), Shri Harish Kumar (A-41), Shri Rajan Mehta (A-42), Shri Ajay Kumar Sinha (A-43), Harish Khandelwal (A-45), since dead), Shri Sanjay

Sinha (A-46), Shri Paresh Chandra Kundu (A-47), Shri Rajesh Verma (A-48), Smt. Shiv Kumari (A-49), Shri Satendra Kumar Mehra (A-50), Shri Rabindra Kumar Mehra (A-51), Shri Sunil; Gandhi (A-52), Shri Dayanand Pd. Kashyap (A-53), Shri Mahendra Prasad (A-54), Smt. Bimla Sharma (A-55), in facilitiating them to withdraw the Govt. funds beyond the budgeted provision, against fake/forged allotment letters, on the false pretext of purchasing feed, fodder, medicines and instruments and, thereby, obtained undue pecuniary for advantage for themselves, accused suppliers and others. The payments to the tune of Rs. 37,30,39,743 were fraudulently and dishonestly made to the accused suppliers who either did not supply at all, or made grossly short supply, and thereby caused corresponding wrongful loss to Govt. of Bihar of the said amount and corresponding wrongful gain to themselves.

The above facts and circumstances prima-facie, disclose commission of offences punishable U/s. 120B r/w Sec. 409, 420, 467, 468, 477 A IPC and r/w Sec. 13(2) r/w Sec. 13(1)(d) of Prevention of Corruption Act, 1988 and the substantive offences thereof.

It is, therefore, prayed that the accused may be summoned and tried in accordance with law.

(A.K. Jha)

Inspector of Police

SPE:CBI:Dhanbad.

Bibliography

Books:

Anderson, R.W., *The Economics of Crime*, London, 1976.

Aristotle, *Politics*, Macmillan.

Arlachhi, Pino, *Mafia Business: The Mafia Ethic and the Spirit of Capitalism*, London, 1986.

Arlachhi, Pino, *Mafia, Peasants and Great Estates: Society in Traditional Calabria*, Cambridge, 1983.

Avineri, S., *The Social and Political Thought of Karl Marx*, Cambridgé, 1968.

Balzac, Honoré de, *A Harlot High and Low*, London, 1970.

Balzac, Honoré de, *Lost Illusions*, Harmondsworth, 1981.

Balzac, Honoré de, *Pere Goriot*, New York, 1962.

Blok, Anton, *The Mafia of a Sicilian Village, 1860-1960: A Study of Violent Peasant Entrepreneurs*, New York, 1974.

Boissevain, Jeremy, *Friends of Friends: Networks, Manipulations and Coalitions*, Oxford, 1974.

Bose, Mihir and Gunn, Cathy, *Fraud: The Growth Industry of the Eighties*, London, 1989.

Box, Steven, *Power, Crime and Mystification*, London, 1983.

Braithwaite, John, *Corporate Crime in the Pharmaceutical Industry*, London, 1984.

Clusterbuck, Richard L. *Kidnap, Hijack and Exportion*, 1987.

Cohen, Bruce J., *Crime in America*, Itasca, Illinois, 1979.

Clarke, Michael (ed.), *Corruption*, London, 1983.

Dickens, Charles, *Lettle Dorrit*, London, 1994.

Douglas, Jack D. and Johnson, John M., *Official deviance: readings in malfeasance, misfeasance, and other forms of corruption*, Philadelphia, 1977.

Dreze, Jean and Sen, Amartya Kumar, *India: Economic Development and Social Opportunity*, Delhi, 1995.

Dwivedi, Surrendranath and Bhargava, G.S., *Political Corruption in India*, New Delhi, 1967.

Engler, *Apostles of Greed*, London, 1995

Fiorentini, Gianluca and Peltzman, Sam (eds.), *The economics of organised crime*, Cambridge, 1995.

Galbraith, John Kenneth, *Economic Development in Perspective*, Cambridge, Mass., 1962

Gardiner, John A., *The Politics of Corruption: Organized Crime in an American City*, New York, 1970.

Geiss, Gilbert. and Scotland, Ezra, *White-Collar Crime: Theory and Research*, London, 1980.

Geiss, Gilbert and Meir, Robert F. (eds.), *White-Collar Crime: Offenses in Business, Politics and the Professions*, New York, 1977

Girling, John, *Corruption, Capitalism and Democracy*, London, 1997

Government of India, *Report of the Commission of Inquiry (Inquiry on the Administration of Dalmia-Jain Companies)*, Delhi, 1967

Government of India, *Report of the Committee on Prevention of Corruption*, New Delhi, 1964.

Government of India, *Vohra Committee Report*, New Delhi, 1995

Heidenheimes, Arnold J. (Ed). *Political Corruption*, New York, 1970.

Hess, Henner, *Mafia and Mafiosi: The Structure of Power*, Hants, 1973.

Hobsbawm, E.J., *Primitive Rebels*, Manchester, 1959

Holmes, Lesli, *The End of the Communist Power*, Oxford, 1993.

Huntington, S., *Political Order in Changing Society*, New Haven, 1968.

International Monetary Fund, *Corruption and the Rate of Temptation: Do Low Wages in the Civil Service Cause Corruption?* IMF working paper, May 1997.

Jacoby, Henry, *The Bureaucratisation of the world*, Berkeley, 1973

Jacoby, Neil *H.: Bribery and Extortion in World Business: A Study of Corporate Political Payments Abroad*, New York, 1977.

Jha, Vikas Kumar, *Bihar: Criminalization of Politics*, Patna, 1996

Kabra, Kamal Nayan, *Financial Sector Scam: Fruits of Liberalisation*, New Delhi, 1992.

Kaplan, David E. and Marshall, Andrew, *The Cult of the End of the World*, London, 1996.

Kohli, Suresh (ed.), *Corruption in India*, New Delhi, 1975.

Kumar, Dharma (ed.), *The Cambridge Economic History of India*, Vol. II, CUP, 1982.

Lenin, V.I., *Collected Works*, Vol. 4, Moscow, 1964.

Levine, Denis B., *Inside Out: An Insider's Account of the Wall Street*, New York, 1991.

Lewis, C.S., *The Screwtape Letters and Screwtape Purposes*, New York, 1961.

Lewis, Norman, *The Honoured Society*, Bath, 1964.

Lloyd, Henry D., *Wealth Against Commonwealth*, New York, 1904.

Long, Robert Emmet (ed.), *Banking Scandals: The S&LS and BCCI*, New York, 1993.

Marcus, Steven, *Engels, Manchester and the Working Class*, New York, 1974.

Martin, John M., and Romano, Anne T., *Multinational Crime*, Newbury Park, 1992.

Martindale, Steven, *By Hook or By Crook*, New York,

Marx, Karl, *Capital*, Vol. I, Moscow, 1977.

Marx, Karl and Engels, Frederick, *Collected Works*, Vol. 3, Moscow, 1975.

Maurois, Andre, *Prometheus: The Life of Balzac*, New York, 1965.

Mishra, Girish, *Agrarian Problems of Permanent Settlement: A case study of Champaran*, New Delhi, 1978.

Mishra, Girish and Pandey, Braj Kumar, *Sociology and Economics of Casteism in India*, Delhi, 1996.

Mittal, S.K., *Peasant Uprisings and Mahatma Gandhi in North Bihar*, Meerut, 1978.

Morris, Albert, *Criminology*, New York, 1935.

Page, Edward C., *Political Authority and Bureaucratic Power: A Comparative Analysis*, Sussex, 1985.

Pantaleone, Michele, *The Mafia and Politics*, London, 1966

Pizzon, Stephen, *et al*, *Inside Job: The Looting of America's Savings & Loans*, New York, 1989.

Prasad, R.C. (ed.), *The Ramayana of Tulasidas*, Delhi, 1989.

President's Commission on Law Enforcement and Administration of Justice, *The Challenge of Crime in a Free Society*, Washington, D.C., 1967

Reed, John, *Ten Days that Shhok the World*, Penguin, 1966

Report of the Banaras Hindu University Inquiry Committee, New Delhi, 1969

Robb, George, *White-collar Crime in Modern England: Financial and Business Morality, 1845-1929*, Cambridge, 1992

Roberts, J.M. *The Mythology of the Secret Societies*, London, 1972

Roosevelt, Theodore, *The Roosevelt Policy*, New York, 1908

Rose-Ackerman, Susan, *Corruption: A Study in Political Economy*, New York, 1978

Scott, James, *Comparative Political Corruption*, Englewood Cliffs, 1972

Shapiro, Susan P. *Wayward Capitalists*, New Haven, 1984

Sharma, Nageshwar Prasad, *Bihar ke Dhahate Vishwavidyalay*, Patna, 1997

Shastri, Sitaram (ed.), *Hitopadeshah*, Banaras, 1955

Simon, Carl P. and Witte, Ann D., *Beating the System: The Underground Economy*, Boston, 1982

Sinha, Ram Narayan, *Bihar Tenantry (1783-1833)*, Bombay, 1968.

Sutherland, Edwin H., *White Collar Crime*, New York, 1961

Sutherland, Edwin H., *On Analysing Crime*, Chicago, 1973

Tarsis, Valery, *The Blue Bottle*, New York, 1963

Tawney, R.H., *The Acquisitive Society*, Sussex, 1982

Thakur, Upendra, *Corruption in Ancient India*, New Delhi-1979.

Theobald, Robin, *Corruption, Development and Underdevelopment*, Macmillan, 1990

Tsuru, Shigeto, *Institutional Economics* Revised, Cambridge, 1993

Ward, Peter M. (ed.), *Corruption, Development and Inequality*, London, 1989

Warwick, Dennis, *Bureaucracy*, London, 1974

Woolner, Ann, *Washed in Gold: The Story Behind the Biggest Money-laundering Investigation in U.S. History*, New York, 1994

Yablonsky, Lewis, *The Violent Gang*, New York, 1962

Ancient Texts

1. *Amarkosa Arthashastra* (Kautilya)
2. *Daskumar Charitam*
3. *Mrichhakatikam*
4. *Mudra-rakshash*
5. *Rajtarangini*
6. *Rigveda*
7. *Sutra Nipata*

Journals and Newspapers

— *American Political Science Review*

— *Finance and Development*

— *Guardian Weekly*

— *Hindustan*
— *Jan Satta*
— *Journal of Economic Literature*
— *Mainstream*
— *New Wave*
— *Prabhat Khabar*
— *Quarterly Journal of Economics*
— *The Annals of the American Academy of Political and Social Science*
— *The Economic Times*
— *The Economist*
— *The Far Eastern Economic Review*
— *The Hindustan Times*
— *The Indian Express*
— *The Newsweek*
— *The Searchlight*
— *The Times of India*
— *Young India*

Index